LOVE AND TOIL

LOVE

AND

TOIL

Motherhood in Outcast London

1870–1918

ELLEN ROSS

New York   *Oxford*

Oxford University Press

1993

Oxford University Press

Oxford   New York   Toronto
Delhi   Bombay   Calcutta   Madras   Karachi
Kuala Lumpur   Singapore   Hong Kong   Tokyo
Nairobi   Dar es Salaam   Cape Town
Melbourne   Auckland   Madrid

and associated companies in
Berlin   Ibadan

Copyright © 1993 by Ellen Ross

Published by Oxford University Press, Inc.,
200 Madison Avenue, New York, New York 10016

Oxford is a registered trademark of Oxford University Press

LIBRARY OF CONGRESS CATALOGING-IN-PUBLICATION DATA
Ross, Ellen.
Love and toil : motherhood in outcast London, 1870–1918 / Ellen Ross.
p. cm.   Includes bibliographical references and index.
ISBN 0-19-503957-2
ISBN 0-19-508321-0 (pbk.)
1. Motherhood—England—London—History.
2. Poor—England—London—History.
3. Working class—England—London—History.
I. Title.   HQ759.R66   1993
306.874′3′pr094212—dc20
92-40849

1 3 5 7 9 8 6 4 2
Printed in the United States of America
on acid-free paper

For my mother, Jeanette C. Ross

and in memory of my son, Zachary Glendon-Ross
October 14, 1982–December 13, 1989

Acknowledgments

The catastrophe of my little son's ghastly three-month-long hospitalization with a brain tumor and his death in December 1989 transformed this project for me and for everyone who knew me. What had been intended as a modest historical monograph took on new layers of significance when I resumed work on it. Like the baseball card collection that gave Zach pleasure and distraction literally to his dying day, this book, after his death, provided moments of enjoyment and a sense of continuity with my happy previous life. At the same time, unfashionable intellectually as these sentiments were, I took solace and sometimes inspiration from my historical subjects, mothers themselves, many of whom had also sat at their children's deathbeds, women who carried on with their own lives after doing all they could for the sick child. Though this book has retained the conventional scholarly form I imagined for it in 1984 when I began its research, in the past three years it has come to mean—especially after it was supplemented (and inevitably partly displaced) by the arrival of our two daughters, Maude and Hope, born in 1990 and 1991—that life still holds intense pleasures.

Dozens of friends and relations helped Zach and have helped us with money, food, games, distractions, love, and now, child care. Dan Polin, Eileen Gillooly, Susan Cohn, and Peter Hellmann, the parents of Zach's two "best friends," not only have done this but also have always offered me encouragement with this book, helping to sustain its special meaning. Among the many other extraordinary friends whose loyalty involved repeated hospital visits as well as ideas and suggestions for this book throughout its life, I especially want to thank Jane Caplan, Temma Kaplan, Ros Petchesky, Rayna Rapp, and Christine Stansell. As the other members, in 1990 and 1991, of a weekly "rescue group" which convened in a Chelsea diner, Cora Kaplan and Judy Walkowitz helped me to fit this project into a historical discipline being turned on its head at a point when any motion at all was painful for me.

At earlier stages of its development, Sally Alexander, Anna Davin, John Gillis, Raphael Samuel, Christine Stansell, and Martha Vicinus read chapters of the book. I benefitted as much from their dismay as from their praise. Leonore Davidoff and Judy Walkowitz read the whole manuscript in its last stages and offered just the right amount of criticism. Jerry White, as the project's "geographer," also read the entire manuscript, and saved it from many of the kinds of errors a foreigner and non-Londoner might make. What errors and weaknesses remain in the book are of course my own responsibility.

When I first began doing research in London in the late 1970s, a naive and inexperienced social explorer myself, my generous and talented guides were Anna Davin and Raphael Samuel. They did not disdain explaining their note-taking techniques and filing systems to me, and both, in different ways, vividly and permanently transmitted their own senses of what one "says" in social history and where the pleasures of the past are to be found.

I would also like to acknowledge the many scholars who shared information, research notes, oral history tapes, and unpublished documents with me: Alan Bartlett; Mary Chamberlain; Dina Copelman; Anna Davin, whose home office has been one of my richest archives; Angela John; Jane Lewis; Rodney Mace; Hugh McLeod; Raphael Samuel, whose oral histories are cited throughout the book; Pamela Walker; and Frances Widdowson.

This project has also benefitted from the superior energy and research skills of a group of extraordinary research assistants, many of whom are now fully established scholars themselves. All were a pleasure to work with: Andrew August (I have also drawn on his dissertation research), Alison Oram, Gretchen Galbraith, Pamela Walker, Jan Lambertz, and Tammy Proctor, for research on the illustrations.

I acknowledge with gratitude the fellowships and grants which have, over the past decade, provided research expenses or relief from a heavy teaching load: American Council of Learned Societies, American Philosophical Society, Ramapo College Sabbatical Leave (1984) and Separately Budgeted Research programs, the Ramapo College Foundation, the Shelby Cullom Davis Center for Historical Studies at Princeton University, and the National Endowment for the Humanities Fellowship for College Teachers.

Libraries and archivists here and in Britain have provided invaluable help and guidance, and I want to extend particular thanks to the staff of the Greater London Record office, particularly Richard Samways, Bridget Howlett, and Jean Kenealy, lovers of London and its history as well as competent and imaginative archivists. It was Ms. Kenealy who suggested that hospital records would be useful for this study, which they were. Ramapo College's library, despite its small and beleaguered staff, handled my dozens of inter-library loan requests with dispatch, and earned my lifelong loyalty. I also want to acknowledge the extra hospitality of Professor John Burnett, who showed me around the wonderful collection of autobiographies he has assembled at Brunel University, and Dr. Gilchrest, the archivist at the Royal Free Hospital, who not only opened the hospital's records to me but bought me lunch on several occasions.

Finally, I want to thank my partner, W. Richard Glendon, M.D., for his unfailing help. Computer installer, hard- and software repairman, and philosopher of the computer, he made certain that the book's infrastructure would remain sound and usable. He also read many of the hospital case records and expedited my making sense of them; his research and experience, I think, kept me from some of the medical naiveté that occasionally appears in works of social and medical history. Having long been a loving and respectful spouse, he sat down with me and urged me to resume work on this book within a week of our son's death; my initial incredulity eventually changed to recognition and appreciation of his wisdom.

Some portions of this book are reprinted from other works by the author, who wishes to thank their publishers for permission to quote from them: " 'Fierce Questions and Taunts': Married Life in Working-Class London," *Feminist Studies* 8 (Fall 1982); "Survival Networks: Women's Neighbourhood Sharing in London before World War I," *History Workshop* 15 (Spring 1983) (Oxford University Press); "Labour and Love: Rediscovering London's Working-Class Mothers, 1870–1918," in Jane Lewis, ed., *Labour and Love: Women's Experience of Home and Family, 1850–1940* (Oxford: Basil Blackwell, 1986); "Good Mothers and Bad: Housewives and Philanthropists in Turn-of-the-Century England," in Kathleen McCarthy, ed., *Lady Bountiful Revisited: Women, Philanthropy, and Power* (New Brunswick, N.J.: Rutgers University Press, 1990); and "Hungry Children: Housewives and London Charity 1870–1918," in Peter Mandler, ed., *The Uses of Charity: The Poor on Relief in the Nineteenth-Century Metropolis* (Philadelphia: University of Pennsylvania Press, 1990). The author is also grateful to Weidenfeld & Nicolson for permission to reprint a short excerpt from Paul Thompson's *The Edwardians;* and to Edward B. Marks Music Company for permission to quote lyrics from the song "When Father Laid the Carpet on the Stairs."

Contents

A Note on English and American Currency and Usage

There is considerable variation in the language of domestic life on the two sides of the Atlantic. To avoid confusing my American readers or offending my British ones, I have nearly always used my native spelling and terminology ("diapers" rather than "nappies," "pacifiers" rather than "comforters"). When I use the British term a parenthetical explanation for American readers is given. American spelling and punctuation are used except in direct quotations and titles.

The ancient English monetary system on which so much of my argument hinges was replaced by a decimal system in 1971. Under the old system:

Four farthings or 2 half-pennies equaled 1 penny (d.).

Twelve pence equaled 1 shilling (s.).

Twenty shillings equaled 1 pound (£).

One guinea was equivalent to 21 shillings.

One half-crown was worth 2s. 6d.

It is futile to assign a dollar value to these sums, as the values of both the dollar and the pound have been drastically inflated since World War I, and standards of living have also improved. As a rough shorthand method, readers may assume that between 1870 and 1914, about a pound a week for a family of five was a poor but subsistence wage, equivalent to the top of the poverty scale today.

Abbreviations

BMA   British Medical Association

COS   Charity Organisation Society

GLI   General Lying-In Hospital, York Road

GLRO   Greater London Record Office

ILP   Independent Labour Party

JRSS   Journal of the Royal Statistical Society

LCC   London County Council

LSE   London School of Economics

MNNA   Metropolitan and National Nursing Association

MOH   Medical Officer of Health

NSPCC   National Society for the Prevention of Cruelty to Children

NUWSS   National Union of Women's Suffrage Societies

PP   Parliamentary Papers

SDF   Social Democratic Federation

TUC   Trades Union Council

Tables

Tables

LOVE AND TOIL

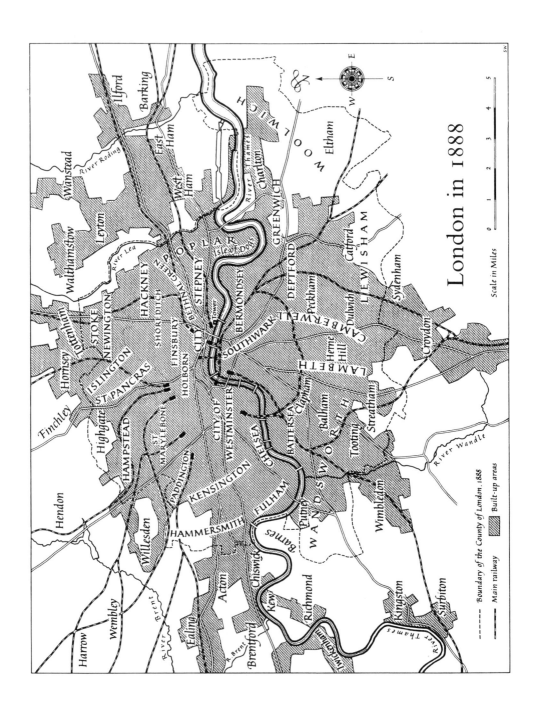

London in 1888

Scale in Miles

0 1 2 3 4 5

----- Boundary of the County of London, 1888

▨ Built-up areas

─── Main railway

"The Other History"
Motherhood

Conceptions of motherhood are at the center of acrimonious public controversies raging today around such issues as abortion, surrogate motherhood, child custody, maternity and paternity leave, foster care, and the rights of divorced fathers. These disputes are seldom openly acknowledged as debates over the imperatives of proper mothering; everyone "knows" what a mother is. As a practical achievement for a woman, a job in the material world, a set of relationships, motherhood continues to be hidden behind veils of desire and fantasy. What is needed to penetrate these veils is public recognition and a discussion of motherhood as a varying series of specific practices (carried out today by women, men, biological and fictive parents, heterosexuals and homosexuals, couples and single people) that are both demanding and socially important. Inserting into public discourse what it really is, concretely, to be a mother to children can clarify some of the hotly contested issues which come up routinely in households, courtrooms, and legislatures.[1]

This book examines the two English generations before (and to a limited extent, during) World War I, when many of the building blocks of contemporary Western motherhood were being laid. As a historian, anthropologist, storyteller, and neighborhood voyeur, I shall try to resurrect the practices of the working people of these two generations and to establish some of the meanings they had for children, husbands, social workers, politicians, and especially for the mothers themselves. I hope that by offering my own portrait of a mother (a woman who could be my grandmother or great-grandmother) I can demonstrate the contingent and provisional nature of our own "motherhood" and help my readers become more critical and intelligent participants in the family politics of the 1990s. The women of working-class London whose lives

I have sketched here built their maternal identities and created a distinct world of mothers and children under the restraints of their time and place: their often antagonistic marriages, their chronic money shortages, their large families of children, their overcrowded living spaces, the sparse opportunities awaiting their children in adulthood, and the growing numbers of "visitors" who appeared in their homes representing new legislation and expectations. The act of examining the way that another era defined and arranged the pieces of "motherhood" permits us to be sharper observers of the fissures and fantasies in our contemporary versions.

In regard to this book's structure I have juggled with the conventions in family studies, in which the starting place is the private realm, the family, later followed by the public realm. Instead, *Love and Toil* begins with two chapters that situate the mother in household, local, national, and international economies ("Food") and in systems of relationships with both women and men ("Marriage"). Two chapters on the distinct ways in which women (often reluctantly) conceived and then bore and reared babies follow, demonstrating the extent to which the custody and care of babies and children was invested in neighborhoods as well as parents. Another chapter looks at the health care resources that state and community provided to mothers, at mothers' care of sick and dying children, and at the meanings of their children's deaths. The final chapter on the Infant Welfare movement of the early twentieth century, an era in which philanthropic and state (both national and local) intervention in motherhood was particularly intense, considers the impact of the new policies on mothering patterns that had endured over many decades.

My stance is at the extreme "social" end of the continuum of positions in contemporary social–natural and nuture–nature debates. Motherhood is, I recognize, both biological and cultural. As the French literary critic Julia Kristeva put it, The mother is "the threshold on which nature and culture confront one another." But there is actually only a little that is truly "natural" about an institution so embedded in social and cultural practices. The dry commentary of British social critic Nikolas Rose permeates our naturalized and sentimental notions of "mother" with deconstructionist logic:

> Motherhood integrates not only certain procreational and interactional processes, not only links sex with both love and children but also is a site of pedagogy and socialisation, exists in a system of transmission of property and status, is a locus of legal rights and obligations, is a unit to which state benefits are disbursed and which carries fiscal implications, plays a key part in the organisation of consumption and cohabitation, is the point of mediation of medical and hygienic norms to homes and males via chil-

dren, is a domain colonised by a range of social agents and practices—doctors, health visitors, social workers, educational psychologists and so forth.[2]

Although many of the elements of modern motherhood (such as its association with sex, marriage, cohabitation, and capitalist consumption) certainly already existed by 1870, when my study commences, those especially having to do with the intervention of the law, state institutions, and the new professions were in flux between 1870 and 1918. The sense in which mothers are responsible to the state and are under its scrutiny, expected to turn out a child schooled in specific ways and cared for as prescribed by medical and associated professionals, was a distinct product of this era, one that is the central issue in the family histories of Foucault and Donzelot.[3] In the decades covered by my study, mothers were "discovered" by social thinkers, and the magnitude of their labors was newly appreciated, though legislators soon used this discovery to make mothers the objects of new kinds of government regulation. (From the 1880s or 1890s, official and voluntary bodies were also at work trying to create a new kind of father: sober, a steady worker, and responsible for his children.) By the twentieth century, in a process intertwined with the epoch's other social changes, poor mothers in London were having somewhat smaller families of children, a pattern that accelerated after World War I and itself represented a striking reorganization of the terms of motherhood.

Other developments in the history of our own form of motherhood are more recent than the period covered by this book. The dissemination of psychoanalytical models of child development since the 1920s and, from the 1960s, theories of early childhood cognitive development has weighted mothers with new responsibilities for their children's formation. The physical work of mothering, the "service aspect"[4] central to the story told here, has been enormously eased over the past century by such varied advances as antibiotics and modern plumbing, but its emotional and social burdens have been greatly expanded. Whereas in the 1940s and 1950s experts blamed mothers for their children's "juvenile delinquency" or "maternal deprivation," today earnest young mothers struggle to head off children's learning disabilities by introducing them to stimulating black-and-white crib mobiles and even vocabulary cards.

Because most scholars are committed to motherhood as a biological given permanent in the human condition, they have been reluctant to examine it as a set of interlocking practices with a history or anthropology of variation and change. At least since the 1920s, psychoanalysis has provided our dominant language for speaking about family relationships, even though it is mainly a science of infant and child development. As such, psychoanalysis grants the mother existence only as an object for the growing child, serving or frustrating the various developmental needs posited by the proliferating schools that Freud's ideas have spawned. The "malaise, insomnia, joy, rage, desire, suffering, happiness" (in Kristeva's words) in motherhood are yet to be uncovered in Freudian psychoanalysis and remain muted as well in the more recent schools.[5] Childbearing and childrearing as phases in a woman's own evolution as a person, as aspects of her emotional life, or as pieces of her wider world of neighbors, kin, work, marriage, and love are invisible, unproblematic.[6] Lacan's version of the infant's development, with its insistence on the entry of children, through language, into the cultural (phallic) world provides an opening to a somewhat more social view of motherhood, as Mary Kelly's dazzling "Post Partum Document" demonstrated in the late 1970s. In her Lacan-inspired exhibit, which included her little son's stained diapers and his early attempts at writing, the artist moved back and forth from her own passion for and absorption with her baby, to discourses about nutrition and early childhood education, and school rules and regulations. Kelly's is one of the stunningly few explorations of what Hélène Cixous called "the other history," that of the developmental lives of girls and women.[7]

In *Of Woman Born,* with a poet's confidence in the authenticity of her experience as a mother and with an analytical framework from 1970s feminism, Adrienne Rich had no difficulty describing "motherhood as experience and institution," the subtitle of her book. But feminists working through the psychoanalytical theories that held out the promise of deeper understanding were more constrained in making mothers subjects. Nancy Chodorow, for instance, acknowledged the importance of the outside world in which the mother moved but it had relatively little practical bearing on the nature of the mother–child diad as she described it. Feminists eventually came to insist on the psychoanalytical telling of the story of the *daughter's* development, either by rethinking the Oedipus complex with the child as a daughter rather than a son or through rich new readings of Freud's famous case studies of women. But only in the most recent years, as Marianne Hirsch has pointed out, have even feminist thinkers broken out of their "daughterly" standpoint to make mothers the *subjects* of analysis.[8]

Feminist scholars inspired by Marx or by the sociological theory once integral to feminist thought rediscovered motherhood and childbirth in the 1960s and 1970s as a poorly rewarded kind of uniquely female labor. Many have devoted their attention to childbirth and the earliest months of parenthood as a period of often traumatic transition for women, or to the new reproductive technologies and their implications. These feminist scholars have fruitfully applied the sociological concept of work to mothering, looking closely at each of its separate operations (housework, health care, education, and the like) and at the satisfaction provided by child care as a form of labor. They argued that this work, seldom classed as "productive" by economists, was demanding and worthwhile, even though the women who did it were chronically undervalued and indeed often miserable and oppressed.[9] The "work" focus has been stretched in the direction of subjectivity, as illustrated by a 1983 anthology entitled *A Labour of Love: Women, Work and Caring* or, in Ann Ferguson's revision of Marxist language, by the concept of mothers' participation in "sex-affective production."[10]

Reflecting the enormous influence of psychoanalysis, historians, until recently, also left mothers and motherhood in silence. In such now-classic works in the history of the family as Flandrin's *Families in Former Times,* Stone's *The Family, Sex and Marriage in England 1580–1800,* and Shorter's *Making of the Modern Family,* women appear mainly as wives, as marriage, romance, and companionship meet in the eighteenth or nineteenth centuries. As mothers, women are included in history only insofar as they understand the developmental needs of childhood, breast-feed their own babies, and discipline children gently. On the other hand, Elisabeth Badinter's remarkable history *The Myth of Motherhood: An Historical View of the Maternal Instinct,* goes against this grain and does examine the activities and emotions of mothers over several centuries. Her contention is that the impulse to love and care for children did not exist for women in Western Europe until imposed on them beginning in about the eighteenth century. Yet Badinter never critically explores what this new institution, motherhood, was, nor does she doubt that she has discovered, once and for all, women's eternal, "natural" feelings for children: boredom and distaste.[11]

With the burgeoning of women's history as a subdiscipline, one small block of color after another has been applied to the canvas left nearly blank by family historians. For just Britain (but something similar may be said for several other Western countries), there are separate studies, from the early modern era on, of parents and children; the impact of state policies in the late nineteenth and early twentieth centuries; infant feeding; the Infant Welfare movement; advice books directed at mothers, childbirth, and its rituals; and so on.[12] Read together, these studies raise the uncomfortable specter with which anthropology has long grappled: cultural relativism. There is no transhistorical vantage point toward which these relationships have been heading, none that is "correct" or best. The vocabulary of parental love, of mother love, is created and meaningful within distinct historical periods and peoples. Motherhood is a historically conditioned grouping of definitions and activities—about which we will inevitably have opinions, but which we should voice with humility. There are some constants in the history of mothering, more variations.

Today's psychic truths about mother and child are seldom questioned deeply, yet a study of the past makes us do this. A hundred years ago in working-class London, intimate elements of this relationship were shaped by the material lives and cultures of the London poor—by their class position. A mother's domestic work—sewing, cleaning, nursing, and especially supplying and preparing food—was often essential to her family's sheer physical survival. Women schemed, struggled, and starved themselves to provide these things; when they failed, they were angry, heartbroken, or depressed. To be of material service was the essence of their maternal identity and to recognize this service a normal requirement of childhood. The emotional balance of the mother-child connection rotated through the child's obligation (owed in money or in kind) to the mother for her hard work and the mother's trust that her children would repay her eventually. The exchange of cash or work during the teenage years when children earned money evened out the balance of debt. Later, there were more spontaneous exchanges between grateful adult children and their aging mothers when the pairs lived long enough and near enough. Today, particularly since the 1960s, with the help of popular advice manuals, consciousness-raising, psychotherapy, and the like, recent generations have tried to free themselves, often with great relief, from much of this emotional rhythm. In late-twentieth-century teachings, the parents' pleasure rather than the child's gratitude is the nexus connecting them; parents need to abandon the hope of "repayment" from their children; children may feel free to avoid this repayment; and guilt (the sense that one has failed one's mother or one's parents) has been banished.

The mothers' story that I will be relating here is not only a piece of the history of the family in modern times but also an essential chapter in the annals of British industrial capitalism. As a population, the poor—children, women, and men—toiled literally night and day for the things they needed. But because the realm of wives was structured as invisible to the working men who were their husbands and to those who were the political leaders of the working-class movement, it has been, until recently, also largely unseen by historians. Working men faced industrial capitalism in its chaotic London form in long, cold walks to the job, exhausting labor, occupational injuries and diseases, and grim periods of unemployment. The wives met the forces of the industrial system at other points: sometimes at their own paid jobs, always at the local market street, with the landlord, with the charities, and with such state institutions as hospitals, schools, and sanitary authorities. In this era, without a reasonably competent adult woman or older daughter, households often "broke up," their members joining those of relatives or neighbors or entering the poor-law system with its cruel separation of spouses, parents, and children.

By thinking through gender as well as class,[13] I want to demonstrate that the family was not really a bulwark against capitalist wage labor, as one school of historians polemically assert and most labor historians have simply assumed.[14] First, it was, in particular, married women rather than "the family" in general whose skill and self-denial dampened the impact of poverty on husbands and, to some extent, children. Second, the disappointment, frustration, and fear that poverty and near-poverty generated did not stop at the household door but penetrated inside, configuring relationships between wives and husbands and between children and parents, shaping the emotions and activities of daily life and the personalities of young people. Carolyn Steedman's biography of her working-class London mother whose childbearing years came in the much more prosperous 1950s rightly aims to prove that many forces—many of them psychic and cultural, not just material deprivation and class position—have structured the lives of workers. Yet one can also read her account as a sophisticated demonstration of the complexity and depth with which class experiences shape historical subjects.[15]

Love and Toil maintains that family survival was the mother's main charge among the large majority of London's population who were poor or working class; the emotional and intellectual nurture of her particular child or children and even their actual comfort were forced into the background. To mother was to work for and organize household subsistence. Reflecting this position, my study is focused on childbearing and childrearing in their domestic contexts and also on the wider contexts—state, city, and neighborhood—in which women were, culturally and politically, assigned specific responsibilities for children and households; given information, social support, and moral rules; and scrambled for the means to carry them out. This survey deals mainly with married women; single adult women (as opposed to widowed or separated women, who were numerous) were rare among these early- and much-marrying populations, but as aunts, neighbors, or adoptive mothers, just about all of them probably carried out some of the functions of motherhood. Paid jobs in the garment industry, as charwomen or launderers, for example, were often part of mothers' subsistence strategies but, to keep a long book from getting longer, are dealt with (in Chapter 2) as only one among many expedients that mothers used to expand, or compensate for, a husband's meager wage.

Writing this book was a process that spanned a decade, one in which there was enormous ferment in historical studies, as the Marxist concepts on which so much social history was built were being questioned and we were barraged with uncomfortable intellectual tasks. *Love and Toil* was written under the diffuse influence of several schools of feminist/literary theory, with their stress on texts as the way in which we learn about reality, on the distinctness of the realm of culture, on the artificiality—albeit all-pervasiveness—of gender roles, and on the renunciation of a "correct" meaning for any document, including the sources used so trustfully by historians.[16] Challenged by Joan Scott, among others, historians have had to come to terms with at least some of this body of thought and its implications for their own work, and I found a dense essay by Robert Berkhofer particularly helpful in that project. Many of my own solutions actually came through looking on while an adjacent discipline—anthropology—reconceived the "truths" about human cultures that fieldwork supposedly uncovered. Always guided by the skeptical feminist commentary of Rayna Rapp, I followed Sherry Ortner, James Clifford, Renato Rosaldo, and Richard Shweder as they salvaged some anthropological traditions, rethought others, and forged a new kind of "artful realism."[17] Eventually I came to accept, though perhaps in new ways, the "epistemological frame of orthodox history," to use Joan Scott's phrase, in particular the assumptions (as I interpret them) of Anglo-American social historians who were inspired by E. P. Thompson: a rhetorical strategy in which many statements are made by accumulating detail; a belief in the significance of the material world to shape individual lives; and an aesthetic pleasure in and respect for the past. The identities of my historical subjects—as women, mothers, and participants in the collective "experience" of their class—I have taken as givens here, though in another kind of study, these might well be open to question.[18] This project combines older with newer ideas about the discipline of history (which often present themselves as incompatible) and is simultaneously a traditional study in the political economy of the family—particularly as lived out by adult females—and an examination of the construction of meanings in working-class culture.

CHAPTER 1

"Miss, I Wish I Had Your Life"
The Poor of London
and Their Chroniclers

LONDON AND ITS POOR

In the years when African voyages of discovery were being recounted in bestsellers like Henry Morton Stanley's *In Darkest Africa* (1890), it was conventional to apply Dark Continent imagery to the slums of London: Remote as "Timbuctoo," these "unknown" and "unexplored" districts were populated by "savages" or "aborigines."[1] Indeed, the imperialists' impulse to explore, convert, help, or conquer brought the friends and siblings of the world travelers to the poor quarters of the metropolis. Their reports emphasized the exoticism of urban poverty and its contrasts with the comfortable and brilliant life of Parliament, the theaters, and the Kensington drawing rooms. As they appear, for example, at the opening of the period of this study, in Doré and Jerrold's collaborative *London: A Pilgrimage* (1869), the wealth and poverty of the metropolis were still being represented in stark contrasts based on urban demarcations: glamorous, glittering West and sinister, huddling East. In the 1880s and 1890s, however, some social explorers set out with a more complex mission to analyze the different grades of poverty and to assess its causes. In the process, they added many new shades between the dusky black of destitution and the gleaming white of carriage-owning, servant-keeping wealth, presenting a new social topography of London.

According to Charles Booth's monumental description and classification, in the late 1880s and 1890s, during a period of general depression spanning the 1870s through about 1896, over a third of the population of East London and Hackney lived in various degrees of "poverty." Classes A through D (the bottom four of Booth's eight groupings) consisted of "the lowest class," "the very poor," and, somewhat better off, two categories of "the poor," households whose means, 18 to 21 shillings a week, were just "barely sufficient for decent independent life." Those in Class E, just above them in the social scale—whose weekly household incomes of 22 to 30 shillings Booth labeled "comfortable" and "above the line of poverty"—comprised another 42 percent. But even these families could easily spend periods of weeks, months, or years in poverty if an employer closed up shop, a wage earner died or was incapacitated, or a cold winter froze out workers who serviced the shipping or construction trades.[2] Many of them shared houses and streets with the poorest Londoners and, especially if they contained many small children, lived by the same expedients as did their poorer neighbors. East London's poverty figures paralleled those of the metropolis as a whole, and when tallied in this way, about three quarters of London's population was, if not totally "outcast," then "poor" and form the collective subject of this book.

London was the administrative seat of an enormous world empire; the cultural center of the anglophone world with a large population of intellectuals, civil servants, and professionals; the country's busiest seaport with almost 20 percent of the country's shipping;[3] and the site of thousands of shifting tiny manufacturing concerns in clothing, footwear, printing, and furniture, all of which had luxury branches, as well as some major industries (brewing, armaments, vehicle building, rubber, engineering, and chemicals). Yet with its royal court and luxury trades, London resembled an eighteenth-century capital like Paris as much as it did an industrial town like Manchester or Birmingham. Describing the social structure of late Victorian and Edwardian London, the explorers used old and vague terms like *rich* and *poor, gentleman* and *working man* (or the plurals or female forms of the latter pair). And these continue to make better sense in describing London's mixed industrial, craft, and court society than do *employers* and *employed, masters* and *hands,* or *proletarians* and *bourgeoisie*. The poor themselves seem to have accepted this nomenclature, though more significant in their daily lives were gradations *among* the poor: between those with regular and those with only casual employment, between the skilled and the unskilled, and between tidy housekeepers and those careless by choice or necessity. These "rough/respectable" divisions, meaningful sources of pride and shame, were highly unstable, as circumstances pushed households into and out of the respectable category and people socialized readily over the rough/respectable divide.[4]

The world's largest city, the area governed by the London County Council (LCC) had a population of 4.5 million in 1901, plus another 2 million in the "outer ring" suburbs beyond the county of London itself.

By 1911, a metropolitan population of over 7 million accounted for nearly a quarter of the whole population of Britain.[5] London was (and is) a cultural reference point and political construction rather than a discrete administrative or even geographical entity. A congeries of separate governing bodies controlled such vital functions as water supply, sanitation, poor relief, public education, and the control of contagious diseases. The size, structure, and jurisdiction of these bodies changed several times during the years of this study. The 118-member LCC was established in 1889, replacing the older Metropolitan Board of Works as the main governmental authority over the county of London but continuing to share power with such other authorities as the School Board for London (1870–1902), the Metropolitan Asylums Board (established in 1867), poor-law administrative districts (unions) staffed by elected guardians, and local vestries (districts for the supervision of health or sanitation, replaced in 1900 by twenty-eight boroughs, each with mayors, aldermen, and borough councils).

Unlike Paris, New York, or Vienna, which had districts of tall tenements and apartment buildings, London's characteristic dwelling was the attached house of three or four stories that, especially in the nineteenth century, proliferated rapidly, creating a huge, sprawling built-up area. The construction of the suburban railroad network enlarged the city still more beyond its 1889 boundaries. By 1914, houses stretched continuously from Ealing in the west to East Ham in the east (to take just one of the city's measurements), a distance of about eighteen miles, and ribbons of suburban villas as well as scattered outlying pockets of poverty extended still farther out into the countryside.

London was a city of children, and its poor districts contained the greatest number of them. During the years preceding and following World War I, working-class streets and courtyards swarmed winter and summer with children of all ages whose shrill little voices could be heard everywhere until dark. In 1871, 43 percent of the population were aged fifteen or under. By 1901, despite a birthrate that had been declining for four decades and the continuing influx of single adults, London's population was still nearly a third children, compared with 20 percent today. Working districts had especially high proportions of children: In 1901 in the East London boroughs of Shoreditch, Bethnal Green, and Finsbury, for instance, children made up well over a third of the whole population, whereas in well-off Hampstead or Stoke Newington, children comprised about a quarter of the whole.[6]

Despite its vast size and the diversity of its pursuits, nineteenth- and early twentieth-century London appears to an American today (or indeed to a Londoner) to have been strikingly uniform racially and ethnically. Its population was virtually entirely Caucasian. A small Chinese population lived along the West India Dock Road in Limehouse, and occasionally a black, Indian, or Arab sailor settled in the dockland districts. The largest group of non-English citizens of London were the children and grandchildren of the 107,000 Irish men and women who had settled in London by 1861, and though they were concentrated in Seven Dials and Drury Lane in Central London, as well as in Whitechapel and Southwark, they could be found in every London borough. A generation later, their Irishness and Catholicism had become a little less distinct. Small Italian communities also flourished, active in the central London garment and food trades. Finally, a sizable Jewish community was taking shape in eastern Whitechapel in these years, as 60,000 refugees from Poland and Russia joined the small and well-assimilated community of Jews descended from earlier Dutch or Spanish Sephardic immigrants in St. George's in the East, Whitechapel, and parts of Bethnal Green.[7]

As the nineteenth century progressed, those with the resources to do so began to leave such inner-city districts as the City, Shoreditch, Whitechapel, or Bethnal Green to the north of the Thames or, south of the river, Rotherhithe, the Borough, or Waterloo. They moved into the new communities being built at Notting Hill to the west, Balham and Tooting south of the Thames, and Holloway or Hackney in the east. After 1871, inner London actually began to lose population. The city's growth separated not only rich and poor from each other but also the better-off workers, who could move away and commute in by rail, from those struggling on the seasonal, sporadic, and piecework male and female wages that had become so common in London by the mid-nineteenth century and were centered in the older inner-London districts. One dock manager testified in 1888 that the size of his daily work force fluctuated by as much as 2,900 men![8] Never sure of their employment, these workers hedged their bets by living near several sources of work for women and children as well as for men.

As Deborah Nord has pointed out, "Darkest London" language was designed both to heighten the drama of London poverty and also to reproach readers for their ready charity for faraway peoples and ventures while a world of pressing need lay almost next door.[9] The realms of the rich and the poor actually abutted each other at many points. The Rev. Harry Jones, planning to move from his post in St. James's, Westminster, to St. George's in the East in the 1870s, discovered that a cab could take him to to this "unknown distant land" in only twenty-eight minutes. As George Sims mischievously observed, the "dark continent" of London poverty was "within easy walking distance of the General Post Office" in Finsbury.[10]

The poor were, in any case, often out of "their place." Every day thousands poured across the bridges from Bermondsey, Kennington, or Walworth south of the Thames or made the journey on foot or in trams or buses from the east to work in the coffee stalls or high-class garment shops in the West End, to build its homes, to drive its cabs, or to clean its homes and offices. Or the poor made their appearance more threateningly. Large Hyde Park or Trafalgar Square demonstrations, often packed with members of London's large network of working men's radical clubs, were common throughout the late Victorian years. The poor were all too visible in the events of February 1886 when members of a Trafalgar Square unemployment demonstration looted elegant West End shops and clubs.[11] In contrast, the orderly West End processions of the 1889 dock strike were greeted by applause and waving hankerchiefs as they reached such landmarks as the Stock Exchange and the Savoy Hotel.[12] In the twentieth century the poor continued as a disturbing collective presence in central London. There were more unemployed demonstrations in the summer and fall of 1905, this time including large and, as the newspapers described them, heartrending contingents of women and children, who in November filled the route along the embankment to Whitehall.[13] The national wave of strikes from 1910 to 1913 (cotton, mining, railroads, and dock, among others) involved London workers, with their accompanying Hyde Park demonstrations and downtown processions. And poor women from London were there in the massive suffrage demonstrations of this era, marching with suffragists who were also slum activists: Charlotte Despard, Sylvia Pankhurst, and Anna Martin.[14]

THE LADY AND THE SLUM

There was also a well-worn path leading from the well-off West End and suburban districts *toward* the slums. It was traveled, first of all, by the kinds of workers who had been part of the charity world for decades: clergymen, church lay workers, London city missionaries (operating since the 1830s), Ellen Ranyard's Bible women who had sold installment-plan Bibles since the 1850s, and representatives of numerous charities supplying coal, blankets, food, and even trusses to the "ruptured poor."[15] The 1870s and 1880s added newer figures: public (board) schoolteachers; school managers (school-based social/charity workers); district nurses; agents of more specialized charities supplying children's boots, eyeglasses, and country holidays or offering job training for the disabled; and Charity Organisation Society (COS, founded in 1869) caseworkers. The numbers of visitors grew with the 1884 opening of the first settlement house, Toynbee Hall in Whitechapel and, in 1887, the

Women's University Settlement in Southwark, followed by others—residences for young people bent on doing good as well as community centers, neutral ground where more occasional visitors could meet the poor and one another. By the twentieth century, new professions, open to females, brought still more women from London townhouses or from country estates to work in poor districts as sanitary inspectors, health visitors, and school nurses. The women who chose London as the focus of their activities are prominent presences throughout this book. Their activities helped shape life for the poor, and their stories of what they saw in the slums—in the form of diaries, journalism, autobiography, and political tracts—form, along with the autobiographies of men and women whom these ladies may have visited as slum children, a large part of the material of which my portrait of working-class mothers is made.

For women enmeshed in Victorian gentility, exploring London poverty added zest and romance to their otherwise staid existences (and indeed, slum life forms the background for numerous literary romantic encounters).[16] And thanks to London's excellent regional railway network, ladies and gentlemen could combine work with the poor with the routines of middle-or upper-class life. Beginning as a young girl in 1875, Constance Battersea, born a Rothschild, journeyed for thirty years from her various country houses to make home visits in Whitechapel and Mile End for the Jewish Ladies' Benevolent Loan Society. For most of 1885, Beatrice Potter (later Beatrice Webb), living in her family's Kensington town residence, regularly made her way by rail to the Katherine Buildings just east of Tower Bridge. Mary Ward, the novelist, began to commute in 1892 from her home in Buckinghamshire via St. Pancras station to the Marchmont Street branch of University Hall, the first of the London settlements with which she worked. Devastated by her husband's death in 1890, Charlotte Despard threw herself into the ladylike charity of supplying fresh flowers to the poor of Nine Elms, a desolate island of riverside poverty in South Lambeth, to which she at first journeyed from her beautiful country house.[17]

No matter how tame the diversion they seemed to provide, Hoxton or Bermondsey could feel as gripping as the Congo River. Young girls, their schooling completed, often yearned for the slums. Katharine Symonds, daughter of the classical scholar, longed in the 1890s to work at Toynbee Hall in Whitechapel but settled for a clerical job at a cos office in Whitechapel Road. In 1908, as soon as she left school, Mary Brinton (later Mary Stocks), a girl who had spent her school holidays helping her mother on her rounds among the West London poor, took a position as the (volunteer) secretary of the Care Committee attached to the Saffron Hill Elementary School in Holborn.[18]

By the later nineteenth century, women from the middle and upper classes had become active presences in the lives of the poor. These ladies helped mothers save up for children's winter boots and for summer country holidays, provided nursery schools and after-school play programs for some of their children, and sat up nights with them when they were sick. In the 1900s, they began to deliver instructions on baby care, nagged mothers to get their schoolchildren deloused, and questioned them about why Jim or Violet at age twelve or fourteen was being placed in a dead-end job rather than an apprenticeship for skilled work. Throughout the Victorian and Edwardian years, politicized by their shocked discovery of the "skeleton at the feast of capitalist civilization" (to use Beatrice Webb's phrase), many of the lady explorers settled down to hard work. They were elected as poor-law guardians or school board members, served as school managers, orchestrated local election campaigns, or they helped striking workers raise funds and joined national organizations like the Fabian Society, the cooperative movement, the Social Democratic Federation, the Independent Labour party, and the Labour Representation Committee (the precurser of the Labour party, which was founded in 1900).[19]

Several kinds of lenses helped the female social explorers focus on the poor as they worked among them. The rose-colored glasses of Lady Bountifuls and the smoked spectacles of masqueraders enjoying a chance to play-act before an audience of strangers were strengthened by ideas from the developing discipline of anthropology, with its antecedents in the traveler's tale of native customs, the collector of artifacts whose uses and meanings were discussed, the student of folklore (*Notes and Queries* began publication in 1874). In the 1890s the anthropology section of the British Association for the Advancement of Science carried out its first ethnographic surveys in rural and village England and Ireland, likening these cultures to the endangered societies of the Pacific Islands that had captured anthropological attention. Even though Henry Mayhew's method, a few decades earlier, has been described as ethnographical, only a few Victorian or Edwardian researchers (like Norman Douglas, who collected children's rhymes and games)[20] actually looked for folklore among the urban poor (more tried to expose slum children to maypoles and morris dancing). In another strand of Victorian thought, the great speculative anthropologists like Lewis Henry Morgan and Edward Westermarck stimulated discussions of the stages of civilization, the origins of marriage, the functions of kinship, and the existence of prehistoric matriarchical societies.[21] Admittedly, neither form of anthropology dominated the language or method of the slum observers (the scholarly Helen Dendy Bosanquet, who married philosopher Bernard Bosanquet in 1895 is the exception), but it did dispose them to find patterns and continuities—to comprehend and respect distinct cultures among the poor—cultures that most earlier observers did not see.

SEEING AND HEARING THE POOR

The peripatetic gentlemen viewers of the slums emphasized the visual, and indeed many of their recorded journeys included pictures, from the Doré–Jerrold collaboration (1869–1872), to John Thomson and Adolphe Smith's photographic *Street Life in London* (1877), to George Sims's three-volume compendium, *Living London* (1902), accompanied by lavish photographs.[22] These descriptions dwell on what was to be seen outdoors in the streets. As COS caseworker Helen Dendy wrote rather scornfully, their often stereotyped views were "the impression of the outsider who confines his investigations to the main thoroughfares, or makes official visits during the business hours." Yet the male spectators, with their cameralike eyes, also include some of the most visually detailed interior scenes of slum life available.[23]

The characteristic mode of the women observers was aural. Many were in professions that required them to listen and to talk: district nurses, charity caseworkers, rent collectors, or, later, school managers and health visitors. The nurse's or charity investigator's case history or the rent collector's weekly knock could elicit a dramatic story of martyrdom and redemption. And the women explorers also quite unashamedly eavesdropped. The anonymous "Sketches of Life in Buildings," published by Charles Booth in his first series of *Life and Labour of the People in London*, are, for example, mostly accounts of what a lady slum dweller overheard (for the buildings' thin walls enabled the author to hear what went on above and below her rooms, and the landing just outside her door was obviously a convenient place for neighbors to meet and chat). One young settlement worker in the 1890s especially enjoyed the invisibility of working at a boys' club refreshment counter, for despite the relative impenetrability of the local slang, "we hear much without listening."[24]

As Bonnie Smith has remarked, women and ladies all over Europe were talking together in these years, often about newly politicized topics: birth control, their husbands' violence or drinking, health care for children, state maternity provisions. The visitors had trouble penetrating the mothers' cautious reserve, their "provoking diffidence," as South London social worker Anna Martin called it. But the ladies were just as guilty of such reserve. They seldom told their own stories; when they spoke it was to ask questions, offer advice, give instructions, provide sympathy, or deliver threats. Margaret Loane, a district nurse who was also a prolific writer on working-class domestic life, despaired of any true communication with her patients. As she admitted, "All my conversations with my patients and their friends have been of an exceedingly one-sided character. . . . [I]n some cases I talked, and in some they did, but we never took anything like equal parts." Maud Pember Reeves, describing the early work of her Fabian Women's Group with a number of mothers in Kennington, a quiet working-class district in Lambeth, recalled the stiff courtesy of the working-class women, who readied themselves to wait out the lectures they expected.[25]

Yet in some cases the barriers were lifted a little, either because the ladies had the authority (as rent collectors, for instance, or midwives) to force the women to speak to them or because some of the pairs found each other attractive enough to make contact, however briefly, across the barriers of accent, dress, dirt, and odor. Ellen Chase, an American who collected rents in Deptford in the 1880s and 1890s, was an outgoing and sympathetic woman who listened to many stories of abandoned families, neighbors' quarrels, romance, violence—enough to fill the book she later wrote. She had been told, and reproduced, the story of the hardworking Singleton family through repeated talks with the mother and her children: about Mrs. Singleton's bad health, her strict and self-denying economies as she worked to equip each of her three daughters for good jobs in domestic service, and the fates of the children after their mother's death.[26]

Training as a midwife in a London maternity hospital and then in a slum district in the 1900s, Katherine Roberts chatted endlessly with her patients; their revealing talk helped me to understand pregnancy, abortion, and birth among the women of "outcast London" and is reproduced later in this book. When she was transferred to night duty at the hospital, the quiet and privacy stimulated still more conversation, and Roberts heard story after story that was "most pathetic." One woman's account "interested me much," she noted, and Roberts encouraged her to talk freely. The mother went on to tell the nurse about her own childhood of neglect and abuse and her plans to work as a charwoman to support her six children. The woman's uncomplaining determination made Roberts feel "ashamed" of her own dissatisfaction with her far-easier life. When Roberts left the hospital to begin her district midwifery training, she found still more opportunities for talk. As the neighbors waited with the midwife during a long labor or prepared a room for a confinement, Roberts explained, "I have had some quite interesting talks with these neighbors . . . and have learned much of their views of life and their way of living." The nurse even grilled one plump and very "costermongery" woman on the mechanics of pawning, revealing an ignorance her interlocutor found most hilarious.[27]

The visitors sometimes complained that their clients among the poor failed to acknowledge their social superiority. But some women did recognize the ladies in their midst. Rent collector Ella Pycroft (a physician's daughter) was treated protectively by local women. She took rooms in the Katherine Buildings in the late 1880s, hoping to forestall the Saturday night fights between husbands and wives that were so common there, but one battered woman good-naturedly urged Pycroft to keep out of it: "You're a lady and ain't used to 'em; we are, you see." In the late 1890s Edith Hogg, carrying out a house-by-house investigation of female home workers near the New Kent Road in South London, encountered a beautiful, defiant, but worn-looking woman who worked at the dirty and difficult trade of fur pulling. She said little while her two roommates chatted with the investigator, but as Hogg and the others exchanged farewells, she lifted her eyes from her work and said, simply, "Miss, I wish I had your life."[28]

Their experiences gave these explorers a mission to serve as interpreters of the East End to the West, an impulse that gives passion, for example, to Maud Pember Reeves's *Round About a Pound a Week*. Helen Dendy, a uniquely uncharitable interpreter, presented a penetrating if harsh view of working-class poverty, whose intricacies she had unraveled during five years of full-time COS work and residence in Shoreditch. Poverty, she said, was not a result of low wages but of the workers' failings in thrift, foresight, and planning, capacities that their social betters should be taking pains to teach them. The weight of these observers' opinion, however, certainly leaned toward sympathy, support, advocacy, and even inspiration from the poor.[29]

For the women whose social work was spawned by their participation in the suffrage movement or socialism, it was a solemn obligation to give a voice to disenfranchised laboring poor women—whether they appeared as workers, consumers, or mothers.[30] In their writings about poverty, they directly quoted the working women (the term they used to designate all working-class women, whether or not they were in paid employment) more than their predecessors did, often, as in the case of Bermondsey settlement worker Anna Martin, giving them large portions of the page. Though the authorial voice was surely the one that prevailed (the women themselves have to be classed as "informants," in the anthropologists' sense), the mixture of voices in turn-of-the-century and early twentieth-century writings is quite new: the scientific statements of the educated women about budgets, infant care, and nutrition; the shopping, family, and street stories of the mothers.

In these mixed texts, the poor women were sometimes, it seems, speaking on behalf of their better-off sisters who were prohibited from vulgar language, talk of sex, or open man hating. The endless stories of cruel and abusive husbands that the social explorers tell us in gruesome detail (fully substantiated by autobiographies, court cases, and judicial figures, to be sure) may have functioned as concealed statements about middle-class marriage. Husbands among the well-to-do inflicted subtler kinds of mental and physical torments, far harder to demonstrate in either criminal or divorce court, as James Hammerton's close study of divorce proceedings during these years reveals so vividly. In another area about which women of all classes had something to say—childbirth—nurse

Roberts rejoiced on her own behalf when a drunken and violent woman arrived at the hospital in labor, was told by the house surgeon to make "less noise," and responded in fury: "Oh, that's you, is it; God d——— you. I wish to heaven it was you had the pain, and I'd stand along of you, and tell you to make less noise." Wrote Roberts, "She echoed the sentiments of us all; and we were grateful to her for expressing them to him."[31]

THE DISCOVERY OF THE MOTHER

By the 1870s or 1880s, London poverty's cast of literary characters—the cat-meat man, the organ grinder, the watercress girl, the fallen woman, the muffin man—was expanded and complicated by another figure, the mother of a family. Mothers could be pathetic rather than frightening or colorful like some of the other classic slum types. Realist artist Frank Holl did several moving paintings in the 1870s of pitiful mothers, some in London and some in country settings: buying medicine for sick babies, abandoning a baby on the Thames embankment, burying and mourning dead children.[32] More often, however, the mother appears as a worn, shabbily dressed, hardworking woman with a practical mind and an awareness of her prerogatives in home and street. In 1871, when the newly formed school board for London, a leader in the nation, began its mission of compulsory education for children up to age ten, working-class mothers became public figures as probably never before. School board visitors (truant officers) and the education authorities whom they represented gradually learned that by and large it was the mothers, not the fathers, who decided whether or not a child would attend school, stay at home to "help," or take a job. COS caseworkers and rent collectors like Beatrice Potter and her coworker Ella Pycroft negotiated with wives over rent arrears and acted on the assumption that they had charge of their households. Charles Booth lodged with and admired these mothers in his private journeys in East London, though their significance is more muted in his *Life and Labour of the People in London*.[33]

But it was not until the 1890s (at least in England) that the middle-class observers had a framework for grasping the wider social significance of wives' domestic labor, the study of household-level consumption. In the 1880s and 1890s, the French sociologist Le Play's method, developed in the 1850s, of carefully recording over the course of a year the income and spending patterns of a few representative families was used in modified form in several major European surveys of workers' budgets.[34] This approach, employed to a limited extent by Booth, was more central to Rowntree's study of York, published in 1901. Rowntree's concept of "secondary" poverty, caused by the way that money was spent rather than by an inadequate wage, was partly based on the significance of women's domestic management.[35]

The budget studies graphically revealed to scholars and policymakers what working-class men, women, and children had taken for granted for decades, possibly centuries: the significance of wives' work in the home to the family's comfort and even survival. In his description of the lives of Londoners living on "small regular earnings" Booth wrote that "the comfort of their homes depends, even more than in other classes, on a good wife" who not only can earn money for the household but also can save it by means of clever and persistent economies. As Henry Higgs put it in an 1893 lecture to the Royal Statistical Society, "Nothing is so striking in the comparison of intensive budgets as the importance of good housewifery, which is often sufficient to turn the balance of comfort in favour of one workman whose wages are much below those of another."[36] Further implications of this discovery were not drawn by any but a small minority of this generation—for instance, that in view of this importance women ought to be granted the vote, family allowances, easier divorce, or access to jobs and professions. Indeed, the insights of this era were nearly lost to the policymaking world sometime after World War I and had practically to be argued anew in the 1945 discussions on the welfare state.

In the early twentieth century, there was a subtle shift in the terms in which female domestic management was discussed. The significance of mothers' work to household welfare was acknowledged and explored in detail in the far more numerous and vivid studies of working-class domestic life carried out in the 1900s and 1910s: the many books of district nurse Margaret Loane, some of Helen (Dendy) Bosanquet's, Alexander Paterson's *Across the Bridges* (1911), the many pamphlets and articles by Anna Martin (published in 1911–1922), Maud Pember Reeves's *Round About a Pound a Week* (1913), Clementina Black's *Married Women's Work* (1915), and V. de Vesselitsky's astute World War I household budget study, *Expenditure and Waste* (1917). Yet in the dialogues on state and local health policy that were part of the Infant Welfare movement, the position that the mothers' advocates laid out was ignored or distorted. The power that mothers exercised in the family was shiftily elided with resources and authority, and the reformers' plans for healthier British children at little or no public cost were transferred to the mothers via a multiplying series of punitive laws.

The "discovery" of the mother was part of the general middle-class recognition that the poor had their own distinct culture. Mothers and their domestic needs were in many ways the key to the order and pattern that the observers began to find in the noisy, bustling streets of the East End.[37] As orchestrators of household survival and arbiters of neighborhood morality, mothers were the figures around whom this working-class culture had coalesced.

What the social observers had discovered has been supported and expanded by recent historians of the working class. Eric Hobsbawm and Gareth Stedman Jones point to a transformation in London's (and England's) working-class life beginning in the 1870s in which home, mother, and neighborhood became the centers of a sometimes politically conservative but always self-defined working-class culture whose outlines remained relatively stable, at least in some districts, through Richard Hoggart's and Willmott and Young's day, the mid-1950s. The Saturday half-holiday in many London trades, the four national bank holidays legislated in 1871, the growth in London of betting on horses and of Britain's densest network of music halls, the foundation of the omnipresent Charity Organisation Society in 1869, the development of the fish-and-chips business, the decline of working-class radicalism, and the compulsory schooling of children all were products of these decades and give a distinct shape to the 1870–World War I period in the history of London workers. In many London districts the consolidation—despite households' endless moves within a radius of a few blocks during the later decades of the nineteenth century—of socially relatively uniform working-class neighborhoods where women ruled the streets and shops was another characteristic of this period. Radical club, union, friendly society, and workshop were yielding their prominence in defining the lives of working men to such neighborhood places as pub, street corner, music hall, and, sometimes, kitchen.[38]

The autobiographies and oral histories of old men and women who were children in London during these decades reflect the larger size and more central place of mothers in working-class life that distinguishes the years of this study. Indeed, the childhoods of several articulate autobiographers—Art Jasper, Dorothy Scannell, Joe Williamson, Alice Linton, and Walter Southgate among them—appear in chapter after chapter of this book as they recount their mothers' lives. The vocabulary of parents' love for their children, and of children's for their parents, as I observed in the Introduction, is a historical product; it has changed many times since the beginning of the nineteenth century. David Vincent's *Bread, Knowledge and Freedom,* a collective investigation of working-class autobiographies from earlier in the nineteenth century, describes many features of poverty that remained constant for more than a century: the association between death and debt, the importance of the family economy and children's labor in household survival, and the shaping of lives by work. But by and large, the earlier autobiographies are structured around the subject's individual struggle for education rather than around a relationship with a mother who establishes the rhythms of childhood and is the one to clear or close a path to a better life. The 1870–1918 childhood autobiographies may also be distinguished from later working-class accounts of childhood, like Jeremy Seabrook's remarkable *Mother and Son,* written in the late 1970s and describing his early years in the 1930s and 1940s, and Carolyn Steedman's *Landscape for a Good Woman,* a discussion of her London childhood in the 1950s and 1960s. Although both accounts are consumed by the figure of the mother (indeed, Seabrook describes his boyhood relationship with his mother as "haunted and obsessive"), the latter are scary figures to be understood with some sympathy but definitely to be escaped as the price of a sane adulthood. For those with late Victorian or Edwardian childhoods, mothers also were pivotal, but as good, or at least "good enough" (to use a term from a later era) figures, whose suffering is described, merit is celebrated, skill and cleverness are noted, and failures are excused. The varied autobiographical accounts of the children's lives from the late Victorian and Edwardian period are at least partly structured by gratitude, the desire to make one last offering, usually to a mother who has long been dead.[39]

As working-class mothers became focal figures in family and class, they increasingly were also objects of national and local policymaking. The care of children, and hence the activities of mothers, was scrutinized and redefined after 1870 by several kinds of legislation focusing on public health, education, or the rights of children. Public standards for parents' material care of their children (often with considerable community assent from organized working men) were being raised; concepts of what could be exacted from children in discipline and labor were becoming a bit more gentle; and parents were increasingly being held accountable to public authorities for their child care. In the late Victorian decades, one of the most important of the acts dealing directly with parents and children was the Prevention of Cruelty and Protection of Children Act of 1889[40] (called the "Children's Charter" by its advocates) plus its later amendments. The Poor Law Adoption Act of 1889 and the Custody of Children Act passed two years later demonstrated the willingness of authorities to take over permanently the care of children who had been removed from home because of their parents' cruelty. National factory legislation and LCC regulations limiting children's paid work further advanced the tendency to place more weight on parents and less on children for maintaining the family.

Of all the measures legislated during these years, compulsory education reached most deeply into the daily lives of the working classes. It is true that over 40 percent of the young children (under ten) of the country were already attending school in some form before Forster's 1870 Education Act. Admittedly also, a London perspective makes the transformation produced by schooling overly dramatic, as London's own education scheme was already in place by 1871, which was a decade before that in many other parts of the country. London's legal school-leaving ages were almost invariably higher, too, than those of most other regions, beginning at ten and reaching fourteen by the turn of the century.[41] But for those households that had for centuries relied on the financial contributions of even young children, compulsory education disrupted a delicate balance.[42]

The 1870 Education Act was actually the start of a process in which, whereas fathers' positions changed less dramatically, that of mothers in wage-dependent households was radically restructured. As mothers lost more and more of their children's help, time, and earning ability, legislators were, especially after 1900, assigning them additional duties. These new obligations—to dress children more "respectably," feed them hot lunches, care for their health in new ways—mothers came to regard as deeply personal. They had entered the modern complex of jobs and emotions that we connect with motherhood. Raising a child was indeed now harder, not only because of what the new legislation actually imposed, but also because of what it said about motherhood and childhood. This rewriting of the terms of mothering was surely, as I explain in Chapter 4, a factor in lowering the fertility rates of the women of the poorest London boroughs, whose reproductive statistics declined little until the twentieth century, with dramatic declines only after World War I.

The lives described in this book spanned two or even three generations framed by two significant pieces of national social legislation, William E. Forster's Education Act of 1870 and H. A. L. Fisher's Maternity and Child Welfare Act of 1918. Historical change in the conventional sense came rapidly during these years. The mothers of the 1870s lived under the reigns of Gladstone and then Disraeli; they witnessed the onset of the first "great depression" in the late 1870s and, sometimes barely literate themselves, coped with the new school attendance laws. Those who were adults in the 1880s and 1890s were ruled by several more Gladstone regimes, lived through national debates on granting more legal rights to married women and extending the vote to new groups of males, and were probably affected by the "new unionism" movement in which masses of unskilled London workers were organized. Socialist and labor-oriented political parties and organizations proliferated during their years of adulthood and were real forces in borough-level politics. The mothers of the early twentieth century might have been the granddaughters or late-born daughters of the first group. In an era of population consciousness and an arms competition with Germany, they were objects of intense municipal activity promoting infant and child health and nutrition. Nationally, a Liberal government goaded by Lloyd George introduced old-age pensions and health insurance for better-paid workers. The street-centered life of the London poor began to fade during their lifetimes as the automobiles of the rich challenged the children of the poor for the control of the throughfares. The domestic world of the poor was utterly disrupted by the outbreak of war in August 1914. Thousands of workers, male and female, lost their jobs in 1914 and early 1915 in the reorientation to wartime production, and then, of course, many of the unemployed men enlisted in the armed services, and others later were conscripted. But many aspects of marriage, sex, procreation, and childhood in the 1870s would have been recognizable in the 1910s, and so I have sometimes treated them in the static mode common (until very recently) in anthropological description. Indeed, the hands of the "family time" clock turn far more slowly than do those of political time.[43]

CHAPTER 2

"There Is Meat Ye Know Not Of"
Feeding a Family

In the chronically hungry London population, providing meals was, more than any other kind of maternal activity, the source of the enormous positive charge that the word *muvver* and its cognates (mammy, mam, mum) carried in cockney dialect. Much of the "awesome responsibility" of motherhood in the years before World War I was played out around a woman's shopping for and preparing food on sums of money over which she had little control.[1] Meals signified maternal service—the safety and comfort it brought—and also, if the food was served and eaten properly, respectability for everyone at the table. Food was obviously also a matter of life or death, for starvation deaths continued to be a regular occurrence even in the kinder years after 1870.[2]

It is not surprising that many of the major political upheavals of the modern West have begun with angry crowds of mostly women insisting on food for their families. Monarchs knew that they could not safely rule without the tacit support of the mothers, the ones who kept their subjects fed, and it was one of the triumphs of the Western industrial states that sometime around the middle of the nineteenth century, they could offer them either a good meal or the hope of it. The attentiveness of the women to their husbands' and children's food, which seems so securely a "private" sentiment, can emerge into the public world at a moment's notice. In the twentieth century, the female sense of "food entitlement" has taken the form of riots at bakeries, support for predominantly male strikers, demands on municipal or national governments for cash and services, the organization of boycotts and cooperatives, and participation in guerrilla and resistance movements. Mothers might be slow to protect their own bodies, but when those of their children are threatened, they can be fierce and forceful.[3]

Though the scientific study of nutrition—vitamin deficiency diseases, caloric needs, and the like—was just developing in the two decades before World War I, the relationship between reduced growth and poor rations was understood at least epidemiologically by turn-of-the-century medical researchers.[4] Mothers, too, understood that there was a direct link between diet and well-being. They knew that they needed to keep their families "full," that milk was good for babies, that meat was good for everyone, that cooked meals were preferable to cold, and that people needed spicy accents in a dull diet.

That food in its many aspects dominated the lives and thoughts of the mothers of London's poor would have come as no surprise to Audrey Richards, a pioneer anthropologist of food and nutrition, or those anthropologists like Mary Douglas, whose work has emphasized food as symbol or metaphor in social relationships. As Roland Barthes put it, food is not only a set of products but also "a system of communication, a body of images."[5] Historians have been reluctant to tackle food as culture in the same way, although caloric intake, and the diet in general for the British working classes, and histories of particular industries (such as those of meat, milk, and jam) all have been well delineated. The historian's prejudice in favor of the material world—food prices, living standards, production methods—provides a good counter to the overly "cultural" approach to food of the Mary Douglas school, which concentrates on meals as ritual. After all, food is produced, sold, shipped, taxed, marketed, bought, and cooked as well as served and eaten. The historical study of the worlds of wives and mothers brings into focus the earlier stages of obtaining meals as points at which families connect with world and local markets.

The ballads and broadsides, street gossip, and public and private quarrels of London's plebeian culture had long reverberated with struggles for money between pub and grocer, husband and wife, and many a fictional woman laid out her weekly food expenses for the edification of an ignorant husband or bitterly complained that the publican's wife was fattening on the cash that would have fed the wife and children at home.[6] Food was a little less scarce at the turn of the twentieth century, and professionals knew more about nutrition, but the broad outlines of the mothers' story remained generally the same.

A woman's responsibility for producing regular meals of a certain kind meant that her emotional equilibrium was on the line at every mealtime. In the austere context of a Charity Organisation Society hearing on school dinners in the 1880s, a Walworth woman confessed that during a period when her husband was ill and she was going out to work, "One day they [the children] had to go to school without breakfast. That was the hardest trial I had." At about the turn of the century, another Walworth child noticed that whether or not his mother actually had a real Sunday dinner to serve her family, she always rattled the plates for the other tenants to hear at the appropriate times. A woman in Wapping, managing to provide her children in wartime with a Christmas dinner that consisted only of a large plain boiled pudding served with the golden syrup that she had cleverly "saved for an emergency," was overwhelmed with misery: "Mother sat and cried as she watched us eat it." In postwar Lambeth, another woman cried in nearly suicidal despair for hours on a Sunday when her family had nothing to eat but a box of Quaker Oats. When some local nuns brought the family a Sunday dinner, she cried all the more.[7]

The matter of food for their children engaged the passions of London wives as did few other matters, passions that they allowed a full range of expression. In 1910, a mother in Hoxton "nearly went mad" when she learned that her young son, Art Jasper, who had worked all day helping a brake driver, had had almost nothing to eat that day.[8] Starving the children was one of the few crimes for which wives were not inclined to forgive their husbands, and accordingly, such charges often figure in the domestic disputes that ended at the Old Bailey, London's highest criminal court. For example, when Eleanor Ey, who was on trial in the early 1870s at the Old Bailey for throwing acid in her estranged husband's face, had a chance to explain her side of the story, she told it not only in terms of the violence to which her husband Amos had subjected her over the twelve years of their marriage in various parts of Marylebone, and his sexual unfaithfulness, but also as a poignant story of food that he had withheld from her and her children. "He would not support me, and has left me with a pennyworth of milk for me and my child," she charged. At one point Eleanor Ey was in the Middlesex Hospital for four months, and "during that time he never came near me to give me even an ounce of tea. The last fortnight he deserted my children and did not give them a loaf of bread."[9] Even in the sanitized form in which the court reporter took Ey's deposition, it is clear that "an ounce of tea" and "a loaf of bread" are signs for the speaker of the husband's most basic duty.

The pressure, the need, and the desire to feed the children appeared in many contexts of women's lives: as they beguiled charities for goods, food or cash; found jobs for their school-leaving children; lent to and borrowed from one another; berated their husbands for drinking or laziness; or frantically scrounged up the food for a violent husband's evening meal.

THE CULTURAL MEANINGS OF FOOD

"Human Occasions"

Autobiographies by both the sons and the daughters of late Victorian and Edwardian London, most of them written in old age and hence fairly recently, abound with memories of meals and recipes. When adopted by working-class writers, the autobiography form has traditionally dictated the conjoining of mother and meals. In Herbert Morrison's autobiography, which has far less on childhood experiences than most, only the formula remains, with its human detail mostly gone. The section on his mother begins: "My mother, who had been a maidservant and also worked as a ward-maid in a hospital, was an excellent cook."[10] In any case, life stories demonstrate—given what is known about the quality of attention that yields short- and long-term memories—the privileging of food in the social experience of these generations.[11]

Acutely conscious as a boy in the 1900s of his widowed mother's struggles to feed her children, Joseph Williamson, who later became a high-church slum priest, includes the basic London stew recipe (3 pennysworth of stewing meat, plus carrots, onions, and celery or parsley, potatoes, and dumplings) in his own autobiography. But food remained the emblem of the Church of England school where he found his calling.

> My first day at school stands out clearly in my mind. A crust of bread and a kiss was my breakfast as I ran across the road to the infants' school of St. Saviour's at the age of five. When I got to school, there was placed before me a white mug of hot milk and a bun; it looked very big. I didn't believe it was for me. I looked up, and there was a big fat man in black, with a funny hat on, looking down at me. He had a big face with a double chin; he was smiling; it was a lovely face. The man put his hand on my head and said, simply, "Eat." That was Father Dolling [a well-known and beloved slum priest], and I think I have felt the touch ever since.[12]

With his memory of Father Dolling's touch and the juxtaposition of the mother's little "crust of bread" and St. Saviour's gigantic bun, Joe Williamson invites us to imagine that devoted and admiring son though he was, he knew from that moment that the church across the street had more to feed him than did his hardworking mother.

Or we might consider the more prosaic use of food in Dorothy Scannell's autobiography, *Mother Knew Best: Memoir of a London Girlhood,* in which recipes help tell the story of the Chegwiddens' cheerful home, its productive father, and its energetic mother. Though her household, where the father's pay eventually reached 2 pounds, was better off than most, food still had great significance. Sixpence would feed the family of twelve.

Agnes [an older sister] would sometimes get the dinner for Mother. Mother would give her sixpence and she would buy half a pound of leg of beef [this represented, of course, less than an ounce of meat per person at this meal], a ha'porth of pot-herbs, a pennyworth of suet, and three ha'porth of potatoes, and for this sixpence there was a dinner for all. I suppose the young ones had gravy and dumplings. Mother used Edwards' dessicated soup powder . . . which she thought "made" the stew. There was, of course, her big rice pudding to follow.[13]

Neighborhood and family solidarity revolved around food and its preparation. Music-hall performers sang of food: Cockney Gus Elen's " 'Arf a Pint of Ale" was just as much about the food that accompanied it; later, Shoreditch-born Harry Champion sang about the virtues of "A Little Bit of Cucumber" and "Boiled Beef and Carrots." Lovers called out edible terms of endearment: honey, sugar, sweetie, "barrel of treacle" (love), "tart" (a girl).[14] At the perimeters of working-class family life there also was food: the neighbor's gift of sweets to the children; the corner mission with its children's dinners or quarts of soup; from the 1880s on, the fried fish whose odors filled the night air; and the banners of striking workers, like those the dockers carried in the 1889 strike depicting "the docker's dinner."[15]

The eating habits of the London poor were by no means organized around the rational principle of maximum nutritional value for minimum outlay (nor indeed is the cuisine of any culture). From a nutritional standpoint, Londoners spent too much of their sparse household money on sugar and meat. Not enough money went into dairy products, green vegetables, cereals, or legumes, the last of which is a cheap source of protein. And this does not even account for the cash that went into such wasteful items as beer, gin, sweetened tea, and tobacco—"drug foods," as Sidney Mintz labeled them.[16] Victorian and Edwardian mothers, the "key kitchen persons" of the working class (to use the valiantly nonsexist terminology adopted by one recent American team of nutrition researchers), resisted efforts to restructure their work as food selectors and preparers toward better nutritional value. Their choices and work in the kitchen were bound to respond to other issues as well: price, taste, ease of preparation, and family power arrangements. Poor as it was, the Londoners' diet represented a focus for the "human occasions"[17] that wives and mothers struggled to maintain.

Of Men and Meals

Londoners spent lavishly on meat. The developed nations' current worries about cholesterol, excess calories, and the ecological extravagance of meat should not obscure the fact that in the past and in most of the world today, meat is a special food—relished and prized more than most others, despite (or because of) its scarcity. Meat is the most compact way of getting protein into the diet, and it contains numerous vitamins and minerals as well. Indeed, many languages have a special word for meat craving, as opposed to ordinary hunger.[18]

London mothers, and children too, believed that meat had special power as a food, though most of the recipes they offered were really only ways of imparting a meat flavor to starches. A Ranyard nurse's duties brought her into contact in 1910 with a woman who, at thirty-four, already had thirteen children and fed them daily dinners of meat stew: "If they get that every day, they won't hurt," was her optimistic view. " 'Basil's beef builds bonny babies,' they used to say," proudly repeated Tottenham butcher Basil Cant's son. Many of the working-class children of this era who lived into healthy old age—probably echoing words they had heard in their mothers' kitchens—attributed this to the meat meals— stews, pies, puddings—they had had as children.[19]

Meat was a particularly eloquent signifier of class. The better-off ate much more of it than did their poorer neighbors. From the 1880s through the 1900s, households with weekly incomes over 30 shillings had fully twice as much meat per person as did those with incomes under 18 shillings (though the amount even in the better-fed households was still under 2 pounds a week per person).[20]

Mushy foods (oatmeal, gruels, possibly pease pudding) signified social dependence and degradation, whereas meat meant independence—a good safe distance from the workhouse. We must think, first of all, of the classic institutional diet—workhouse, prison, poor-law school—with its bread and gruel menus to grasp one reason why London household budgets among the poor were prodigal with meat or fish despite the high cost of these foods relative to other nourishing fare like cheese or beans. Oliver Twist's insubordination, declared the workhouse beadle, could be squarely blamed on his eating a food unsuitable for paupers: "meat." The "privation of animal food" was one of the routine punishments at a boys' asylum at Hackney Wick in the 1830s. "Work'us stuff" was indeed what some of Margaret Nevinson's East London neighbors in the 1890s called oatmeal when presented with her well-meaning suggestion for a cheap and nutritious meal. Even workhouse residents were not resigned to their low-meat diet, and guardians hoping to improve the inmates' morale without raising the rates were active in trying out the cheap, new imported meats that had begun to arrive on the British market in the 1870s and 1880s.[21]

Meat was equally powerful in marking gender distinctions and prerogatives. Men's greater access to meat, a truism in modern anthropology,[22] was a feature of working-class London domestic life as well. A skilled and orderly wife struggled to indicate the special place of the father in the family with his special chair by the fire and his superior, meaty food. Beside their share of meat-flavored family hot pots, women's and children's diets were not so different from those of bread-eating workhouse inmates. It was actually the men who ate meat, as was well known to contemporary students of family budgets, from Friedrich Engels (in the 1840s), to Dr. Edward Smith (in the 1860s), to early twentieth-century infant-welfare workers. From the detailed dietaries collected by Dr. Thomas Oliver from various points in Britain in the mid-1890s, historian Derek Oddy tabulated the daily calorie and protein intakes of men and women, with dramatic results. The men not only consumed many more calories, on average, than did the women, 3,320 to 1,870, but also more than twice as much protein and almost three times as much fat. Most of this contrast is due to the men's much greater consumption of meat.[23] When a meat-starved little girl, daughter of a cranky and selfish casually employed dock laborer, saw a saucepan full of bacon bones at a neighbor's house, she readily proposed a game of "Mothers and Fathers." Playing the father, Mrs. Benjamin (the woman the little girl became) got the biggest bone to chew before she went off to "work," and the biggest when she returned, saying: "Well, I've done a hard day's work, what have you got for my tea?" Eventually, "We had every bit of meat off all the bones."[24]

The rationality (in terms of group survival) of such disproportionate amounts of meat going to men is defended by Marvin Harris as the "breadwinner effect," which ensures that when family resources are scarce, "the principal wage earner gets fed well enough to go to work, even if this means that other family members are hardly fed at all." Pember Reeves's formulation was that "the wage-earner must be fed."[25] Yet the "breadwinner effect" explanation is not very convincing, as countless feminist scholars have noted. First, as a result of pregnancy, lactation, and heavy domestic and/or waged labor, women's caloric needs were generally not much lower than those of their husbands. In any case, in hundreds of cultures in the world, women in fact do heavier labor than men; women in Africa, by and large, work longer hours than men do,[26] yet even men who do relatively little labor get extra meat.

The "breadwinner effect" can explain men's often superior meals only if that term is understood to designate not the breadwinner's greater caloric requirements but his (and occasionally her) higher status and the housewife's sense that she has to propitiate the wage earner(s). In a London clerk's household, there was plenty of food for all, and presumably the man's caloric needs were not enormous, but "we always saved the best for father." Working teenaged children often got extra food as well. A young boy in Hackney whose evening meal was usually bread or toast and dripping sometimes got a contribution of something special from his employed older brother's plate: "Probably a little bit of fish

. . . something like you know, he was at work." The contrast between the two meals a Limehouse mother made in succession, bread and cheese for her unemployed carter husband, a hot meal carried to her employed daughter's workplace, makes the point best. The man's loss of work also brought with it the decline of his domestic status.[27]

When a London wife served her husband his kipper, saveloy (a kind of sausage, of German invention), or chop, she was simultaneously acknowledging his value as a worker, his privileges in his household, and the power of the meat to hold a place for him in the separate world of men. A phenomenological study of men's workplace lunches, packed at home by their wives but eaten where other men could see them, would be a good supplement to this chapter's study of food in its domestic context. In Poplar in the 1900s, Leah Chegwidden daily packed her husband a huge Cornish pasty to take to work (both partners had spent their childhoods and young adulthoods in Cornwall), which "he used to say . . . was the envy of all his mates." But Robert Roberts knew of many husband–wife quarrels over workplace packed-lunches in contemporaneous Salford factories: "Some men [demanded] fillings which the family budget could not sustain. One mechanic, I remember, after a violent quarrel with his wife found next day that lunch consisted of the rent book between two slices of bread."[28] This wife's provocative gesture was her assertion that helping her husband establish his place in a coworkers' pecking order would have to take a back seat to her most central obligation, to maintain the household.

The events surrounding the hardships of the 1889 dock strike suggest that a disjunction between the rations of men and women was an accepted fact of working-class life. The meager vegetarian "docker's dinner" of bread crusts, vegetable tops, or half-rotten onions—a common piece of iconography in the strike's daily parades and processions[29]—represented the meal the dockers themselves could eat on their inadequate hourly wage. (And in his speeches, John Burns assured his audiences that the men were striking for money for food, not for drink.) The strike fund was used to provide (very inadequate) meals for the men only, leaving their families to fend for themselves. The union policy was never criticized, but East London newspapers were full of reports of starving women and children and of the efforts of charitable groups to feed them.[30] For the charities, too, accepted the dietary division of households by gender, and in any case most were unwilling to support the dockers directly. During the 1912 strike, the Stepney poor-law guardians were looking for ways to aid the dockers' children without helping their parents, and a School Care Committee in Poplar determined to offer extra school dinners in that borough and were fully supported by the LCC. On the other hand, it was a matter of honor for the men to avoid eating their wives' food. "The general rule among men," according to Anna Martin's observations of the 1911 dock strike, "was to touch no food indoors. What the wife manages to secure is held sacred for her use and the children's."[31]

In more comfortable periods, the separation of household spending streams by sex meant that extra household money was spent not only on the husband's meat, but also on his larger quantities of all foods and special additions to his meals, like shrimp, winkles, celery, and eggs. What the inequality in diet between men and their families meant might be imagined from a look at the first three days of a Lambeth household's meals. Mrs. X., whom Maud Pember Reeves judged a good household manager, got roughly a pound each week from her husband for running the house; she had four preschool children. Mr. X., a carter, took only a shilling as pocket money and ate his dinners at home every day.

SUNDAY. Breakfast: One loaf, 1 oz. butter, ½ oz. tea, a farthing's-worth of tinned milk, a half-pennyworth of sugar. Kippers extra for Mr. X. Dinner: Hashed beef, batter pudding, greens, and potatoes. Tea: Same as breakfast, but Mr. X. has shrimps instead of kippers.

MONDAY. Breakfast: Same as Sunday. Mr. X has a little cold meat. Dinner: Sunday's dinner cold, with pickles, or warmed up with greens and potatoes. Tea: One loaf, marmalade, and tea. Mrs. X has two eggs.

TUESDAY. Breakfast: One loaf, 1 oz. butter, two pennyworth of cocoa. Bloaters [lightly smoked whole herrings] for Mr. X. Dinner: Bread and dripping, with cheese and tomatoes [tomatoes were very rare in working-class dietaries before World War I and were viewed with suspicion in Salford, according to Roberts, but as they were cheap and recommended for their vitamins, they mark Mrs. X. as the good manager she was]. Tea: One loaf, marmalade, and tea. Fish and fried potatoes for Mr. X.

At just about every meal, as these samples show, the husband ate dishes different from those on the table for the other five members of his family.[32]

The London fathers and elder brothers who routinely dined on fare for which they had worked hard but over which their wives and children were literally drooling were not monsters who enjoyed tormenting their families; their dietary privileges and their families' deprivation were simply on the edges of awareness. Children hung about them begging tidbits: the top of the father's egg, or the "ears" (a euphemism for the uneaten corners) of the haddock.[33] To eat better than one's family often obviously meant eating alone. As Dorothy Scannell remembered, her father, Walter Chegwidden, often took his superior meals in private, for he disliked the "pairs and pairs of intensely staring eyes" that accompanied him as he bit into "some delicacy which the rest of us had not received." "Sometimes," Scannell continued, "he would rub the top of his head uncomfortably and say to Mother, 'Haven't the children had their dinner? Have you given them enough to eat? They are looking at me as though I have robbed them.' " Chegwidden, indulged and serviced by his lively and elegant wife, fanatical about his particular chair and about the dangers of "smells," proud of his homemade truss, is an endearing, quirky figure, a faithful earner, a fond husband, and a vivid presence in the lives of his ten very happy and extraordinarily upwardly mobile children. Not selfish, greedy, or cruel, Chegwidden was simply a husband, a father, and a worker who unthinkingly exercised the several prerogatives attached to these positions.[34]

The Oatmeal Wars

As her household's "key kitchen person," it was a wife's responsibility to negotiate between household needs and power relations, her own abilities and facilities for buying and cooking, and what the market—local and world—offered her. She was, in addition, the focal point of nutritionists and food reformers of all stripes: temperance workers, vegetarians, pudding ladies, oatmeal aficionados, brown bread campaigners, and infant-welfare workers keen on breast feeding. Especially near and after the turn of the twentieth century, working-class wives in London and everywhere in Britain found themselves at the center of a low-grade class war in which even their competence at feeding their children was called into question. We can see this struggle especially from the 1880s in some of the rhetoric of the middle-class figures who were involved, mostly in their capacity as school managers, in providing schoolchildren with cheap or free dinners. Among the managers' many and mixed ambitions were reeducating the children out of their "slum tastes" and, through the children, reforming the food habits of their mothers. That is, getting the children actually to like poverty foods like puddings, oatmeal, rice, and macaroni and teaching them good table manners would eventually change the way their mothers cooked and served the food.[35]

By the early twentieth century, "Why do not the poor use porridge?" was an "ever-recurring question," as one social worker sarcastically phrased it.[36] The synechdochic bowl of oatmeal hovered about all discussions of "the social question" as a statement about the refusal of the poor to improve themselves and, more pointedly, about the refusal of the mothers of the poor to use their limited housekeeping funds wisely. Oatmeal is indeed nutritious, especially in B vitamins, and is inexpensive. But from the seventeenth century, oatmeal "pottages" had become more and more confined to the north and west of the country; confirmed Londoner Samuel Johnson considered oats suitable only for feeding horses. Although the upper classes in the south of England had begun to enjoy oatmeal for breakfast from about 1870, eating porridge was nonetheless not a London tradition among the poor. When a Ranyard superintendent in Bow recommended it at a mothers' meeting in the late 1870s, the suggestion was not met with excitement: "They seemed to think bread and potatoes better, and sometimes a little fish."[37]

Fabian feminist Maud Pember Reeves wholeheartedly supported the Lambeth mothers' negative position on "the gospel of porridge," recognizing it as an alien intrusion into the working-class home. Several of them, Pember Reeves wrote, had indeed tried serving porridge but had found, because they could not afford milk for it and because their few cooking pots tended to retain odors of earlier meals, that when they gave it to their families, "they 'eaved at it." Pember Reeves not disapprovingly tells her readers that a husband contemplating a meal of porridge commented, "Ef you gives me that stinkin' mess, I'll throw it at yer."[38]

An encounter between a working-class child in particular and a social worker would—sooner or later, it seems—involve oatmeal. A group of boys at a summer camp in 1908 were required to eat "at least part" of their porridge, though some only "stared at it and messed it about." An East End school manager and Toynbee Hall resident wholeheartedly believed that London children would eat porridge if it were accompanied by a lot of milk and sugar. Some school-meals workers reported hopefully that children who had come to like school porridge were persuading their mothers to make it.[39] In general, though, oatmeal was a food that middle-class officials of various kinds attempted literally to stuff down the throats of the workers, a nauseating reminder of their social status. Refusing the porridge, throwing it at the provider (even when it was a beleaguered mother pressured by local social workers), or simply "messing it about" were defenses of bodily and social integrity, as indeed were the cockneys' preferences for their customary foods, however thriftless and nutritionless they may have been.

The Sunday Dinner

Another choice that housewives made as a kind of reflex was a seemingly odd one: to spend a good portion of the week's food money on a single meal, the Sunday dinner, even if it meant risking semistarvation by the end of the week. The Sunday meal was not, properly speaking, a ritual if that term means (as Bocock defines it) a "bodily action in relation to symbols" that, like those involving the church, the monarchy, or the military, are formally acknowledged as such.[40] Without calling it a ritual, though, we might say that the Sunday dinner was exceptionally meaningful. It is significant that two of the examples of wives' passions revolving around meals that began this chapter involved Sunday meals: the Walworth wife in a bad week who rattled the dinner plates for the neighbors' benefit, as if a Sunday dinner were in progress; and the Lambeth mother who could not face an oatmeal meal on Sunday.

The Sunday dinner contributed to the distinctive atmosphere of working-class life in London. In Edwardian Battersea, in a district of railway employees—crewmen, drivers, firemen, engineers, plate layers—the park on Sunday mornings was completely empty of women. Only men could be found rowing on the lake in Battersea Park, for their wives all were at home preparing dinner. On Sunday mornings, the street markets all over London, too, were far more a male preserve than they were at other times. And the pubs, heavily populated with men at most times, were exclusively so during their Sunday morning and early afternoon opening hours. Even the steady and respectable Battersea railway workers stopped in at the pub before dinner, though they were "careful" to arrive for the meal on time, as Edward Ezard, a "Battersea boy," explained, alluding to the thousands of nasty Sunday husband–wife confrontations that the men's drunken, tardy arrival at their dinners generated.[41] (World War I's shorter Sunday morning pub opening hours supported the wives' position.) Although the well-paid railway workers did not have to worry where their next meal was coming from, they, too, would eat much better at Sunday dinner than at other meals.

Some of the day's formality was associated with going to church, and although the London working classes were notorious for their religious indifference, their children, from the very poorest to the most prosperous homes, were sent to Sunday school at least once during the day. For adults and children, the day was marked off by special clothes, and "anyone who appeared on Sunday in work-a-day clothes was beyond the pale," as Fred Willis wrote of respectable working-class life at a fictional 101, Jubilee Rd, S.E.[42] The girls' newly starched white pinafores or best Sunday dresses, hats, hair ribbons, boots, and even gloves; the boys' uncomfortably stiff Norfolk suits, and restrictions on children's outdoor play all marked Sunday as a special, if not a necessarily pleasant, day. The solemnity of the day was heightened by the use of the parlor for the dinners—in those households that had them—and for the Sunday tea later on in the day. In those households that could afford it, special foods were served at dinner and also at breakfast and evening tea, often but not always reserved for the father: bacon or eggs at breakfast and winkles, watercress, shrimp, or celery at tea.

A Sunday dinner could seem desperately significant. In a grim 1876 Old Bailey case that had ended with a distraught mother's murder of her little girl, a Barnsbury couple reduced to near-destitution pawned the children's shoes to provide enough for the Sunday dinner. The St.

Pancras "Pudding Lady" who spent hours in the kitchens of the poor of her district attempted to characterize the neighborhood's position on Sunday dinners: "All these families feel poverty most if it deprives them of their Sunday dinner; they do not mind living on tea and bread all the week if they can have a good Sunday meal. . . . Also they all have time to enjoy the meal, the memory of which lasts till the next Sunday." The heaping up of expenditure on just that one meal might be simply viewed as an example of high-handed, improvident spending, as the meal happened to take place the day after most men on weekly wages were paid. But there was more to it. We need to think of the week's meals syntagmatically, that is, as a patterned cycle, in which the parts are endowed with meaning partly because of their place in the whole week's chain of meals and perhaps also in global terms. Writing about Sundays and Sunday dinners, Willis commented that in school geography lessons he had learned that "the Indian can live on a handful of rice a day," which made him and his classmates "feel a particularly opulent race" during their Sunday dinners.[43] A good portion of London's population, around a third, lived in poverty and ate something like the British equivalent of the Indian's "handful of rice." As Florence Petty sympathetically observed, the "memory" of the Sunday meal, plus the daily bread, tea, and a few other condiments, allowed even the very poor to feel like respectable human beings all week long, despite their harsh material lives.

The male headship of the household was acted out through the Sunday meal even if subverted at every turn during the week, for another function that ritual (or semiritual, in this case) fulfills is to obscure conflict or disorder. By carving the meat on Sundays, fathers dramatized the fact that the money for the Sunday joint had come from their work, even though the meat had been in their wives' hands through the many earlier phases of shopping, cooking, fire building, and so forth. The fathers' dominance over their children was on weekdays a theoretical rather than a practical fact, as the mothers were normally the disciplinarians.[44] On Sundays, though, the authority of the father was often exerted at dinner; the children at table were variously required to remain silent, eat everything on their plates, say grace, request permission to leave the table, and observe the proprieties in table manners. "Oh you ate with your knife—Gawd help you. Get a smack with—with a—with a carving knife. . . . the flat end of it of course," was one man's vivid memory of the penalty for one kind of transgression in his Battersea household in the 1910s. Another woman remembered her father's mealtime (daily) discipline as a real nightmare: "Because father was so strict at the table . . . our lives were a misery—they were really a misery at the table. We wasn't allowed to look up, speak, breathe or anything else."[45]

MONEY, FOOD, AND THE MARKET

Shopping in the World Market

Though her own thoughts were focused on bloaters and butter, the housewife setting out to the shops was a participant in a world market that, in the years we are considering here, had begun to work enormously to her advantage. Britain's present and former colonies were providing cheap meat, butter, tea, sugar, chocolate, and fruit, and steam power was getting the food to London before it spoiled. Especially in the last decade of the nineteenth century, the amount of meat imported from South America and New Zealand, for example, was expanding rapidly, doubling between 1888 and 1897. By the 1880s, the British fishing industry had begun, thanks to refrigeration combined with steam trawling, to supply the metropolis liberally with its characteristic treat, fish and chips. Industrial food-processing methods were providing the London housewife with cheap, new, and fairly tasty foods: margarine, cheap jams, golden syrup (a processed form of molasses)—all of which could be used to make bread seem like a meal. The food was cheap because it drew increasingly on the enormous grain-growing prairies of North America; by 1914, 80 percent of wheat consumed in Britain was imported.[46] Sweets added zest to the lives and palates of London's poor children, for Britain's confectionery industry also "took off" during this period.

In a minor triumph of government intervention regulating the contents and manufacture of some foods, what the shopper bought during these years was less adulterated and less likely to be rotten than were the goods her mother had purchased: Her bread was less apt to be mixed with alum or sawdust, her tea with harmful dyes or elm leaves.[47]

Money was much more likely to be transformed into food for the table when it came in the form of savings from cheaper commodities than in the form of higher wages. In one decade, from 1877 to 1887, the retail prices of the sorts of foods for which working-class wives were shopping fell by almost a third, a result of both increasing imports and lower taxes. Mutton, bread, fish, tea, sugar, and fruit all were becoming less expensive for late Victorian housewives from the 1870s through the late 1890s. From the late 1890s to 1914, on the other hand, there was a small decline in the wife's purchasing power. Several economic slumps early in this century affected London's economy, especially after 1902. The cost of living actually rose somewhat in the country as a whole, and real wages in London, according to one calculation, declined by about 7 percent between 1900 and the outbreak of World War I.[48]

The new or newly affordable foods characteristic of the years after

1870 represent, as many food historians have observed, a real transformation in the daily diet of workers in Britain. Sidney Mintz less sanguinely notes that slave-produced and colonial products, especially tea and sugar, made it possible during the years of industrialization for workers to survive and even to feel well fed on incomes that were otherwise below subsistence. The labor of the slave or, later, the contract laborer or overworked self-employed Jamaica sugar worker supplemented the toil of the metropolitan workers in priming the industrial capitalist pump. The London housewife, choosing foods for her family with her few shillings, was able now to stretch them with "drug foods": former luxuries like tea, coffee, sugar, and tobacco—all of which satisfy or allay hunger while providing little actual nutrition.[49]

Food and Rent in Household Budgets

Food was the largest single item of household expenditure. As much as 60 percent of British working-class income between the 1880s and the start of World War I went for food, as the many family budget studies carried out in those years demonstrate.[50] But among a substantial part of the population in London and elsewhere, with low incomes, high rents, and other fixed expenses that devoured the weekly wage, the proportion of income available for food fell considerably below the averages calculated in the budget surveys. Sociologist Hilary Graham observes that because food is more elastic than most other items in the household budget, it is actually "at meal times that the meaning of poverty is most acutely felt" among the poor today—meals skipped, especially by parents, and a monotonous high-carbohydrate diet.[51]

Some of the London household budgets that I selected at random from my own files actually indicate less spending on food than was the national "norm," somewhere between 40 and 50 percent, at least ten percentage points lower than the figures calculated for the 1890s.[52] This difference demonstrates not more discretionary income but higher rents than elsewhere in Britain. London's expensive housing kept poor households short of food. A housewife in Bow who kept accounts early in the twentieth century prepared a detailed and readable weekly budget that, like the others I have described, involved spending less than half of the man's weekly pay on food. More than 9 of the wife's 23 shillings were committed to rent and fuel, and the costs of insurance, clothing, and cleaning materials left her only about 10 shillings with which to feed a family of eight. Or to take a particularly harsh case: In the early 1890s, the household of a young jobbing plumber, his wife, and their three children aged eight and under who lived near Loughborough Junction in South London survived and ate on enormously fluctuating sums. The husband had become ill with lead poisoning and was hospitalized in the winter of 1891. Two weeks' delay, both husband and wife were sure, in getting on outdoor parish relief while the man was at the hospital and during which they had "nearly starved" (and frozen, too) cost the life of their smallest child, who contracted lung disease in their unheated room. From early in 1891 through the spring of 1893, their weekly household expenditures varied from about 7 shillings to occasionally over 26 shillings. The amount spent on food varied, too, ranging from 3 shillings for a very bad week in February 1891 to 10 shillings for several better weeks throughout the period.[53]

Rent absorbed far more income in London than in most other places in the country. Unlike most other prices, rents did not decline in Britain as a whole in the last quarter of the nineteenth century. Urban house rents in England and Wales doubled between 1845 and 1910, according to one careful researcher, with the highest increases in the 1860s and 1870s and again around the turn of the century. In 1885 Edith Simcox calculated that 60 percent of the workers' wage gain over the previous half-century had gone to pay rent. This was certainly the case for many of the households in St. Georges in the East, a crowded and poor district of inner East London, whose wages and living expenses were surveyed in 1848 and again in 1887. In a borough like Hackney, under pressure both from its resident population and for industrial space, rents went up by a third in the eight years between 1894 and 1901. It is easy to understand the appeal of Henry George to London artisans during this period, men whose wages were being devoured by landlords.[54] Inner-London rents at the turn of the twentieth century were, in general, one and a half times or double those of comparable sections in Manchester and Liverpool.[55] Over 85 percent of London workers paid more than a fifth of their income for rent, the Royal Commission on the Housing of the Working Classes found in 1885, and nearly half were paying over a quarter. Another notorious symptom of London's high housing costs, aside from its peoples' curtailed food budgets, were the enormous numbers living in one-room flats, nearly 7 percent of London's population in 1905, compared with well under 2 percent for the country as a whole. In fact, in 1891, more than 18 percent of all London households lived in just one room.[56]

The Battle over Alcohol

The husband's alcohol represented another, though more variable, charge on the wife's food budget. The poor man's drink was at the expense of his family's food and sometimes his own. A violent drunk whom a missionary persuaded to take the pledge proudly, some time later, displayed a pig in its sty: The unused drink money had been transformed into (future) food. Not surprisingly, the wives from "a slum in the vicinity of the docks chiefly inhabited by dockers" who were the subjects of a budget study in the winter of 1915–1916 mostly tended toward temperance positions.[57] Even a moderate beer drinker, having two pints a night at a 2½ d. each, plus an extra one on Saturdays and Sundays, would be spending nearly 3 shillings a week on beer; on that sum, the wife could serve meals to a family of five or six for two or three days. Wives' drinking could also, of course, be a drain on income, but arrests for drunkenness, pub watchers' figures for the proportions of women entering pubs, and family budgets show that married women spent much less on alcohol than their menfolk did.

The budgets gathered between the 1880s and World War I, with their modest 1 or 2 shillings withheld by the husbands, seem uniformly to underestimate the amount of money that went for drink. When it was later compared with national statistics on money spent on drinking and smoking, a Ministry of Labour survey carried out in 1937–38 was found to have reported only 14 percent of the total working-class consumption of alcohol and tobacco! We can safely assume wild inaccuracies in nineteenth- and early twentieth-century budget studies as well. The domestic budgeting arrangements of British workers were most accurately registered in national patterns of spending on alcohol. As Dingle has shown, it was in periods of rising money wages (as opposed to real wages) that the peaks in spending on drink were manifested, as men took their extra earnings directly to the pubs.[58] National figures show that the last third of the nineteenth century registered a peak in the amount of alcohol sold per capita in the United Kingdom, which then began a slow decline in the years before World War I. The annual per-capita expenditure on beer and spirits reached a high of £4 9s. in 1876 and another high of 4 pounds in 1899. Rowntree and Sherwell estimated in the late 1890s that about a fifth of working-class income in Britain as a whole was spent on alcohol. Reporting on a study of over 9,500 working men in various trades, they calculated that a good-sized minority, about 23 percent, spent 5 shillings or more on drink per week. A full 30 percent spent between 2 and 5 shillings; another 31 percent spent under 2 shillings; abstainers comprised only 17 percent.[59]

Alcohol, especially beer, was obviously a way of life for Londoners. In 1902, one house in every seventy-seven in the metropolis was a public house; according to 1896 figures, there was a pub for every 393 persons in London (making pubs sparser there, remarkably enough, than in any major English city).[60] The battle between the wife and the publican for men's wages, described in so many pre-Victorian street ballads and broadsides continued into Victorian and Edwardian pubs as well. Around 1910, Jack Welch's mother stormed into the Diss Street, Hackney Road, pub where her husband spent a goodly amount of his earn-ings. In response to her demand for money, her husband pushed her out of the door into the street, where she fell and fractured her elbow. Mrs. S., one of Anna Martin's Rotherhithe clients, describing to the settle-ment worker how she domesticated her husband, explained that when he was spending money she needed, "I've gone into the public and tipped up the table where he was drinking, and once when he struck me I gave him a black eye, then and there, and he's never touched me since." Ann Jasper had an understanding with the local publican, who, when he saw her at the pub with her heavy-drinking husband, would push his change repeatedly in her direction.[61] More struggle, of course, took place at home, where the men arrived minus big portions of their wages. They thus could enjoy the pleasurable oblivion and male camaraderie that al-cohol provided only at the expense of feeding their families.

Wages and Food

It took constant worry and unremitting labor to transform inadequate, sporadic wages into regular and satisfying meals. In Charles Booth's view, it was not so much men's low wages that created poverty in Lon-don but, rather, earnings that were irregular, fluctuating seasonally or with trade cycles. Some of the largest metropolitan trades were seasonal, laying off some workers and putting many others on short time in the slack season. Building, for example—brick makers and bricklayers, ma-sons, carpenters, joiners, painters, plumbers, and the like—employed almost 135,000 men in London's twenty-two census registration dis-tricts in 1881 and was slack after Christmas and again in June and July. The wood and furniture trades, with 53,134 men, were seasonal too, as were clothing, brewing, many branches of gaswork, and of course nearly all the waterside trades. Food and drink work (bakers, butchers, food processing) was less seasonal, but the 278,000 road and railway laborers were also subject to cold-weather layoffs.[62] In 1887, during one of the periodic recessions of this period, a survey of 29,000 working men in London found that more than 70 percent of the workers in some trades—dock workers, building trades workers, tailors, and boot makers—had been unemployed that winter, and most had been out for at least two months. Of members of the larger London occupations, only clerical workers, merchants, and public employees like police could feel that they had secure, year-round employment.[63]

Households could be fairly well fed if their main earner's wage was at the 1893 median of 31 shillings for London men in regular employ-ment (provided that the men turned most of it over to their wives). Skilled London building trades workers, at least, earned relatively good wages, an average of 43 to 46 shillings for a fifty-hour week in the early twentieth century, plus overtime pay, and could weather periods of unemployment. But unskilled building workers earned under 30 shillings a week, and of course, men in other trades earned still less, even when they had full-time work. Boot lasters and finishers, for example, got between 25 and 30 shillings for a fifty-four-hour week between 1902 and 1906. In 1892, a few years after the great dock strike, average wages in the docks were still estimated between 13 and 17 shillings per week. In Britain as a whole, in 1886 and twenty years later as well, a quarter of employed adult workmen earned under a pound a week, and about two thirds (in 1906) earned under 25 shillings weekly.[64]

Earnings by wives and children were "a frequent resource" of the unskilled, according to Norman Dearle. Bowley's 1911 study of working households in twelve British towns disclosed that only about 5 percent of unskilled workers' households could survive on the man's wages alone.[65] Wives of low-waged men were joined in the labor force by thousands of deserted wives and by women whose husbands were ill, disabled, or simply "bad." About 13 percent of the married women in London on census day 1911 were listed as employed, though the proportions in specific inner-city districts were much larger: 26 percent in Shoreditch, 24 percent in Holborn, 22 percent in Bethnal Green, and 19 percent in Westminster. The proportions of working widows, listed at around 50 percent in many censuses and 40 percent in 1911, must have been in reality still higher.[66] The large married women's work force in London, often unlisted by census enumerators either because the male "household head" failed to mention it or because the census taker viewed the wife's work as insignificant, has remained largely invisible even today.[67]

The waged work that married women did varied enormously by district, as it was related to both what jobs local industries could offer and the seasonal layoffs in male trades. In 1911, for instance, about a third of employed wives in Kensington worked in laundries, whereas only 4 percent of those in Bethnal Green did that kind of work. In Soho, where, as Arthur Sherwell observed in the late 1890s, more of the men were unskilled than in comparable East London districts, the laundry, confectionery, and dress trades hired wives, widows, and daughters. Here Crosse and Blackwell's had its pickle factory, hiring unskilled women workers. Charring in adjoining Mayfair and Belgravia also engaged many of these Soho women eager to put food on their tables. The peaks in Kensington laundry work, in the late spring and early summer social "season" and again in the fall with the opening of Parliament, fit well into the slack periods of several male North Kensington industries: notably the big gasworks at Kensal Green, the smaller gas enterprises, and the building trades.[68] Similar relationships between wives' work and that of husbands were found in Poplar and Whitechapel, where wives' sweated garment work filled in their husbands' slack seasons in the waterside trades, or in Rotherhithe, where fur pulling, leather work, and confectionery factories supplied work for wives whose husbands were casual dock laborers. After the turn of the twentieth century had brought downturns in many male trades and a rising cost of living, working-class wives were entering the labor force in numbers greater than ever before, and James Schmiechen estimates that—despite much lower census figures—probably half of London's working-class wives did paid work of some kind.[69]

Money moved very quickly from hand to mouth. In poor districts, boot clubs (through which children made installment payments toward wholesale boots) had to be collected not weekly but daily in farthings, from households where tiny amounts of cash came and went every day. Observers in the board schools were astonished to find a sprinkling of women bringing their children breakfast in midmorning, having just earned enough through morning street selling or cleaning to buy it.[70] A moment of carelessness could generate a catastrophe. In "Ditcher's Row" in northeast London, a woman who, sometime probably in the 1860s, had seen her life fall apart as her husband went through debtor's court and bankruptcy prison, relived a bit of that horror when her eight-year-old son lost a desperately needed half-crown piece in the street. The accident elicited, another of her sons remembered, "a look of something like blank despair on my mother's face" as the children, aided by many neighbors, patiently scraped up the street's surface dirt in their futile attempt to recover the coin. Later, around 1910 in Hackney, another mother (whose self-mocking, expansive good humor radiates from her children's accounts of her) severely beat a daughter for losing her "last shilling" on a shopping errand. An older sibling's intervention finally rescued the girl.[71]

When the money did not go far enough, the women reached into their familiar bags of tricks. They found odd jobs for school-aged children, helping with home industries, running errands for neighbors, delivering milk, cleaning steps, selling newspapers. They pawned household goods from the "bank" of ornaments on their mantles that were indeed there to be cashed in during hard times.[72] Anything marketable, from jam jars to old clothes, they quickly turned into food. And they turned old, less edible food into current meals: dripping from the Sunday meal served on bread or used in a steamed pudding; stale bread mixed with raisins and margerine and turned into bread pudding. There also were the invaluable contributions of wage-earning teenagers.

Turning too little money into a meal was a routine trick, and the pawn broker was the magician. Around the turn of the century there were 41,520 million pledges per year in London, according to the *Pawn-*

brokers' Gazette, which averages out to more than six annually per person! The pawnshop assistant could transform goods not needed at the moment (like a man's Sunday suit or an extra pair of sheets) into cash for the next meal. That pawning was so heavily a female domain in Victorian and Edwardian London tells us something about the sorts of things commonly pawned—clothing and household goods—and also that pawning was often an early stage of meal preparation.[73]

Working-class autobiographies and oral histories, and conversations between housewives and the social investigators of the prewar years abound with accounts of the daily miracle of the loaves and fishes: They advertised triumph over adversity in general, and the particular genius of particular mothers. In Bow, Mrs. W. told settlement worker Clara Grant how she could construct a tea for her family out of a single penny, buying a farthingsworth each of condensed milk, tea, sugar, and wood for fuel. In an East London industrial suburb, another account describes the direct translation of a mother's labor (two kinds of paid work, plus shopping and cooking) into a meal.

> My mother earnt a penny farthing for making [trousers] . . . with a hand machine, a Singer's little one. She'd try and get two pair done in a day and then she'd get tuppence ha-penny. She'd take them to Stepney on the tram (where the rag trade was). Round the back there was watercress beds. She'd pick the watercress and sell it ha'penny a bundle, then she'd come home and she'd say, "Well, we'll have a nice boiler full of shackles" (my father came from Berkshire and called a stew "shackles").[74]

Whole districts, stretching for miles, lived a weekly cycle of plenty and want written out mainly in the changing food on their plates. The men got their wages on Saturday afternoon or evening. Good eating (and drinking) followed for at least twenty-four hours. A former pawnshop assistant in the West End witnessed the Saturday night's high living each week as people, many of them showing signs of an evening of drinking, came in to redeem their Sunday clothes. "Some was eating fish and chips, some was eating tangerines, some had pease pudding and faggots. Cor blimey it was like Mother Kelly's doorstep in there," he commented. It was later in the week that the hard times arrived. A male worker boasted to economist Henry Higgs in the early 1890s that "he lived as well on a Friday as on any other day of the week." In a relatively prosperous family with nine children living in The Island, an enclave of poverty in Clapton, a mostly lower-middle-class district of Hackney, the weekly cycle of meals petered out by Thursday or so. The Sunday dinner, based on a "joint" (roast), was followed on Monday by soup, cold meat (Sunday's leftovers, no doubt) and bubble-and-squeak (pan-fried sausage and potatoes). "Tuesday was sausages, Wednesday was liver and bacon, Thursday would be whatever Mum could afford by that time in the week and Friday would be rice for the kids and perhaps fish for those who went to work."[75] Surveys of board school children in January 1895 found striking differences between the children's diets at the beginning of the school week, on Monday, and toward the end, on Thursday. In two very poor schools, where fifty-six older girls were questioned, forty-three had had meat with their Monday dinner, but only thirty-five had had it on Thursday. Of the fifty-six girls, thirteen had had nothing to eat on Thursday after their tea (which would have been at four or five o'clock), whereas only four had had to endure this on Monday.[76]

For children and adults, money meant, above all, food. As the weekend's food supply was exhausted, working families were reminded of the precariousness of their daily bread.

Cooking on Ten Shillings a Week

A mother's skilled and crafty food preparation provided the warp of the only "safety net" available to the London poor. One basic hot meal per day was supplemented by two other bread-based repasts. For the hot dish, the general strategy was to use potatoes or grain (usually rice, rarely macaroni, lentils, or oatmeal) as the base starch, with onions, turnips, or carrots as the major flavorings and meat as a "relish" or minor flavoring. For the starch to acquire a meaty taste, it had to be cooked at length in stews or soups. A recent American experiment conducted by the *New York Times,* in which a famous gourmet chef and food columnist tried to shop and cook for a family of four on a poverty income, confirms the logic of the stew-and-soup London dinner pattern. The cook, Pierre Franey, was able to use meat "mainly as a flavoring for beans and grains."[77]

Although after the 1870s per-capita bread sales had ceased to rise, bread was still a central object of household spending, second only to meat, according to an 1881 national study carried out by the British Association for the Advancement of Science. In terms of weight, bread provided a much larger proportion of the diet than meat did. For example, Charles Booth's London budgets from the late 1880s show an estimated 6.5 pounds of bread eaten per person each week, but only 1.6 pounds of meat.[78] Bread was, of course, the food that stood between children and hunger. "Mammy, ain't there a bit of bread?" journalist Olive Christian Malvery heard a small child ask her mother during the school dinner hour as the mother sat sewing buttons on waistcoats in the 1900s. In 1878, a five-year-old boy in a home in John Street, Marylebone, asked his mother, another home needleworker, "When are we to have our bread?" The mother answered that they would have to wait until the father came home with some money. As the central starch of the London diet, bread became the nearly exclusive food when households were in great poverty. As nursery educator Margaret McMillan put it, describing the diets of children, "Bread, bread, and always bread in surfeit is their portion."[79]

Bread was (and is) also a convenience food needing neither cooking nor eating utensils. The new white, light, roller-milled flours of the late Victorian decades from which the nutritious wheat germ and bran had been removed were baked into sweetish, fluffy, seductive loaves. At 5 or 6 pence for a gigantic four-pound (quartern) loaf, bread was cheap as well. Schoolteachers, school managers, and other charity workers who became involved with providing children's dinners after the late 1870s pitied the board schools' "bread children" and disapproved of their mothers for giving them so much of it. A survey of 310 pupils at the Bay Street School in Haggerston one day in the winter of 1908 revealed that the great majority had had a bread breakfast, and less than a third had had "a relish" (such as cheese, egg or bacon) with their meal. More disapprovingly, but just as graphically, a junior inspector of schools in West Ham testified before the Inter-Departmental Committee on Physical Deterioration:

> Well, the children come to school, and they have no regular breakfast; they have, perhaps, bread and butter as they dress, and they get some bread when they start, and they have very cheap butter. They bring lunch to school, but it is only bread they have, and they get bread only till they come home at dinner-time and in the evening. It is bread and butter, jam, and tea.[80]

The extent to which a mother ventured from bread meals, in fact, had less to do with her character and more with her plumbing and her facilities for cooking. A large part of the housing stock in which London's working population lived had been built in earlier days for grander households. Only some of the flats into which they were later subdivided had real kitchens and ranges, usually the more expensive ground-floor flats. Thus hundreds of thousands of households had only fireplaces, provided with grates and perhaps Dutch ovens, for cooking. Gas stoves, one solution to this problem, were being introduced in the 1880s, but they were expensive to run: In the 1890s, a pennyworth of gas lasted about five hours. Gas was declining in price during the last quarter of the nineteenth century, it is true, but gas cookery for the poor, Pember Reeves noted, led to "underdone food." At Maidstone Street School, in a poor Hackney district, fewer than half of the pupils' homes had gas stoves in 1902. The expense of running a gas stove, or the trouble of making and maintaining a fire in a coal stove or grate, restricted the amount of cooking that wives did. Frying and grilling were certainly the most common, as they were quick and required little fuel.[81] The puddings that nutritionists were trying to make popular needed to cook from two to four hours, soups and stews even longer (Pierre Franey recommended two hours, but his readers were cooking on modern gas or electric ranges). No wonder women boasted of their stews and hot pots to outsiders and prepared them only once a day, if that.

The lack of piped-in water could further dry up a housewife's enthusiasm for cooking. Before the 1870s the many private companies that controlled London's water supply were the bane of local medical officers, and there were still eight left in 1902 when the Metropolitan Water Board was finally established and authorized to buy them out. The water supplied was notoriously polluted, even in the later decades of the nineteenth century, and unreliable as well. It might be turned on for only a few hours a day, and some companies supplied no water at all on Sundays. A large house off Tottenham Court Road in the 1880s that had had its water supply cut off for "some time" was surely not an anomaly. According to an inquiring school board visitor, the tenants had to get their water from a woman next door who let them traipse through her house. A continuous water supply throughout the city (as required by the Public Health [London] Act of 1891) did not exist until well into the 1890s. (The newer "by-law housing" built after 1880, much of it in such fast-growing working-class suburbs as Willesden, West Ham, Leyton, and Tottenham, was more likely to have piped-in water.) Octavia Hill's controversial idea of a model workers' apartment building, in the 1880s, had only one water tap per floor, nonetheless a great improvement over the facilities in hundreds of thousands of nonmodel dwellings in the central city.[82] Smith's Place, Pentonville, a little court of ten tiny two-room houses, each one occupied by a separate family, was probably no worse off than most inner-London slum districts before the turn of the twentieth century. In 1884, it was equipped with one common tank in the center of the court, shared by the thirty to sixty people who lived in the houses.[83]

Not surprisingly, such districts were richly provided with stalls and shops selling ready-cooked food: smoked and cured fish of all kinds, hot sausages and meat pies, and fish and chips. For a small fee, cook shops would carry out the slow, long cooking that a Sunday dinner might require but was impossible when wives had no really usable kitchens. In 1910 an LCC food inspector made a survey of what the cook shops in St. Pancras had to offer: "fried fish and potatoes, canned goods, brawns made from coarse parts and trimmings of good sound meat of all kinds; jellied eals, trotters, tripe, and treacle, jams, pickles of the cheaper kinds, all of which can be bought in farthing, halfpenny, and pennyworths ready to eat, and are good wholesome food, well cooked."[84] Bethnal Green, with a population of about 125,000 in 1910, housed twenty-seven fried-fish shops; in Southwark, in 1900, 58 percent of the population had eaten fried fish in the month before the health officials carried out their survey; and in Bethnal Green, nearly two thirds of the residents of certain streets had done the same. Children and teenagers were the principal fish eaters, and mothers told sanitary investigators of their children's passion for it.[85] But the whole community needed the cook shops as supplements to the home-cooking efforts of its wives.

Market Relations

Money management was, as acknowledged by both men and women, the special talent of women. Men had a poor reputation indeed, especially among women, as shoppers. A Walworth woman unwittingly revealed her views on male domestic economy at a rummage sale in which district nurse Margaret Loane was selling a handmade bedspread for 4 shillings. When the woman was asked whether this was a fair price, "she appraised it carefully, and then said slowly, unwilling to hurt my feelings, 'P'haps a nusban' *might*.' " (Loane finally priced the bedspread at 2s. 9d. and got rid of it.) When food tastes had to be reconciled with material limits, shopping was of course, a crucially important material stage in food preparation, and one central in housewives' consciousness. Marketing researchers have demonstrated for recent years the energy with which poor housewives hunt for good deals in far-flung stores.[86] For women, shopping was an outing, a social occasion, but also a matter of strategic importance.

The shoppers' choices took into account more than the nutritional value of the food or even its anticipated taste. Certain shops and kinds of shopping sold safety, health, status. The butchers, who proliferated in the late nineteenth century, were of many grades, from the "best" to the lowest, selling such poor people's cuts as sheep's heads and tripe, along with the new frozen meat that, in Salford at least, was considered very "low." But these meanings in these generations were mainly created by the shoppers and shopkeepers themselves. Edwardians were the last to do their marketing largely outside the context of nationally advertised products. The 1890s and 1900s constitute a period of intense competition among tobacco brands, whose purchasers were virtually all men, but the products on which working-class women spent most of their money were usually not sold by brand name. Of the national and international brands that were being mass marketed before World War I, only patent medicines, condensed milk, and some soaps and cleansers— Monkey Brand, Brasso and Bluebell metal polish, Zebra grate polish, Sunlight Soap, Reckitt's starch—were bought with any regularity by working-class housewives. The breakfast cereals, warm beverages (Bovril, Rowntree's cocoa), baby formulas, and biscuits (Carr's, McVitie's, Huntley & Palmer's) aimed at a mass market were quite beyond workers' pocketbooks and almost never appear in their family budgets. The major daily newspapers read in workers' homes, *John Bull* or *Reynolds' Newspaper,* were beginning to earn significant revenues from brand-name food advertisers; Bovril was advertised in lights at corner of Trafalgar Square from 1896 onward. But compared with her granddaughter, the late Victorian and Edwardian woman was an innocent as a food shopper. Rather, her choices originated in another kind of rationality.[87]

Buying in small quantities—coal by the hundredweight or even by the pound, tea or sugar by the ounce—not only was a product of very limited flows of cash but also—despite the higher costs of this method per unit—could save money because it would keep always-hungry families from eating up the next day's provisions. With perishable items like meat, it reduced the risk of spoilage. On a hot weekend in June 1895, a Homerton housewife unwittingly demonstrated the advantages of daily shopping for small amounts. She had bought enough meat for a large pie intended to last for two days but created a tragedy when her entire family of nine became deathly ill with food poisoning. The pie intended for the second meal had obviously spoiled overnight.[88]

Saturday night marketing was almost sure to be a part of any housewife's routine. The noisy, exciting, and convivial Saturday evening markets were the focal point of the housewife's week: Hoxton Street, swarming with rough children from its poor but lively neighborhood; Chrisp Street in Poplar with its theatrical sellers of patent medicines and gadgets, fortune tellers, and escape artists; Bell Street in Southwark; and Rye Lane in Peckham Rye, where a Salvation Army band competed with the "foot doctor" and a pianist playing the latest popular tunes. In 1893, the LCC listed over a hundred of these street markets, consisting almost entirely of barrows and movable stalls. All the markets had service shops as well as street stalls and, lit by naphtha flares, were kept open until midnight or later. Toward the end of the evening, some of the most expensive elements of the next day's meal, meat or fish, were sold or auctioned off cheaply to those who had waited around the longest. The widely separated major market streets often required a long walk, but they offered bargains that merited the extra trouble. For a number of foods sold in her district, nutritionist Florence Petty calculated the differences in cost (1909–1910 prices) between some grocery items in the local shops and in the street markets: stewing steak, 4d. per pound versus 2.5d. in a market street; potatoes 1d. for three pounds in a shop versus five pounds for the same price in a market street.[89]

Relationships with stall- and shopkeepers were central elements in housewives' marketing strategies.[90] All shop owners, but particularly the smaller ones, depended on regular customers in districts that, unlike the working-class quarters of Paris or Vienna, were often relatively lightly populated. Those on the smaller turnings blended in socially with the working-class families around them, as Hugh McLeod's study of shop-keepers' intermarriage in Lewisham suggests. Obliging merchants per-mitted buying on credit and offered good deals on such items as bruised fruit, broken biscuits, or soup bones. Based on his visits to neighbor-hoods where the poor lived, the journalist George Sims wrote about the cash value of having established a "character" with local shopkeepers, an advantage that often cemented poor households to particular districts. The East London funeral procession of Mrs. Sayers, in honor of whom there were closed shutters or drawn blinds "in nearly every house in the road," revealed her importance in the neighborhood. The deceased, as the wife of Mr. J. Sayers, "the well-known potato and vegetable sales-man of Cambridge Road," probably worked behind the shop's counter many hours each day and, to judge from the number of mourners, was generous and fair with her customers. With a hearse and five mourning carriages, her funeral was a fairly substantial proceeding.[91] Shoppers and shopkeepers lived in a symbiosis that ultimately benefited the shoppers' families.

The ability of wives to buy on credit had a still wider significance in sustaining whole neighborhoods during strikes. A combination, per-haps, of public relations and powerful community ties generated enor-mous support for, in particular, the 1889 dockers from East London shop owners. Abbott Brothers dairy in Limehouse distributed free milk during the strike; other merchants, like a group in a side street off Com-mercial Road, displayed banners and flags to show their support, and still others wrote letters to the local newspapers or donated money to the strike fund announcing theirs.[92] During the 1911 dock strike, a West Ham household living on 10 shillings in strike pay was maintained for some time by buying on credit: "If it wasn't for our grocer we would have definitely starved" was the memory of the son who was a teenager at the time. Indeed, a *Star* editorial in 1889 suggested that the strike's success owed something to both the support and the generally adequate resources of the local shopkeepers.[93]

BOUND TO FAIL

The historical record, not very forthcoming about housewives' struggles and occasional victories in their campaigns to feed their households, is most fulsome in documenting their failures. Medical officers, school doctors, and charity clinics all could see that the babies and children of the working people were badly fed. Thin, anemic-looking children who admitted that they were hungry were a scandal in the board schools when they first began to arrive in 1871, and they continued to exist, in fact and in propaganda, into the next century when they were central figures in the 1904 interdepartmental hearings on "physical deterioration." School dinners programs, in which public officials and private charities served a quintessential maternal function, were, among other things, a reproach to the mothers, and many of them knew it.

The new charitable clinics that had begun to appear with the twentieth century documented repeatedly that the health problems they most often found in children were related to diet. At the Women's Labour League's Baby Clinic in North Kensington, founded in 1911, the most common ailments were "nearly all the diseases of malnutrition." In 1912 and 1913 the City of Westminster Health Society's children's clinic in Golden Square, Soho, registered rickets[94] in 19 percent of the infants and in nearly a quarter of the one- to two-year-olds. At the society's other clinic, in Pimlico Road, a poorer, largely unskilled district, "wasting," "improper feeding," and "rickets" were the problems most commonly reported by Reginald Jewesbury, the clinic's volunteer physician. In one East London elementary school, in a poor district formerly the center of London's thriving weaving industry, only the children of publicans or shopkeepers had really good "physiques," according to the school physician.[95]

Working-class urban children throughout the country were, on the average, smaller and lighter than better-off children. This "growth faltering," though not actually a health problem, was recognized then, as it is now as well, as a symptom of lifelong nutritional deficiencies.[96] The slum schools of the metropolis were filled with children smaller and lighter than the average, whereas the suburban schools had larger, heavier children.[97] In 1910, the London medical officer for education could map huge areas of urban poverty simply by plotting the schools where boys and girls had the lowest heights and weights at ages eight and twelve. They could be found in the riverside districts on both sides of the Thames, North Kensington, and "a central area extending from the Strand district to Bow and Bromley." The twelve-year-old girls enrolled in LCC secondary schools, themselves specially advantaged in comparison with most twelve-year-olds in London, were almost seven centimeters shorter than the girls at the fashionable North London Collegiate school. Their age mates in Worcester, Massachusetts, and in Berlin and Stockholm all were larger as well.[98]

Her limits as a food provider were finally written on the mother's body itself; she was probably worst at feeding herself. The mother's "auto-starvation," as one not particularly sympathetic physician put it in 1904, was partly a sign of a struggle for control resembling in some odd way anorexia as it appears today (indeed, anorexia was identified as a syndrome during this period), partly perhaps a statement about being a woman. For women rich and poor as portrayed by nineteenth-century novelists almost never ate: Dickens's heroines ate or starved offstage; Trollope's presided at dinner tables over empty plates. Women's hunger was unmentionable, an indecent subject.[99] Women activists viewed the starvation of England's mothers as a reflection of their low status and disenfranchisement. The staff of the St. Pancras School for Mothers wrote in 1907 of "the extraordinary tendency of women to starve themselves," which they linked with women's political nonage. "They never treat themselves, either in the home or in public affairs, as of any importance, and consequently no one else thinks them important. One of the first steps needed to effect the political and social emancipation of woman is a crusade on the part of man calling upon her to eat." Just after the war, Beatrice Webb also connected women's silent domestic deprivation with their low public status, noting in particular their prewar "starvation wages." She hoped that the high wages and well-balanced canteen meals of the wartime women factory workers would permanently "raise the standard of women's meals" and mark the end of women's resignation to going hungry.[100]

"I can't see them want" was the mothers' natural reply when well-wishing social workers urged them to eat more of the family food. From Anna Martin's vantage point, closer to the kitchens of Rotherhithe, it was the other household members, especially husbands and grown-up working children, who held women to a standard that was simply beyond their resources.[101] It was safest to give others her portion. When the rest of the family had a meat dish, like stew, mothers often ate bread. In a household living on very good munitions-work wages in Woolwich, it was the mother's eating bread and butter on Thursdays and Fridays that marked the difficult days at the end of the week. A Poplar woman was in the habit of dining on a "kettle bender," "a cup of crusts with hot water, pepper and salt, and a knob of margarine," clearly meant to kill off her hunger while others were eating more appetizing food, for her daughter remembers: "She always had this meal just before father came in for his."[102] Joseph Williamson, with his extraordinary biblical sense of the meanings of food, described the same process, one that was repeated daily:

> How my mother existed is a mystery. I am reminded of the Lord's saying: "I have meat ye know not of." She would sit at table watching us eat, and she would make little balls of dry bread and put them in her mouth. One of us would urge her: "Have some dinner, Mother," and she would reply quite cheerfully: "I'll have mine presently." I cannot remember her having a proper meal with us when we were children.[103]

CHAPTER 3

"A Gamble You Have to Take":
Marriage

I fell in the cart with marrying him, but still, it's a gamble you
have to take.
"Emmie Durham,"
in Paul Thompson, *The Edwardians*

Lord knows, miss. It 'appens to most women wot don't look out.
A battered wife, mother of five, and waistcoat maker,
in Olive Christian, Malvery, *Baby Toilers*

Wedlock "happened" to most people in London's industrial districts,
but these marriages seem decidedly embattled: cemented together by
powerful forms of material interdependence but pulled apart by gender
divisions and hostilities. Family life provided the settings for some of
the sweetest moments in the hard lives of London workers, and cockney
humor softened marriage's harsh edges.[1] But sexual antagonism was an
openly acknowledged party to the contract.[2] Husbands' authority in their
households was a wobbly fixture, one that was always on the verge of
breaking down. Wives could easily be found who were neither ladylike
nor deferential, and their husbands had to struggle, often violently, to
maintain their authority over them.

Many of the tensions of married life were expressed through the vocabulary of the music hall which was so much a part of London workers' lives. These lyrics provided a way of processing the greatest of the
contradictions in London's working-class gender relations: husbands'
privileges and peremptory demands at home and their poverty and
powerlessness outside it. Husbands and fathers became comic figures;
when not odious or dangerous, their attempts at domination were sim-

ply funny. When a Walworth carman in the 1900s, for example, threatened his wife with a stick, his daughter pushed him backward into an
open cupboard. As he landed "on his back with his legs up in the air,"
the rest of the family enjoyed a hearty laugh. Laughter, affectionate or
bitter, open or secret, was one of the many ties that united a wife and
her children against her husband, women in general against men. As for
the men, the "dignity" of their position in the home made it nearly
impossible for them to laugh at themselves there, but in the music halls
they were ready to grin at the pretensions of "swells" who lived on
clerks' salaries or "noblemen" who were barbers' sons.[3] And men as
well as women were treated to another stock music-hall figure, the hen-
pecked husband, the man who had lost the battle for authority at home.
"It's a Great Big Shame," was Gus Elen's classic of this genre: the pairing of a gentle giant with a little harpy of a wife.[4]

Husbands' claims to competence and mastery in the home were a joke,
as expressed in the hilarious ballad sung by Nelson Jackson in 1899,
"When Father Laid the Carpet on the Stairs":

> We all of us enjoyed it, it was bliss without alloy—
> Although to show our mirth we were naturally coy,
> And mother went behind the pantry door to hide her joy—
> When the carpet laid poor father on the stairs.[5]

It was part of music-hall style to construct scenes and situations modeled
on real life. But the music-hall formulas structured the way that people
viewed their lives, as suggested by this sketch—the product of a daughter's late adulthood—of a parallel incident in the lives of the Chegwidden family in Wapping in the years before World War I. The much
loved father was the object of laughter but took himself far too seriously
to join in the fun. Seeing an advertisement in the *News of the World,*
Walter Chegwidden was determined to get rich by raising mushrooms
in his backyard, though his wife opposed the plan. He solemnly warned
his ten children to keep their distances from the growing box he had
constructed. When, "with the air of centuries of mushroom-growing in
his blood," he finally opened the lid, there was nothing inside but mouse
holes and cobwebs.

> Mother turned and walked slowly into the house, Father gazing after her
> with a look of intense hatred. . . . Then all hell broke loose, we all scat-
> tered into the house finding various secret corners where we could let loose
> our hysterical laughter. Mother was under the table shaking and pretend-
> ing to dust the floor. Someone else was hanging on to the roller-towel in
> the scullery, and laughter, albeit choked laughter, came from all parts of
> the house.[6]

Working-class marriages, with their peculiar framing of male power, diverged considerably from those of the British middle class, in which husbands and wives alike were constantly aware of the authority that both the law and economic realities accorded men over their mates, and the essence of a lady was her smooth and courteous deference toward men of her own class, often based on a genuine respect for their political, professional, or financial expertise.[7] Cockney marriages were probably also different from those of working populations in rural or mining England, where husbands' wages were less insecure than were those of men in large parts of London, or pockets in Lancashire (such as Preston), where married women's well-paid textile employment plus religious nonconformity produced more peaceful and cooperative marital arrangements.[8]

In large parts of pre–World War I working-class London a number of circumstances tended to undermine husbands' legal and economic power. The economic bedrock of husbands' claims to domination, their earning power, was, as noted in Chapter 2, highly precarious for perhaps as many as half of London's working husbands. Trade slumps, old age, illness, or injury could leave a man dependent on his wife or children for survival.[9] Children's wage contributions were therefore counted on by their parents, and wives would serve as earners at some point in the life cycle of most families. Furthermore, when children went to work as young teenagers, they viewed themselves as "working for" their mothers, as their earnings entered and strengthened the female part of the household exchequer.

In addition, London working men, despite the two reform bills, were largely disenfranchised; perhaps a tenth of working-class men in the metropolis, even after the Second Reform Act, were registered voters during this period. Being on poor relief disqualified them; moving to another house delayed registration; and lodgers (the great majority of London working-class heads of household) had to reregister every year. Court decisions and legislation improved the situation somewhat, and Battersea and Southwark in the early twentieth century were especially conscientious in easing registration for lodgers, but it is fair to say that the dignity of citizenship was one that most London working men did not fully possess.[10]

Another situation that weakened the domestic power of London working men was that many fathers were losing or had already lost their stake in their sons' futures, as their own trades—saddle making, hemp-rope weaving, hand shoemaking—were industrialized, and a father had no other power to shape his son's livelihood. Although the system continued in some towns—Birmingham, for example—apprenticeships were rapidly disappearing in London, and men could no longer dream of bringing their sons into their own trades. By 1906, according to an LCC study, apprenticship as a system had disappeared from most London industries. A 1910 survey of the teenage sons of Lambeth widows found that only 1 percent of the boys had been taken on at their fathers' workplaces. The unskilled jobs available to teenage boys in the metropolis, where errand boys or helpers in shops were in great demand, were now likely to be found for them by their mothers through neighborhood contacts.[11]

On the other hand, wives' status in inner London's closely settled neighborhoods was enhanced by the supportive presence of neighbors and relatives. Women's neighborhood networks fostered a language of female need and interest as acknowledged in Jenny Hill's earnest lines: "I've been a good woman to you, / And the neighbours all know that it's true."[12] We get a glimpse of the effect of neighbors' intervening between wives and husbands in a courtroom scene in the early 1900s in which a large group of local women, their prams parked outside, encouraged another: "You stick to it," "Go on wiv' it," "Get your separation." Or in a back-fence conversation between a Bethnal Green woman (probably in the 1920s) and her sister, overheard by a child the morning after a husband had attacked his wife: " 'The old man was in a bloody temper last night, wasn't he?' Auntie Liz would say over the garden wall, next morning. 'I wonder you're so daft as to stay with him. I'll be damned if I would.' "[13] The "cheeky" factory girls who so offended their more respectable fellow workers, the London schoolgirls whose swearing shocked their rustic hosts when they went away for country holidays, grew up into no-nonsense wives and mothers who would fight and curse when angry and who could laugh at a husband's pretensions.

MARRIAGE IN LONDON

In working-class boroughs, marriage was a far more central part of adult life than it was in better-off districts. For one thing, young women born in London tended to avoid domestic service, with its years of enforced celibacy. In the late Victorian years, only about a quarter of London servants had been born in London. Compared with their social betters, the poor in London married earlier and "more often." One measure of a population's marriage rate is the proportion that married in their early twenties (ages twenty through twenty-four). If we compare prosperous, servant-keeping Hampstead in 1881 with Bethnal Green, and look at men rather than women to eliminate most of the servants from the figures, we will find that nearly a third of the Bethnal Green men (32 percent) but only 15 percent of the Hampstead men were already married; the contrast among women, of course, is even starker because of domestic service: About half of Bethnal Green's had married by age twenty-four, but only 14 percent of Hampstead women were wed. Hampstead's figures were much lower than the national figure of 22 percent for men and 33 for women in 1881; Bethnal Green's were much higher. The 1911 census shows that the proportions of couples marrying in their early twenties were considerably lower than those of earlier censuses, but the contrast between the marriage habits of wealthy and poor London boroughs continued into the twentieth century (see Table 3–1, A and B).[14]

We can also measure London workers' commitment to marriage by looking at the proportions who were still single in their late forties and early fifties, those who were unlikely to marry, as Table 3–2 illustrates. The contrasts by borough are, of course, enormous in the case of women: In 1881, nearly 30 percent of women of this age in Hampstead but less than 7 percent in Bethnal Green were single (and many of them were or had been living with steady "tally" partners). But even among men, very few of whom were servants, there are significant differences between rich and poor boroughs: About 10 percent of older men in Kensington were single, 9 percent in Hampstead, 6 percent in Bethnal Green, and 7 percent in St. Olave's Southwark.

Although comparatively few Londoners married as minors (in the 1880s London's figures for marriages of minors were among the lowest in the country), they did tend to marry two or three years younger than the national averages for England and Wales.[15] As Table 3–3 illustrates, marriage ages were clustered in the early twenties. For example, at churches in two very poor districts, St. Matthew's (Bethnal Green) and St. Peter's Liverpool Street (Walworth), the median age at marriage during the period of this study ranged from twenty-one to twenty-three for women and from twenty-four to twenty-five for men at the two

TABLE 3–1A. Percentage of Londoners Ever Married, Ages 20–24, in 1881 and 1911

Census Year	Men Ever Married		Women Ever Married	
	Percent	*Numbers*	*Percent*	*Numbers*
1881*	22.2	78,118	32.0	132,105
1911†	13.7	26,194	22.0	52,336

*London, including metropolitan Middlesex, Surrey, and Kent.
†County of London only.

Sources: 1881 Census of England and Wales, PP 1883, vol. 80, Table 7, p. 9; 1911 Census, PP 1912–1913, vol. 113, Table 12, p. 374.

TABLE 3–1B. Londoners Ever Married, Ages 20–24, in 1881 and 1911, by Borough: Two Wealthy and Two Poor Boroughs Compared *

| | 1881 | | | |
| | Numbers | | | Percent
Ever Married |
Borough	Single	Married	Widowed	
Hampstead				
men	1,391	244	0	15
women	3,564	483	18	14
Kensington				
men	9,126	1,852	15	17
women	18,334	3,356	62	16
Bethnal Green				
men	3,850	1,793	15	32
women	2,796	2,741	38	48
Poplar				
men	4,898	1,685	15	26
women	3,301	2,978	38	48

| | 1911 | | | |
| | Numbers | | | Percent
Ever Married |
Borough	Single	Married	Widowed	
Hampstead				
men	2,974	281	1	10
women	6,405	601	8	10
Kensington				
men	5,349	803	3	15
women	11,158	1,574	20	13
Bethnal Green				
men	4,324	1,004	6	19
women	4,574	1,855	6	41
Poplar				
men	5,733	1,109	7	16
women	5,117	2,117	11	30

*Census divisions are not entirely comparable between 1881 and 1911.

Sources: 1881 Census, PP 1883, vol. 80, Table 7, p. 9; 1911 Census, PP 1912–1913, vol. 113, Table 12, p. 374.

TABLE 3–2. Singleness in the Later Years:
Proportions Ever Married, Ages 45–54, and
Contrasts Between Wealthy and Poor Boroughs

Borough	*1881*	
	Number Single	*Percent Single*
Hampstead		
men	124	8.5
women	619	29.5
Kensington		
men	902	9.7
women	3,740	26.1
Bethnal Green		
men	275	6.0
women	353	6.9
Poplar		
men	520	8.0
women	349	5.8

Borough	*1911*	
	Number Single	*Percent Single*
Hampstead		
men	462	11.9
women	1,942	33.2
Kensington		
men	1,038	13.8
women	4,074	34.1
Bethnal Green		
men	544	10.0
women	473	8.5
Poplar		
men	818	11.2
women	503	7.0

Sources: 1881 Census, PP 1883, vol. 80, Table 8, pp. 10–11; 1911 Census, PP 1912–1913, vol. 113, Table 9, pp. 231–35.

TABLE 3–3. Marriage Ages at Two Inner London Churches, 1879–1912

	St. Matthew's, St. Matthew's Row, Bethnal Green					
	1879–82 *388 couples*		*1893–96* *463 couples*		*1909–12* *211 couples*	
	Men	*Women*	*Men*	*Women*	*Men*	*Women*
Median marriage age	23–24	22	24	21	25	23
Percent married at age 20 or younger (numbers)	11.0 (42)	29.6 (115)	6.5 (31)	22.4 (104)	5.4 (11)	12.7 (27)

	St. Peter's *Liverpool Street, Walworth*			
	1887–88 *233 couples*		*1902–3* *206 couples*	
	Men	*Women*	*Men*	*Women*
Median marriage age	24	22	24	22
Percent married at age 20 or younger (numbers)	13.6 (29)	31.3 (73)	6.0 (13)	24.3 (50)

Sources: Marriage registers, Greater London Record Office: St. Matthew's: P72/MTW/70, 73–74 and 78 (August 1, 1879–August 1, 1882; August 1, 1893–August 1, 1896; August 1, 1909–August 1, 1912). St. Peter's: P92/PETI/42 and 48 (January 1, 1887–January 1, 1889; January 1, 1902–January 1, 1904).

churches.[16] In 1911 (when marriage ages nationally were higher) the mean age at marriage for Hampstead men was thirty, whereas in Bethnal Green and Poplar it was twenty-seven.[17]

The official figures, high as they are for workers, actually underestimate the proportions of cockneys living as couples because a significant minority of these twosomes avoided legal marriage. Older customs, in which couples formed and lived "tally" without benefit of clergy, breaking up and reforming once or twice in each partner's lifetime, were quite slow to die among the poorest Londoners and within some subcultures. In the late 1860s and 1870s costermongers (hawkers of fruits and vegetables) and other members of the so-called rough poor were still practicing their customary form of serial monogamy.[18] In the 1890s, the "rough poor," especially those who lived by street selling, were apparently still pairing off in this way, and Charles Booth commented on the tendency of young couples in some slum districts to marry after a period of co-habitation. Parliamentary testimony in 1903 and in 1910 reported the same thing. In the case of a pregnancy, the cohabiting couples married, or sometimes the technically illegitimate child was absorbed into the woman's own natal family. As Robert Moore, a barrister who worked as a volunteer poor man's lawyer at Cambridge House Settlement in Camberwell Road, put it in 1910, his clients had "no sense of shame in acknowledging their irregular sexual arrangements."[19]

Church marriage registers do support the notion of distinct sexual arrangements among the poor, in which marriage followed a period of cohabition. The marriage registers in three poor London districts, Walworth, Poplar, and Bethnal Green, for various years between 1879 and 1912 show an astonishingly high proportion, ranging from 45 percent to 89 percent, giving the same street or even the same house as the address from which they married. In some of these cases, as with Guy Aldred's mother and her second "husband," whom she married bigamously at the Finsbury Town Hall in 1897, the husband had been living as a lodger at the wife's parents' home.[20] In others, it seems clear, parish regulations required that couples give a local address, and they did so. But a great many marrying couples were actually cohabiting when they set out for the church. How this might happen is revealed in an 1870s Central Criminal court case. Sarah Ann Rodwell lived with a man at Earl's Court "as his wife" in a room at the man's mother's house. The couple were planning to be married very soon, "the day after tomorrow," Rodwell reported in her Old Bailey testimony, but their plan was thwarted by a horrible accident in which the future husband accidently killed the infant girl his partner was caring for as a nurse mother.[21]

Older couples, at least one of whom was already married but separated or deserted, "remarried" readily without benefit of clergy, a phenomenon that remained on the edges of middle-class awareness and commanded official attention only during World War I when thousands of unmarried "wives" claimed separation benefits. As Booth put it, second unions among older people were more respectable in neighborhood terms than were similar unions among young couples. Matthew Peters, for example, in his forties and long separated from his wife, had cohabited comfortably with Catherine Smith for nine years in Woolwich when they finally decided to get married in the early 1870s. His new responsibility for his dead sister's five children seems to have precipitated the belated, and redundant, wedding.[22]

Parish visitors, COS workers, and poor-law officials usually made the production of a woman's "marriage lines" (the certificate that documented her marriage) a prerequisite for aid, but the state welfare programs of the early twentieth century—old-age pensions, national insurance—would subject more and more marriages to public scrutiny, and those living tally would find themselves under increasing pressure to get married.

CHOOSING A HUSBAND

Marie Lloyd made her music-hall debut in 1885 with a revival of a Nelly Power number from the 1870s. A song of extravagantly hopeful courtship, its fantastic premise was completely undisguised: "Now if I was a Duchess, and had a lot of money, / I'd give it to the boy who's going to marry me; / But I haven't got no money, so we'll live on love and kisses / And be just as happy as the birds on the tree."[23]

Lloyd's song gets much of its spice from its contrast with the rest of the music-hall canon with its decidedly skeptical view of courtship and marriage. Vesta Victoria's "Poor John" raises the issue of the hypercritical future mother-in-law; her "Waiting at the Church" is the tale of a courtship swindle. "At Trinity Church I Met My Doom" (sung accompanied by ominous chords and featuring the line "like a salmon I was speared") is a classic of the reluctant-husband genre, and Gus Elen's "Me and 'Er" sardonically makes "a black eye now and then" a token of marital affection. The music hall's few romantic songs (usually of thwarted love) are countered by harsher tales of rotten husbands like "We All Go to Work but Father," and Vesta Tilley's sly "Following in Father's Footsteps" of 1902, in which the schoolboy son—Tilley in stage drag—ingenuously recapitulates his father's secret philanderings.[24]

Courtship, as John Gillis has pointed out, was a negotiation between fantasy and reality, a period of testing and fact-finding to which not only the young couple but also their peers and parents were parties. For most of the teenaged years, courting was an affair conducted by parallel groups of girls and boys who gave each other courage and whose seen or unseen presence policed the boundaries of sexual propriety. Early boy–girl contact involved playful anticipations of the hostilities of real marriages: slaps, punches, and a variety of unintelligible sounds caricatured by Arthur Morrison in his story of East London courtship and marriage, "Lizerunt," or, more gently, in Albert Chevalier's "The Future Mrs. 'Awkins," which conveys some tenderness amidst the roughhousing. Indeed, a seventeen-year-old's playfully meant blow to a girl's stomach as they chatted on Highgate Hill one evening in 1874 was interpreted by an adult walking down the other side of the street as a life-threatening attack.[25]

Girls were, however, more likely than boys to view their sweethearts through romantic lenses. They lived and courted in the earliest years of the modern commercialization and magnification of love and romance. It was the girls who hummed romantic music-hall tunes, consulted palm readers and sellers of love potions, and even had crushes on such un-likely figures as the local vicar. Girls wrote love letters; indeed, the Jewish girls of Whitechapel were noted for the flowery missives that theyhired local scribes to write for them.[26] A few women made a point throughout their married lives of saying that they had "married for love," obviously a respectable option among the many reasons for marrying.

Boys were the main senders of the obscene comic valentines that ar-rived on the British market in the late nineteenth century, cards ob-viously aimed at diffusing the high emotion of courtship. However, the records of the Old Bailey, where only the most serious cases—like mur-der and attempted murder—were tried, contain many examples of high romance among London men, many of them at the courting stage: sex-ual jealousy, broken hearts, frustrated desires, and clumsy, violent ways of dealing with these feelings. Surely one of the major projects for young men, given how emotionally close and how long working-class mothers "kept" their sons, was to distinguish their future wife from their mother. This is the age, after all, that produced the frankly oedipal "I Want a Girl Just Like the Girl That Married Dear Old Dad." One Hampstead man movingly recorded this conflation in his autobiography, which de-scribes being haunted during his courtship by sweet memories of child-hood walks on Hampstead Heath with his mother, who had died when he was still a boy.[27]

The role of suitor was very different from that of husband. "Never again would a man be so careful with his language and appearance, or be so chivalrous or romantic," as John Gillis put it. For these months or years, these men were as close to their mates as they ever would be; after their weddings they would very likely be back in the pub. Their sweetheart was, for the moment, someone to be wooed and pampered, not the woman of all work she would become after her marriage. As a wise West London thirteen-year-old told Emmeline Pethick (later, Pethick-Lawrence) during Pethick's stint as a West London girls' club worker in the late 1880s and early 1890s, men were different once they were married: "If you don't belong to 'em body and soul, you get it on the 'ead."[28]

Not all young women entered marriage with their vision blocked by images of perpetual "love and kisses." When Marie Welch, born in Norfolk Gardens, Hoxton, in 1904, was being courted by the mild-mannered person who became her husband, she remembered her moth-er's old warning: "Be careful who you marry." The daughter had shrewdly responded: "Well you may not have known father was going to do all that to you until you married." Yet Marie never told her mother what else she was thinking during these discussions, thoughts that revealed the depth of her rage against her father, a violent, even sadistic man who almost deliberately starved his family: "If my husband does that, I'm going to look round for something heavy. I don't care if I go to prison." Other young women, quite aware of the risks and dangers of marriage, used the courtship period to test their young men. A laundry worker in Battersea sometime around the turn of the century was closely watching her fiancé, a tram conductor. As her brother told the story, "He lost so many days through laziness or drink that—she didn't care whether she had him or not." She continued the engagement until she met an ex-soldier who had a sizable capital on which they could marry; then she broke off her relationship with the layabout. Another girl whom Emmeline Pethick got to know through her West London work tested her suitor by deliberately keeping him waiting for a half-hour while secretly observing him. Because he waited patiently without cursing or shouting, she agreed to marry him. "I didn't want to put up with things the same way as my mother had to," she told the settlement worker.[29]

Among both skilled and unskilled laborers, Londoners tended to court and marry their own neighbors. Neighborhood endogamy was replacing marriage within the same trades, a process occurring throughout industrial Europe during these years.[30] Marriage within a considerably smaller radius (which I call *street endogamy*) predominated among the Londoners who produced autobiographies and oral histories. Mr. and Mrs. Mac, born in 1894 and 1905, respectively, both of whom lived in various streets in Hoxton, Shoreditch, and vicinity, had known each other since childhood. Ethel Vango's parents were both raised in Pope's Head Court near Brick Lane, and met and married there. Alice Linton, who married in the 1920s, chose the son of the family who had lived opposite her own in Shoreditch during World War I. Edward Ezard, born in a Battersea railroad district in the 1890s, may have been describing an overlapping of trade and neighborhood intermarriage when he wrote that there was considerable hostility toward men who courted "a girl from outside" and also "when an outsider walked off with a local beauty." Should the couple decide to reside in the bride's parish, "that took years to live down."[31]

Parents in general managed to maintain a control over their daughters' sexual lives nearly as complete as that of the middle classes, regulating not only the time the couple spent together but also the length of their courtship. A combination of an adult child's sense of filial duty and the parents' need for the child's continued wage contributions could keep courting couples waiting for years to marry. The strict curfews, nine or ten o'clock, imposed on daughters, even when they were well into their twenties, are a recurrent theme of stories about Edwardian times. Mrs.

Henman, telling about her East London Edwardian childhood, reported that even when she was twenty she had a 9 P.M. curfew. While she entertained beaux in the parlor (which had no door!) her mother sat in the kitchen nearby, and at 9:30 the mother began urging the suitor to leave. "You wasn't allowed to kiss one another in front of her—used to 'ave to kiss 'em on the doorstep." Mrs. Henman was not interested in telling a tale of working-class rectitude, however; she went on to point out that her younger sister was allowed to frequent the local pub with her suitor and speculated that he had been clever enough to bribe his future mother-in-law for this privilege.[32]

Yet especially in the later stages, courting couples were normally granted, and expected, special privileges and amenities. Girls who had mothered their little siblings and donated their wages to their families found the reins of the family loosening. The parlor was tidied and the tablecloth laid in many homes when older children were keeping company. A young Camden Town woman whose usual curfew was 9 o'clock got it extended to 10 when she began her courtship (she married in 1922 at the age of twenty-three). May Surrey, who moved to Custom House in East London with her family in 1906 or so, had a rather austere childhood considering that her father, a lighterman, was quite a good earner. She went to her first dances and on her first walks when she was courting in the 1910s and 1920s and saw the West End for the first time in her life (and possibly the last) during those years.[33]

The series of courtship and marriage rituals that among the middle classes and most prosperous workers created a sharp demarcation between the newly forming family and the old—engagement, "white" wedding, honeymoon—barely existed among most of London's working-class districts during these generations. A formal period of engagement, marked by a ring or other formal gift giving, was also rare among workers throughout this period. Alice Linton's courtship, which led to a long and happy marriage, might stand in for many others: "He never actually proposed to me, we just began to look in furniture shops and talk about being married, taking it for granted." Working-class brides did not begin to marry in white in significant numbers until the 1930s. Before that, the rule was quick and unceremonious church weddings, sometimes in mass marriages arranged by zealous clergymen hoping to make honest women of many brides at once. Clergymen polled in 1883 commented that couples actually preferred to marry away from their own parishes to ensure "a quiet wedding."[34] Small, simple receptions in the home or pub followed. The reception ham and the beer finished, the couple moved into their new quarters and found themselves day by day assuming more of the gestures and postures of husband and wife.

THE DUTIES OF WIVES

The reciprocal obligations of spouses were widely recognized in working-class communities. Wives' responsibility for child care and domestic labor are spelled out in numerous ballads and songs. "They darn up all our stockings and they make our buttons fast, / And comfort and console us throughout life," announces one music-hall song, "Angels Without Wings." An old bachelor, advertising for a wife in an earlier street ballad, complains:

No wife have I, my bed to make
To wash my shirt or fry my steak;
I am forced to dine at coffee shops,
To scrub the room, and emp' the slops,
   O what is more than that, alack.
No wife have I to warm my back.[35]

These formulations created a pleasant illusion of order and fixity, but the rules of the sexual division of labor rested on unstable foundations. Their artificiality was far more patent in these households than in middle-class districts where servants and spatial arrangements could maintain sexual distinctions. Many working Londoners had to suppress knowledge (for example, men's familiarity with laundry procedures or women's with shoemaking) to maintain an illusion of profound sexual difference. Working-class London boys, unlike their middle-class counterparts, tended to have considerable domestic experience with child care, laundry, and cleaning in particular. Men who had been to sea, plentiful in South and East London, were expert at routine sewing, and some could knit and embroider as well. During childbirth or in households where no children were old enough to help, husbands could be seen scrubbing floors and washing dishes. In one, two, or three-room dwellings, domestic labor could not, in any case, be hidden from the man of the house as it was in Kensington townhouses. The sexual division of labor had to be negotiated from moment to moment. Loving wives protected their men from the indignity of falling into female roles; yet in moments of anger, wives could force husbands to sample woman's work, sticking a husband with child care or forcing him to do the week's marketing.[36]

   Men sometimes had to go to dramatic lengths to demonstrate their right to and need for specific services from their wives. The Ranyard nurses on their rounds in the early 1870s met a husband who had willingly starved himself rather than do his own cooking while his wife was crippled with badly burned and infected arms. The wife was intensely grateful for the nurses' successful treatment. As she wrote, "Now my husband likes to have something cooked for his dinner; before, he would often be content with a bit of bread and cheese, as he did not like to eat anything which I had handled." A generation later, a Bethnal Green man, though a high-class French polisher (a skilled furniture finisher) and no doubt manually dexterous, refused to put jam on his own bread or peel his own oranges, leaving those tasks, too, to his wife.[37]

For a wife to fail to offer proper meals, even for very good reason— such as the husband's refusal or inability to provide the money—was to court a violent retaliation: These wife beaters were fighting not only for food but and also for domestic deference. Those of South London pawnbroker John Small's female customers who demanded quick service because "they had to get the old man's supper ready, or wouldn't they catch it!" were probably not exaggerating.[38] Wives' domestic lapses were a major theme in the serious assaults tried at the Old Bailey. For example, overcome with rage, Robert Plampton stabbed and killed his wife Emily Maria after a series of confrontations one afternoon which began with the man's discovery, when he went to take a nap, that his blankets had been pawned. Emily Plampton apparently pawned a saucepan as well as the blankets—thereby delaying the preparation of her husband's dinner—as she stopped for several drinks with her neighbors on her way to borrow another pot. The wife's supply of meals was a hot topic, too, in the strife-torn Jasper household in Hoxton in the decade before 1918. The husband's expectations about his dinners were in no way moderated by his knowledge of how little money he was giving to his wife. At Sunday tea, if there were no winkles and watercress on the table, the son reported, "I've seen him create something awful. He would come downstairs, sit down at the table and say, "No cress; you know bloody well I always have them.' " And he would then lash out violently.[39]

A good wife knew how to orchestrate a response to her husband's demands that was compatible with family survival in general, and being conciliatory was often part of it. "If you can't make peace don't make trouble," was one wife's motto. "It is better to give points away for peace," announced Leah Chegwidden, who believed that it was bad for children to see their parents arguing.[40] It was the mother who generally lost the points; her apportionment of food, her superhuman efforts to discipline the children during their father's dinner hour and Sunday nap, and her silence when he wasted money all were more or less conscious elements of the peacemaking process.

But keeping the peace with a man meant that he became an object of household routine rather than a part of it, someone to be either shielded or feared. A Bethnal Green wife did not even have to warn her daughters to keep quiet when she rescued her husband's steak from the cat who had already begun to gnaw it: "What eye don't see, heart don't grieve over," was her motto. Another mother quickly shooed her daughter away as the girl exploded with laughter at the sight of her father napping with a red handkerchief over his face that puffed out like a balloon whenever he exhaled. Walter Chegwidden, though a loyal and fond husband and father, nonetheless often complained that his wife "made him an ogre to his children." Another author admitted that she had been "scared of me Dad" as a child. "I don't know why. Mum used to say 'you wait till you father comes home.' " The husband's privileges and dignity could well make him an alien in his household.[41]

The work of a "good" wife was not exactly analogous to that of a good husband, for the woman had far less room for error. Sobriety, consistency, and at least some cleverness were built-in requirements for wives, and the absence of these qualities was much more likely to be noticed than their presence. After all, even the most drunken and neglectful husband usually had someone to take care of his home and children. Drinking (and therefore often heavy-pawning) wives were subject to literal battering by their husbands and to figurative battering by the poor-law, the COS, and other agencies. Mothers' heavy drinking and their concomitant neglect and mismanagement of their infants figure in many Old Bailey cases, for their derelection had dire consequences for their families. Women consistently made up around a fifth to a quarter of those arrested on drunk and disorderly charges, but they vastly outnumbered those incarcerated under the Habitual Inebriates Act of 1898, which mandated confinement in detoxification "homes" for as long as three years for those charged with drunkenness at least four times during one year. After eight years under the act, 375 men but 1,902 women had been hospitalized nationally under its provisions. In 1913, when the asylums were closed and the experiment ended, the final national figures showed that more than 80 percent of those sent to the reformatories were women. In some cases drunkenness associated with child neglect was their specific charge.[42]

Alice Neale was definitely a bad wife and a bad mother; the eight months' imprisonment that was her punishment in an 1887 Old Bailey case for manslaughter seems an awfully light sentence. Her inability or refusal to carry out her basic duties led to a death in the Neale family and great misery for the survivors. Neale had clearly refused to keep house for her husband and to care for her children, whom she left alone day after day, the baby constantly crying and covered with filth. Her landlady and neighbors in Kentish Town and, to some extent, her wayward husband William had kept the children alive and occupied while Neale was out drinking, and it was the landlady who, after many warnings, swore out a complaint against her.[43]

A much larger group of "bad" wives, far larger than that of drinkers, were women who had "lost all hope," as the saying went, women who, to use Beatrice Potter's terms, were "very dirty and untidy" or "untidy, incapable and careworn," dragging themselves as best they could through their days and carrying out minimal domestic functions in a weary, depressed state.[44] These symptoms could express a variety of underlying states: overwhelming fatigue, illness, depression, or rebellion. What they meant in one particular case is clear in Edith Hall's autobiography describing her childhood in the engineering district of Southall, West London, before and during World War I. Hall had a neighbor who quite suddenly and deliberately gave up trying to be a good wife. Mrs. Lane had ten children and worked as a charwoman, sometimes for well-off women with few children and large beautiful houses. Was it this contrast that put her into a rage that reduced her to total inaction? In earlier days, she returned home each day from the charring, cleaned her own house, and would "then sit, unwashed, on her front doorstep, with her hair in curlers." "Then, without warning, she turned lazy. She went out no more a-cleaning, nor did she bother about her own children. She stayed in bed all day and it was rumored that Mr Lane poured cold water over her, but it made no difference; still she wouldn't get up."[45] Mrs. Lane exercised one of the few forms of rebellion she had available. But their powerful ties to dependent children or aged parents made it unlikely that many mothers would, like Mrs. Lane, simply quit.

THE PROVIDER ROLE[46]

East London Federation of Suffragettes neighborhood worker Malvina Walker heard one woman's view of marriage and its meaning in Bow in 1914, and it came down to the husband's wage and the way he offered it: "It's true [men] have to work and earn the few ha'pence they get, but when they dub up on Friday, they think they're giving you a fortune; 23 shillings mine gives me and four babies to keep. . . . Do you know what? I would rather he'd stick to the few ha'pence, and he keep the home, but there, *he couldn't do it*."[47] Husbands' primary obligations were to work and to hand over a customary amount of their pay to their wives. Being a husband was synonymous with providing support. A woman's court testimony in the 1870s suggests the close association between husband and earner: "He has been a good father to his children, and a good husband to me as far as his means would let him."[48]

Although this money exchange was experienced as a personal one between wife and husband, it was also structured by forces far beyond the control of individual couples. Obvious among them are the availability and regularity of work for men and women, wages, prices, and rents. The period of this study also witnessed a series of new claims on men's income. Professional soccer and boxing and organized betting on horse races (the latter attractive to women as well) joined the older attractions of the pub as powerful competitors for men's pocket money, drawing on the new moments of working-class men's leisure and surplus cash of the 1880s and later. By the 1890s professional boxing (as opposed to bare-fisted prizefighting, which had been illegal for some time, and as opposed to the more gentlemanly sport of amateur boxing) had become a popular spectator sport for residents of some parts of the metropolis: inner East London; and especially Bermondsey where the area's dockers, tannery workers, and sawmill employees paid admission fees at pubs and small halls to watch the bantam- or featherweight matches that generated so many champions. Beer, winkles, and gambling added to the costs of such evenings. Particularly in West Ham, Tottenham, and Millwall, where there were good teams, men also went to professional soccer matches in the 1890s, where food, drink, and betting again snared their pocket money.[49]

Before World War I, working men were much more likely to gamble on horse races than on either boxers or football. Betting on horses had been democratized and expanded into a national system in the mid-Victorian years as the electric telegraph made racing news and daily odds accessible to men in urban pubs or street corners, and railroads facilitated the movement of horses to distant racing sites. From 1853 onward, off-course cash wagers were illegal, and this gave slum betting its particular structure of street bookies, touts, lookouts, and runners in working-class districts (and scrupulous honesty to bettors), a structure that appears to have taken shape by the 1880s, one on which masses of working-class men (but not, apparently, the poorest third or so) were apt to spend small sums regularly.[50]

"Good" husbands surrendered most of their pay each week despite these temptations. They were seldom violent, offered extra help like boot repair or potato peeling on Sundays, and (to read beneath the many layers of euphemism in which this issue is hidden) made only limited sexual demands. Such men were common enough, sociologically speaking. One social worker attempted a primitive estimate of the proportions of "good" ones among the Somers Town households, many of them one-room dwellers, with whom she worked in the 1900s. In her "sample" of twenty-one husbands, there were only two really "bad" ones, one of whom, when in one of his periodic rages, "will not think twice of lifting the bed and throwing it out of the window." Seven husbands were good, in the combined judgments of their wives and the social workers, four were "middling," and eight were mentioned by their wives without further comment and were thus dismissed by the pollster as "quite harmless."[51]

As magistrates of this era testified repeatedly, the single thing that wives wanted from their husbands was money: Insults, violence, and sexual infidelity all paled in comparison. Thomas Saunders's memoirs of his work as a Thames Police Court magistrate in the 1870s and 1880s reveal his bewilderment and impatience with the dozens of women who approached him each day for aid in getting money out of their husbands. A bricklayer's wife complained to Saunders that her husband allowed her only a pound a week; a young wife, married only three months, requested a divorce after discovering that her husband, who earned 2 pounds a week, brought her only half of it; and another woman reached the breaking point when her husband yelled at her for pawning his best coat "when she did it to get the Sunday dinner."[52] What relief the law could provide was not structured to meet the needs of working-class wives. In 1878, magistrates were empowered by the Matrimonial Causes Act to grant separation and maintenance orders to women who could prove that they had been physically assaulted. The 1886 Maintenance of Wives Act permitted magistrates to grant and enforce maintenance orders for wives who had been deserted. The Summary Jurisdiction (Married Women) Act of 1895 permitted separation on the grounds of the husband's persistent physical cruelty or his imprisonment for at least two months. In the 1902 Licensing Act, the husband's (or wife's) "habitual drunkenness" was added to the grounds for a separation order. Wives by and large did not want either separations or divorces; indeed, court observers and judges were amazed that most of those who were legally separated were soon reconciled and that nationally, separation figures were fairly small (about eight thousand a year around the turn of the century). Women actually wanted maintenance orders without separations, something that became legally possible only in 1924. Meanwhile, in the courts, the women continued to appeal to men in authority simply to make their husbands give them more of their money.[53]

A husband's unemployment could thus generate almost intolerable domestic tensions, as it still can today, and seems to have been a factor in a large minority of Old Bailey assault or murder cases. Unemployed men were angry and frustrated. Their wives' material deprivations could lead to taunting, reproaches and a decline—by choice or necessity—in the quality of service they performed for the men. Because wives of unemployed men usually went to work themselves, it was not only their lack of time to perform their usual domestic services but also, it seems likely, their sense of their own rights as wage earners that infuriated their husbands. In one assault case from the late 1870s in which a husband attacked his wife, it was her employment and his unemployment that created the conflict. Because he had threatened and attacked her several times, Emma Tritner was living apart from her husband William on Mile End Road. On the day of the attack, he knocked at his estranged wife's door. "I opened it and said I was in hopes he had got a place, because he was out of work, and I was paying the rent," Emma testified. In the fight that sealed William Tritner's determination to "do for" his wife, Emma—angry at being dragged out of bed by her idle husband so that she could go to work, worried by William's rough treatment of the baby, and furious at her husband for letting her leave the house hungry and with no food for the baby—had shouted at her husband and thrown a cup at him.[54]

When men who did have regular work came home with wages badly diminished—usually at the pub—their wives felt entitled to retaliate. In the 1900s, Margaret Loane reported that she had met a number of wives who did not hesitate to beat up their husbands when they returned home missing "an undue proportion of their week's wages." More common, it seems, as domestic-violence patterns today confirm, the wives fought in the way they knew best—verbally. Their less articulate husbands responded as they also knew best and as they felt they had a right to: physically. Jack Welch describes a 1911 fight his parents had had when he, the eldest child, was eight and they lived in Waterloo Place, Haggerston. The children were in bed when late at night the father returned from the pub and "a quarrel started as mum upbraided him with boozing money away that she needed to pay rent and buy food." As Welch continued when he was interviewed in the 1970s, "She was giving him a good tongue lashing, when suddenly I heard furniture being bowled over, a scream cut short, and a bump. I leapt out of bed and scrambled fast down those stairs, with Peter [age six] screaming after me." The boys found their father on top of his wife, "both hands locked round her throat." Jack grabbed his father from behind while his little brother pried at the man's hands and probably bit him. Suddenly loosing his grip, the elder Welch got up silently and walked away.[55] The historical record does not tell us why the senior Welch suddenly relaxed his grip on his wife. His youngest son's sharp teeth may have done it or perhaps his knowledge that he had done wrong to drink away his family's subsistence.

Theft was one way that women could exact their due from husbands who were bad providers. Such men were the victims, and mothers and children were the partners in this frequent but probably heavily underreported crime. In a desperate version of wifely theft, which ended in her murder, Mary Ann Ford infuriated her husband when she took his entire week's pay. "We had a few words about money matters," the man told the court at his trial for murder (here presented in typical courtroom understatement). "I never meant to kill her, she should have kept her hand out of my pocket."[56] The dead woman would surely have said (and probably had) that the money she took was owed her.

In the Jasper family in Hoxton, when the husband gave his wife only 7 or 8 shillings a week, a small part of his fairly large earnings, the wife stole money from her husband whenever she could, it appears, and so did some of the children. The son Art Jasper's autobiographical versions of these incidents use the mode of the music-hall comic ballad in which wives regularly go through their drunken husband's pockets, as in James Fawn's "Woman, Lovely Woman" ("By who up the stairs are we carefully led, / And when we're asleep and our senses have fled, / Runs through our pockets, when we are in bed? / Woman, lovely woman.").[57]

> I remember my father going to his own bed. As he took his trousers off, his money fell out of his pocket. He was so drunk he couldn't bend down to find it. I was going upstairs as this happened and looked in the door and saw some cash on the floor. Knowing he always kept Mum short, I dived under the bed and picked up a two-shilling piece. . . . I slid out, found Mum and gave her the two shillings I managed to pick up. She asked me how I came by it, and I explained what had happened. "Good boy," she says, and upstairs she went. Dad was now out to the world, so she had all the silver and left him the coppers.

In a later incident, Ann Jasper found her husband's "panel money" (his disability payment under the National Insurance Act of 1911) at the bottom of the bed and hid it in her nightdress. The next day, while the father ordered the whole household to hunt for the cash, the mother went on a shopping spree: new boots and clothing for the kids. The new clothes advertised the thief's name, but old man Jasper let the matter drop. His wife had called him all the foul names she could lay her tongue to, but this time he was simply the family fool.[58]

THE WIFE'S "WAGE"

The internal "wage" system was in many ways the key to sexual separation within families. The custom of paying wives "wages" for housekeeping expenses, from which the male earner's "pocket money" was reserved, was widespread throughout England and Wales by the mid-nineteenth century.[59] In this system, husbands generally kept wives in the dark about their total actual earnings but assigned them total responsibility for household subsistence. There were other methods of apportioning household income, such as the "tip-up" or "whole wage system" in which the man's unopened wage packet was publicly deposited in his wife's lap for her to distribute as she saw fit, or the still less common arrangement in which the husband kept most of the wage and organized the household spending himself. Budget studies from the 1930s and 1940s uncovered enormous regional variations that probably date back several generations. In Slough, just west of London, for example, only 5 percent of the husbands gave all their earnings to their wives, compared with 49 percent in the Lancashire industrial town of Black-burn. This north–south contrast has continued into the present. In the early 1970s, a sixth of households in the north followed the whole wage system, whereas only one fiftieth of London households did. The house-holds in our own generation that most resemble those under study here—poor, urban, and with many children—are the ones most likely to use the pocket money system that predominated among Edwardian and late Victorian Londoners.[60]

In pre–World War London the pocket money system was nearly the rule. In the Somers Town homes in which nutritionist Florence Petty was a regular visitor for a few years before 1910, only one of twenty-one husbands kept the money himself and did all the paying, and the rest apparently used a pocket money arrangement. In the second winter of World War I, researchers under V. de Vesselitsky who were trying to assess the impact of inflation and separation allowances on the bud-gets of Limehouse residents found that most men kept pocket money as they saw fit. In a smattering of homes, however, the husband gave his wife his entire wage, making his own spending money the object of negotiation. These men thought themselves so remarkably virtuous that they took "particular delight in explaining that all they have is what the 'missus allows them.' " The size of the wife's wage was determined in part by husbands' tastes and drinking habits, in part by local custom. As for the East London dockers, carmen, general laborers, and factory workers in Vesselitsky's study, about half of whom had only casual em-ployment, they gave their wives, on the average, about three quarters of what they made; none kept less than 5 shillings a week, including men earning only 25 shillings. Obviously what the men spent on luxu-ries like tobacco and beer was way out of proportion to the family's expenditure on food.[61]

Wives used a variety of ways of penetrating their husbands' secrecy about their actual earnings, such as listening attentively to street orators during strikes, but most would have to be content with what they got. A. S. Rowntree, frustrated in his York budget analyses by the knowl-edge that the wives could not give him accurate figures on their hus-bands' income, finally used his personal influence with employers to get wage figures directly from them. Young and Willmott's Bethnal Green research in the 1950s found a few wives who did not know even ap-proximately what their husbands were getting, and more recent studies done in other towns suggest that male wage secrecy remains the practice of a determined but good-sized minority.[62]

Wives' wages declined with husbands', and disappeared altogether with their unemployment, but many arrangements were so rigid that they remained unchanged throughout the man's wage-earning years, without regard to inflation, the birth of additional children, or special emergencies.[63] George Acorn's father gave his wife 18 shillings a week "when he first married [probably in the 1870s], and never increased it" despite the arrival of about half a dozen children. Much later, when Alice Linton's father took a high-paying war job, he "still didn't give mother much share of his extra money, and she still needed to go to work." Mrs. Z, one of Anna Martin's neighbors in Rotherhithe, had nursed a sick working daughter for several months and then fell ill herself, having accumulated enormous debts to finance the daughter's care. The husband, thinking that the details of survival were "always the wife's business," had never inquired how his wife was coping with the extra medical expenses and the loss of the daughter's income. Recent investigations demonstrate that wives' household allowances continue to lag behind husbands' wage increases.[64]

The author of a recent sociological study of household finances concluded that "when money is so very short . . . managing the family's income should be seen as one of the chores of the household, rather than a significant source of power." Victorian and Edwardian husbands knew they were well rid of this burden. Yet the responsibility for food and care generated in wives a sense of entitlement that was expressed in domestic confrontations with husbands, in dealings with charity workers, and occasionally in the public arena. To the children, the mother's control of the purse strings appeared absolute: "Children always speak of the family income as belonging entirely to [the mother]," District Nurse Margaret Loane reported.[65] Children might well have perceived their mothers' money management as a sign of their power; it was their mothers who told them whether they would have stew or only rice for dinner, whether they could go on school outings (which usually cost something), and whether they could have new clothing. Standing between the husband's wage and the child's desire, it was the mothers who taught their children the meaning of poverty, a poverty shaped in part by their parents' marriage contract.

GENDER DIVISIONS AND JURISDICTIONS

Household jurisdictions and even physical spaces apparently were sharply divided by gender. Children's language, for instance, showed a vivid awareness of masculine and feminine household divisions. Asked to report on their activities one Saturday in May 1905, East London schoolboys used wording that suggested their own place in female territory. One referred to his "mother's fire," for which he got some wood, and another labeled the errands he had done as "my mother's work." Children spoke of "mum's moves" when describing the family's frequent removals to new quarters, for which women did the decision making and negotiating.[66]

The rather extensive "farming" carried on in East and South London basements, yards, and vacant lots—raising chickens or rabbits or cultivating small garden allotments—was, on the other hand, definitely a male activity. Although these side employments certainly augmented the men's wages (according to one sensible estimate, at the turn of the twentieth century at least 40 percent of the working-class households in Great Britain engaged in them, and another 10 percent lived entirely off such informal sources of income), the money did not necessarily mean higher living standards for the households, for the men used the proceeds quite variously. Alice Linton's surly father in Shoreditch raised chickens and kept the money from his egg sales for himself; indeed, he stored the eggs in a large wooden trunk "which had a secure padlock on it." Walter Chegwidden, on the other hand, supplemented his regular wage with a series of backyard ventures that he hoped would make the family's collective fortune—the unsuccessful mushroom-growing scheme already described, plus attempts to raise chinchillas, rabbits, and chickens. Mr. Griffiths, a tram employee in Poplar, raised rabbits and chickens with more success in his back garden off St. Leonard's Road. The poultry ended up on the family table at Christmas, and the profits from his egg sales were deposited in an unused teapot on the dresser, a public place, where they were at his wife's disposal.[67]

Mending the family's boots was an ancient male responsibility, and even cantankerous and neglectful fathers looked after their children's feet. Boot repairing enlisted skills that boys were taught in the board schools and required materials (leather, awls, nails) that husbands usually bought out of their own money. Mr. Griffiths in Poplar mended his household's thirteen pairs of boots in his garden shed. The leather, soaked in water to soften it, was sewed to the damaged boot, and Blakeys—noisy, uncomfortable, and even dangerous steel tips—were nailed on to protect the new soles. Doris Bailey's tyrannical father took his children to a good shop near Liverpool Street every Easter to buy them expensive shoes; the Easter bank holiday was a time when he found extra work polishing bank counters, and nasty as he might have been, he did care about his children's feet. One of the hardships that Edith Hall in Southall suffered during World War I when her father was at war was perpetual foot discomfort: "My mother just could not repair our shoes properly; I walked on little leather-patch platforms during the whole of the war."[68]

The parlor, if there was one, belonged to the wife. It housed her treasures—family photos, mantlepiece drapery, ornaments, furniture, and plants. Indeed, in Walter Southgate's household, the genial radical father dubbed the mantelpiece "mother's altarpiece" for it "kept company," wrote the son, "with the vases and tall oval glass shades, under which she kept the bridal ornaments of her once radiant girlhood."[69] Unlike the father's chair, for his use alone, the parlor was available to others, though at designated times and on specific conditions. Many parlors had to be used as sleeping quarters at night; most were opened for Sunday dinner and Sunday evening gatherings; and mothers also turned them over to courting daughters and their young men.

Clean steps, sidewalks, windowsills, hearths, and pristine parlors, the work of wives or their children, demarcated women's space in houses and streets, precincts that were destined to be invaded. A young boy entrusted by his mother with domestic chores in his family's home in Wellington Place, Bethnal Green, in the early 1900s, angrily noted that his father and brothers showed no respect for the household interior's feminine territory, the polished grate and swept-out hearth: "My father used to tap his pipe and empty its contents all over it, and my step-brothers threw their cigarette ends over the hearth." Octavia Hill reported with great satisfaction a successful lesson in cleaning as a claim of female turf in one of the "rough" Marylebone buildings she superintended. "One little girl was so proud of her first cleaning that she stood two hours watching her passage lest the boys, whom she considered as the natural enemies of order and cleanliness, should spoil it before I came to see it."[70] The whitened circles, squares, or oblongs outside house doors all over working-class London before and after World War I—patches that would eventually be dirtied by passersby—are poignant attempts of housewives to extend their turf just a bit beyond their own four walls.

In many homes, "father's chair" by the fire was kept sacrosanct, a reflection of his extra material comfort at home and a symbolic statement of his headship there. In J. C. Heffron's song, "We All Go to Work but Father," the father, a comic villain, in fact refuses to let the family move his chair during a midnight "flit." As Grace Foakes wrote about her father: "He was the only one to have a comfortable chair in my home. It was a tub-shaped wooden chair with railings along the back and sides. . . . No one could sit in my father's chair when he was home. We always tried to, but were turned out." Alice Linton described in similar terms her living room in Allerton Street, Hoxton, in the years before 1914: "A round table stood in the centre of the room and dad's old wooden armchair held the place of honour in front of the fireplace. No one would ever dare to sit in that chair, sacred to father alone." Thus there was little doubt as to who belonged in "the empty chair," the lavish and popular wreath gracing so many London funeral processions.[71]

Some fathers may have fought for their chairs, but more had them supplied almost invisibly by their wives, like most of the husband's other

domestic privileges. Walter Southgate, an SDF member and lifetime Labour party and trades union activist, artfully noted this in his autobiography. Describing his childhood home in the 1890s in Cambridge Heath
along the Regent's Canal, Southgate tells the "father's chair" story twice,
the second time subtly undermining the chair's sacredness by delineating
its construction in sexual politics and political economy: "My father,
too, would declaim on such matters [as Tory misrule, Charles Bradlaugh, Gladstone, and Henry George] from his armchair by the fireplace. . . . That armchair was held sacred for my father's use and we
children were not allowed to sit in it while he was home." In the next
paragraph we learn, however, something about the way in which the
mother financed its purchase and managed to keep it there by defying
the forces of the capitalist state:

> It was an ordinary Windsor chair, of the type turned out in their thousands
> and costing eight shillings paid weekly. Mother never paid cash for furni-
> ture for the good reason that she never had the cash to pay in full for
> anything in that line. . . .
> Father was once summoned to the county court over payments due on the
> chair. The registrar ordered a court payment of two shillings per month.
> The debt collecting firm could have taken the chair away (and kept the
> installments) but they preferred a judgement summons. The debt collect-
> ing agency sent threatening letters on vivid blue paper. Mother tore them
> into narrow strips and she made pipe lights of them for father who bliss-
> fully used them unaware of what they were.[72]

Southgate's attention to the layers of domestic detail required for the
maintenance of that central symbol of male dignity gives the father's
(seated) position a decidedly comic turn: The chair on which the pater-
familias sat declaiming on Gladstone and Henry George had feet of
clay.

PAWNING AND POWER

At the pawnshop women transformed and traded household resources
outside the gaze of men. The publicity of the whole pawning process—
which was known to neighbors, pawnshop countermen, music-hall
songwriters, but not (officially) husbands—suggests an effort to belittle
the wage earners while affirming the community of wives with one another and their neighbors. Pawning, really a metaphor for marriage itself, could variously be a desperate attempt at survival, a women's game
in which the men were "it," or a "comic disaster" on the music-hall
model.[73]

Pledging household goods was a normal part of London working-class life through World War II. In a district like Hoxton, pawnshops were extremely plentiful: At the end of the nineteenth century there were ten within a particular half-mile area in Kingsland Road. The 1902 London figure of six annual pledges per capita amounted to one pledge per family every two or three weeks brought to one of the 692 licensed pawnbrokers. It was not "grandmother's diamond brooch" that was being pawned but skirts, boots, and blankets. The average pledge was worth 4 shillings, and only a tiny proportion of London pledges surveyed for *The Pawnbroker's Gazette* in 1902 were worth more than 10 shillings.[74]

Pawning was a part of the female domain all over Britain by the 1870s at least, when a parliamentary investigation uncovered and worried over this fact. Women accumulated pawn tickets, fretted about losing them, and gathered at magistrates' courts to sign affidavits remedying the loss.[75] COS caseworkers investigating the assets of households applying for aid were invariably shown bundles of pawn tickets by the women with whom they spoke. Women giving depositions at London's Worship Street Police Court in Shoreditch often reported thefts of pawn tickets, and they appear to have stolen them more than men did. Lent, stolen, or honestly obtained pledge tickets were transferred and traded in complex patterns among groups of women, as various court cases show.[76] Indeed, it was the recognition of the significance of pawning for women as organizers of weekly household survival in poor districts that prompted Margaret Llewellyn Davies of the Women's Cooperative Guild to propose to a stunned male national leadership that the Coop open its own pawnshops (to be given the businesslike title of "Loan Department"), a plan they quickly rejected.[77]

It required skill and experience to know which shops paid best for pledges of different categories and how to fold, arrange, and package them to get maximum value, and women were far more likely than men to have cultivated this skill. An embezzler in Barking used a female midwife to pawn some of the hundreds of pairs of stolen boots that he suddenly acquired in 1888. The rings of thieves who invariably employed women to pawn their stolen goods paid homage to this female expertise.[78] Pawnshop countermen could be shrewd and bullying, as it was in their interest to belittle the articles offered as pledges, and it took nerve to stand up to the countermen's harsh patter. Helen Bosanquet reported that she had seen pawnshop assistants "chaffing the women on the quality of their clothing, and holding some well-worn garment up to ridicule; see him take the wedding ring from some poor woman, try it on the counter and sniff contemptuously that 'there ain't much gold in that.' " Art Jasper recalled his mother's shrewd bargaining with a practiced opponent at Long & Doughty ("a long time in and doubt if they ever come out," the locals quipped) in Bridport Place, Hoxton.

One went into a cubicle where the gent behind the counter usually knew his customers. "How much?" were his first words. "Ten shillings," says Mum. "Seven," said the gent behind the counter. "Oh Christ," says Mum, "Don't be like that, Sid." "All right," says Sid. "I'll make it eight bob, but don't forget it's the last time I take this lot in."[79]

Jasper certainly classed pawning as one of his mother's many superior survival skills.

Because of their potential as pawnable goods, most household possessions were claimed by wives as their own. Men's clothing was prime material for the pawnshop, as it was better made than women's and did not go out of style. When John Blake's father wore his good suit to the pub near their Poplar home, he was sharply instructed by his wife to avoid spilling beer on it, which would lower its value at the counter. A music-hall song, parodying "After the Ball" and sung by a husband, ruefully recounts a man's gradual realization that his best Sunday trousers were the parcel that his wife had placed on the pawnshop counter "after the shawl."[80]

Pawning was a family joke, with the father as the straight man. A boy growing up in Bromley-by-Bow before the war took items to the pawnshop for a neighbor who often urged him to hurry " 'fore the old man comes in." Dorothy Scannell recalls that in her Poplar household in the 1900s, extensive pawning was carried out by mother and children without the father's knowledge. She also notes that "no other fathers seemed to know of their wives' and children's visits to this establishment." A local girl pawned her father's watch every Monday in the winter, "for then her father arose in the dark and went to bed in the dark so he didn't see that the watch was missing." Victorian photographer John Thompson in 1877 snapped a posed shot of a "Dealer in Imitation Jewellery" who told Thompson that he often sold two dozen brass wedding rings in a single night, many of them "to wear in place of the genuine wedding-rings pawned for a drink, so as not to let the husband know."[81] This formulation, no doubt meant to please the curious photographer of London street life, also suggested that through pawning, wives gained some independent access to cash to use for their own pleasure.

Sensible husbands probably did their best to keep the pawning out of awareness or to keep silent about their own knowledge of it, as a Hackney story describing a weekly routine suggests. When a burly cab driver awoke from his nap after Saturday dinner, soon after World War I, he expected to put on his good boots. As his wife always pawned the boots on Mondays, it was a family ritual to speedily fetch them on Saturday afternoon while the father, getting up from his nap, visited the outside lavatory. The father's role obviously was to delay long enough for his wife and children to successfully carry off the sleight of hand.

> Dad didn't know where his boots were. While Dad was in the lavatory Jackie had to run like hell down to Grout's with the pawn ticket . . . before Dad came out. He was always a long while in there—I don't know what he did because there was nothing in there, no windows. He might have been studying form, with the bum paper [which was made of cut-up racing journals]. I don't know. But whatever it was, he was always a long while, which was greatly to Mum's relief. . . . Why he wore 'em on Saturday I don't know, but he did.[82]

Even the child who reported this weekly scene many years later had realized that the father was as much in on the steps in this routine as were the mother and children.

VIOLENCE

Domesticated as it might have been in countless neighborhood and music-hall songs and jokes, the threat of male violence was one of the daily fixtures of married life for women. Husbands were, practically by definition, violent. Indeed, one woman brought a warrant out against a man who had "knocked me down as if he was my husband." A West Londoner told her settlement worker in the 1890s after her husband took the (temperance) pledge and stopped beating her up: " 'E ain't like a 'usband at all—'e's more like a friend!"[83]

Husband–wife violence was indeed a privileged form in a culture that permitted a wide range of physical expressions of anger and in which violence was a prerogative of those in authority. Parents slapped, spanked, and whipped children, as did police, neighbors, and teachers; fights broke out in pubs and streets not only between men but sometimes between women also. Nancy Tomes's estimate, for London in a slightly earlier period, the 1850s and 1860s, was that in any neighborhood of two hundred to four hundred houses, ten to twenty men would be convicted of common assaults of women during any one year. Although figures for all kinds of violent crimes, including assaults, had declined in London by the end of the nineteenth century, there is no evidence that the proportion involving husbands beating up their wives had fallen.[84] On a street off Brick Lane in the 1870s, where a coster had attempted to murder his mother-in-law, a slipper maker told a court that he "heard cries of murder, but that being such a common occurrence in that neighbourhood I took no notice of it." Magistrate Montague Williams wrote in the early 1890s that on a Saturday night, the waiting room of the London Hospital, Whitechapel Road, had sometimes had as many as fourteen battered wives, with faces or bodies bruised or bleeding. The majority of wife-beating incidents, 99 percent in Anna Martin's estimation in the 1910s, were never reported to the police. Mrs. C., one of Martin's informants, estimated: "I should say seven out of ten of the wives down my way feel their husbands' fists at times, and lots of 'em are used shocking." Police court waiting rooms were filled each morning with injured women. "If I were to sit here from Monday morning till Saturday to protect women that had got drunken and brutal husbands, I should not get through half of them," complained Montague Williams.[85]

Community behavior in wife-beating incidents acknowledged the inevitability of violence between spouses and the "right" of husbands to beat up their wives. Neighbors in the same house or street were acutely aware of nearby conflict, often because they could easily hear or see it; the sound of shouting and blows would cause them to collect on stairs and landings and at windows, but they would normally allow the fights to continue. Only the presence of a really dangerous weapon, the sight of a lot of blood, or sounds of real terror would persuade them to intervene. William Hancock's murder of Elizabeth Glover, whom he had probably just met, outside the Black Swan Tavern in Bow Road in January 1879 serves as a dramatic case in point. Hancock repeatedly threw the young woman to the ground as a crowd of six or seven gathered. He kept them from interfering by saying, "It's my wife, and I want to take her home, she is drunk" (which Glover was meanwhile loudly denying). Both a waiter from the tavern and a policeman who had been spectators testified in court that they had avoided intervening "because I thought [said the policeman] they were man and wife."[86]

Fighting between men, or between women, was usually public and ritualized. Both parties had to agree on the match; coats were removed; seconds were chosen; and a place "to spar" was found. Domestic collisions were far less orderly and more dangerous as a result, especially to women who were usually, though not always, the weaker fighters. The fights normally took place at home. Couples did not decorously exchange punches but wrestled, slapped, kicked, bit, and threw household objects. Although a few shootings were the result of premeditation, most assaults were products of uncontrollable rage. In their court testimony both women and men commented on their inability to cope with it. "I got into that way I did not know what I was doing," said one woman who had knifed her husband. The image of wives as delicate and passive, immobile victims of brutal husbands, which dominated nineteenth-century campaigns against wife beating—and still prevails in some of today's literature—was probably inaccurate. Cockney men were small and wiry (East and South London boxers were concentrated in the light–featherweight and eventually bantamweight categories),[87] whereas a good many married women were stout, and their heavy domestic labor had developed their shoulders and biceps. Although women were usually the losers in fights with their husbands, many were often willing to fight nonetheless.

Violent aggression itself would not bring wives to the "threshold" of tolerance for marriage or husbands; such fighting was, after all, only to be expected. What did cause women to seek legal separations or to leave their husbands informally were threats of murder, physical attacks on the children (rare according to all observers), refusal to provide income, and sexual insults. "I would forgive anything," a woman told William Fitzsimmons, a famous police court missionary in the 1900s, "but the filthy names he calls me." At age twenty-three, she had been deafened in one ear and had had her nose broken in a long series of attacks by her husband.[88]

Wives hated and feared the injuries they received, some of which left scars or disabilities. But all the evidence we have on domestic violence in this era suggests that its social meaning was different from today's. If marriage did not mean trust, sharing, and intimate partnership, then it was far from surprising that conflict should frequently erupt. Because men's and women's competing desires were an acknowledged part of their culture, it was to be expected that men might use violent means to secure their wives' obedience. Marriage created no sacred or separate space. There was nothing secret or shameful about a Saturday night fight.

Philanthropic agencies, poor-law officials, and jurists had made numerous efforts from 1870 onward, when the first Married Women's Property Act was passed, to use the law to protect working-class women from male violence, and much of late nineteenth-century English family law was posited on the proposition that the men of the working classes were brutes. Although the divorce law that applied to middle-class couples was deeply involved with matters of sexual fidelity and illegitimacy, reformers legislating for the poor thought much more in terms of physically protecting wives. The product of a campaign against working-class male violence in which Frances Power Cobbe was active, the Wife Beaters Act of 1882 was built on notions of working males' loutishness. It allowed courts to confine wife or child beaters in the pillory for up to four hours and permitted long prison sentences and whippings for a second offense.[89] Formal divorce as a recourse for abused wives continued to be off limits to working-class couples until well after World War I, but legal separations for battered, abused, and abandoned wives became increasingly accessible. This legislation, though providing little practical relief or protection for working women, did reformulate a new official position on the rights of wives, however poor.

PLEASURE

"Good-bye Mum. I'm off."
"Good-bye. Have you got your bag Dad?"
"Yes my dear."

Every morning at seven o'clock in the 1880s and 1890s Charles Welch heard this reassuring interchange between his parents as his father set off from their home in Rotherhithe for his job in an Old Street leather bag factory. In his autobiography (published in 1960) Welch tells a familiar story of London poverty: a father whose trade of hemp-rope making was being undermined by the development of steel ropes; the family's reduction to a one-room dwelling; infants left with a grandmother while the mother went to work; and children leaving school at fourteen to find employment. But as an adult, Welch had become a devout Christian. His question, which he could never resolve in print, was why his large, poor family could be so happy, so generous, so fun loving, so sweet tempered, and yet so ungodly. His mother saved money from her earnings at a silk factory for the family's annual beach holiday, spiced by recurrent hilarious disasters. At home, when the parents had loud arguments, the father later padded into his eldest son's room "to assure me all was well, and that he was forgiven." On Sunday evenings, which were more serene, Welch senior read aloud Dickens's novels to his cheerful family in the parlor.[90]

The English working classes as a whole were among the best off in the world in their time, and their better pay, cheaper food, and greater leisure translated into happy moments of eating, drinking and music. If the Sunday dinner made a statement about family order and hierarchy, holiday outings and Saturday and Sunday night parlor gatherings communicated the pleasure, even joy, that could be captured when the week's struggles were put aside. Such collective amusements as sing-songs, evenings of cards, ludo (a board game), and snakes and ladders told of the satisfaction that family life could offer.

Outings for recreation are not so uncommon in accounts of London working life after 1870. Saturday nights were one time that couples went into pubs as twosomes, and the loud closing-time singing that caught the attention of settlement house residents included the voices of respectable matrons, at least on Saturdays. Trips to Hampstead Heath or Epping Forest on bank holidays suggest a taste for space and greenery that Octavia Hill worked energetically to satisfy with her movement to save the commons in and near London. Sunday visits to London parks or walks along the Thames, for example, lightened the days of the family of Frank Galton's father, a morose saddler whose trade was being destroyed by factory production in the 1870s.[91]

Music was the anchor of cockney family events; it offered a pleasure that Dubliner Brendan Behan was able to share fully with his London mates in Holleslay Bay Borstal during World War II. Piano sales were apparently brisk in London's industrial districts well before World War I, and the hunger for pianos was satisfied during the war by the "munition worker's piano," a symbol of the domestic prosperity of the war years. "Many people could play the piano in those days, in varying standards maybe," as Hackney shoemaker Arthur Newton put it, but accordions, concertinas, and banjos could also be heard in working-class parlors. From the rather refined Sunday gatherings with a select few relatives described (for the 1900s) by Edward Ezard in *Battersea Boy,* for which the family dressed up and actual sheet music was supplied by an aunt; to the raucous, drunken, and often violent contemporaneous events at the Jaspers in Hoxton; to the Sunday night parties in Battersea in the 1890s when a Battersea cab maker would "fetch his pals round,"[92] music—and usually the tunes of the music halls—supplied the leaven in these moments of family pleasure.

Although Christmas gift giving was modest among London workers, by late Victorian times the holiday was certainly a moment of family celebration with its special dinner, decorations, and often a Christmas tree. In the 1880s and 1890s, a Battersea household celebrated the holiday by hanging stockings into which Santa put apples, oranges, a new penny, and perhaps a penny toy. Charles Booth's investigator found many traces of Christmas celebrations when he toured a section of East London in the weeks after the Christmas of 1897. In West Bethnal Green he noted street litter containing traces of recent Christmas festivities, and "there were a great number of small Christmas trees fully decked out with sugar plums and candles in the front windows—especially noticeable in the poorer streets."[93]

For all their differences and divisions, marriages could foster loving feelings between wives and husbands. Many of these calmer relationships are invisible to us now: households in which angry men gave their wives killing looks rather than beating them up, households in which no one was ever arrested for violence or drink, in which philosophical acceptance of the spouse's failures or even delight in his presence dominated. These happy families were by no means all alike.

When she was an old lady of seventy-nine, Elizabeth Rignall, born in Lavender Hill, Clapham Junction, in 1894, recorded her childhood in a cheerful, odd family of Salvationists. The father, a painter and decorator, was often out of work, but the household had considerable resources in the mother's Yorkshire-based relatives and the father's siblings and parents, stewards at the Shaftesbury Club on Lavender Hill. Clara, the mother, took in lodgers, many of them students whom her husband loved to show around the metropolis in his spare time. The parents did not quarrel, and the angriest that Elizabeth ever saw her mother was over a relative's breach of hospitality. The husband was devoted to his wife and family. He cooked the midday meal on Sunday morning (he appears to be the only adult male in the city to have done this) so that his wife and sister-in-law could go to morning service, played energetically with his children, and was an ardent believer in birth control—which we know not only from accounts of his views but also from the very wide spacing of his children.[94]

Or for a very different kind of happy marriage, we might turn to the calm, productive, and intensely upwardly mobile household of the Bermondsey hatter James Ashley. Born in north Wales in 1833, he moved to London in the 1850s and there, in 1857, met his wife at one of C. H. Spurgeon's revivalist services at Surrey Gardens. They were married the next year and lived together amicably, adopting an eight-year-old orphan girl and also presiding over the phenomenal success of their biological sons Percy and Will, who were awarded scholarship after scholarship.[95]

"He's always been a good man to me" and "'e's all right" were statements of warm praise, cockney-style, by wives. But social workers or children occasionally heard more specific assertions of marital love. Walter Southgate's mother always told her children that despite offers from richer men, she had "married for love." Another woman informed her children that there was no other man for her "in the whole wide world" but her husband. A woman told Pember Reeves's workers in Kennington of her love for her husband: "My young man's that good ter me I feel as if somethink nice 'ad 'appened every time 'e comes in."[96]

Displays of husbands' attachment to their wives turn up in the historical record more often in violent contexts—assault, murder, or suicide. Guy Aldred's grandfather Holdsworth, who had probably married in the 1860s, was a Clerkenwell artisan, freethinker, Gladstonian radical, and autodidact. A devoted family man and a loving grandfather, he began every day of his adult life rising very early and preparing breakfast for his whole family. But after his wife's death in the late 1890s, he became deeply despondent and committed suicide in 1900. In 1879, a Kentish Town carpenter—whose wife of only a year had yanked off her wedding ring and told him she was going to leave him—said, according to the wife's testimony at his trial for assaulting her, that "he would do all as was in a working man's power to make me happy." Tormented by jealousy, the man had been having dreams in which his wife made cutting remarks, dreams from which he awoke crying bitterly. In another case from the 1870s, James Cranwell, a carpenter who lived just off Lisson Grove, had been happily married and lived "on very affectionate terms" for over thirty years with his wife when she died in the early 1870s. The two had survived the painful deaths of their two children, and during the last fifteen months of his wife's life, Cranwell had attentively and kindly (in the landlady's words) nursed her. After her death, the widower, who was fifty-four, was "very low spirited and very miserable," missing his "poor old lady." (He was in court, however, for killing a new mate in a jealous rage.) A Walworth meat porter, James Rick, was rescued by a policeman in a rowboat from the Thames when he jumped in at Wapping in a suicide attempt. When questioned at the police station, he answered, "I have lost my wife, and everything has gone wrong. Everything seems to have gone wrong with me."[97]

Songs of married bliss are rare in the music-hall canon, and given the performers' fondness for cross dressing, the sincerity of even these lines was frequently in doubt. Yet some of the longest-lived songs ("I Want a Girl Just Like the Girl That Married Dear Old Dad," "Daddy Has a Sweetheart [Mother Is Her Name])" are celebrations of married love. And probably the single most-loved music-hall song, Albert Chevalier's 1892 "My Old Dutch," celebrates—with "oleaginous dollops of sentiment," in Colin MacInnis's words—forty years of married love.[98]

By the 1880s the music halls, now more "respectable," their performances by and large less "blue" and their audiences better behaved, were catering to a wide London public that included nannies and their little aristocratic charges, schoolteachers, and the denizens of London's newly sprawling villadom. But however sanitized it had become, the music-hall genre gave voices to women as well as to men. Man hating as well as misogyny were music-hall conventions: Both the woman who wants those wages on Saturday night and the man who wants to drink them away were standard music-hall characters.[99] Cockney women heard similarly varied voices in their streets and shops; they formulated their thoughts about husbands and marriage in regular doorstep gossip and could count on support for their claims from their neighbors, kin, and children. No expectation about "privacy" or marital "unity" clouded their thinking about their differences from their husbands. Indeed, the vocabulary available to those who felt intense attachment to their mates was far more limited. The elaboration of a mass culture of romantic love, domestic virtue, and marital bliss, still in its early stages, had not yet created a voice more powerful than those of daughter, neighbor, or comic music-hall tune matter-of-factly describing the divisions and hostilities that belonged with the pleasures of marriage.

CHAPTER 4

"What Is Fated Must Be"
Having Babies

Now you're married I wish you joy,
First a girl and then a boy,
Seven years after next November,
You'll have something to remember.
   Twins at once,
   Triplets twice,
   Honeymoon all over.

London children's round game, played by girls and boys, about 1900,
in Elizabeth Rignall, "All So Long Ago"

Ah, well, Nurse, thank God, I am not married. I won't be 'aving
one every year like 'er, por thing.
Patient in a Central London maternity hospital, 1903,
in Katherine Roberts,
Five Months in a London Hospital

Music-hall jocularity about being "in a family way," the sing-song of children's street chants, and even women's matter-of-fact stories of the material strains of pregnancy represent the dominant "mustn't grumble" version of continual maternity. In the 1910s and 1920s, though, birth control and maternal health advocates began to ask women new questions about gynecological health, about sex, and about "wanting" babies. When they did, they heard a less-told story of childbearing—of fear, pain, and resentment.

Nineteenth-century doctors and midwives heard the frightening version, too, when they listened to their patients. Dreams described in doctors' case notes from the General Lying-In Hospital, York Road, Waterloo, dating from the 1880s, convey the anxiety of childbirth, even women's terror of children. These have come to us (via a little-seen medical archive) because for a time, the hospital staff believed that emotional distress could account for postpartum fevers (the record of dreams disappeared during the next decades as the doctors lost faith in this view). The case notes of Sarah Chessum, for example, an Edmonton woman having her eighth child at age thirty-one, a very premature girl who died the next day, reported as Chessum began to convalesce: "Strength being quickly regained. Sleeps without dreaming now, formerly always dreamt—'falling over precipices.' " Mrs. Smith, a sewing machinist, was plagued by bad dreams after having her second child at the same hospital in early February 1884. On her fifth hospital day she broke out in a rash that looked like scarlet fever, and on the sixth she complained of "funny dreams" and a headache. By the eighth day she was feeling better but was still having the "funny dreams, e.g., 'that there was a beast of a dog in the bed instead of a baby,' not of a pleasant kind," as the doctor editorialized.[1] Both dreams provide us with fit metaphors for the experience of repeated and seemingly unavoidable pregnancies ("falling" was a synonym for pregnancy) and the arrival of infants whose needs profoundly threatened their mothers.

HONEYMOON ALL OVER

As a biological condition as well as a set of social definitions, motherhood was all-encompassing for inner-London women throughout the two generations between 1870 and 1918, this despite the fact that the early twentieth-century mothers were beginning to limit the number of their pregnancies. To be an adult woman was practically tantamount to being a "mum." Figures for England and Wales as a whole show that in the cohort of women who married in about 1860, 63 percent had five children or more but that only 12 percent of those who married in 1925 had this many children. The 1911 Fertility Census of England and Wales found that 20 percent of the married women who had completed their childbearing by that year (and whose husbands were still alive) had had eight or more children.[2]

Such unrelenting childbearing had increasingly become the fate of poor women only, as the middle classes had begun perhaps as early as the 1850s to have smaller families. The contrast in fertility—a term that technically means the proportion of married women aged fifteen to forty-five giving birth in one year—between rich and poor was far greater in 1901 than it had been fifty years earlier in England.[3] The 1901 census revealed enormous contrasts in London fertility rates by borough and thus by class. They ranged from an annual rate of 283 births (per thousand wives aged fifteen through forty-five) in Bethnal Green, 295 in Stepney, 283 in Shoreditch, and only 183 in well-off suburban Hampstead. Thus to describe these figures in another way, in the poorest boroughs, nearly a third of wives of reproductive age had babies each year in the later decades of the nineteenth century, whereas in better-off boroughs like Lewisham or Hampstead, the proportions ranged from a fifth to a fourth.[4]

The records of London midwifery charities provide an opportunity to look at the childbearing histories—at a time when working-class fertility rates remained close to their peak—of a special sample of London's poor women, that is, those who at age thirty-five or older were still actively fertile and who had probably married somewhat earlier than the London average. Their reproductive experience is summarized in Table 4–1, A and B. The 256 women, mostly from North Lambeth, who had signed on with the General Lying-In Hospital's midwifery service for an impending birth, already had an average of seven births, counting stillbirths; most would, of course, soon have yet another child. Only about 17 percent of the women had had four or fewer previous births; just about half had already had between five and eight children; and about a third had had nine children or more! Records kept on over 1,300 patients by the Guy's Hospital outpatient Lying-In Charity tell a similar story for a Southwark catchment area farther east along the Thames a little over a decade later. The women thirty-five or older who signed on in 1892, 1893, and 1894 had had an average of 7.66 children and were undergoing yet another pregnancy. Nearly 40 percent of the women had

TABLE 4–1A. Births to Women Aged 35 and over Using General Lying-In's Outpatient Midwifery Service, 1877–1882 (not including next expected birth)*

Number of Births (live and still)	Percent of Women with this Number	Number of Women
0 to 4	17.18	44
5 to 8	50.78	130
9 and over	32.03	82
Totals	99.99	256

*Women aged 35 and over constituted nearly a quarter of the total number of patients using the service.

Source: General Lying-In Hospital, York Road, Outpatient Registers, July 1877–November 1882, GLRO.

TABLE 4–1B. Births to Women Aged 35 and over
Using Guy's Outpatient Maternity Service, 1892–1894
(not including next expected birth)

Number of Births (live and still)	Percent of Women with this Number	Number of Women
0 to 4	13.24	174
5 to 8	47.49	628
9 and over	38.88	512
Total	99.9	1314

Source: Guy's Lying-In Charity (Outpatient) Maternity Record, GLRO.
The casebook runs from 1892 through early 1896; calculations are taken
from early 1892 through late 1894. The Lying-In Charity's name was
changed to Maternity Charity in 1897.

had nine children or more, and only about 13 percent had four or fewer previous births.

Although fertility had begun to drop in all classes from the 1880s on, as both parts of Table 4–2 illustrate, the decline in poor boroughs was rather small in the last decades of the nineteenth century compared with the much faster drop in more middle-class boroughs. Between 1880 and 1901, for example, the fertility rate in a solid working-class district like Poplar fell 6 percent, but the rate of decline in Hampstead was nearly 30 percent in those two decades, and in Kensington, about 21 percent. In the first decades of this century there were much more dramatic drops in fertility rates in all London boroughs, though the decline continued to be faster in those that were better-off. All together, the London fertility rate, combining legitimate and illegitimate births, fell nearly a third in the period of our investigation: The 1910 rate was 31 percent lower than the rate for 1870–1872.[5]

Stillbirths and late miscarriages, linked with maternal health, were also common among the London poor (see Chapter 6). Although the records do not reveal full-term pregnancy outcomes, about 12 percent of all the pregnancies recorded by the General Lying-In Hospital's midwives apparently ended in second- or third-trimester miscarriages.[6] Stillbirth rates have declined over the past century, but there remain huge gaps today between figures for rich and poor, gaps that also may have existed in the past.[7] As the variable findings outlined in Table 4–3 suggest, we cannot precisely fix these rates for the past, as late miscarriages and infant deaths, even days after birth, were often classed as stillbirths. Many

TABLE 4–2A. Fertility Rates for Some London Boroughs, 1880–1934 (number of births per thousand married women of reproductive age)*

Borough	1880–1881	1890–1891	1900–1901	1909–1911	1922–1924	1934
Bermondsey	306	290	273	223	175	105
Bethnal Green	313	298	283	226	166	101
Hackney	291	257	233	169	130	91.0
Hampstead	261	222	183	121	100	71.7
Kensington	255	226	201	149	121	87.4
Lambeth	284	266	243	164	125	87.6
Paddington	255	227	203	151	114	83.6
Poplar	302	286	282	219	173	108
St Marylebone	288	280	276	148	105	64.9
Shoreditch	297	277	272	225	183	115
Southwark	279	261	252	201	155	100
Westminster	238	210	174	124	87.9	66.6

*Legitimate and illegitimate births combined (the legitimate rates are about 1 percent lower than the combined ones). For the years 1880 to 1901, "reproductive age" is 15 to 45; for the following years, it is 15 to 49.

Source: Based on T. A. Welton, "A Study of Some Portions of the Census of London for 1901," *Journal of the Royal Statistical Society* 65 (1902): 493, Table VIII; and John W. Innes, *Class Fertility Trends in England and Wales 1876–1934* (Princeton, NJ: Princeton University Press, 1934), app. II, p. 134.

TABLE 4–2B. Declines in Fertility Rates in Some London Boroughs, 1880–1911 (calculated from Table 4–2A)

Borough	Between 1880–1881 and 1900–1901 (percentage declines)	Between 1890–1891 and 1909–1910 (percentage declines)
Poplar	6	23
Hampstead	30	45
Kensington	21.3	34
Southwark	9.6	22.9
Lambeth	14.4	38

TABLE 4–3. Stillbirths Recorded by Various London Agencies, 1910–1915

Agency and District	Dates	Numbers, when Available	Percentages
Westminster Children's Health Society, cases handled by visitors (A)	1910	986 births; 39 stillbirths	4
Maternity wards, metropolitan poor-law unions, plus Croyden and West Ham (B)	1914	2,213 children born	just under 9
Royal Free Hospital, maternity outpatients, childbirth histories for patients 35 and older (C)	recorded in 1914–1915	1,053 patients	3% had had at least one still-birth in repro-ductive lives
City of London Maternity Hospital, outpatient service (catchment area Shoreditch, Islington, Hoxton) (D)	1913–1915	1,479 patients; 25 born dead or died within a few hours	1.7
Kensington medical officer of health's study (E)	1910	1,487 pregnant women studied; 67 stillbirths, of which 42 were premature	4.5
London, figures compiled by the London medical officer of health based on registered births (F)	1910		2.3★

★Compulsory notification of stillbirths was not required until 1915, and so these figures likely are lower than the actual ones.

A. Westminster Children's Health Society, *1911 Annual Report*, Table IA, p. 22.
B. Local Government Board, *Annual Report 1914–15*, pt. I, p. 30.
C. Royal Free Hospital, *Obstetric Casebook, Outpatients, 1914–17* (this book looked carelessly kept).
D. City of London Maternity Hospital, *District Case Books*, no. 1 (October 1913–September 1916); figures based on October 16, 1913, through October 18, 1915.
E. Kensington MOH, *Annual Reports*, 1910, p. 11.
F. Report of the MOH of the County [of London], in LCC, *Annual Reports*, 1910, vol. 3, p. 13.

were simply not reported, as there was no legal requirement for registering stillbirths until 1915, and women often simply forgot to mention them when describing their reproductive histories. Thousands of unregistered stillborn babies were unofficially buried by private arrangement with undertakers without funerals and at greatly reduced fees.[8] Today "fetal deaths" (from the end of the fifth month of pregnancy through birth) account for about 1 percent of pregnancies; nineteenth- and early twentieth-century figures appear to have been far higher.

Until after World War I, the women of London's miles of poor streets lived their adult lives undergoing numerous births, even more frequent pregnancies, and years of baby and child care. With their last child so often born in its mother's fifth decade, many women thus lived and died as full-time, active mothers of infants and small children.

"NOT A CAREFUL MAN": SEX, CONTRACEPTION, AND ABORTION

Whereas in late twentieth-century marriage there is a structured conflict between romance and parenthood, nineteenth-century unions were posited on babies coming. Working-class women and men had often had many years' experience caring for their own young siblings and so knew a lot about babies. In Lambeth, Pember Reeves suggested, a first birth was usually a welcome one for both parents. Fathers were apt to be fondest of their first and possibly second children, a point supported by Alexander Paterson's observation that paternal interest among the South Londoners he knew dropped off rapidly after one or two births.[9]

Yet most of the London working women, for most of the period before 1918, had many more than three or four children. Did the women want so many children? We should note that the question of "wanting" children is anachronistic, as it is based on an idea widely disseminated by the birth control movement after World War I. Were the language and assumptions of the prewar decades, by contrast, those of a fatalistic acceptance of conception and birth?

The birth control and sex education advocates were, before and after World War I, consciously introducing a new vocabulary for speaking about sex and childbearing, one through which a woman's desire for sex, for a child, or for no more children could be articulated. The middle-class health professionals and others who circulated in the London slums used this vocabulary very naturally. ILP activist Katherine Bruce Glasier used the term sometime around the turn of the century in the birth control movement's sense, that is, distinguishing wanted children from "regrettable accidents." Speaking of her own pregnancy in 1894, she wrote, "For many sakes we don't want it yet." Katherine Roberts, who had begun her midwifery training in 1903, was convinced that "life is a dreary . . . place for any baby not wanted." Though she may have been the one to teach them how to say this, Roberts heard many of her hospital patients speak readily of not wanting their babies. One woman, for instance, after recovering from the chloroform after her birth, sighed,

"The baby was dead; I'm glad, because I didn't want it, but I'm thankful it's over."[10]

Birth control rhetoric in the 1920s associating sexual intercourse with "wanting" actual babies introduced a new self-consciousness about older reproductive practices. The letters that Marie Stopes received in the 1920s, for instance, often echoed Stopes's own language. Mrs. E. T. wrote to her in 1923: "I think us poor Mothers was more of a victim by suffering the strain of constant childbearing year after year. What do our lives become we get broken in health, have sickly babies and too often have to go out to work to make ends meet." A woman in her forties, sick with worry that her family of seven children was about to be increased again, wrote bitterly that it was "a shame that pore people should be dragged down with families fed up with life keep having children."[11]

The language of fatalism endured as well. Even in the 1920s when birthrates were plummeting, doctors and nurses were struck by some women's seeming resignation to continuous pregnancies. E. P. Blacker, a physician and eugenicist who worked in the Guys' Hospital catchment area, heard such phrases of homey resignation as "We must take what comes without grumbling," and "What is fated must be." But this fatalism had long been the safest posture for the women to adopt with middle-class professionals. Pregnancy, childbirth, and newborns were, after all, legally and politically sensitive areas, as, for example, seen in the "overlaying" controversy described in Chapter Seven. When Somerset Maugham's autobiographical Phillip Carey delivered twin babies in a South London slum whom their parents greeted with undisguised infanticidal rage, his response was to threaten a coroner's investigation should a death occur.[12] A sudden miscarriage or an unexpected infant death would lead to a coroner's inquest if a woman had complained too much, too publicly.

Women's actual behavior in the late Victorian and Edwardian years suggests anything but universal resignation to repeated pregnancies. Women took many steps—many of them unsuccessful, to be sure—to control their bodies and to avoid motherhood at the several points where this was possible: keeping away from sex or making sex "safe"; aborting pregnancies; and even—especially in the case of desperate single women—killing newborns or letting them die. Demographers often forget that reproductive behavior is not a specific life compartment, but a part of sexual and social relationships between women and men and within communities.

Sexual intercourse itself was, in the prewar generations, actually a fairly difficult point at which a woman could try to prevent conception. The fissures in the family, dividing women's sphere so totally from men's, help explain husbands' widespread inability to consider sex or conception as a joint responsibility. Though biological fatherhood was, of course, understood, conception was still vaguely "blamed" on women. Music-hall songs like "I'm Very Unkind to My Wife" jocularly view the arrival of a pack of children as one of the many annoyances that a wife brings to a man. Lilly Morris sang "Don't Have Any More, Missus Moore," holding the mother solidly responsible, it seems, for the Moores' twenty children.[13]

Snatches of slum conversations reveal husbands who shared this view. A Poplar man at home sounded like a music-hall husband when he was overheard complaining to his wife sometime around the turn of the century: "I can't hang me trousers on the end of the bed that you're not like that [pregnant]." Living in workmen's flats in Whitechapel in the mid-1880s, Margaret Nevinson, eavesdropping on her neighbors, heard a woman say: " 'E was awful angry because I had another baby. . . . ['E] swore at me shocking, and now 'e's taken 'isself to the public 'ouse because there's no dinner for 'im."[14] Indeed, Ranyard nurses and others who circulated in and out of the homes of the poor were aware of many cases of wife battering during pregnancy, when wives, caught up in the demands of the pregnancy, neglected their husbands' needs, and the men in turn were totally disconnected from the fetus they helped create. In one emblematic case that a clergyman had witnessed, the battering began after a woman in labor could not get up to cook her husband's dinner.[15]

The possibility of pregnancy was seldom far from the mind of any woman, whether married or single, who was having sexual intercourse. In a culture that was not very conscious of time, in which many households did not even have clocks, women nonetheless kept close track of their menstrual periods. All but a very few of those patients queried by the General Lying-In house physician in the 1880s and 1890s remembered the time of their last period, at least in general terms ("Just before Christmas," "early in May") A handful of the women, most of them single and with restricted opportunities for sex, could even date to the day their conception. Lydia Bartlett of Brixton Road, for example, had good reason for such alertness: "Had connection with husband 5th May. Married 5th June." At least two women (both single servants) cited "Jubilee Weekend" (1887) as the time of conception.[16]

By the later decades of the nineteenth century, sex was a mysterious and forbidden arena for working-class girls in London whose mothers were struggling to keep them sexually ignorant and thus "respectable." As a neighborhood woman, a local prostitute or abortionist might be accepted into her community, but her actual profession was surrounded by silence. As an East London teenager in the years just preceding World War I, Elizabeth Flint was aware only that the adults around her were whispering about sex and pregnancy. A mother's vague but ominous warning to her sixteen-year-old daughter to avoid the Territorial troops billeted nearby during the war shows the ways in which language kept sex off limits to young women. The girl's behavior had alarmed her mother, her daughter later remembered: "Somebody told her I was round the school where the boys were—I know she came round and told me they're not the sort of things you should do—it will lead to wrong things and trouble and not only that I remember her words were 'You don't know what to do to those boys.' " Another woman, the wife of a Thames lighterman, frightened her young daughter into silence after the girl talked with enthusiasm about a book on gestation and birth. "I came home full of it and told mother. Oh she frightened the like out of—she was going to put me in a home. If I said anything or told anybody, and I was scared. I never did tell her anything after that." A South London mother and grandmother together silenced another teenager just as emphatically. The only disagreement between the two older women was over the best punishment for the girl's mentioning a neighbor's pregnancy:

> I said, 'ere, gran, you know Mrs. Bibbs? I said, she's going to have another baby. So my mother said, oh? How do you know that? Oh, I said, Mollie Davis said you can always tell Mrs. [B]ibbs with a white apron, she's got a big belly. My mother gave me one spank there on the ear. Oh I can always remember that. She said you'd better keep away from [Mollie] Davis. My old granny said, never hit 'em round the ear 'ole, she said, hit 'em on the leg.[17]

As a result of this silence, maintained against so many odds, the sexual knowledge of most working-class young people was extraordinarily limited. An amazing chorus of wives, and husbands as well, expecting babies in the prewar decades and even later, did not know how the first child would be born. Mrs. Mac, a woman born in Hoxton in 1905, told an interviewer that at her marriage she knew absolutely nothing about sex; her mother, always "very modest," had told none of her children about the facts of life. During her first pregnancy, Dorothy Scannell expected that "my tummy would open out" to let the baby out. (As one woman in the 1930s explained when her confused husband visited her in the hospital after childbirth, "It's come from the same place as you put it in.")[18]

Because sexual talk was suppressed in the working-class Victorian and Edwardian cultures of most regions, sex was one arena in which it was nearly impossible for wives to develop a collective sense of where their "rights" or "interests" lay. Women who fought furiously over a husband's wasted shilling would yield regretfully to an unwanted sexual advance. Many of the descriptions we have about sexual attitudes come from the years just before World War I when maternity, venereal disease, and sex education were already being politicized by reformers.

Women's sexual passion, however, had no place in these discussions, was not heard, and is not a part of "history."

Those who were sympathetic to working women viewed sexual victimization as one of the several crosses they bore. In 1911, as one newly pregnant Rotherhithe woman told settlement worker Anna Martin, who had helped found what must have been one of England's first birth control clinics in 1908: "I knew how upset you would be . . . but what is a woman to do when a man's got a drop of drink in him, and she's all alone?" Intercourse was initiated by men, submitted to by women. Thames Police Court missionary William Fitzsimmons implied in 1912 that even the wives of men who had venereal diseases had no choice but to submit to their husbands, as long as the two lived together.[19] Music-hall songs of courtship and early marriage celebrated brides' pleasurable anticipation of sex with their sweethearts, but some version of sexual martyrdom was a staple of real married life and was not spoken of tragically. A Poplar mother and her sisters were heard whispering about a butcher's wife, "poor woman," who "had to be ready for him every day when he came home to dinner." The same mother included among her large repertoire of homey phrases, "It wasn't the lustful man who had the children" and "A man must have his pleasure." Said a suburban wife blandly on a Christmas eve some time around World War I, about the husband she was expecting to arrive home drunk, "I do hope he doesn't make another beer baby." Stories of the inevitability of female sexual and reproductive suffering made the South London protagonist of *Jipping Street,* a girl growing up in those years, determined to avoid men altogether. The ways in which so many women from all over Britain told their stories in the Women's Cooperative Guild's *Maternity* illuminate the dominant version of sexual intercourse as something that "belonged" to men and from which women defended themselves. As one wife explained a decade later to Marie Stopes, she had had numerous pregnancies because her husband was "not a careful man in that respect."[20]

The sexual partition did make life easier for a few very determined women, who could use such contraceptive methods as a diaphragm or pessary without comment from their husbands. These devices were certainly employed in the 1890s and 1900s but were much more widely available after the war. At the Women's Labour League Baby Clinic in the 1910s, patients often raised the subject of birth control with the clinic's women physicians, probably hoping for access to these "women's methods" of contraception.[21] Some wives, as Lella Secor Florence reported from Cambridge in the 1920s, rejected these methods as "an unwomanly invitation to pleasures which are supposed to have been designed for her husband alone." But others knew that they could use a pessary or diaphragm secretly, without inspiring their husbands' curi-

osity about the sudden and sometimes permanent decline in their fertility. One of the selling points in 1890s advertisements for these devices
was indeed the possibility of a woman's using them "without the
knowledge of the husband." One Lewisham woman, determined to avoid
being trapped at home with many babies, got a diaphragm fitted at the
Marie Stopes clinic in the early 1920s. Her husband never knew about
it and never appeared curious about why he had only two children.[22]

One way or another, with or without their husbands' support, women
were finding ways to restrict their childbearing, at least a little. This
does not mean that they made extensive use of contraceptive devices or
coitus interruptus. Lewis-Fanning's 1946 study (based on a national sample
weighted toward London and toward the "less well-to-do") looked at
these standard birth control methods and concluded that only 15 percent
of the 161 women who had married before 1910 had used "any form of
birth control" but that a higher proportion, 40 percent, of the 361 women
who had married between 1910 and 1919 did so. Of just those few women
whose husbands were semiskilled or unskilled manual workers, only 4
percent of the pre-1910 cohort had used methods of birth control that
the researchers recognized. But a 1905 study by two medical officers of
health, based on a borough-by-borough analysis of London fertility statistics, more helpfully concluded that among the richest tenth of the
London population, contraception is "systematically and largely practiced"; among the poorest one-fourth "the practice is probably almost
unknown"; and the rest of Londoners, including hundreds of thousands
of working-class couples, lay somewhere in between. Here wives tried
homemade pessaries or kept sex at bay with separate beds or numerous
children in the marital bed, through invalidism, or through extralate
bedtimes; husbands occasionally bought a condom or practiced withdrawal; and local abortionists were busy. Even the most fecund of London boroughs had a fertility rate much lower than that of England and
Wales as a whole in the early twentieth century. Obviously only a relatively small proportion of London women were producing babies at
any sort of "biological maximum." As the slowly declining London
fertility figures for every borough after 1880 or so further demonstrate
and as the two medical officers noted, even among unskilled and semiskilled London workers, "there is some voluntary avoidance of childbearing."[23]

Contraceptive devices certainly had a part to play in this behavior.
Angus McLaren has demonstrated that the 1890s represented a turning
point in their commercial production, advertisement, and sale: condoms, diaphragms, pessaries, and syringe equipment all had been improved by the new vulcanization techniques of the previous decade.
Though many of these products were effective, their primary value was
probably in communicating the idea that sex did not have to lead to

conception. Sir Francis Champneys, for many years in the late nine-teenth century the obstetrics consultant at the General Lying-In Hospi-tal, observed that his patients commonly used quinine and cocoa butter pessaries. They were widely available in London, having been devel-oped in 1885 by a Clerkenwell pharmacist and packaged in the red box in which they are still sold. A Finsbury general practitioner also was impressed with the frequency with which condoms (presumably) were advertised. In many districts, he told the 1904 Interdepartmental Com-mittee on Physical Deterioration, "You cannot go into a single public urinal without seeing an advertisement which has been gummed up there." At 2 shillings a package, condoms were sold legally in pharma-cies throughout the metropolis and the country.[24]

Abstinence and withdrawal, probably the most common methods of restricting conception, of course demanded male support, and this in turn meant redefining the husband's relationship with both his wife and his children; that is, the children had to "belong" to their father as well as to their mother.[25] The couples who consciously cooperated in limit-ing the woman's fertility—a small and quiet minority around the turn of the century—eventually increased in number. In the *Maternity* letters, gathered in 1913 and 1914, there are occasional references to couples' joint determination to limit their families' size. In some cases, the couple had determined that their "means" permitted only a few children. In others, the husband was willing to compromise his sexual needs to pro-tect his wife from the threat to health or life that other pregnancies might bring. One man felt that by helping spare his wife he was honoring his mother, whose violent, drunken husband had made her pregnant many, many times.[26] These couples were not always more loving than others; rather, what distinguished them was the father's assumption that the children to which his wife gave birth were his responsibility as well as hers.

Among these family-limiting couples were London-born Elizabeth Rignall's Yorkshire-born parents, described in the previous chapter. With their small child they had spent some years with the wife's parents in Howarth, where the husband took a mill job. Some years later, Eliza-beth's mother told her about a conversation between her husband and some of the other men in the 1890s as they left the Yorkshire mill after a day's weaving. They were talking about the wife of one of their co-workers, who had just had her tenth child, and one of the men re-marked that she "seemed always to be either ailing or carrying." The men teased Rignall's father for having only one child who was already three, and he retorted, according to his daughter's account, "Sooner than subject my wife to such misery, I'd—and referred to the solution handed out to Peter Abelard." Elizabeth was about five years younger than the oldest child; another brother was born when she was ten and another a few years after that—a pattern suggesting coitus interruptus with its occasional failures. All four of the children got secondary school educations.[27]

The decision to intervene after conception had occurred belonged to the woman herself, which has not only lent abortion a complex of meanings related to the refusal of motherhood and the murder of a "child" but has also tied it to fears of female autonomy and self-determination.[28] During the years of this study, women who wanted to abort often spoke simply of "putting themselves right," that is, restoring their normal periods and their usual bodily functioning.[29] This attitude made perfect sense in an era when quickening, in the fourth or even fifth month, was what usually announced a pregnancy; thus a woman who had missed a period or two did not define herself as carrying an unborn child.

Women's ideas about what they were doing when they tried to end a pregnancy and the methods they used to do this have their own history and geography, which are only now being charted by historians.[30] In the early modern centuries, European women who wanted abortions had used herbal medicines. Pennyroyal, a member of the mint family; savin, a bush related to the juniper; and ergot of rye were most often mentioned in seventeenth- and eighteenth-century English sources. These and many other herbs do have abortifacient properties and can be safe to use if taken in doses of just the right size, often over a period of days. Because of the plants' different growing patterns and properties, abortifacient knowledge was relatively local. In the nineteenth century, when millions of now-urban women were cut off from both the local networks and the flora that had provided them with medicines of all kinds, new patterns of abortion and new methods began to emerge. They included quinine, a drug imported into England in large quantities only in the 1870s, lead compounds, apiol (extracted from ordinary parsley through a method developed in the mid-nineteenth century), and, toward the later decades of the nineteenth century and in the twentieth, instrumental abortions that involved puncturing the amniotic sac. These new methods, like the older ones, were disseminated through local and fluctuating women's cultures. Thus, taken internally, lead diachylon, which was contained in the plasters that pharmacists sold for small wounds, was widely used in Birmingham, Leicester, Nottingham, Doncaster, and a few other towns in the early 1900s but was apparently seldom used in London.[31]

There was thus a "widespread tradition of abortion based on folk remedies" in England in the later nineteenth century.[32] The women whom Katherine Roberts nursed in a Central London maternity hospital in 1903, most of them single, spoke openly of their obviously futile and extremely varied attempts to bring on miscarriages in the early months of their pregnancies. (Those who had resorted to competent professional abortionists never appeared at this hospital, of course.) The women had thrown themselves down steps, lifted heavy tubs, taken pills, immersed themselves in steaming hot baths, and drunk many different concoctions; one music-hall dancer "had gone on with high kicking" throughout her pregnancy in the hopes of inducing a miscarriage. Ted Willis's mother, desperate to avoid another birth in a household in which the husband was a drinker and unemployed, tried many obviously ineffective methods, including hot baths, running up and down stairs, and eating gunpowder mixed with margarine. The enormous sales of (unfortunately usually useless) "female pills" in the late nineteenth century by firms based in London and elsewhere suggest the compatibility of chemical methods of abortion with the popular female view of the meaning of abortion. In the 1920s, medical workers in South London found that the older women patients were accustomed to trying reputedly abortifacient drugs such as lead, ergot, or quinine.[33]

The "first [European] abortion revolution" (the second came after its legalization in the early 1970s) of the 1920s, as Edward Shorter sees it, was the product of the rise of "mechanical" forms of abortion, effected with syringes, curettes, or other sharp objects stuck into the uterus. Infection and perforation of the uterus were the main risks of a procedure that was generally more effective and safer than drug abortions. A Birmingham social investigator speaking at a 1914 conference on the declining birthrate was convinced of the frequency of abortion, often involving the newer mechanical methods. She speculated that about a quarter of working-class women in her town had had an abortion at some point in their lives. By the 1910s, she believed, when artisans and "respectable" working-class couples were beginning to use contraception, the poorest women "very largely" practiced abortion. Marie Stopes argued that abortion had contributed significantly to the fall in the British birthrate, at least by the 1920s.[34] Oral and written recreations of working-class London street life in the later nineteenth and early twentieth centuries show that most neighborhoods included a woman, sometimes an unlicensed midwife, who was known for her willingness to perform abortions. South London mothers whom Blacker knew in the 1920s used the local abortionist and, as a backup, the nearest teaching hospital, to which the abortionists had obviously begun to gear their practices: "Such a person, after practicing his *[sic]* art, is in the habit of instructing the woman as soon as she feels the pain or notices an haemorrhage, to report herself to a medical man or present herself at a hospital where she is taken on as an ordinary case of threatened abortion."[35]

Obviously, both in the prewar and postwar generations, women generally did not "want" eight, ten, or twelve pregnancies and so tried in various ways to limit them. But before 1918, neither abortion nor contraception had yet fundamentally transformed the worlds of working-class mothers, whose lives were devoted to pregnancy, birth, and child care to an extent that their daughters and granddaughters soundly rejected.

"OFTEN WEAK AND LOW SPIRITED":
PREGNANCY

A pregnancy did not really begin for a nineteenth- or early twentieth-century woman until she felt the sensation of the fetus moving, some time in the fourth or fifth month. The closely mapped three-trimester pregnancies of recent advice manuals detailing fetal development nearly day by day define pregnancy as something a woman *does,* a project that requires careful attention to diet, exercise, and the use of medicine, drugs, and cigarettes. London pregnancies a century ago *happened to* women; the mothers were conscious mainly of getting fat and of eventually feeling fetal movements. As the pregnancy progressed and the reality of another baby's arrival was more palpable, anxiety about life and health merged with intensifying material cares: the need to pay for birth attendants and baby supplies and the running of the household during the mother's convalescence.

Women were especially attentive to the moment of quickening, the only diagnosis of the pregnancy that most of them would get; few would see a midwife or doctor until their labor had actually started. Prenatal care was rare even for upper-class women before the twentieth century.[36] The fact that quickening so often provided the first news of a pregnancy is what led so many women, I believe, to "faint" or to have "fits" (reported equally often) in response as the perhaps only dimly suspected conception announced itself unequivocally. A Westminster woman who had already had two premature stillborn babies fainted when she felt a third quicken and had a slight "hysterical fit," she told the General Lying-In doctor in 1888. As the numbness in her hands probably indicated, a thirty-nine-year-old single nurse from Chelsea began to hyperventilate (a symptom of anxiety) when in 1883 she felt her fetus move. A woman in her forties with three children who wrote to Marie Stopes in 1926 described a moment of quickening that brought the frightening news that she was pregnant at a time when she was already quite ill. "You can imagine my horror when I felt a movement in the body, in fact I was so unnerved that a friend of my sister's took a sample of my water to a water doctor."[37]

The anxiety of pregnancy was certainly heightened by the first-time pregnant woman's utter ignorance of the transformations her body was to undergo. (Perhaps a fifth of pregnancies were first pregnancies among the working classes around the turn of the century, compared with a rate about twice as large today in Britain as a whole.)[38] Though ubiquitous, pregnancy was also invisible, as illustrated so well by the slap the South London girl described earlier in this chapter that she received from her mother for just seeing the pregnant Mrs. Bibbs. The word *pregnant* itself was not used outside medical settings. Among working people, the condition was described more obliquely: Women were "carrying," had "fallen with a child," were "going to have another one," or were "in a family way."[39] Grace Foakes, whose mother had twelve children after her own birth, never learned to spot the pregnancies; she was genuinely surprised at each of them, unless she had happened to notice her mother buying baby clothes at jumble sales and clothing stalls! The women who wrote for *Maternity* in the 1910s attributed their lack of sexual knowledge to the fact that their mothers were faraway or dead or unusually reticent. Whereas upper middle-class mothers and daughters exchanged reasonably informative letters and conversation about sex and the female body, such sexual talk rarely passed between working-class generations. (The *Maternity* writers nonetheless consistently assigned the job of girls' initiation into sex and reproduction to their mothers, a fascinating exercise in fantasy.) East Londoner Leah Chegwidden, a talkative and loving mother to her many daughters and sons, said only one thing to her daughter Dotty about sexual intercourse, and that was after the younger woman's honeymoon (and in the 1930s at that): "I could have told you it was overrated."[40]

In most pregnancies the women's anxieties were a compound of economic struggles and health problems. Mrs. Layton, whose moving life story was collected by the Women's Cooperative Guild in 1931, became pregnant for the first time in the early 1880s after months of unemployment for her husband, who did not find work until shortly before the baby's birth. "My health was becoming impaired with work and worry," she wrote, and she was afraid that her own bad food and exhaustion would undermine the baby's health as well. To those who had observed working women's lives closely, the months of pregnancy indeed seemed the grimmest of their lives. Some of the "saddest cases," wrote Evelyne Bunting of the St. Pancras School for Mothers, were women in the last months of pregnancy, weak with hunger: "The extra expense of the coming confinement hangs over her like a black cloud." As Pember Reeves put it at a 1912 conference on infancy and infant care, because of the hardships of pregnancy, during these months "motherhood is hanging over them like a curse."[41]

Like those who wrote a generation later to the Women's Cooperative Guild, depression and wearinesses were part of the normal experience of pregnancy for the General Lying-In Hospital's patients in the 1880s. As one Old Kent Road mother in her forties responded when asked about her ten previous pregnancies, the only problem was "feeling weak and that we don't reackon [*sic*]." "Much mental depression throughout" was the report of a single domestic servant who had a child at age twenty-six; "sometimes depressed, had a great deal of trouble," responded another single woman, and depression indeed marked the pregnancies of more single than married women. "Often weak and low spirited," reported a young married woman having her third child; "rather low spirited last 5 months, has had trouble," said another married woman. "Not more low spirited than usual," was the noncommittal remark of a Kennington Park woman in her third pregnancy at age forty-one. In one group of sixty-five patients admitted to the hospital in 1884, twelve complained of depression or low spirits during their pregnancies.[42] The problem was considered routine enough by the staff to be listed on the printed admission forms later used by the hospital for maternity patients.

Getting enough food to meet the powerful appetites of pregnancy was often a lost cause. A large minority of the General Lying-In Hospital's patients appeared to the intake doctors in the early 1880s as "sickly," "anemic," or "pale." One patient admitted that she "has been half starved"; another more cautiously confessed that she had "not had good food during her pregnancy." The case notes of a thirty-three-year-old woman having her sixth child reveal: "She cried on this question being put to her."[43] The queries of a physician with an interest in food cravings during pregnancy elicited a cornucopia of working-class London delicacies: apples, watercress, grapes, oranges, oysters, pineapple, crab, and faggots (the hospital record even included the full recipe for these spicy loaf-shaped sausages, which were obviously not part of the doctor's regular menu). About two dozen of 151 questioned in the early months of 1888 reported food cravings during this or earlier pregnancies. One woman who had lived in India as a soldier's wife dreamed of "currie," and another wanted lobster, but the others had had more realistic longings for apples, pears, potatoes, cucumbers, gooseberries, oranges, or pork.[44] Even in fantasy, the women had little capacity for self-indulgence.

The women knew that the new baby would represent a substantial expense. A professional nurse mother interviewed by an LCC inspector reported that a ten-month-old, for example, consumed well over 2 shillings in milk each week and also required additional household spending on food, soap, starch, fuel, and sometimes rent. (The child thus cost her more than she could collect from the mother, which was, in the 1890s, 5 shillings per week.) A 1915 estimate (made just before the ravages of wartime inflation) of the costs of a cot, flannel clothing, and a perambulator, was £2 9s., assuming that the baby clothes were the secondhand variety available in bundles at pawnshops. Other expenses included the midwife, whose fee ranged from 5 to 10 shillings in the early 1890s and close to 10 shillings in 1910; possibly a nurse to help at home; and the mother's lost wages and housekeeping skills.[45]

So just as the pregnancy itself was taxing a woman's physical energy, her work increased as she took on extra paid jobs to meet the expenses of her confinement. Mrs. W., one of Anna Martin's Rotherhithe clients in the 1900s, told Martin that whenever she was "carrying" she took jobs "at the fur pulling," working five days a week and paying a baby minder out of her wages. "I used to do my washing after I came home at night, and was often up til twelve or one." As a West London Bible woman described one of her neighbors: "Her husband was a bricklayer's labourer, and the woman did rag-sorting to help with the living, and used to wheel sacks full of rags on a sack-barrow to the warehouse. The wonder to me was that the babies were born alive."[46]

The General Lying-In Hospital's case records register the very heavy work women did during pregnancy. Few of the patients with paid employment stopped their work in the weeks before delivery, and housework, of course, continued throughout pregnancy. Overwork was frequently the reason that the women gave, or the doctors used, to classify causes of miscarriages or premature labor. A Camden Town woman who went out "scrubbing and cleaning" despite her three children and fourth pregnancy, reported to the Lying-In doctors in January 1884 that she had been bleeding since before Christmas: "Had been working very hard and carrying up trays and coals up and down stairs." A cook reported that she had got a prolapsed uterus a few years previously by "lifting a tub of water," an experience apparently fairly common among women laundry workers, according to G. F. McCleary, who cited "uterine displacement" as a special health problem of women who worked in large or small laundries. A GLI patient from Newington Butts, Southwark, a charwoman married to a cabman, reported that she had begun hemorrhaging for three days before the birth of her fifth child "through working a machine," probably a heavy mangle.[47]

Toward the end of the nine months, women began to scrub and tidy their homes and readied their supply of linen and nightclothes. For childbirth, no matter how frequent, was also a literal rite of passage. It turned the home into what it normally never was, a public thoroughfare, through which might pass a midwife, a nurse, neighbors, and possibly a doctor or a medical student. The bed, the room, and the baby's things all would be, for this period, part of the public realm. In her "anxiety to make the best appearance possible . . . [the pregnant woman] gives the whole house a special clean down, in view of the strangers who will come in to take control of it when she is incapacitated," wrote Sylvia Pankhurst of this moment. Women from West Ham described the starched and frilled valances they put on their beds to hide chamber pots, basins, and other childbed equipment before the midwife arrived.[48] A district nurse in 1905 noted that there were women who preferred the more anonymous district nursing agencies to local midwives because they were ashamed of what neighbors would say at their lack of bed and baby linen. As an East London woman who had her first child in 1915 noted proudly: "I could get everything done before I had my babies, even to the last day I would wash if there was any dirty clothes about so that they wouldn't be left for the—woman to have to do when she came in." Obviously, by the time these women went into labor, they were utterly exhausted. One Old Kent Road woman who wisely arranged to have her eleventh child at the hospital in 1881 alarmed the hospital staff by sleeping practically around the clock for several days after the birth.[49]

A disaster like a husband's unemployment could entirely wipe out the results of a pregnant wife's planning. Bible women in Lambeth Walk met a woman in 1897 who had been preparing for a new baby by sewing its clothes, but when her husband lost his job, she had to pawn all the new things. When E. W. Morris, head of the London Hospital, went out on rounds with the district midwife in December 1922, he met a Mrs. Smith of Florida Street, whose husband had lost his job during her pregnancy. "The patient had saved up a pair of clean sheets and clean pillow cases and little odds and ends to be 'nice and respectable' when the nurse from the hospital came. But alas! 'out of work'—empty stomachs, pinched and hungry children's faces—and the clean sheets had to go—a week before the day of their glory—where all pretty and nice things go in the East End." Midwives during World War I reported that mothers' preparations had generally been more successful than Mrs. Smith's. Perhaps this was a result of the 30 shillings in maternity benefits that many women received after 1911, or perhaps it was related to wartime full employment. Fewer women were delivering their babies on bare mattresses, without linens, blankets, or clothing for the newborns.[50]

Pregnancy exacerbated other common ailments such as colds and coughs, only adding to the miseries of these months. In the late winter months of 1886, 20 of 135 patients at the General Lying-In Hospital, or about 15 percent, had coughs or colds bad enough to be noted in their case records; some found them particularly painful and troubling during labor itself. Many of the maternal deaths that occurred in the hospital were actually the result of preexisting conditions such as consumption or kidney disease. Thus in 1885, of 395 women giving birth as inpatients, there were four maternal deaths, one from septicemia, two from consumption, and one from kidney disease. Elizabeth Garrett Anderson's figures from greater London hospitals and maternity charities from the mid-1890s show that about 16 percent of maternal deaths were from such diseases as cancer, heart disease, or lung diseases.[51]

Surely among the strains of pregnancy was the very ancient belief, shared by both the women and their medical personnel, that impressions in pregnancy would affect the health and character of the fetus. "Frights," dreams, or other strong emotions, even foods eaten (which is why we know so much about food cravings) were noted with worry or interest by the women and their medical attendants.[52] Agnes Reed, a thirty-year-old needlewoman who had her fifth child in the hospital, told the doctor that its red face could be explained by the large quantities of brimstone and treacle (presumably for constipation) that she took in late pregnancy. Mrs. Lambert, about to have her eleventh child, related to the admitting physician the reasons for her ninth child's being born without one of its hands: "When about 6 weeks to 2 months gone a beggar in street uncovered his arm without a hand and gave her a fright and was always dwelling on it, does not know which arm it was." When the eleventh child, a healthy girl, was born with a slight deformity of the left foot, Mrs. Lambert was again questioned about her pregnancy and eventually remembered slipping on a curbstone on a wet night "a fortnight before Christmas" spraining her ankle. But by that time, the baby's foot was looking much better, and the doctors lost interest in it. In 1888 a Borough woman was convinced that her fourth-month miscarriage was caused by being "frightened by some bullocks, and gave birth to a bullock's head," and a widow having a seventh child related how her second premature child had died: "Was frightened by a cow and child had cow's feet."[53]

CHILDBIRTH AS "RUPTURE": MATERNITY RITUALS

When one of her hospital patients, a woman convalescing after delivering her ninth child, asked Katherine Roberts to write a letter to her husband, the nurse was both touched and educated by the writer's intense concern for the family from whom she was temporarily separated. Roberts described the letter's contents:

> She made no allusion to past suffering or present bliss, nor to the baby's looks, nor the joy of re-union; she merely stated that "she and the baby was doin' nicely" and she hoped to be back on Monday to "see to" things again, after her "bit rest," and hoped the children were well, and that Jeanie's cold was better and her sister had been able to step in now and again to give a hand.[54]

The nurse, momentarily aware of the empty sentimentality of her own language of maternity, came up short against her patient's powerful connection to her home and her sense of the hospital birth as a problematic interruption in her domestic routines.

For most births, which were at home, childbed rituals helped cut off the mother as surely as a hospital stay did, if only for a short time, from her boundless responsibilities. During the days or hours of childbirth the mother was symbolically separated from her children and husband. In the children's memories, the births of siblings were always silent, secret, and unexpected. One of the clearest duties of neighbors was to help remove the older children from a household during the hours or days of a birth. Women tried to give birth as quietly as they could; older children were sent away when labor began; and younger ones were bundled off to another room. Katherine Roberts wrote in her district nursing journal of "a baby of two years old [who] sat on a broken down sort of cot and stared at us with wide open eyes," but Roberts disposed of slightly older children by offering them pennies to go out and buy sweets.[55] Ann Jasper in Hoxton sent her five-year-old son out to a playground with an older sister for a large part of the day on which she went into labor; when the children returned for their midday meal, their baby sister had arrived. As Lillian Hine recalled the routine (repeated eleven times) of her Poplar childhood:

> Every time a baby was born, my father would be pacing up and down, waiting anxiously to see if it was going to be another girl or a boy. . . . We all used to wait outside our house, watching for the nurse to arrive with her little black bag. . . . We were allowed into Mum's room afterwards to see our new baby. I have lovely memories of this: Mum sitting up in bed holding the baby for us to see and the bedroom smelling so nicely of talcum and soap.

The London Hospital's professional midwives were used to working in one-room dwellings with large numbers of children about and knew how to establish at least the forms of separation for the births they attended. They sent the older children out onto the landing, while the younger ones were packed into an improvised tent made of chairs and the nurses' large cloaks. "Suddenly there is a little baby cry, and 3 or 4 little curious faces poke through the curtains. 'Whatever was that?' "[56]

The wives of political leaders during the late Victorian and Edwardian years were nearly always accompanied by their husbands at their births. Although upper-class men had been involved in childbirth since about the 1830s, the labor room remained off limits to working men. As a district midwife Katherine Roberts took it for granted that husbands would not be present at confinements. Only one man objected to this practice, saying that he was determined to "stay where he was" (in the childbirth room). Roberts removed him only by threatening to leave without helping his wife. A woman writing in *Maternity* ingeniously got her husband away from the childbirth by giving him a sleeping pill when she went into labor.[57]

"Good husbands" helped pregnant or birthing wives in other ways, however. In the 1870s, some bought them the supplies they would need for the confinement: "a pair of sheets" or some calico. Another husband, to spare his wife worry, hid for many weeks after a new birth the fact that he had lost his job.[58] Husbands were most commonly the ones to fetch the childbirth attendant, and the complaints of drunken or overbooked midwives working for the General Lying-In Hospital show the seriousness, indeed desperation, with which husbands carried out this duty, running miles through the streets of London to find a substitute for the midwife who could not come to help.

Citing the danger of uterine prolapse, medical opinion supported the popular custom of women's remaining in bed for two weeks after giving birth; to get up sooner was viewed by all childbirth practitioners as disastrous.[59] Medical and nonmedical attendants alike wrapped the new mother's abdomen with a "binder" of cloth bands and served her special sickroom foods, "water gruel and toast." To further separate the woman from normal routines, changing the bed linen or indeed washing her at all was frowned on by folk practitioners, at least in the earlier decades of our period. "In some instances the poor unfortunate patient was not allowed to have her face and hands washed for days," recalled Mrs. Layton, who had helped at childbirths off and on from the 1870s before she became a full-time midwife; "I remember hoping I should never have a baby if I could not be washed."[60]

Childbirth gave mothers the prerogative of the sick: a period of (at least apparent) freedom from work. Midwife Emilia Kanthack reported that East End women stayed in bed for about ten days after each birth, and a Peckham woman who had the first of her nine children in 1898 always looked forward to her ten days' of relative leisure. Only 12 of 638 housewives surveyed by the Christian Social Union in 1905 had "got up" before the tenth postpartum day, but after a fortnight three quarters were "up." Of the 385 women with paid work whom the researchers surveyed, only a handful actually resumed their work before two weeks had elapsed.[61] Women who worked outside the home tended to remain in the house a few extra days after their getting up. But it was less the need to return to factory or home paid work that got women out of bed and more the pull of their domestic responsibilities. With a ten-day convalescence, a woman could indeed boast, as Clementina Black heard many do: "I never missed but one week's wash with any of my babies." Even from her sickbed a new mother could continue many of her domestic duties. As Alice Linton described the nine childbirths of her neighbor across the street in Shoreditch in the early twentieth century, the mother's postpartum week in bed was still productive. "It was surprising how much she managed to do even if she was in bed. She cut the bread, did the vegetables, all the mending and managed to give the orders and keep them all under control."[62]

The "getting up" from the immobility of childbed was marked by little formal ceremony among working-class women, though occasionally it was commemorated by a ceremonial meat meal. "She's 'ad her chop," in Whitechapel in the 1900s meant that the mother had resumed her usual routine. Discharging the nurse who had been hired to preside over the household for the lying-in period or terminating the doctor's brief postpartum visits were other ways of "getting up." Most women well remembered their "gettings up," to judge from the precision with which they could recall these moments for investigators of all kinds. For the mid-nineteenth-century aristocrats in Judith Schneid Lewis's study, the transition from childbed to normal life was made gradually over a four- or six-week period, as women moved from bed to sofa, opened the blinds after the darkness of the postpartum days, and gradually were given more kinds of food and drink.[63] The leisureliness of the process not only protected the mothers' health but also gave special emphasis to the process of childbirth as a phase in their lives. For the working-class mothers, the short period of convalescence was dictated by material demands and also underscored the meaning of birth as a beginning of a new kind of work.

CHILDBIRTH ATTENDANTS

The invasion of the home and the break with daily work that a birth required made childbirth an assault on domestic survival strategies. The care of other children and of the husband himself had to continue; few husbands could, or would, run their households during their wives' lying-in period. As the Women's Cooperative Guild put it in its 1917 Memorandum on the National Care of Maternity, one of the most pressing needs was "reliable help in the home—in cooking, washing, looking after the children. Such help is additional to the services of a midwife and is much more important to working women than nursing at such a time." These years saw fierce politicking and shifting alliances among nursing, midwifery, and medicine, culminating in the 1902 Midwifery Act mandating training and national registration for midwives. The medicalization of childbirth and the fate of midwifery in its various forms are the issues that historians and women's health advocates trace in these struggles. But the working-class women who were the invisible subjects of these debates thought more of the housekeeping help the birth attendants could offer than of their formal qualifications, medical or not. At one point, the head of the Obstetrical Association, acknowledging this need, argued for a plan to license women with minimal training who could serve simultaneously as birth attendants and home helpers. The Midwives' Institute, on the other hand, representing professionally trained midwives, fended off all schemes requiring midwives to do housework.[64]

The recruitment of childbirth helpers of any rank was, and had to be, very local in an era when telephones were unknown in working-class homes; cabs were hired only in the most dire circumstances; and the speediest medical personnel often traveled by bicycle. Each borough, even parish, was a different universe in regard to care during childbirth. There were many different obstetrical systems, some old and some new and modern: hospital programs using medical students, maternity charities staffed by trained midwives, poor-law services of widely varying quality and accessibility, private doctors, formally trained freelance midwives, informally trained neighborhood "granny" practitioners, and "nurses" who did only the housework at confinements.

London's chaotic mixture of childbirth services actually provided among the best care in England in its time, even in the world. Statistics collected by Elizabeth Garrett Anderson demonstrate that London was a relatively safe place in which to give birth in the late 1890s (see Table 4–4), even for the very poorest women, a fact Anderson attributed to the better training of all childbirth personnel in the metropolis and to the availability of expert medical backing. The average maternal death rate in England and Wales during the decade ending in 1910 was 4.1 per thousand live births, still frightening but one of the best figures in the world at that time. This general figure remained about the same from the middle of the nineteenth century until the mid-1930s when antibiotics all but erased the risks of puerperal septicemia, the infection that had accounted for about half of maternal deaths, and the death rate for childbirth began to descend toward its current infinitesimal levels. By the early twentieth century, London maternal mortality statistics were lower than the national average, and in most London boroughs there were declines between 1901 and 1915 so that by the war years, many of the poorest boroughs had substantially lower maternal death rates than did the better-off ones, as Table 4–5 illustrates. The outpatient maternity departments of six London general hospitals providing care for poor women, for instance, had a collective average of only one maternal death in every 549 deliveries (thus a rate of under two per thousand). Unlike just about any other kind of death statistic, female death rates in pregnancy, childbirth, and the four weeks that followed were higher among middle-class women during these years than among working-class women, an endorsement of both the value of reputation and neighborhood contacts and the well-run charities that served the poor.[65]

To help a neighbor alone in childbirth, or in the days following a

TABLE 4–4. Maternal Death Rates in Outpatient Maternity Departments of Six General Hospitals in London, 1895–1897

Hospital	Total Number of Deliveries	Maternal Deaths *	Ratio of Deaths to Deliveries
St. Bartholomew's	4,999	6 (4)	1 in 838.1
St. Thomas's	6,816	15 (13)	1 in 454.5
Guy's	10,100	24	1 in 420.8
Middlesex	3,210	6 (5)	1 in 535
Charing Cross	917	4	1 in 229.2
King's College	1,955	3 (1)	1 in 651.6
Total	27,997	58 (51)	1 in 482.7†

*Figures in parentheses represent maternal deaths directly related to childbirth. Anderson considered that seven of the total number of maternal deaths, the former due to phthis, typhoid, and the like, were not directly related to childbirth.

†Subtracting the 7 nonchildbirth-related deaths from the total of 58, Anderson calculated a ratio of 1 death per 548.9 deliveries.

Source: Elizabeth Garrett Anderson, "Deaths in Childbirth," *BMJ*, September 17, 1898, p. 839.

birth, was a powerful imperative among working-class women, and nearly all who gave birth managed to get some help. Doctors and nurses who went out among the poor often registered this fact with surprise. G. A. Simpson, who worked in the late 1880s as a surgeon to the Acton General Dispensary, delivered "at least two hundred babies" in the space of a year, mostly to women employed in local laundries. But only "on one or two occasions" did he also have to "act as nurse, wash the baby and look after the mother's welfare." A Bible woman remarked on the "perpetual streaming in and out of friendly neighbours" during confinements, and Katherine Roberts noted in her diary during her first stint as a district nurse that to her surprise, "I almost always find a friend has 'stepped in' to help, and they do all they can in spite of their own work." The women whom district nurses found alone and unaided in childbirth or postpartum days were invariably recent migrants to a street or temporary lodgers there. Indeed, even country women who, utterly alone, came to the city to have illegitimate babies secretly, were often cared for by their landladies or other tenants in the houses in which they took up residence.[66] To rely entirely on the services of compassionate neighbors was, nonetheless, a last resort. It was normal for an older child of the mother, a sister, a grandmother, or a paid "nurse" to preside over

TABLE 4–5. Maternal Mortality in the Early Twentieth Century in Selected London Boroughs and English Towns

Borough or Town	Number of Deaths per Thousand Live Births, Annual Averages		
	1901–1903	1911–1913	1915
Bermondsey	3.2	2.1	2.8
Camberwell	3	3.1	2.2
Chelsea	3.8	3.8	2.2
Finsbury	3.12	3.09	3.19
Hackney	1.9	2.6	1.6
Hammersmith	2.93	3.2	1.9
Hampstead	4.3	4.1	3.7
Holborn	★	1.5	1.5
Paddington	3.3	3.3	1.4
Poplar	★	2.7	2.1
Shoreditch	1.8	2.4	3.9
Southwark	1.4	.9	1.7
Stepney	3.27	2.56	1.98
St. Marylebone	3.4	4.4	2.1
St. Pancras	1.8	3.2	2.3
Wandsworth	4.2	3.6	2.5
West Ham	3.29	1.81	2.14
City of Westminster	2.77	4.13	4.53
Woolwich	3.4	2.02	3.2
Bath	.66	1.74	6.64
Liverpool	2.7	2.8	3.1
Oldham	5.4	6	6

★Figures not available.

Source: Compiled from figures in Janet Campbell and E. W. Hope, *Report on the Physical Welfare of Mothers and Children*: England and Wales (2 vols.) (Liverpool: Carnegie U.K. Trust, 1917), vol. 1.

the household during at least part of the ten or so days before the mother "got up."

Nearly all women from the ranks of shopkeepers' wives and up the social scale used private physicians as their childbirth attendants and had been doing so throughout the nineteenth century, but among the rest of the female population, at least until the commencement of national health insurance in 1911, private doctors were the one kind of practitioner not used. Yet medically trained personnel were common as childbirth attendants to poor and working-class women. London was unique in England in this respect, for to instruct doctors, nurses and midwives, the city's many teaching hospitals required thousands of "volunteer" mothers. Because it needed the cases, the Royal Free Hospital, for example, made it a policy to extend its outpatient services, staffed by female medical students, to any woman who applied for them.[67] The poorest women used poor law infirmaries or the forty-four London poor law dispensaries whose attached physicians could issue orders for home attendance by a midwife or physician. Others used the free outpatient services of the huge London teaching hospitals, services staffed by midwives or medical students occasionally supplemented by nurses. In 1898, eleven of the teaching hospitals handled 15,444 outpatients; in 1901, 15,532. Medical students or their supervising doctors delivered large proportions, even the majorities, of babies in several large poor boroughs. Guy's handled the largest numbers, almost 3,000 in 1891 and nearly 3,500 in 1901. These eleven large hospitals accommodated nearly 12 percent of the registered births in London in these years.[68] If we consider that this list does not include dozens of other maternity charities as well as the smaller hospitals and the poor-law maternity services, we can get some sense of the involvement of formal medicine in London childbirth before the twentieth century.

Although hospital-affiliated midwives carried out deliveries that would today be classed as too "complicated" for them, they could count on support from their hospital's obstetrical specialists. In fact, the 1902 act required that midwives call in physicians in any case of "abnormality" in childbirth, and the number who did so began to increase after 1902. An estimate in *Nursing Notes* in 1907 was that midwives called in doctors in about 3 percent of cases. Yet in one midwife-staffed outpatient maternity program run by the City of London Maternity Hospital, there were only a miniscule number of such referrals between 1913 and 1915.[69] Credentialed midwives were obviously leery of calling in doctors. For one thing, the medical men expected to be paid at rates that were beyond the resources of most of London's poor. Furthermore, the doctors did not always appreciate requests to attend births at odd hours and so made life hard for the midwives who had sent for them; those who resented their competition occasionally openly refused to help.[70]

Throughout this period, the physicians were as a body not better practitioners than their trained or untrained female rivals; possibly they were worse. What distinguished the medical men's deliveries from those of other practitioners was their frequent use of forceps. According to one national estimate, in 1899 doctors were using instruments in more than a quarter of their cases, a trend probably encouraged by the widening use of chloroform, as instrumental births (especially in the hands of the inexperienced) were often excruciatingly painful. Antisepsis, practiced universally in hospitals by the 1880s—and more necessary than ever with such dramatic invasions of the mother's body—was, however, "still little used in private midwifery practice," the president of the Gynaecological Association charged in 1897. The director of outpatient services at the Chelsea Hospital for Women also asserted in 1892 that "a very large proportion" of their cases were "women whose health has been injured by careless or inefficient treatment during their confinements: forceps, surgical interference, septic mischief." The poor obstetrics training required of medical students was scandalous but well known. A typical student in a great London teaching hospital in the early 1890s had only the one week of clinical training required to obtain a certificate in obstetrics from the Royal College of Surgeons. During this week, as one student complained, he witnessed exactly one labor and was not permitted, despite his urgent requests, even to view the obstetric instruments. Another physician smugly testified in 1892 that blood letting was the best treatment for a woman who developed convulsions at the end of labor. Obstetrics training became more rigorous in 1896 when the General Medical Council began to require medical students to spend three months in lying-in hospital wards as well as to be present at twenty home labors, five of them supervised. After 1906, the students were required to complete their hospital instruction before undertaking the district cases.[71]

On the other hand, Harry Roberts, the admittedly remarkable Whitechapel Road Fabian general practitioner, provided his childbirth patients with more service than did most midwives, charging them a half-guinea for a home confinement (a whole guinea for first births). Soon after Roberts opened his office in 1908, the Welsh proprietor of a local general shop called him in at short notice for her unexpectedly early labor: "By noon of the following day, hardly a house within a mile of the surgery but had heard of the new young doctor who had not only attended Mrs. Powell without a fee in advance or even an hour's warning, but had got the baby single-handed, washed and dressed it, 'changed' the mother and—last and most wonderful of all—made her a cup of tea." Not surprisingly, Harry Roberts became extremely popular with childbearing women in Stepney, and in his first year there, he tended "just over 500 confinements—11 in 36 hours was his record," with no maternal deaths. His burgeoning practice in the 1910s, though, had a great deal to do with national health insurance, which for the first time provided a way for working-class women to have private physician-supervised births.[72]

Trained midwives, instructed in hospital programs or through the Obstetrical Society's Examination Board (established in 1872), were extremely competent but did not always meet the needs of the poor. The midwives dispatched by the General Lying-In Hospital in 1886 tended to be quick and efficient, devoting an average of only three and three-quarters hours to each birth. They certainly did not stay long enough to help mothers afterward with the domestic jobs that so weighed on them, though their services did include daily visits for nine to fourteen post-partum days (though the Guy's medical students did the same).[73] It was the poorest women who were most often served by trained midwives, as they were usually eligible either for the maternity charities that employed them or for poor-law maternity care that in some boroughs (Islington was one) was also offered by trained midwives in patients' homes. Credentialed women birth attendants were relatively few in number throughout the late Victorian and Edwardian years (see Table 4–6 on their activity in 1917), for women who trained as midwives tended not to stay in the field long. Of over 3,500 London women registered as midwives in 1910, only 420 were actually practicing midwifery at that time. For example, most of those who had received the very good mid-wifery training provided by the General Lying-In Hospital in the early 1900s continued their careers in the less difficult job of "monthly nurse" in private homes. Sometime in the eighteenth century, midwifery had lost the battle for the easier trade of the well-off, and whether salaried or operating freelance, midwives were usually paid modestly and worked long hours.[74]

Maternity "nursing" and "granny" midwifery were extensions of the patterns of female nighborhood-based self-help that were mobilized during childbirth and other emergencies. One kind of informal care giver, usually called a nurse, did the cooking, cleaning, and child care without actually supervising the birth and often served as a supplementary attendant. "Going out nursing" within a radius of a street or two from home was a common way in which needy women could earn some money. Taking on maternity work of this kind marked a woman as being from a "lower social stratum," as a West London woman put it, and such nurses tended to be widows or old women. According to those who grew up in the early years of the twentieth century there, Peckham bustled with such informal nurses whose livelihoods depended on their neighbors. They charged between 5 and 15 shillings per week before the war, including beer and food; a generation earlier the price had been as low as half a crown.[75] On the Isle of Dogs in East London, a woman

TABLE 4–6. Proportions of Births Attended by Licensed Midwives in Selected London Boroughs and a Few Other English Towns, 1917

Borough or Town	Approximate Proportion of Deliveries by Midwives
Bath	55
Liverpool	78
Oldham	65
Bermondsey	20
Camberwell	55
Chelsea	40
Finsbury	16
Hackney	50
Hammersmith	50
Leyton Urban District	45
Shoreditch	70
St. Marylebone	only 5 regular midwives working in borough
St. Pancras	31
Wandsworth	48
West Ham	60
City of Westminster	28

Source: Compiled from figures gathered by Janet Campbell and E. W. Hope, *Report on the Physical Welfare of Mothers and Children: England and Wales* (2 vols.) (Liverpool: Carnegie U.K. Trust, 1917), vol. 1.

did nursing for confinements "only in our own street, more or less." In Cambridge Heath, Walter Southgate's mother, Elizabeth, called in her neighbor, Tiny Henshow, a woman who had often acted as an unofficial local midwife, to help her when the doctor was late in arriving in May 1890; Elizabeth Southgate in turn nursed her Cambridge Heath neighbors on similar occasions.[76]

The line separating "nurses" from "midwives" was a hazy one. For example, the East London woman just mentioned who went out nursing for neighbors in her own street was sometimes the only one present when a child was born. But she clung to her self-definition as a "nurse" rather than a midwife by refusing to use a scissors to cut the umbilical chord after births at which she was the only attendant. Other women

121

gradually made the transition from nurse to midwife over a period of years. During her husband's illness, Elsie Lambert of Tottenham combined cleaning for neighbors with work as a home help during confinements. Once widowed, she "used the knowledge she had picked up at various confinements" to become a successful, if uncertified, midwife and nurse.[77] Mrs. Layton, whose autobiography is included in the Women's Cooperative Guild's collection, *Life as We Have Known It,* also crossed in her career the blurred line dividing neighborhood nursing from midwifery. She had had her first experience of childbirth when as a teenager in the 1870s, she helped with the birth of her sister's fifth child. In the 1880s as a young wife with a sickly husband, she did washing and ironing for a living in South London, but when her household moved to Cricklewood, she took up maternity nursing informally, referred from one Women's Cooperative Guild member to another. As the "nurse" at many births, Mrs. Layton met many medical men who taught her how to handle births, showed her how to use forceps, and even took her to postmortems. "Quite a large number of young married people came to live in Cricklewood [probably in the 1890s] and I had sometimes as many as a hundred cases a year. The doctors left so much to me and did so little for their fees, that people asked me to take their cases without a doctor," she wrote. A medical man to whom she turned for advice gave her encouragement and promised to back her up in difficult cases; eventually Mrs. Layton was known throughout her district as a trustworthy midwife.[78]

In the negotiations leading to the 1902 Midwives Act, many voices were raised defending the neighborhood arrangements that poor women made for childbirth and cautioning against new legislation. The act finally hammered out after decades of controversy controlled midwifery as a profession with an almost vicious stringency (closely regulating the equipment, clothing, and private lives of midwives) but was actually quite lenient toward women practicing midwifery without formal training. Those who by 1905 had been in "bona fide" practice for at least a year and who "bore a good character" could be enrolled as midwives along with those who held certificates from the London Obstetrical Society or various teaching hospitals and institutes. Indeed, in 1905, the roll of midwives in England and Wales who could legally practice under the act included 12,521 bona fide (informally trained) midwives, the last of whom retired in 1947, compared with 9,787 certified midwives. The bona fide practitioners had until 1910 to take the certification examination.[79] But neighborhood-based midwifery had by no means disappeared after the Midwives' Act went into effect, for the bona fide midwives were, in their turn, supplemented by thousands of maternity "nurses" invisible from the Houses of Parliament.

"FALLING OVER PRECIPICES":
CHILDBED FEARS

Behind women's anxiety over household arrangements was, as the two bad dreams that introduced this chapter revealed, literally fear for their lives. Some of the "fits" that women experienced in pregnancy should be attributed to sheer terror of the possible maiming or death that each pregnancy represented to all women until at least the 1930s. A quarrel between two sisters in the early 1870s (probably) in Bow Common suggests the pregnant sister's chronic anxiety about her impending birth. Mrs. W., a young woman married to a railroad employee, had an unmarried sister in service whose illegitimate child she had been caring for. The sisters quarreled, and Mrs. W.'s curse encompassed both her sister's infant and her own childbirth ordeal. She "took a dreadful oath, and wished God would never let her get through her own near time of trouble if she kept the child in her house after Friday in that week." Among the women who gave birth at the General Lying-In Hospital, panic was similarly always close to the surface. Some of the patients said they had lost mothers or sisters in childbirth—6 of a group of 101 patients in 1881—and they had likely sought the hospital birth attended by renowned specialists as a safer one, though statistically it was not. But most of the Lying-In Hospital's patients were not women at particularly high risk. Many had managed to get a hospital letter simply because their homes were overcrowded or because they had no one to care for them there. Hospital routines and personnel, it is true, must have—just as they have continued to do—exacerbated the women's fearfulness. Given enemas and antiseptic douches before labor, confined to one often-uncomfortable position on their backs during labor, drugged heavily if noisy or too physically active, many women must have succumbed to panic who might have been able to contain it in more reassuring surroundings.[80] Yet just because these women were so closely observed, their hospital records provide invaluable descriptions of the mothers' emotional lives during their two postpartum weeks.

New pains, fever, or bleeding in the days following a birth terrified the women. When Harriet Noakes felt a pain in her abdomen two days after the birth of her first child, she "got frightened," and a number of other women were described as inclined to be "nervous" about themselves during their hospital stay. In 1882, the hospital matron was concerned about the patients' widespread "nervousness," which she believed could be attributed to the intrusive street noises of York Road, carrying traffic to and from Britain's largest railroad station at Waterloo. The ward setting itself increased this tension, for when one young woman began to hemorrhage, several others in her ward became anxious for themselves as well as for her. On her fifth hospital day, in the winter of 1881–1882, Amy Jennings's temperature went up to 104 degrees, and she became very frightened. "Patient has been fretting," read the house physicians's notes. "Thinks she is very bad and is going to die." The next day, after a short period of continued hemorrhaging, she was still more terrified. "In spite of all I said to her, she firmly believed she was going to die and talked to that effect." Seventeen-year-old Charlotte Wanding, a single servant from Peckham Rye, kept up all night by her neighbor's hemorrhage, became "rather nervous" herself.[81]

The distress of the postpartum weeks at the hospital was closely related to the material situation in which the new mother found herself; many "nameless" fears actually had names, which were poverty and helplessness. The signs of grief and worry that the General Lying-In physicians noted—crying, "fretting," inability to sleep—were concentrated among the women having babies without men to help support them. Although some of the single women who gave birth seemed to have made unproblematic plans to place their babies with agencies or nurse mothers and go back to work, or to stay with their own families while caring for the newborn, more of them were, during the days after the birth, engaged in negotiations with the babies' fathers, with their own mothers, or with future employers, which would determine their fates and those of their babies.

Among married women, those living apart from their husbands were the ones most likely to feel distressed during their hospital days. Thus Mary Barrett, of St. George's in the East, having her third child at age twenty-six, "cried a good deal" on February 13 and again "cried at night" on two later nights, though her new baby girl was healthy, her labor had been short and easy, and all her other children were well. The doctor's notes on February 16 reveal the probable cause of her distress: "Patient has been fretting a great deal since admission. Cries very often. Husband in prison." Mrs. Colson, a Pimlico cook married to an engineer's laborer, became "hysterical" on her ninth hospital day. As the doctor described it: "Patient was very hysterical, had a regular fit. Shut eyes when spoken to, talks in weak voice, has *clavus hystericus*." The next day he noted that she exhibited further hysterical symptoms: "Complains of pain when just touched, but can tolerate great pressure on abdomen when attention is distracted." Mrs. Colson was in fact more profoundly under pressure. Her baby was irritable and "troublesome," and the staff believed it was syphilitic. (Three previous babies all had died within a few months of birth.) Her relationship with her husband was by no means a stable one, and in fact when he came to the hospital to fetch her home, he "was in great distress to find his wife had gone off to the friends of some soldier with whom she had been cohabiting." Lydia Bartlett was another married woman who "fretted greater part of the time" according to the record. Her first child, a baby girl, was well, and the pregnancy had been easy, but the fact that she was separated from her husband probably contributed to the tension she felt in her postpartum days. On the first day she became "hysterical" when she learned that the house physicians were going around the ward, and she was upset again a few days later by a baby's crying in the ward.[82] For all these new mothers, the physical terrors of parturition were compounded by more mundane fears about providing for a new life.

WORN OUT

Leaving the care of the babies to the next chapter, let us briefly consider the physical effects of continuous childbearing on the mothers. The medical officer for the county of London calculated that for the decade of the 1890s, life expectancy at birth for women was about fifty-four years, for men about fifty years.[83] It was only during the generation described in this book that maternal mortality, despite the continuing high rates by our standards, had ceased to make the depredations on women of childbearing age that for centuries had kept their life expectancy lower than men's. Yet women survived childbirth only to be burdened with physical and mental health problems.

If there was any point in a childbearing life that was likely to plunge a woman into serious depression or other kinds of mental illness, it was not the birth of a *first* child, which researchers in women's health today often point to as contributing to depression or a state of "shock."[84] Rather, for late Victorian and Edwardian mothers, trouble was more likely at the arrival of a fifth, seventh, or ninth child. Later births, especially those coming before any siblings reached working age, were the ones likely to keep an exhausted woman up at night worrying about how she would feed yet another child. The apathetic, dulled women whom social workers met do seem to be concentrated among mothers of many children, and married women before and after World War I were far more likely to seek abortions for later than for earlier pregnancies. Eleanor Rathbone thought that she could easily distinguish the mothers of many children from those who had had just one: The former were always haggard and thin. Margery Spring-Rice's survey, carried out among British working-class mothers in the late 1930s, found only 31 percent in good general health. The figures gathered by the Peckham Health Centre at about the same time were similarly grim. A study after World War II found that even in very poor families, first children were likely to have had good care, which I read here as a sign of reasonably good maternal morale. Care that was only "fair" or even "poor," as rated by health visitors, was more common in households with four or more children.[85]

Giving birth itself, of course, contributed significantly to women's illnesses. Perineal tears, both small and large, were quite common in deliveries with attendants of every type. The smaller tears could heal quite easily if the mothers rested several days after childbirth, clearly what Clementina Black was delicately alluding to when she said that so many working-class mothers suffered "permanent injury" from getting out of bed too soon. A Dublin physician writing in 1872 was convinced that both perineal tears and prolapsed uterus were more common among poor women, "wives of our artisan and labouring men," who "undergo far more hardship and privation, and at the same time perform as much labor as their husbands." A surgical treatment for prolapsed uterus was developed in the 1920s, but before that, women with this problem who sought treatment were given metal or rubber pessaries that kept the uterus in place, at least until they slipped or became corroded, causing fresh misery.[86]

Doctors' case records are a study in long-suffering womanhood. A sixty-year-old woman in 1912 saw a doctor at the Royal Free Hospital's woman-staffed gynecology service (at the old Gray's Inn Road location) complaining of "lump in front passage" that caused pain and of urinary frequency, both of which had troubled her for six years! Multiple pregnancies must have contributed to her condition; she had had ten, including three miscarriages. At fifty-two, another woman had had uterine prolapse for nineteen years after the birth of twins; a much younger woman had been having "exceedingly painful periods" for five years, having to remain in bed each month for several days. Another woman, aged thirty-eight, came to see the Royal Free's doctors after sixteen months of "painful micturitions" after the birth of her eleventh child and, when questioned, reported still worse problems, including "something coming down at the vulva, especially in the evenings, or after hard work." The doctor found a ready explanation for this woman's miseries: Her perineum had been disastrously torn during the last birth, causing "rectal and uterine prolapses."[87] Yet she waited well over a year for treatment. Sarah Chessum of Lower Edmonton, though only thirty-one, had suffered acutely as a result of childbearing. Married for ten years, she was about to have her eighth child at the General Lying-In Hospital in 1881. Her case history describes bad health that no amount of medical treatment could cure: "Has heard noises in head last 12 months. . . . Health very bad; couldn't eat a piece of boiled chicken; sinking at chest; very weak; indigestion so bad: has had neuralgia 9 months at a time—whilst suckling one of her children—thought she would have gone mad with it."[88]

A London waistcoat maker might have represented thousands of other mothers: Though she had begun adulthood with a "very strong consti-tution," at age fifty she felt "worn out," according to Clementina Black. Her life had been a grueling combination of childbearing (she had had thirteen, though only five remained alive, three of them still at home) and long hours of housework and tailoring at home or in a workshop. Although she still worked steadily at her sewing, she seldom managed to leave the house. The combination of poverty and motherhood had taken its toll.[89]

CHAPTER 5

"I'll Bring 'Em Up in My Way"
Child Rearing

For aristocratic English women early in the nineteenth century, motherhood had meant mostly the painful act of giving birth to heirs to their husbands' estates. Later, childbirth anesthesia obliterated the pain (or its memory), while many aristocratic and upper-class women were coming to view motherhood in a new way, as a tender and enriching emotional experience.[1] For working-class women of our period, the transmission of blood and property were not central issues, and the pain of childbirth was seldom openly voiced. Motherhood mainly meant labor, not only in giving birth, but also in sustaining the child's life. Some London mothers were nurturing, some affectionate, and some playful, but these were only incidental qualities of good mothers. A good mother was mainly a good worker.

Child labor and the political controversies over it, the games, the learning, and the fears of childhood are pieces of English social history that have found their excellent chroniclers.[2] In this chapter I try, though many of my sources are children's autobiographies, to keep the less-told mothers' story (both in separate homes and more collectively in neighborhoods) at the center. The final section on "school stories" is, however, a composite account by grown children of the chances for a better life that mothers made them pass up, which (though many other subjects would do the same thing) demonstrates the inevitability, under conditions of poverty, of disappointment as well as fierce loyalty (much of it focused at mothers).

In *Working-Class Childhood,* Jeremy Seabrook spoke of childhood for the working classes in the 1980s as "the last resting place of dreams and visions"; Viviana Zelizar has called this process the "sacralization" of babies and small children, a process that had begun much earlier among the middle and upper classes. Seabrook pointed to something that for most of the population of Britain probably changed only in the 1950s or 1960s: Late Victorian and Edwardian working-class mothers' conception of childhood and of their relation to it had remained quite different from that of their upper-class contemporaries. Many well-off mothers, some of Beatrice Webb's married sisters in the 1870s and 1880s, for example, closely charted their children's motor skills, language, and social development and were deeply involved in their achievements.[3] Such conceptions of the central place of female nurture in children's spiritual development circulated in middle-class advice books. But working-class mothers in the same period more unsentimentally viewed their children in terms of the resources they required or contributed. They knew their love was vital to their children, but they acknowledged that young children meant hard work, which the children could later reciprocate—a vision closer to that of preindustrial families.

BEING A MOTHER

Those whose travels brought them to the mothers of the London poor recorded, though very sparsely, their more general comments about being mothers. A Mrs. Price, obviously tired and frazzled, in the spring of 1897 told a visiting Bible seller that with the twins screaming and the other children messing up things she would never get her rooms cleaned up, and she knew exactly what would help: "I wish I had plenty of money, then I should be happy." Mrs. Williamson, newly widowed at thirty-five with eight young children, firmly told the Poplar Board of Guardians, also in 1897, that a mother, no matter how poor, was indispensable to her children. The guardians had offered to put her four youngest in the East London orphanage and asked, "What would they not have [there] that they have got now?" As she later told her son (for her statement was for the children as well as for the guardians), Mrs. Williamson's simple response was, "A mother's love." Another mother, in a quiet moment at dusk probably in 1915, sadly told Sylvia Pankhurst of the future sorrow from which she could not protect her children as they nestled around her: "Poor things! . . . When they're little's the only joy they get."[4]

Laughter was a help in handling the demands of motherhood. Mrs. Bennett's miserable weekly chore of mangling the wash in early twentieth-century Walworth was lightened by her son's Charlie Chaplin imitations ("It was good to hear her laugh," he wrote). Wives laughed at their husbands, the comic figures of the working class, sharing the jokes with their children and neighbors. Leah Chegwidden joked with her children over her cocky husband's mushroom-growing fiasco, his penchant for hot curries, and his ugly homemade chair and handily placed spitoon; and she acted out her own comedy routines, such as her madcap attempt to rescue, with the aid of a huge pair of fire tongs, two little daughters from the terrors of an escaped pet eel.[5] The grim silence of George Acorn's Bethnal Green mother in the 1870s and 1880s and the harsh tongue and hand of the South London mother in Kathleen Woodward's *Jipping Street* have to be set against the ability of some women to laugh at themselves. In the 1890s or 1900s, Elizabeth Rignall's mother in Lavender Hill, Clapham Junction, in a fury at two of her children whose loud morning game had awakened her lodgers, first threw a shoe at them, then, seeing the shoe fly out of the third-story window, "collapsed on the bed with laughter." The Hoxton mother—whose fierce outbursts of rage in the decade before World War I were vividly recalled by her daughter—was still capable of laughing at herself. One night, her husband away, she shared her bed with two of her daughters. The mother was fat, and the bed, none too sturdy, collapsed under the weight of the three females, all three joking with great hilarity that it would take a "crane" to get the mother off the floor.[6]

Martyrdom was another, though less common, way in which women could construct their lives as mothers. The sentimental versions of motherly self-sacrifice that appeared in parlor songs like "Queen of the Earth" or preprinted mantlepiece mottoes like "What Is a Home Without a Mother" could certainly have structured the way that some women saw their lives and work. Leah Chegwidden, who presided so competently and with frequent laughter over her family of thirteen, was probably tempted by images of sainthood. Neatly dressed in black, with white lace collar and amber brooch, she was always waiting at the door at four o'clock when her children came home from school. Only once, seriously injured and immobile, was she not there. As her daughter wrote, instead she was "lying at the bottom of the wooden steps, not moving, and looked different somehow, but even then when I patted her face and called she opened her eyes and smiled [beatifically?]." The daily self-starvation of vast numbers of hardworking London mothers lends itself to a "sainthood" explanation, and certainly some of the children—for example, Joe Williamson (the boy whose mother defied the Poplar guardians), who became an Anglo-Catholic slum priest—writing as adults about their mothers, did describe them worshipfully.[7]

Rearing children involved talk. Mostly women told their children about their daily work: how they got money out of their husbands, bought their food, and cooked their meals. Only one subject, though a large one—the mysteries of sex, birth, and the body—was off limits. Women's regrets over or satisfactions in their marriage and anger at husbands were not kept private, however. Some related how they had rejected other suitors in favor of the men they married, gave daughters advice on selecting spouses, and itemized their grievances against their husbands. Ann Jasper, for instance, unromantically told her son that she had married his father because the two had been turned out by her mother when they returned late from a date; they went to the senior Jasper's place instead. She got pregnant, so they had to be married, and with a brass wedding ring to boot.[8] The women spoke openly to their children of their money worries. Sometimes Joseph Williamson and his sisters would hear their mother crying, "I can't go on," and they would hug her head, saying, "Don't, Mother." Once they heard her exclaim, "I must go and drown myself." And it was this kind of talk more than direct orders or requests that made children want to earn money to help.[9]

Much of this motherly talk took the form of maxims, whose familiarity and repetition gave them the power to shape their children's lives. Taken all together, they described a world in which destiny had to be accepted, corners cut, and hard work faced. When a fifteen-year-old Limehouse girl married without her parents' consent in 1878, giving a fake age, her mother eventually helped her find a room when the first baby was due but admonished her: "You have made your bed; now you must lie in it." Said the woman who had just rescued her husband's Saturday steak from the cat: "What eye don't see, 'eart don't grieve over." Dotty Scannell's mother surrounded her children with such aphorisms: "Cleanliness is next to godliness"; "God wouldn't send a child into the world without a crust of bread"; "Little pitchers have big ears"; "A man must keep his pride"; "Never fish one and fowl the other"; "Half a loaf is better than none"; "Where there's a will there's a way." Dotty heard her mother's proverbs of cheerful resignation and "accepted them without question."[10]

MOTHERS AND THEIR BABIES

Being the mother of an infant, a schoolchild, or a working teenager called for different kinds of work and skills, involved different community resources, and mobilized different passions. A woman with a stepladder of children would, of course, be exercising them all simultaneously.

Rituals of the Postpartum Weeks

Naming the baby, officially part of the christening ceremony, placed the infant in its social world. The custom of giving the oldest child of each sex the name of the same-sex parent, indicating the continuity of generations, remained intact during this period. Children's names were generally drawn from a very short list. Traditional biblical or English names inherited from· parents and grandparents were repeated, for example, over and over again in the 1871 census for Three Colts Lane in Bethnal Green: Ann, Emma, Sarah, Eliza, Catherine, George, William, Alfred, Charles, Thomas, Henry, and so on. When Clara Grant first arrived in East London in the late 1890s, it seemed to her that all the boys were named William, Thomas, or William Thomas; the girls Emily, Emma, Elizabeth, even Ellen Nellie and Betsy Elizabeth. There was only a little room for creativity, for the expression of excitement at the thought of a new child: a Poplar woman, and one in Hoxton too, whose many daughters each had the name of a flower (Rose, Lily, Poppy, Primrose, Daisy, Violet); the women who, during the Boer War, had named their children Paul Kruger or Pretoria; the playful Mrs. Heydinnick in South London who named her triplets born in 1886 Alpha, Beatrice, and Omega. Clara Grant contrasted the restraint of her early East London parents with the profusion of imaginative names that began to appear in the 1920s, stimulated by the international culture of the cinema: Shirley, Carole, Valerie, Allan. By the early 1950s, offspring in Bethnal Green were carrying such glamorous transatlantic names as Lana and Marilyn, Glenn and Kevin.[11]

In many ways, the mother's "getting up" after childbirth, described in Chapter 4, was the most significant of the postchildbirth ceremonies, if the least public and formal. Churching and baptism, often perfunctory, were public rituals involving mothers and infants. Almost universally, the mothers went to their parish priest sometime between the twelfth and twenty-eighth day after a birth for "churching," a brief ceremony—theologically suspect and unpopular with clergymen—in which mothers gave thanks for having safely negotiated a childbirth. The sense that before churching, women were in a kind of semipregnant state appeared in such popular English notions that a woman who went outdoors without having been churched would have another child within a year or would cause the women of any house she visited to get pregnant immediately. In two Lambeth parishes in the 1890s, on the other hand, mothers expected that their churching would prevent later miscarriages.[12]

Christenings were very small affairs, with their meaning as the initiation of a two-week-old infant into the church more or less ignored. Mid-Victorian London city missionaries were astonished to find that people thought of baptism as a form of magic, conferring health or luck on children. The godparent relationship formalized at the christening was also not a very important one for working-class children.[13] In one Bermondsey parish, an estimate for the 1870s was that for every baptized baby there were three who were not, as much "through want of clothes and suitable sponsors" as through principled indifference. In the early twentieth century, a few Bermondsey clergymen, using more modern methods—beginning with birth notifications from the local registrar of births and then followed up by door-to-door visiting campaigns—had more luck, according to historian Alan Bartlett, and the proportion of babies baptized grew. Bartlett's Bermondsey research, however, reveals that the rising numbers may well have simply reflected in the 1900s a female population accustomed to directives from professionals. Baptism, like vaccination, school attendance, and so on, was something that was being insisted on for their children: "Just rules and regulations," said a Bermondsey mother when pressed to explain why people who never went to church still had their babies baptized. Indeed, these processes appear to have been associated in some mothers' minds. "I've had him vaccinated and I've had him Christened and I can't do more than that," nursery teacher Muriel Wragge heard from well-meaning mothers in Hoxton.[14]

Women were in charge of baptism as of other rituals of infancy, usually bringing female friends to the church on a weekday evening for the ceremony. Even though the Church of England defined infant baptism as a public event centering on the two parents and three godparents, fathers were rarely seen at workers' christenings in this period. Few clergymen actually refused to perform the quick ceremony, but without the fathers' presence, these baptisms were not liturgically correct. Perhaps an inverted sense of propriety explains why a father and grandfather in Hoxton in the 1910s, having attended a christening followed by a boozy party, appeared at the local pub that evening dressed as women.[15]

Foundlings, Informal Adoptions, and Community Child Care

The common practices of taking a newly christened baby around the neighborhood to show to each household in turn (silver coins were sometimes pressed into its hand) and of encouraging children to call adults "auntie" and "uncle" are a few indications of an implicit, common adult relationship with the local children.[16] Many babies were even reared by local people who were not their biological parents. The legal machinery of adoption did not exist until the 1920s, but especially on the poorest streets, informal adoptions—some permanent, others temporary—by neighbors were not unusual. Henry Nevinson's fictional "Mrs Simon's Baby," in which a neatly wrapped bundle is deposited anonymously at the door of a childless woman, was repeated at 7 Smart's Buildings in the late 1880s, where Booth's investigators found a woman shopkeeper who had been given two foundlings and had permanently adopted one, and in Whitechapel Road in the 1900s when a German baker and his wife out for a stroll saw a "parcel in a doorway," a baby girl that they picked up, took home, and raised along with their other children. In a Battersea district in the 1890s, illegitimate children whose mothers were in service were often adopted by their aunts or grand-mothers and thus absorbed into existing families, rather than being sent out to paid "nurses."[17] Other babies got homes with non relatives. Mrs. Taylor, of Grove Road, told the Bethnal Green guardians in 1889 that nineteen-year-old Sarah Taylor was her adopted daughter; the biological mother, now in Canada, had given the child to Taylor when she was "three or five weeks old." An Italian woman working as an organ grinder around New Cross, South London, found a blue-eyed female bundle on a park bench sometime in the 1880s and kept and reared her. When the adoptive daughter, one of the few English organ grinders on the Lon-don streets, grew up and married, she and her husband in turn "adopted a little waif—a boy, picked up from somewhere, the Italian woman's charity being passed on in this way,"[18] according to journalist Olive Christian Malvery.

Descriptions by middle-class observers stress, as motives for these adoptions, women's compassion for needy children or their affection for them, rather than articulated notions of community obligation. George Sims, touring a very poor South London neighborhood with a criminal reputation, encountered a woman sharing a "wretched room" with six children, two of whom she told him were "only staying with us." They were, she explained, the children of a widow living upstairs who had been sent to prison for assaulting a police officer. "She intended to keep them if she was able till the mother came out. 'It was only neighborly-like, and my heart bled to see the poor young 'uns a–cryin', and that wretched and neglected and dirty.' " The desire to "keep" children near their homes and under the protection of their own kind, children who would otherwise be sent away to "the parish," must have indeed been a powerful motive in both long- and short-term adoptions.[19]

The readiness to help was also a statement about the indispensability of mothers to small children, one that reflects the assumption that babies and toddlers, more than other young children, needed intimacy with a woman. When households broke up, it was usually the bigger children who went into the workhouse, while their baby siblings were absorbed into the homes of neighbors or relatives. As one Rotherhithe woman who, despite her poverty, had decided to take in her husband's three-year-old orphaned nephew, explained her decision: "When he is older I shall be obliged to let the Guardians have him; but I can't let a baby like that go where there is no woman to love him, as long as I can find a bit for his mouth." Ada Bennett, born in Chatham Street, Walworth, in 1901, was one of three children orphaned by their mother's death in

1904. The youngest, a baby ten months old, was adopted by "friends of the family" who brought her up as "their own"; the two oldest, three and five, were shuffled among an aunt, their father, and the workhouse. A Poplar woman's decision to adopt a three-year-old orphaned girl, though she already had ten children, not only affirmed the importance of motherhood but also raised her credit with her older daughters. As one of these older daughters explained, "Mum—being the angel she was—decided to look after her. We never regarded Kathy as anything else but our sister."[20]

Mothers who needed daily child care help looked to a variety of non-family helpers, paid and unpaid. Nearby neighbors watched one another's children; such networks were closest among families sharing a house (thus two to eight families), extending also to those "opposite" and next door. The small catchment area for cooperative child care suggests both the relative population density of most poor London streets and the limited physical mobility of adult women with children. Some child supervision was formally arranged and was paid for by the parents. Working mothers in early twentieth-century Hoxton were most likely to leave their infants with local women, whose price was only 2s. 6d. a week. An early twentieth-century report on employed Lambeth mothers showed that a large group had formal child care arrangements with neighbors, and a still larger group with no formal plans for their children may well have relied on informal supervision by women living nearby. Another survey of London working mothers of infants, made a few years earlier, found that half left them with relatives, 30 percent with neighbors.[21]

Paid baby nursing was actually another form of community-based infant care. This practice, normally netting the nurse mothers about 5 shillings a week for a new baby for most of the period we are discussing, had an evil reputation because of a few notorious trials of "baby farmers" who took in dozens of infants simultaneously and had clearly murdered a succession of infants in their charge, sometimes with the tacit consent of their parents. Three detailed parliamentary investigations of the nurse–mother system (1871, 1890, and 1896) demonstrated, however, that this murderous form of baby minding was a rare crime. Most of the women who took in babies for cash had only one infant under age one at a time in their care, possibly together with one or two somewhat older children. The high death rates among infants cared for by paid nurses were paralleled by similar rates for bottle-fed infants living in poverty and cared for by their own mothers. Legislation dating from 1872 established a system of inspecting baby nurses but exempted those with only one infant, the result of a campaign by Lydia Becker and the Women's Vigilance Society to protect this female income-producing activity. Like babysitting, baby nursing was a poor woman's occupation whose practitioners were mostly widows or older women with grown children who took in babies as an alternative to taking in laundry or doing daily charring.[22]

The "commercial" baby nursing system was, however, difficult to disentangle from other kinds of neighborhood child care. A group of 256 Battersea families surveyed in the 1890s by members of a local deaconesses' house contained only sixteen "real" nurse children, most of them illegitimate. But a larger group of households in the district had also taken in extra children, such as those of sisters or daughters, and these also usually involved some cash payment, confounding the investigators' assumption that "family" child care would be free while the same service from neighbors or strangers would be paid.[23]

Most of the paid baby nurses were recruited through word of mouth. When a pregnant West End servant rented a room in Battersea in the 1890s to await her confinement, "It would be known among the women in that street or in those few houses near, that she wanted to leave the child and that she had promised to pay a certain amount and to find the clothes," as one of the deaconesses told an investigating committee in 1896. A Kent servant who had come to London to give birth, for example, used her landlady's daughter-in-law as a nurse for the baby. Describing the ways in which women might take in a baby "casually in different cases," the deaconess continued: "When a girl has been confined these poor women know everything that is going on; one will say that she will take the baby."[24]

The 1896 Bermondsey case of eight-year-old Ethel Wakefield provides a good example of paid baby nursing and its intermingling with informal adoptions. Harriet Wakefield, Ethel's mother, had her illegitimate child in the workhouse, and a Mrs. Barnes agreed to care for her for the customary 5 shillings a week, which Wakefield managed to pay for a year. Later she claimed the child but returned to the workhouse with her to give birth to a second. At that point, since Mrs. Barnes "had become so attached" to Ethel, she applied to the mother to "adopt" her and got her consent. A few years later Harriet Wakefield married a coachman, but she never laid claim to the child.[25]

The acknowledgment that care for children gave adults rights over them generated many ambiguities about the definition of parenthood. Some of the paid nurses became very attached to their babies, and officials found many who had sacrificed dearly to support infants whose mothers had ceased making payments. Understandably, many of these nurses labeled themselves mothers and refused to part with their charges.[26] Biological and nurse mothers regularly found themselves in battles for custody in the Old Bailey or involved in assault cases that terminated in magistrates' courts.

Powerful emotions fueled these "child-stealing" court cases. A routine child nursing arrangement that began in Spitalfields in 1878 ended less routinely at the Old Bailey in 1884, for in this case the nurse had actually kidnapped the child. Abigail Jacobs was a single dressmaker living in Commercial Street when she arranged for Elisabeth Francis, who lived nearby in Acorn Street, Bishopsgate, to keep her eighteen-month-old son Barnett in exchange for 3s. 6d. per week. The mother and the nurse agreed that the mother could visit the baby whenever she wished. After only three weeks, Abigail Jacobs announced that she was about to get married and that she wanted the baby back, at which point the nurse disappeared with the baby. Jacobs "tried to find the child day after day and night after night" without success. But five years later, she spotted the ex-nurse in a Brick Lane fish shop and confronted her: "This is the way you have served me, you have ruined my heart after so long a time." The nurse, Elisabeth Francis (who was sentenced to six weeks in prison without hard labor), had explained her actions to herself in the vocabulary of the community: "I don't think I stole the child, he has cost me a lot of money." To her obviously mistaken but logically consistent way of thinking, her years of financial support for the boy legitimized her claims to him. She told the arresting detective that "she liked the child, and kept it," and indeed, she had taken good care of little Barnett, who was enrolled in a nearby board school when his adoptive mother was finally tracked down. In another 1884 case, the parties were an illegitimate child's grandmother (the mother having died in childbirth) and the nurse mother, an acquaintance of the grandparents. The nurse was a professional who combined paid child care with a small laundry business. Though she had a few other babies in her charge, she was deeply attached to the disputed baby. The women were involved in fierce quarrels and extensive litigation, a process that began when the child was about two. Both "mothers" were in jail at various points.[27]

"Working for" Baby

However she had acquired her child, the new mother faced a heavy round of tasks. A speaker at a British Nurses' Association meeting in 1891 calculated that a woman living in a third-story flat who carried water and slops up and down from a ground-floor tap was doing "the equivalent of a day labourer's work." A Manchester City Council survey in 1918 concluded that it took close to ten hours per week (much of it very heavy labor indeed) to do the laundry of a family of just five people.[28] To take just laundry as an example: To heat the water for doing laundry in the "copper"—a large immobile cauldron that some houses had in their own sculleries, some in shared laundry rooms—a fire had to be built under it. "Very often the fire would go out," grimly recalled a West Ham man born in 1891. "Then she would get a sack and try to beat the copper hole where the fire was, to make the coal and wood catch alight." The next steps were pushing the clothes around in the hot soapy water with a heavy stick, rubbing them on a washing board, changing the water for rinsing, wringing them out by hand, mechanical wringer, or mangle, and then hanging them up to dry. The Ranyard nurses understandably boasted in their journal of a compliment they received, that unlike other district nurses who "made washing," they actually "saved the washing."[29]

The voluminous diapers (which could be made cheaply by using the tails of worn-out men's shirts) used by all classes, which folded over several times, with loops and ties sewn on, must have been the scourge of washdays, and one unpleasant shortcut was merely to dry out wet ones rather than laundering them. Early nineteenth-century baby care books had recommended two changes daily for babies, but by the end of the century the advice books were urging that diapers be changed whenever wet, which meant as many as two dozen times a day. Few working-class mothers had the time or the linen or the hot water for such a standard of infant hygiene, and as Wapping-born Grace Foakes remembered of that era, "The child was almost always soaking wet and smelly."[30] Another nappy-saving trick was to "hold out" the baby over a potty at regular intervals during the day, sometimes even stimulating the child's anus, a procedure in common use among all classes almost into the present and recommended in most nineteenth-century editions of Pye Chavasse's ubiquitous child care guide, *Advice to Mothers*. Even Susan Isaacs, the first of the Freud-influenced popular childrearing-manual writers, also urged conventionally in 1929 that babies be put "on a vessel after each feed," though unlike her predecessors, she warned her readers not to expect children to be "too docile."[31]

The long, flowing clothing of a new infant, usually worn until the third or fourth month—as late as nine months if poverty interfered with the supply of "shortening" garments—spelled itching and overheating for the babies and work for the mothers. The *British Journal of Nursing* in 1905 directed midwives and district nurses to follow the new "light" and "modern" plan for dressing infants, which still left a staggering number of layers, straps, and tabs. The first layer consisted of a soft woolen vest with long sleeves and a large diaper over the buttocks, covered, if possible, with another flannel triangle. A long flannel "back wrap" laid down the baby's back with arms passing through shoulder straps was the next layer. Finally came a "monthly" gown, flowing to well below the baby's feet and often pinned, and a "head flannel." Many mothers added a night dress over the whole parcel, plus a veil.[32] The nurses' 1905 outfit omitted the "binder," still ubiquitous on working-class babies. Wound many times around the child's middle, it was thought to "strengthen" its back. At the St. Pancras School, where the staff discouraged binders, one woman complained that her husband found the new method unsatisfactory; it left the baby "too soft." "There's nothin' to catch 'old of," he had complained. Women attending mothers' classes in Westminster in 1914 still insisted on binders. Later in their first year, boy and girl babies were changed into "short clothes," dresses and petticoats, with neck, arms, and lower legs bare.[33] Boys were "breached"— dressed in the short trousers that signaled their status as boys—and their baby curls were cut off sometime between age two and five.

Extra feeding, holding, and cuddling were essential to working-class infant care; schedules were rare; and babies lived closely surrounded by adults and other children. This approach was totally at variance with that of both conventional and progressive middle-class opinion, both of which, despite their differences, prescribed schedules for vital functions like eating, sleeping, and elimination and recommended chilly rooms, a bland diet, many baths, and a good deal of physical separation from adults in cot, playpen, and nursery.[34] Conversely, from birth until they were replaced by another newborn, working-class infants were in nearly continuous contact with their mother's body. Especially in the nineteenth-century decades of this study, prams were not a routine household appurtenance for workers. Rather, they were rented by the hour for special occasions, such as trips to the park. Babies were normally carried everywhere their mothers went: to shops, music halls, and pubs, indoors and out. When Grace Foakes's ailing mother went out, she took her most recent baby with her, using a cumbersome but ingenious method for carrying its supply of diapers: "Taking about half-a-dozen nappies, she would pin them one at a time to her petticoat, near the waist. They hung down around her, covered by her skirt. When a dry nappy was needed she took one and changed the baby, replacing it with the wet one." Or to cite a particularly grotesque example, even a woman coldly determined on murder had to take her babies with her. Ann Sarah Hibbard had been carrying her youngest child, aged two and a half, in her arms all afternoon and had a four-year-old at her side as she went into a Custom House pub in 1894 to track down her stevedore husband, followed him out into the street, and stabbed him.[35]

Crowded quarters and thin walls meant that one baby could disturb dozens of people in several households. Babies were thus held partly to keep them content and quiet, in deference to wage earners or school-children. Court testimony documenting admittedly extreme situations demonstrates the carrying range of a baby's cries. Three different witnesses from different parts of a Peckham house easily testified at the Old Bailey about the morning in March 1888 when a lodger must have suffocated his crying baby: The baby's cries had been heard throughout the house since he moved in, and the other lodgers all remembered exactly when the crying stopped.[36] Among a wife's normal duties was protecting her husband from the noise of babies and children, and failure could well lead to a battering. One of W. J. Brown's earliest Battersea memories from the 1890s was of his mother begging her two sons to stop their loud, cheerful nighttime play. "She said that unless we kept quiet she would have to 'go away'," and the boy guessed that his violent and irritable father had, once again, attacked his wife. A St. Pancras woman in the 1900s whose husband worked nights took her two preschool children outdoors in any weather to keep them out of the way while he slept, and when they were at home, according to a nurse's report, "the mother is in a rather nervous state, and worries if the slightest noise is made."[37]

The temptation to administer a quieting drug to a crying baby must therefore have been great, as opiates, an integral part of Britain's colonial trade, were popular, widely used medically, and easily accessible until the late Victorian years. Thus Mrs. Winslow's Soothing Syrup for Teething Infants, a common remedy, originally contained morphine, as did Chlorodyne and Godfrey's Cordial. After decades of debates and legislation, only partially effective, a series of court cases in the 1890s established the requirement that patent medicines containing narcotics be labeled as poisons and be sold only by pharmacists.[38] As a result, many of the patent mixtures dropped the opium from their formulas, with some even proudly advertising that fact. The observers of working-class motherhood who invaded East and South London in the 1900s were nearly silent on the question of mothers' doping their babies, and the issue seldom came up even in the 1904 "deterioration" hearings, otherwise so critical of working-class mothering.[39] For with the arrival of the twentieth century, the new panic was not drugs but maternal alcohol drinking, which temperance advocates like Joseph Rowntree and Arthur Sherwell and, a few years later, journalist George Sims described as a grave threat to the nation. But even Sims expounded on pub-floor germs and the evils of crowded drinking places more than on the use of alcohol or other drugs to keep babies quiet.[40]

The labor-intensive methods continued to be the most popular ways of soothing crying infants: carrying them, giving them to bigger siblings to watch, putting them to sleep cuddled next to their parents, and feeding them as often as they were hungry.

Feeding the Baby

"Feeding the baby," the quintessential maternal function, is even today in affluent countries the topic of intense discussion and study and of a copious popular and medical literature. A century ago feeding was a topic that, among the poor, was even more crucial. Food was scarce. Even breast milk was not very plentiful, and a woman with a "good breast of milk" was often pointed to with praise or envy. One whose breast milk failed knew that her child's life had become more insecure. As with many poor cultures, plump babies were viewed as healthy ones: "As fat as a little pig" was a phrase of appreciation describing a baby.[41] Also, many diseases of infants, some congenital, were manifested by such symptoms as insufficient appetite, poor digestion, or wasting. One of the worst killers of infants before World War I was a digestive disease, summer diarrhea, which alone was responsible for about a quarter of all infant deaths in most of the years we are describing.

Early twentieth-century figures demonstrate that like those in the rest of England, well over three quarters of working-class London women breast-fed their babies for their first three to six months. The proportions of breast feeding ranged from 77 percent of the 862 Paddington women interviewed by health visitors in 1904 or 1905 to 63 percent in St. Pancras. Another 10 or 11 percent of babies in both boroughs were getting a combination of breast and "hand" feeding.[42] The hard work of infant care did not (and often still does not) harmonize with the body's work of lactation. The Fabian visitors in Lambeth, for example, recorded the daily schedule of Mrs. B., a thirty-eight-year-old woman (who looked fifty to the visitors) with eight children under thirteen and a husband who worked nights. The youngest child, a nursing baby of three months, was "small and hungry." The child had to be kept quiet and comfortable, yet the mother's milk was not plentiful; so she usually gave the infant eight daytime breast feedings and two more during the night.[43]

The women, draped with some of their many tiers of clothing, appeared comfortable doing the breast feeding at home with their families. An Old Kent Road boy, age eight, called on to testify at the Old Bailey in 1879, spoke quite unself-consciously of his mother's breast feeding his eleven-week-old sister in their one-room flat. One evening the parents had a quarrel, he said, the mother went out, and when she returned she "sat down and gave the baby some tittie." Later the mother picked up her baby at the upstairs neighbor's, returned and again "gave it a drop of tittie." Lilian Westall, born in 1893 into a large and poverty-stricken family who lived in Kings Cross, was the second eldest of the children. There was little privacy in their three-room house. "My mother always seemed to have a child at her breast, and, as the second eldest, I would often keep her company, sitting on the edge of the bed with her until late at night, as she nursed the baby and waited for my father to come home."[44]

London women generally weaned their infants during the last months of the babies' first year, having already begun to supplement heavily their breast milk. One year was the average weaning age among the Lambeth mothers in Pember Reeves's study, rather later than she and other health professionals thought healthy. Some women, of course, nursed longer than this, either to save money or to capitalize on the contraceptive reputation of long nursing. Jewish women in East London, while praised by health officials for their high rates of breast feeding, were also criticized for prolonging it into the baby's second year. An observer at a Whitechapel infant clinic in 1910 found the mostly Jewish children in the crowded waiting room clean, chubby, and cheerful, and did not appear to share the doctor's views about the importance of early weaning: "A woman sits shamefaced before the doctor. 'Eleven months old and baby still given the breast, mother?' The woman makes no reply; and the interpreter whispers, 'Afraid of unemployment. Is keeping one breast going as a safeguard.' They pass out, the wasting mother and the thriving child."[45]

Between 1870 and 1918 a number of new issues made infant feeding newly complex and controversial. By the late nineteenth century, with the spread of knowledge of basic sterilization techniques, it had become quite possible for a bottle-fed baby to survive and flourish. Middle-class households, where it was easy to keep things clean and cool, did this in large numbers with low infant death rates. Nursing pioneer Agnes Hunt's mother, in the 1860s and 1870s, successfully bottle fed all but two of her eleven children after one of her first babies bit her breast while nursing. Advice books and even medical writers after about 1870 often recommended giving babies the bottle.[46] At the General Lying-In Hospital in the early 1880s, for instance, the staff ordered a high proportion of the babies to be fed supplementary bottles or to be entirely bottle fed, and this was true also of the Bell Street Clinic's practitioners west of Regent's Park a generation later.[47]

Pressure for bottle feeding came not only from medical workers but also from the infant-formula advertising that, from the late 1860s when Liebig's was introduced, was creating a multinational market for the new infant products. By 1883, there were twenty-seven different brands of patent foods available in England.[48] The products' main ingredient was either dried milk (as in Benger's and Glaxo) or, more commonly, cereals of various kinds, which were to be mixed with milk or water. Among workers, to judge from the 1898 survey made by the Limehouse medical officer, Nestle's, Mellen's, and Ridge's food were the most popular, though many other brands were also in use. Condensed milk, which could also be bottle fed, reached the British market in the 1870s, but its sales jumped dramatically there only in the 1890s. Nutritionally, condensed milk left much to be desired; it was usually heavily sugared, and the cheapest brands also contained inadequate amounts of fat or protein.

Although the contents of each tin were sterile, they were often opened at the shops, as many households lacked can openers.[49] Fresh cow's milk (mixed with water for small babies) provided the best infant nutrition, but the purer the milk the higher its cost. It was thus not often given even to infants, and after the age of one, English urban workers seldom tasted fresh milk at all.[50]

When bottle feeding was popularized among the poor, who lacked facilities for sterilization or refrigeration, it presented health problems that its early advocates had not anticipated. The bottle's association with summer diarrhea was suspected from the 1870s but was established definitively only in the early twentieth century. The isolation of the *E. coli* bacillus in 1945 provided only a clue to the causes of diarrhea, for although some subtypes of *E. coli* do cause serious disease, *E. coli* are found in all human digestive systems. What is known is that the bacteria that make infants so sick are dangerous only if plentiful. They can multiply very easily in unsterile bottles, nipples, or formula, spread by flies or contact with contaminated feces in the soil or water.[51] Death rates from infant diarrhea, which had climbed in the mid-1880s, began to decline during the 1900s, especially after 1911, as infant death rates in general fell, and the Infant Welfare movement's campaign to "educate" the mothers has been granted credit for the change. Education regarding domestic antisepsis clearly played a role in the drop, as did better sanitary conditions, a real achievement of this era—water supply, street cleaning, and plumbing arrangements. But we might also argue that the Infant Welfare movement was most effective in educating health personnel about the dangers of bottle feeding for working-class babies, making them more responsible about advising it.[52]

Poor London mothers began to give babies solid food months sooner than medical practitioners advised, a pattern that has continued to the present. The Finsbury Infants' Milk depot, opened in 1904, counseled that no solid food should be given to babies until they reached ten or eleven months, but working-class women were giving their babies ham bones to suck on at one or two months and were feeding them bread-and-milk mixtures. Cereals, such as barley, or biscuits, or groats soaked in water or milk were introduced equally early, in the hopes that the baby would be "satisfied."[53] (In the 1970s, British working-class mothers were introducing solid food at an average age of four months; over 40 percent started their babies on solid food at under three months.) Investigators for the City of Westminster Health Society noted, however, apparently with some surprise, that "entirely unsuitable food, such as cheese or fried fish" was not being fed to very young babies there.[54]

The idea that infant feeding should take place at timed intervals, first proposed by doctors and health visitors in the 1890s, had not penetrated working-class women's culture in this period. In the 1900s, nurse Katherine Roberts earned the gratitude of her maternity patients when she determined to avoid waking the mothers and babies at the mandated two-hour intervals for night feedings. Rigid feeding schedules were quite incompatible with mothers' work or with life in overcrowded homes. In any case, many households also lacked watches and clocks. The Fabian Women's Group's Lambeth researchers supplied the daily schedules of a number of mothers with small babies for sometime between 1909 and 1913, which demonstrate the way in which feeding and infant care were adjusted to the rhythms of housework, husband, and children. Such care was easier if the baby were fed as soon as it cried. Mrs. B., the exhausted thirty-eight-year-old mentioned earlier in this section, tried, by feeding her baby ten times a day, to cope with a house full of young children and a printer husband who needed to sleep during the day. Another mother, whose four children ranged from infancy to age eight, nursed her baby if it woke up early, hoping to keep the other children sleeping while she helped her husband get off to work as an LCC carman. Other nursing sessions later in the day calmed the baby and provided time for the mother to give the two schoolchildren their meals and to care for the three-year-old at home.[55] The Lambeth feeding patterns tell of mothers' generosity toward their babies but also of the imperative that infant care fit the mother's central work of caring for the family.

"Dowager Babies"

In a great many cultures, the break with the mother that comes with weaning or a new sibling is a notoriously agonizing one in a child's life cycle. This separation from the mother often engenders the child's first sense of its distinct consciousness, and the earliest memories of many working-class London autobiographers cluster around moments of separation, most often the result of another baby's birth.[56]

Hoxton-born A. S. Jasper became an ex-baby very late, at age five (a series of stillbirths or abortions perhaps putting off the moment for some time), in about 1910. His recollections of his confrontation with the new situation communicate a sense of loss, rage, and dislocation. As soon as he saw his new sister, in fact, Jasper began to cry, and his mother got him into bed with her to comfort him. "She had always made such a fuss of me, and I suppose I must have realised my nose had been put out of joint. I never left my mother all that day." But the moment of reckoning came at bedtime.

> My mother told me I would have to sleep with my sister Jo' as I was now getting a "big boy." Also, I could not sleep with her in the big bed because of the baby. I cried and cried my eyes out. It was understood. . . . I had always slept in my parents' bed. In the end, I must have been pacified and

went with my sister Jo'. She laid me in her bed and quickly got in beside me and tried to cuddle me off to sleep. I must have gone to bed sobbing my heart out at leaving my mother.

That first night, the boy awoke later and "cried out in fright," waking the whole household and stimulating a series of curses from his father. The mother then arranged a pillow at the foot of the bed for the large ex-baby to sleep on. "Feeling her next to me, I soon went off."[57] Jasper was eventually able to deal with his loss through his relationship with a nurturing and generous teenage sister and by sharing his mother's work caring for his new sibling. But his autobiography, with its references to mediums he visited as an adult in order to talk with his mother, now dead, about her reasons for remaining with her terrible husband, demonstrates the ex-baby's lifelong refusal to part from his mother, a woman who had turned away from her son to a new job, the care of yet another baby.

There is no English word to describe a baby with a still younger sibling, and the linguistic improvisations used by everyone involved with these intermediate beings reflect their vague status. The bigger infants were called "ex-babies" or "dowager babies," at least by health and social workers. Newborns were known as "born babies" or "just-born babies." A very small child with two younger siblings, one eighteen months old and one just born, made the distinction in this way to her nursery school teacher: "I've got two babies at home, one's born and the other isn't born!"[58]

The second year of life continues today to present health problems in poor countries. Kwashiorkor, the protein deficiency disease prevalent among Third-World children, translates from Swahili as "the disease of children who have ceased nursing," and weanling diarrhea has remained a serious problem among poor populations in which the disease's danger is greater because of malnutrition.[59] London's ex-babies were said to be thinner and more poorly nourished than their younger siblings. It was in the second year of life, rather than the first, that poor children generally began to grow "delicate" and fall behind in growth, wrote nutritionist Florence Petty. Although the year-old baby ought to be the "most expensive person in the household to feed," she wrote, instead one thin and ricketty nineteen-month-old was fed "chiefly on bread and potatoes from the time it was weaned, and this is the history of hundreds of babies in the poorer districts of London." Some of the maternity centers founded in the decade before 1918 responded to the needs of ex-babies by providing meals for them, and the St. Pancras School permitted mothers to bring another child to its cheap dinners, interfering only if the toddler ate up too much of the mother's own food.[60]

There was little room in a mother's world for the experimental activity and high spirits of a one- or two-year-old. A helpless baby was the object of work, as it had to be fed, changed, and held; a competent five- or six-year-old could become a mother's junior partner in household survival. But a toddler cried out for adult time, patience, and playfulness, resources that only a few remarkable mothers could supply. The curiosity and mobility of ex-babies were also totally incompatible with the family's small quarters, its open grates, basins of hot water, and supplies for home industries.

During much of the day, toddlers were often confined to high chairs or strapped into ordinary seats, waiting in frustration for an older sibling to return from school and take them out. A Ranyard Bible seller in Bethnal Green in 1883 visited the two-room home of a badly paid cobbler's wife and saw the woman, her small children all around her, making matchboxes. The mother was assisted by the six-year-old, who glued pieces of emery on the sides of the boxes for striking. The four smaller children, twins aged three, a two-year-old, and a newborn infant all were sitting on the bed, because, the mother explained, if they played on the floor they would disturb the piles of half-made matchboxes that covered it. Confinement of this kind was painful for Dorothy, one of the Lambeth ex-babies in the Fabian Women's Group project. At age two, she was "seething with restlessness and activity" yet had to be confined for hours at a time to a high chair, in which she also slept during the day. "Her mother declared that it was not safe to have her up stairs on the bed or she would be out the window or down the stairs directly she woke." An old woman in a North London suburb in the early 1900s simultaneously minded half a dozen toddlers by keeping them tied into seats. (Clementina Black's only comment on this child care method, which she encountered often when doing her prewar survey of married women's work, was that it "must be bad for their backs"!) In a London case that came to the attention of a district nurse early in the twentieth century, a three-year-old actually appeared paralyzed as it sat or lay passively around while its mother did homework, only too glad to be left undisturbed. A professional masseuse whom the nurse called in had the child walking in six weeks simply because she played with the child, got it excited, and encouraged it to move.[61]

Not surprisingly, the anomalous position of the ex-baby captured the imagination of educators and settlement workers. In middle-class nurseries, the years from two to five were set aside for at least some physical experimentation and education. The Montessori methods that progressive child workers were exploring, as well as the Froebel-based training available by the turn of the century at a number of training colleges, recommended mildness, playfulness, and a willingness to foster each child's individual development.[62]

The slum toddlers could be deeply appealing to visitors. Though they declared the children inarticulate and lacking in imagination, youth workers in the 1900s were struck by how well behaved, considerate, and affectionate inner-London children were.[63] Though grubby and rough spoken, these children were, after all, mostly English, and to many of the Socialist-leaning women who worked among them, as Carolyn Steedman notes, they represented a new racial birth. Margaret McMillan (whose lyrical references to "the children of tomorrow" were not entirely typical) enjoyed the physical blossoming and increasing social skills of the young charges at the Deptford nursery school that she founded before the war. In a moving fictionalized sketch of an encounter between a Deptford boy and his harassed, overworked mother, McMillan described the boy's efforts to get his mother to share his excitement at seeing the stars for the first time after sleeping outdoors. McMillan's writing, like that of many early twentieth-century educators and social workers, betrayed a muted rivalry with the working-class mothers whose children they cared for. She observed proudly that Jack, a six-year-old pupil at her nursery, had become quite a problem for his mother, a "delicate" woman who worked at home sewing. Before he started attending the school, Jack used to sit "quiet as a mouse" near his mother all day winding spools or putting pins into a cushion. But after some months at the nursery, the boy had become so noisy and spirited that his mother threatened to remove him. "He used to sit still for hours but now he has that much life in him that I can't abide him in the room," was the mother's explanation.[64] The mothers demanded quiet and control, whereas the educators wanted to encourage imagination and self-expression.

The reformers opposed physical punishments and reproached mothers who hit young children. Nurse Honnor Morten's *Tales of the Children's Ward* describes a running conflict over discipline in the 1890s between the mothers and the nurses, with the mothers claiming that the nurses spoiled the children. When a little boy threw a boiled egg across the room, his mother shocked the indulgent nurses by shouting, "Leather 'em." Another mother, apparently "one of the bad characters of Woolwich," whose boy attended the Woolwich Mission Kindergarten in 1901, encouraged a teacher who was making a request of her inattentive son: "Go on, beat him: I should!" The boy obeyed without a beating, the teacher reported triumphantly.[65] The mothers were indeed often tough on small children. One boy remembered well into adulthood, but without bitterness, his mother's giving him sharp raps on his head if he squirmed while she did his hair into a topknot (a style worn by some boys still in petticoats and removed variously at ages three to five). Another boy, who at age three was not toilet trained, was often dunked into cold water when he wet himself. His mother, a West London laundry worker with five children and a rigid disciplinarian seemingly obsessed with respectability, was, at least in this case, operating only somewhat outside the community's norms for dealing with problems of toilet training.[66]

There was a powerful, though unorganized, pressure from the London mothers themselves for help with ex-babies, as, for example, the feeding programs demonstrate and as the Women's Freedom League Settlement in Nine Elms came to recognize when it established in 1916 a guest house for children from age two. In this account from the league's newspaper *The Vote,* the identification of a need is coupled with a subtle condemnation of the Nine Elms mothers:

> The Guest House for children was started by the Settlement to supply a want that seemed to have been hitherto overlooked—a home where mothers send what have been called the "dowager babies" to be cared for while they themselves were laid up during the advent of a new baby, or in hospital for an operation. The workers here watched the results in our street, where new babies arrive with alarming frequency, and their elders, often only just able to crawl, spend their time on the doorstep, eating frequent unvaried meals of bread-and-margarine, or taking adventurous walks in the gutter.[67]

It was the needs of mothers that led the school board for London to provide almost from the start what we would today call custodial care, in groups of up to sixty, for children as young as two and a half. Before such care was offered, the infants were being sent to school with the bigger siblings who were their traditional caretakers. Having created a rift in the household and child care systems of the poor, the board was pressured to repair it at least partially, and as early as 1872, the *Charity Organisation Reporter* recommended infant classes as the only thing that would enable compulsory education.[68] At its peak in 1901, about 43 percent of all the children aged three, four, and five in the country attended school. Children two through four (five was the age when compulsory schooling began) comprised a tenth of the London elementary school population by the time the school board disbanded in 1904. The LCC Education Committee, which took over the old, more progressive board's duties in 1904, discouraged the toddlers' school attendance, and so the numbers declined somewhat in the next decade.[69]

CHILDREN HELPING AND WORKING

Daughters and Sons "Helping Mother"

Major domestic contributions by children are universal in nonurban cultures, and carrying water and gathering firewood tend to be children's jobs in societies in which these tasks have to be done daily. Despite their modern urban setting, these mid-industrial London households generally required no less labor from their children.[70] The mothers' demands, though enormous, were specific and concrete and could be formulated in terms of tasks done, or pounds, shillings, and pence offered. "Working for" mother would earn her love and discharge the obligations incurred during the dependent years of babyhood.

Women expected their children to work hard. They were their mothers' errand goers, often the ones to fetch things that required a long wait in line, such as the penny-a-quart soup served by a local mission off Russia Lane, Bethnal Green, where Walter Southgate often waited in the 1890s with his empty jug, or the free disinfectant distributed in the workhouse yard for which Dorothy Scannell walked every Saturday down the Poplar High Street in the 1900s. The long lines during World War I outside bakers or grocers included many cold, tired children. Mothers sent their children shopping, usually to specific shops with discrete sums of money, partly to save time and partly to get better value from kindhearted merchants. A girl raised in a Camden Town family with thirteen children woke up extra early every morning in the 1900s to line up outside the baker's for the stale bread and cakes that he sold cheaply.[71] Many schoolchildren, especially boys, found or were given paid jobs delivering milk early in the morning, lathering chins in barber shops on Saturdays, assisting in shops, or hailing taxis for people in the street. For girls, the choices were fewer—cleaning steps, running errands, doing housework, or minding babies—the pay worse, and the employers even more commonly their mothers' neighbors and friends. However, "the severest work, the longest hours, and the hardest conditions" were probably found among those working with their parents doing home manufacturing, wrote Catherine Webb in 1904.[72]

For both boys and girls, having to "care for baby" had been a standard excuse for missing school since well before compulsory education and continued to be one. Indeed, though school attendance in general was higher in the early twentieth-century than in the nineteenth-century decades of compulsory education, it was always lower in poor districts. Mothers from the 1870s through the 1890s, whose written excuses for their children's absence from school were recorded by board schoolteacher Thomas Gautrey, sometimes kept their children home because they lacked boots or other clothing, but just as common was the mother's statement of her need for the child's domestic help. As one mother wrote, "Sir, Thomas stayed away while I went to the house spittle [hospital]."[73]

Despite the frequency of the threat, "Wait 'til your father comes home," discipline was primarily a female activity. Mothers' frustration and irritation as they tried to extract work and cooperation from children who wanted to play sometimes bristles through their children's autobiographical writings, which are otherwise suspiciously silent on maternal anger. Mothers were more likely than fathers to discipline with screams, slaps, and cuffs, as opposed to fathers' formal spankings. In North Street, Cambridge Heath, in the 1900s, Mrs. May, a large woman with a deep voice known for her colorful cursing and rages, yelled at her daughter Minnie when the girl made a fuss about going to school: "I'll skin yer alive, yer little bugger"; "Let me git 'old of her, an' I'll break every bloody bone in yer carcass"; "I'll wring yer bleedin' neck when yer comes 'ome, yer jes' wait." Another girl, at about the same time, whose Irish mother worked at a laundry near their home in Kensal Green, was often the object of her mother's wrath when she played in the street rather than doing her household chores. "Me mum used to drag me in and make me do it. . . . She'd swear like blooming hell at me. Call me all the blackheaded old cows that ever!" One woman, who in the early 1890s insisted on hitting her children often, openly claimed this right when her husband protested: "Mind your own business. "I'll bring 'em up in my way."[74]

In many households, mothers made a point of their husbands' authority—to use Max Weber's term for the form of power that is considered fully legitimate—by serving up naughty children for sterner paternal punishments. A year or two before World War I, a Hackney mother acted as the disciplinarian but talked as if that role were her husband's. She often lost her temper with her five children. When a daughter's response to a request was too slow, she threw a potato at the offending child (and missed); when her children failed to comb their hair or wash their faces for school, she boxed their ears. It was she who (in Chapter 2) beat the daughter who had lost the last shilling of housekeeping money. Yet the mother pretended that her husband was the disciplinarian of the family, often threatening the children with "You wait till your father comes home." Though he actually seldom touched them, his children were afraid of him. It is true, as Alexander Paterson wrote and many working-class autobiographers agreed, that fathers were the ones "to administer punishment in its most severe forms," so that "the child is brought up to fear the parent he sees so little."[75] But the task of daily discipline nonetheless belonged to mothers.

The Hackney mother, with her nasty temper and quickness to resort to boxing ears and throwing objects, was, however, well within community standards of decent treatment of children. This is evident if we compare her with a mother whose violence was totally unacceptable to her neighbors. Louisa Murphy, abandoned by her husband with two school-aged children, was criminally cruel to both of them over a period of months in 1876. The dreadful screams (as one neighbor put it) of her little girl and boy as she burned or beat them could be heard throughout the house in Queen Street, St. Pancras, and no fewer than five neighbors, two of them men, testified in just one of the two Central Criminal Court cases against Murphy that they had gone up to her room repeatedly to remonstrate with her. Mary Boyd had threatened Murphy, for instance, that "if she did it again I would pull her head off." William Lovell, another neighbor, warned Murphy that this treatment would surely kill the children and that if it did he would gladly testify against her. A third neighbor took the badly injured children away from their mother to the police station; they eventually received medical treatment and recovered.[76]

Schoolchildren were mothers' junior partners in organizing household survival. They responded to coercion, but also to the pleasure of being grown-up enough to help. Many schoolchildren took on their mothers' economic worries and could be found making independent efforts to get goods or cash. As a schoolgirl in the early 1900s, Lilian Westall often confronted her father in the pub, in the image of the famous temperance song, begging him to come home and stop spending the household cash. Henry John Begg's formulation of his boyhood dream "to help" might stand for many others: "That was my one prayer, if I could only find some money or get hold of some money to help my mother. Yes. I used to feel so very sorry for poor old mum you know. Perhaps I'd see her sitting there crying, you know, well, don't know what her trouble was you know." Jim Bushnell, to take another example, was the son of a Canning Town gasworker who earned extra money by hailing taxis or carrying packages for prosperous people in the street. One of the boy's clients accidently dropped a half-sovereign, and after she disappeared, he picked it up, "whipped it in me pocket quick, and run. . . . I thought of me mother. That'll do my mother a wonderful good turn that will."[77]

The pressure was greatest on eldest children. An eleven-year-old Stepney girl, her "father's darling," told a visiting Bible seller in the spring of 1883: "I am sorry for mother; she does have to work so hard. I wish I could work for her, but I don't think it will be for a year or two yet." Oldest children, according to Stephen Humphries, were more likely to be caught thieving, as the pressure to "help" was heaviest on them. Studies in the 1920s demonstrated that thirteen-year-olds, boys not quite old enough for jobs, committed more property crimes than did boys of any other age.[78]

A part of "helping" was to make few demands on mothers. Some women simply refused to cope with their children's problems. Rose Albert, who grew up near the Elephant in the 1900s, learned that her mother, who had been abandoned and robbed by her husband [Rose's father] in about 1910, had little sympathy to give Rose: "I don't want to hear your troubles, you know . . . you sort it out between yourselves." More children censured themselves. Frank Steel, describing a North London childhood in the 1860s and 1870s, wrote that as the family slipped into poverty and food became scarce, the children at first cried for food; later they displayed a "mute endurance" for which their mother, years later, told them she was very grateful: "You were *kings* of boys!" she told her sons, "Otherwise I never *could* have gone through those times." In the 1900s, journalist Olive Christian Malvery, investigating children in East London at work in sweated home industry, witnessed an example of children's forbearance in the home of a waistcoat maker with five young children. When the children, home from school for the dinner hour, asked their mother if they could have some bread, "Mrs. Jennings made no reply, and the children did not press the question."[79]

Early twentieth-century children probably had easier lives than did their peers in the 1870s and 1880s. The older people in settlement worker Anna Martin's district, Rotherhithe, spoke bitterly to her in the 1900s and 1910s about the constant labor of their childhoods. Marie Kelly Welsh, growing up in the grimmest East London poverty in the 1900s and 1910s, listened to stories of her grandfather's far harder Bethnal Green childhood, when after-school play was always forbidden, for at four o'clock he immediately had to get to work with the rest of his family, stitching the shiny peaked caps that were his family's livelihood. The school-leaving age—only ten in London in 1871 when compulsory education began there—was gradually raised to fourteen by the turn of the century. Children in the 1870s and 1880s thus took on full-time jobs several years earlier than their own children would have to. Indeed, many middle-class youth workers saw compulsory schooling mainly as a way of preventing parents from putting their children to work. The 1889 Prevention of Cruelty to Children Act prohibited children's night street selling, and the LCC, especially in the early twentieth century, made more and more jobs off limits to youngsters. Edith Hogg's Women's Industrial Council survey in the late 1890s found, rather dubiously, that only about 5 percent of London's board school pupils had paid jobs like street selling, delivering milk or newspapers, or doing home piecework such as artificial-flower making, beading, or chair caning. Yet at the turn of the century (the 1901 census was the first to measure work done at home) there were probably well over 100,000 homeworkers in London, more than half of them women. Many of those with children got them involved in their work, and the controversies over sweating in the 1900s uncovered thousands of them. The need to help mother thus continued to dominate the lives of cockney children into the twentieth century. For the majority it was errands and other forms of "mother's work"; for the poorest it was the drudgery of home manufacturing.[80]

Throughout the years from 1870 to World War I, boys as well as girls lived in the world of their mothers. Sons were intimately involved with child care, cooking, cleaning, laundering, shopping, and even nursing the sick. Middle-class observers were always moved as well as surprised by the nurturing behavior of rough little boys toward their little siblings, as the boys wiped noses, passed the little ones extra food, or insisted on remaining with the younger ones on school and camp outings. The autobiographical and oral history literature is studded with the memories of today's old men of the intricacies of diapering a baby, getting a wash white, or making a tasty stew for under sixpence.[81]

The movement of boys out of the hands of women is problematic in any sex-polarized culture. Although cockneys are famous for their comfortable adult mother–daughter relationships (though this is not such a tidy story, either), mother–son ties and the issues they raised about gender and intimacy were even more problematic. In the United States, researchers like Nancy Chodorow have argued that the process of creating men for whom it is natural to dominate women takes place gradually, when mothers push their sons in early childhood away from female behavior and from themselves. Working-class London mothers in earlier generations, however, especially in inner-city worker households, kept each of their sons close to them for almost two decades. Thus the eventual separation began rather late. It was marked externally in adolescence, first by the boy's wearing of long trousers and then by the declining proportion of his pay the young man offered to his mother as he moved through his late teens, his greater expectation of services from his mother, and his increased leisure hours spent with his peers.[82]

Many cultures have structured puberty rites, men's houses, and seclusion rituals to mark the transition from son to husband or potential husband, from child to man. The London equivalents were provided by mass culture and public and private family-shaping agencies. The semicommercial male world of street betting on horses or soccer that was developing in the 1880s was one for which boys prepared through years of playing betting games like "tippy-cat" and "pitch and toss." Board schools, too, from the late 1870s, self-consciously began to teach working-class boys "manliness," dropping, for example, needlework for boys from the curriculum and stressing woodworking and math. As Alexander Paterson commented in his 1911 study of life in South London, "The primary object of a school is not to convey knowledge or to teach a trade, but to make boys into men. . . . It is made more difficult by the absence of cooperation in the home. . . . With many boys every hour at home is a step back." School military drill and team sports were designed to link boys into a national male culture. Boys' brigades and boys' clubs in the 1880s and later, in the 1900s, boy scout troops aimed at the same thing.[83] Boys' magazines and comics, filled with imperial adventure and sports stories, began to proliferate during the late Victorian and Edwardian years: *Boys' Own Paper, The Boy's Friend, Magnet,*

Gem, and the comic magazines known as "penny bloods." Boys who could not afford to buy them new borrowed their favored reading, inherited old ones from cousins or neighbors, or bought them cheaply from street stalls.[84]

Mothers generally expected more of their daughters than of their sons. Or perhaps we could say that girls' tasks, like those of their mothers, were never finished. And still more than their brothers, girls identified with their mothers' worries. When Mollie, age twelve and the eldest of eight children, was ill with pneumonia in the winter of 1906, she told her nurse "I must not die; mother couldn't spare me!" When Clara Grant asked two little girls what they thought they would like to do when they got to heaven, their answers were good descriptions of their lives: " 'Run errands for God,' said one. 'Carry pails to wash up the floor,' said the other." Girls' work for their mothers restricted their freedom to play, limited their access to girls' clubs, Band of Hope meetings, and other organized evening activities; and, as Anna Davin has demonstrated, kept them out of school more often than it did their brothers.[85] Because schoolgirls earned less cash than boys did, it was harder and slower for them to "pay back" their mothers. The unlimited, unending work of their mothers was their fate also as daughters.

Practical-minded, careworn, vigilant girls as young as ten or eleven—known throughout London (and New York as well) as "little mothers"—were a common sight in working-class areas as they supervised one or more smaller children. May Craske, a Central London settlement worker, described in 1908 "the little girl, aged from nine to fourteen, who is the drudge of the family. She nurses the baby, she helps with the washing and charing, she runs the errands; her work, poor mite, is never done."[86] At a gigantic hall on Marshalsea Road in the Borough, Charles Morley watched in the late 1890s as dozens of wily "little mothers" used the same energy to get food for their "babies" as they had witnessed in their own mothers. Their small charges in tow, the bigger girls persuaded the janitors to let them in for the last school dinner sitting of the day. "They look at the authorities—and between the mouthfuls fill the spoon with gravy and pour it into the baby's mouth." Violet Harris, born in 1900, who had lived in Vauxhall as a girl, told historian Mary Chamberlain with much bitterness about her childhood as a little mother: "I can say, really, dear, I never had much of a childhood. . . . I was always at their beck and call, lugging them out. We had to up the park all day long when we had our holidays, so my mother could get on with the washing. . . . Used to be up there about nine o'clock, send us home about six at night."[87]

On the children's side, resentment and hostility toward mothers mingled with gratitude and affection. Some boys and girls, at least as they confessed much later, did not love cold, strict mothers, however much

This stylized young mother selling what looks like watercress on an East London street appeared as an illustration in *London: A Pilgrimage,* the 1872 collaborative work by French graphic artist Gustave Doré and *Daily News* journalist Blanchard Jerrold. (Reprint, New York: Dover Books, 1970.)

Realist painter Frank Holl's "Doubtful Hope" (1875) is one of his many extraordinary portrayals of desperate and pathetic mothers. The woman here, at the pharmacist's, is urgently hoping that his abortifacient mixture will be effective. (Courtesy of The FORBES Magazine Collection, New York.)

John Galt, a member of the London City Mission, photographed scenes of neighborhood and work life mostly of Bethnal Green in the 1880s and 1890s. This one, titled "Backyard Blacksmith," like many of them, is also a family portrait. It is likely that the woman next to the blacksmith is younger than she looks; the young woman in the background is probably the daughter of the household, holding its youngest baby. (Courtesy Galt Collection, Photography Library, the Museum of London.)

"Sunlight"

(above) Pears' Soap had been on the market since the early nineteenth century, though it was not mass produced until 1862. It was known for its innovative publicity schemes and advertising. Here the housewife is being invited to clean up these cute though grubby little boys. (John Johnson Collection, Bodleian Library, Oxford.)

(above, left) Detail from Paul Martin, "Market Stalls in the New Cut, New Laid Eggs, 1894." Shoppers at one of London's largest street markets, just east of Waterloo Station, photographed by Paul Martin, pioneer of unposed everyday London sights. (Courtesy of the Gernsheim Collection, Harry Ransom Humanities Research Center, the University of Texas at Austin.)

(below, left) Sunlight Soap, manufactured by William H. Lever beginning in 1885, was one of the most popular laundry soaps in Britain ten years later. In this advertisement, the clean and pretty baby is being sold with the soap. (John Johnson Collection, Bodleian Library, Oxford.)

"Commercial Street 1907" conveys the intensity of street life in East London and its fast pace, even at a point when motorized vehicles were exceptionally rare. (Courtesy of the Greater London Records Office.)

"Children Playing, c. 1910," a much-reproduced photograph from the Greater London Photograph Library, conveys a flavor of children's street life. The big girl in the foreground appears to have a supervisory role over the smaller children. (Courtesy of the Greater London Records Office.)

"The Queue." This expressive 1918 print of people waiting to buy scarce provisions in the last months of World War I, is by C. R. W. Nevinson, son of social explorer Margaret Wynne Nevinson and journalist Henry Nevinson. At first an ambulence driver, C. R. W. Nevinson was eventually appointed an official war artist, turning out many works in this semi-cubist style. (From Geoffrey Holme, ed., *Londoners Then and Now as Pictured by Their Contemporaries* [London: "The Studio," 1920]. The original of this picture could not be located.)

they knew they owed them.[88] But whereas fathers were fair game, anger and resentment at mothers was seldom openly expressed. Even Rebecca Jarrett, the recently converted Salvationist who served as an intermediary in Stead's famous 1885 white slavery "Maiden Tribute" case, whose mother had prostituted her as a young teenager for drinking money, refused to condemn her as a "bad Mother"; rather, she blamed her father for abandoning his wife. Jarrett avenged herself by later entrapping another woman who was doing the same with her daughter, for this anger often had to be redirected. Folklorists like Peter and Iona Opie have discovered the hostility toward adults, especially mothers, threaded through children's games and chants. "One of the things that play is about, intermingled with all the others, is conflict with the adult world," according to Colin Ward. Making noise and banging on doors so as to annoy adults, as in the ubiquitous prank/game "knocking on ginger," were popular features of children's games. Boys played "Upsetting Mother's Gravy" and "Pulling Up Father's Rhubarb" and also "Ducking Mummy," in which two little boys tried to hit a stone (mummy) with their pebbles. More girls' games involved domestic themes, such as "Turning Mother's Wringer," "Looking for Mother's Thimble," and "Follow Your Mother to Market," whereas other games labeled the figure who was "it" the mother. "Mother May I Go Out" requires hostile, cheeky responses to the mother figure who is "it." Or consider this girls' rope-skipping rhyme, with its cheerful hatred:

> Cold meat, mutton chops,
> Tell me when your mother drops.
> I'll be there to pick up her—
> cold meat, mutton chops.[89]

Collective Care of Children

Not only parents but also neighborhoods set detailed standards for maternal and juvenile conduct. In an East London model dwelling, a girl's teasing and harassing of other children were the subjects of much unfavorable comment in the building's daily gossip. On a poor street in Deptford in the 1880s, neighbors circulated rumors that a woman had allowed several of her children to be buried by the parish, talk that cut the woman to the quick.[90] Some pressure took more public forms, however, as when in the late 1860s a woman accused of killing an infant for whom she had been caring was mobbed outside the courtroom by an angry crowd of neighborhood women or when a large group of Mrs. Lane's friends from Olga Street, Bethnal Green, packed the courtroom at the Worship Street trial of Poplar clergyman James Mellor Evans for abducting her fifteen-year-old daughter Jane. The "settled notions," as one London magistrate put it, that so many London women held of their prerogatives and rights in relation to their husbands had their counterparts in collectively stated and enforced standards of child care.[91]

Neighbors and neighborhoods also functioned as auxiliary parents whose care demonstrated the youngsters' community affiliation. Adults in nearby dwellings fed and treated children, as did the old couple who regularly supplied one girl with the only farthings she had to buy herself sweets. A less frivolous woman served bread pudding to the many hungry children of a large household nearby. The three young children of Annie Higgs, a widow who was found dead of starvation in Long Street, Shoreditch, in the summer of 1905, had been kept alive for many weeks with offerings from the surrounding households. A Rotherhithe woman just before World War I was incredulous at the possibility that a child could starve to death in her own district, though it was one of the poorest in the metropolis. She was sure that "someone would have certainly given it something" to eat. A Poplar neighbor bandaged Dorothy Scannell's cut thumb and took her to a hospital, and the ragged trousers of a boy in Bromley were patched up by a neighbor.[92] NSPCC reports of deserted or neglected children almost invariably referred to neighbors who had fed and nominally cared for the children for days or even weeks.

Along with adult kin, neighbors were available to children as protectors against angry or unfair parents or as supplements to parents as teachers of the ways of adult life. An East London girl's unease with her mother was strengthened by her friendship with a more refined neighbor. Elizabeth Flint's autobiography describing her childhood at 3 "Waterloo Row" near Commercial Road, Aldgate, at the beginning of the twentieth century tells the story of a girl vaguely uncomfortable with but also very attached to her mother's casual housekeeping and breezy way of making do with the proceeds of her husband's work as a casual porter at the Spitalfields market. Nearby, Mrs. Polly Hackett, whose husband had died at sea, lived impeccably on her widow's pension and enjoyed the companionship of the sweet-tempered daughter of her frowzy neighbors. She taught the girl to read and write before she started school, showed her how a cup of tea was properly drunk, and displayed the fine points of dusting furniture. "Only careless housewives forget [to dust] the legs of things," she often said, an innocent enough comment that set off a complex chain of ideas in Mrs. Hackett's little guest, who was discovering a world beyond the one that her mother had defined for her.

> My throat would fill with a lump at this point, but I would say nothing.
> If I had spoken it would have been to say that Mum never dusted ours,
> and I must never say that.

So I knew for a fact now that Mum had faults. She did not dust chair legs, and she could cuss your ears and shout if she felt in the mood.[93]

As she became more aware of what her own mother stood for, Elizabeth's relationship with her lost its transparency. She was tempted, for instance, to tell her mother about the many issues involved in proper dusting, "but something told me that I had better not. Like as not it would only have earned me a cuffing." Later, with the support and help of Mrs. Hackett, Flint got a scholarship and remained in school through age fifteen. Her neighborhood had supplied Elizabeth Flint with an alternative mother, just as Southwark provided Kathleen Woodward with Jessica Mourn, also a widow, the sweet and affectionate counterpart to her own embittered mother described in *Jipping Street,* her fictionalized autobiography.[94]

Landlords, and especially landladies, as Leonore Davidoff has shown, in exercising general superintendence over their tenants, kept a casual eye out for children and old people living in the house.[95] A London landlady who figured in an Old Bailey case in the 1870s had been feeding her destitute tenants' children for six or seven weeks. In his case notes from the 1900s on a young deserted wife with three preschool children, the Hackney Union relieving officer observed that without the landlady's kindness, Mrs. T. would have been unable to manage. "Her landlady seems to have been a mother to her, and to have helped her all through" her many trials with sick children, unemployment, and the workhouse.[96]

Mrs. Potter, George Acorn's landlady during his Bethnal Green childhood, was an important minor character in his life. Her placid and cheerful marriage with Mr. Potter, which Acorn described with irony when he published his autobiography in 1911, was a counterweight to the daily surliness and violence of his own parents' life, and many times the Potters managed to create temporary peace in the Acorn household. Among Acorn's bitter tales of childhood is an incident in which his mother commanded him to carry a heavy bottle of water three times in fast succession from a downstairs tap up the narrow and winding stairs. On the third trip the small boy blacked out and fell down the steps, breaking the bottle and landing in a heap in the hallway below. Rather than offering sympathy and concern, his mother whipped him severely for breaking the bottle. Mrs. Potter was available, at least, to listen sympathetically to the child's bitter complaints, though she refused to take his side in the dispute. Acorn's relationship with his landlady was followed by later childhood alliances with teachers and settlement workers.[97]

As auxiliary parents, neighbors supervised and disciplined the children who came into their line of vision. A child growing up near Millwall

Basin was aware that should she stray too far from home, unseen women would surely report her movements to her mother. A Stepney woman stopped a fight between a local girl and boy, scolding the latter: "Don't you know it is wrong to hit a little girl?"[98] Accompanying this protection, however, were widespread rights to punish children. These rights were shared not only by policemen and school personnel but also by such ordinary residents as housewives at their wit's end with games of "knocking down ginger." One schoolboy reported in an essay on "What I Did Last Saturday" in 1905 that after one round of this game—the fun of which was in fact based on disturbing neighbors by manipulating their door knockers with a string—"one of the boys got court by one of the women and got a good hiding off of her."[99]

The right of nonparents to strike children was not agreed upon and quarrels over this issue figured prominently in the enormous amount of women's neighborhood conflict that came to the attention of the courts. One Tower Bridge magistrate, reviewing his long career in the 1920s, complained that "many more than half of the total applications for summonses . . . are made by women against other women, and arise out of idiotic quarrels about idiotic trifles." The courts had been heavily used, he was sure, as a forum in which a woman could "pour forth in public a stream of violent abuse of her next-door neighbour." Thus the Stepney woman just mentioned who stopped two children from fighting ended up at Arbour Square, the home of the Thames Police Court. The boy whom she admonished called his mother, father, and other relatives, and a huge row ensued that the magistrate made no real effort to disentangle.[100] A child growing up in Tottenham in the 1890s and 1900s reported both that the neighbors whipped one another's children and that his own mother and some of her friends were outraged at that practice: "I'm the one that does the hitting of my child, you leave my child alone." In the early 1950s, when James H. Robb conducted his community study of Bethnal Green, the ambiguity that had led to such bad feeling was gone, and punishing a neighbor's child was, he thought, "very definitely against local custom."[101]

Wage-earning Children

Children who left school to become wage earners reached a new milestone: They had become their mothers' partners and breadwinners. All or most of the new earner's cash, according to "some unwritten law," as Alexander Paterson wrote, ended up in their mothers' hands. As we have seen, mothers as often as fathers by the late Victorian years found their children—even sons—their first position in the work force. The unskilled jobs available to their sons as errand boys or helpers in shops (both dead-end jobs providing no skills or stake in an adult trade) could now be found just as easily through mothers' neighborhood networks as through fathers' job contacts. The pleasure and relief of mothers when their first child found a full-time job was proclaimed in many ways. Women fought with the London school board over the right to install children as earners. Also, the many budget studies carried out around the turn of the twentieth century show that women in households in which teenagers had begun to earn wages experienced their first leisure and comfort (such as a glass of beer at a pub, better food for the whole family, a larger apartment, new furniture, or freedom from taking in extra laundry work) since the earliest years of their marriage.[102] Mothers mourned dead teenaged wage earners more demonstratively than they mourned their babies, as Chapter 6 shows, and their "lamentation for the wage-earning children" was a striking reminder to middle-class social workers of the difference between the way the poor loved and the way they did.[103]

Having children at work did entail extra domestic responsibilities for the mother, especially in regard to providing better food and more space for the wage earners. As a mother of employed teenagers told Anna Martin, "They expect such a lot for the money they give you, and a mother doesn't like to fall short." A waistcoat maker told Clementina Black in about 1908 that she probably spent on his food most of the 10 shillings her twenty-three-year-old son gave her. David Nasaw, in *Children of the City,* his study of the American working children who were the peers of these young Londoners, emphasized the compromises that parents made to keep their working children, even rather young ones, living at home and contributing wages.[104] The London mothers' control appears firmer than this, but older children, especially men in their late teens and twenties, gradually kept more and more of their income for themselves. Indeed, at some point, given their superior "breadwinner" food, their contributions to their mother's household income would level off, and so at marriage their income was not so badly missed.

The financial obligations of the working child were usually clearly spelled out. A Deptford mother, who had worked extraordinarily hard over a period of years to equip her teenage daughters to go into service, confidently expected specific contributions from them in return. She told Ellen Chase, her rent collector: "I gave all the girls except Hannah just a half fit-out, and they gave me their wages until they were seventeen; after that they kept their money and finished out their sets of clothes. Deb is nearly through this now."[105] Or look at the shorter-term exchange carried out daily in the Old Nichol in the late 1880s: At 12, Half Nichol Street, according to notes kept by the Rev. Arthor O. Jay on his parishioners, a sixteen-year-old daughter working full time for only 4s. 6d. per week had a carefully worked-out arrangement with her mother.

For each of the five weekdays, the mother (who received the girl's whole wage weekly) returned fourpence to the girl for her dinners. The daughter also got bread and butter for lunch and tea and, it was also specified, had her breakfasts and suppers at home.[106]

Boys in their early teens similarly exchanged set sums with their mothers. When George Acorn got a factory job as a shop boy in the 1880s, he earned a weekly wage of 6 shillings. A young teenager at the time, probably about thirteen, he gave his mother all but sixpence of the total. E. Robinson, who had spent his childhood watching his father struggle in his failing trade as a hansom cab driver, got his first job in about 1904 working for an artificial-limb maker in South London. The pay was 8 shillings per week, and his arrangement was the traditional one: "My mother was very pleased about this and allowed me 3d. pocket money per week." Soon afterward, when he got a half-crown tip for the peculiar errand of delivering an artificial leg to a Chinese restaurant owner, he was "elated" but did not cheat: he kept only sixpence for himself and gave his mother the rest of his windfall.[107]

Stories about helping mother appear without fail in working-class life histories of all kinds. Told in the published autobiographies of boys who rose from working-class origins to prominent positions in politics or the labor movement, they function as symbolic declarations of continuing class allegiance. The 1889 dock strike leader and later member of Parliament Will Crooks, describing his childhood in the 1850s and 1860s in Poplar, recounted to his official biographer George Haw in 1911 his memory of waking up at night to see his mother crying "through wondering where the next meal is coming from." The boy whispered to himself: "Wait till I'm a man! Won't I work for my mother when I'm a man!" Indeed, when at age thirteen he earned his first half-sovereign, he came running home with it: "Mother, mother, I've earned half a sovereign, and all of it myself, and it's yours, all yours, every bit yours!" The helping motif appears repeatedly in other kinds of autobiographical literature, in pieces composed with the support of local social history programs and in autobiographies produced in many other ways. It is clearly a part of the vocabulary of these generations. The description of a Pentonville girl, born in 1896, and collected by University of Essex interviewers in the 1970s, is similar to Crooks's, yet she was the sixth child, clearly not the first to take a paid job, and had, unlike Crooks, lived life in obscurity. After working for a few shillings as a learner in a garment factory for six months, she finally graduated to better earnings: "Oh—the first—the first time I earned ten bob. Oh I had a little thin—ten shilling piece, I wasn't half pleased when I brought it home to my mum. She gave me sixpence out of it."[108]

Things could certainly go wrong with the bargain between mother and child. Mother could fail child, or child could fail mother. Daughters

as well as sons "cheated" their mothers in small ways, by not "declar-
ing" tips and overtime pay, for instance. But such small naughty acts
did not fundamentally challenge the mother's right to the child's earnings. To take a less common example of a total rupture, however, the
Ranyard nurses in the Kennington district in 1878 met a heartbroken
woman whose sixteen-year-old daughter was exceptionally disobedient.
The girl, confined for three months in a lock hospital as a suspected
prostitute, was released and stayed out all night with her first freedom.
When the mother remonstrated with her, her husband defended the girl
and "said she should do as she liked." The girl stole things from her
mother to pawn, and when the latter complained, the daughter, encouraged by her father, actually slapped her face. In another failed mother–
daughter relationship, Daisy Cordell was a working teenager in the 1890s
living in "The Island," a pocket of poverty in comfortable Clapton,
when her widowed mother announced her plans to remarry. "What, to
that?" Daisy rudely asked. Disgusted at the match, Daisy announced
that she was moving out and taking her wages with her. In an attempt
to prevent what to her was a disastrous loss, the mother stripped her
daughter's room of all her furniture and possessions, but Daisy turned
to her fiancé and his family, who helped her equip the new room in
which she was to live for three years.[109]

Teenaged sons could be considerably harder to keep within the maternal fold than daughters were, though the problem appears to have
been no worse in 1914 than it was in the 1870s. The "discovery" of
adolescence in the decade before 1914 was accompanied by a panic over
juvenile delinquency, the establishment of a juvenile justice system, and
the social work campaign to place working-class children in jobs with
good future earnings. As John Gillis has argued, using materials from
Oxford, although males in their teens were probably better behaved in
public, less rowdy, and less violent at the end of the nineteenth century
than a generation earlier, their behavior was more closely scrutinized by
vigilance groups and youth workers; courts were more willing to pros-
ecute for very minor thefts; and there was pressure on magistrates to
order more whippings for young offenders. It would be wrong, however, to see this conjuncture simply as the imposition of middle-class
ideas about adolescence on a passive working-class public. Throughout
the two-generation period ending with World War I, despite shifts in
official policy and rhetoric, mothers and fathers whose sons were errant
did what they could both to protect the children and to get them to help
their families. They prosecuted in the police courts, trying to use the
judicial system to get bad children put away. Magistrates in the 1860s
and 1870s were in fact so deluged with requests from parents to have
wayward boys sent to reformatories that they retaliated by charging the
parents a weekly maintenance fee for their children. In the 1910s, Ann

Jasper, seeing that her none-too-bright eldest son Bert had taken to burglary in the years before World War I, got him placed on an industrial training ship. At about the same time, a mother in North London, tired of her sons' rough pranks, decided to let them spend the night in jail when they were arrested for gambling in the street. During the war, women even used the meddlesome Women Police Volunteers to help round up their sons (and daughters).[110]

School Stories

The mothers had the power, generally speaking, to command most of their children's time and labor until their late teens or even longer, and they expected teenagers to make great sacrifices of their own pleasures and ambitions to the household's requirements. The dramatic failures ended up with social agencies and the judicial system. The more subtle conflicts were expressed especially eloquently when children did well in school and were encouraged by teachers to remain past the legal school-leaving age or to switch to secondary schools. The educators viewed their pupils as individuals rather than as family members and encouraged the children (or at least those whom they singled out as gifted) to make something of themselves. The "school stories" of successful pupils who had to leave, stories retained into adulthood, carry a variety of meanings: that one was clever and promising, that a chance in life was lost, and, finally, that the comfortable and reassuring power of mothers has a harsh edge. These school stories, embedded in countless autobiographies and oral histories, have nothing in common with the tales of upper-class boarding-school pranks that usually bear this label. They all are moments in which working-class children were schooled to disappointment, and it was usually the mother who, mediating between the child and its poverty, restricted her children. The small child might be denied the country holiday, the new dress, or the Christmas presents or might be refused time for reading or play. For young teenagers, school stories are parallel, if starker, narratives. Although they present good cases for anger and rebellion, they also convey the hopelessness of defying mothers.

Most of these stories date from the twentieth century. Although the higher-grade schools run by the London school board (and boards throughout the country) multiplied rapidly during the 1890s, after 1902 there was still greater expansion in secondary school provision in Britain. By 1907, the number of secondary pupils had more than doubled (to sixty-six thousand for the whole country), and the "free place" system introduced by the Liberals that year, providing financial incentives for secondary schools that reserved places for graduates of public elementary schools, encouraged more schools to admit working-class young people. Yet it was mostly the lower-middle-class children who benefited from these reforms. Among boys born between 1910 and 1929, 40 percent of the middle-class, but only 10 percent of the working-class boys, reached secondary school. High proportions of the working-class children selected for grammer schools refused the places they were offered, a commentator in 1926 revealed.[111] Thus there are many, many school stories, and they make particularly poignant statements about the psychic injuries of poverty as mediated by mothers.

Each story is a variation on the theme of school versus family and especially mother, with the conflict just beneath the verbal surface. A socialist plumber's daughter, an East London girl born in 1897 and pressured by her father to make something of her brilliance in school, found "rather funnily the very week I was going to sit the scholarship I was taken ill, and whether it was nerves or what it was I don't know . . . so of course I never sat for it." Marie Kelly Welsh described a 1918 confrontation with her mother at their home in Walthamstow, not over education, but over the chance to emigrate to America with an older sister. "Mother still wouldn't let me go because now I was just getting to the age when I could earn some cash. You can understand it really."[112]

The household rows created by an older daughter's secondary schooling convinced a Hoxton mother that her other children, all clever scholars, should get out of school as quickly as possible. The older girl, the only scholarship student at Bishopsgate School in Spitalfields, could find no place at home to do her lessons and was in a state of constant worry over it. "She used to end up in tears nine times out of ten," said a younger sister interviewed as an old woman in 1974. So the mother refused to let the next daughter even try for the scholarship, and she harassed the eldest girl until she, too, left at fourteen. Another brother on a trade school scholarship left at thirteen to get a job. "Mother wanted us to leave school as soon as we could really," the sister mildly told the interviewer.[113]

The "school story" of another East London woman, born in 1905 near London Fields in Dalston, is far harsher. The household lived in the direst poverty on the wages of the father, an ailing casual dock laborer, and on whatever work the mother could get. Evictions and semi-starvation defined Mrs. Benjamin's childhood. Here is her bitter account of her thwarted attempt to continue at school:

> In 1916 [when she could have been eleven] I went in for a scholarship and I won a scholarship to the Bluecoat School, and my parents never told me. One day the teacher told me I'd won. She said "only rich children can go

to the school where you've got a place, you're very lucky; but you're very unlucky to have the mother that you've got, because she won't say yes or sign her name."

The girl would have received a grant, and an aunt had promised to help pay for her books. As she learned more about the school, near Brighton, and the career as a schoolteacher that it promised her, the prospect looked more and more attractive. Supported by her teacher, the girl appealed to her mother to let her go to the Bluecoat School, but the mother's cold response was: "You take your chances like the others." From this position there was no appeal: "There was nothing else that I could do."[114]

For Elizabeth Flint, the Aldgate-born girl who later published her autobiography, *Hot Bread and Chips,* school occupied a treasured retreat from the rough and blowzy world that radiated from her mother's warm kitchen. Mrs. Hackett, the neighbor, or sometimes Flint's gentle father shared the girl's enthusiasm for her school lessons: "Long ago I'd learnt not to talk to mum about school. 'Lot of rubbish they tell you there,' she said." Only when she was in the most indulgent of moods did the mother listen to the daughter's school chatter. As a serious scholar, Elizabeth Flint was always fighting for space and quiet in which to do her lessons, but when she made any open demands, her mother would threaten to remove her from school entirely. Very reluctantly—because the older children were already earning and the father was doing well, Flint's mother let her daughter compete for a scholarship that would extend her education by a few years. The girl begged her mother to join the audience at the new school's first speech day, and sitting at the front, Elizabeth scanned the room eagerly for signs of her. She desolately returned home to find her mother still there, dressed in her Sunday clothes. "It was them other mothers, Liz, that's what. Why, some of them came in cabs, they did, right up to the door. I couldn't go in with them I couldn't." As an adult, Flint commented on this childhood incident: "The school was to be forever between her and me—the school and what I learned there. It was a long, long time before I could put it into words."[115]

School stories are especially compact ways of expressing the complexity of working-class family feeling as experienced, in their turn, by elder children: the pull of love for mother or of gratitude, from which followed the need to help and provide for her; the lure, for a lucky few, of other worlds, resources and pleasures—lonely and risky. Family life exacted its price not only in endless work and in physical want but also in the suppression of the self. To sentimentalize the Victorian values of the "close-knit" and "sacrificing" families of the past or (as Carolyn

Steedman has warned) to posit "poverty" as their only significant influence trivializes the intense and contradictory emotional and material bonds connecting mothers, fathers, and children in the generations we are describing as they negotiated the scarce resources and limited choices offered by London poverty.

CHAPTER 6

"She Fought for Me like a Tigress"
Sickness and Health

A child's illness, no matter how minor, was a cause of dread and worry. An innocent-seeming cold might mark the first stage of a lethal case of bronchitis or pneumonia, or a baby's poor appetite might indicate the onset of the deadly summer diarrhea that carried off so many babies in the years we are describing.[1] After the vital topics of food and money, the women talked most about illnesses, healers, and remedies. As guardians of children's bodies, mothers in working-class London drew for advice and help on an enormous range of very different, and often mutually hostile, resources and cures. They looked to such neighborhood figures as pharmacists and spiritualists, other mothers, and also local medical doctors and nurses and a rapidly expanding network of public and private medical institutions as the allopathic framework gradually began to dominate the other theories of disease.[2] This chapter considers health care both as an issue in the social history of medicine and as a form of nurture, an aspect of maternal duty and love.

Maternal thinking about children's health revolved around the possibility of a child's maiming or death. The heroic mothers who figure in family histories and contemporary accounts, watching night after night over feverish children ill with typhoid, whooping cough, or scarlet fever, were battling against death itself. Conditions that brought children only discomfort, such as itching or chronic pain, made little claim for this sort of effort. By ignoring such symptoms themselves, parents taught their children to do the same. Late Victorian and Edwardian medical workers were astonished at the success of an entire culture in not seeing such problems as perpetually running noses, decayed teeth, squinty eyes, infected sores, and rashes. Children afflicted with these conditions ran about cheerfully, apparently without distress and without worrying their mothers.[3]

As medicine in this era could do little to treat most diseases, skilled and constant home nursing was often the only hope for the seriously ill; a child's life was often literally in a mother's hands. The ordeal of caring for a very sick or dying child was one that most mothers probably experienced many times. Even in a magazine for middle-class women like Ada Ballin's *Baby,* many pages are devoted to nursing techniques such as building an elaborate "croup tent," providing steam for a child with respiratory disease, or caring for a feverish child. But in households without servants and with few cash reserves, it was the mother who not only nursed the sick one but also assembled the extra money needed for doctors, supplies, and medicines. "After a long illness of a member of a poor household it is a common thing for the mother to break down from scanty feeding and anxious watching," wrote an East End doctor in the early 1890s. This excerpt from the Women's Cooperative Guild's 1915 *Maternity* collection is a mother's account of the exhaustion that overcame her while nursing a sick daughter (who did survive). "I watched by her couch three weeks, snatching her sleeping moments to fulfill the household task[s]. The strain was fearful, and one night I felt I must sleep or die—I didn't much care which; and I lay down by her side, and slept, and slept, and slept, forgetful of temperatures, nourishment or anything else."[4]

This strenuous devotion was hard for observers to associate with the mothers' linguistic frugality. Pember Reeves was struck by the contrast between one Lambeth woman's sparing words when her baby was near death with pneumonia, around 1910, and the dramatic statement that her actions made: "She sat up night after night, nursed him and did all the work of the house by day, but all she ever said on the subject was, 'I'd not like ter lose 'im now.' She looked more gaunt as the days went on, but everything was done as usual. When the baby recovered she made no sign." Another woman who visited her hospitalized two-week old baby night after night in the 1900s until it died made a similar statement in equally spare language. The night nurses were disturbed by her stoic silence, and the mother never spoke to or looked at the newborn. "She had long ago forgotten how to caress or show affection," a sympathetic nursing staff member wrote in 1906, "but her love dumbly expressed itself by a regular nightly attendance till the night nurse grew ashamed of her own hardness." It was the mother, not the nurse, who witnessed the baby's death on its twenty-first night and broke her silence: "Nurse, e's gorn, poor little dear, Gawd 'elp 'im!"[5]

George Acorn's 1911 Bethnal Green autobiography recreates the moment of crisis and grief when he realized that the endless work of his taciturn and grumpy mother was a sign of love. His account of his boyhood, published in 1911, also makes clear the limits of what social investigators could see and know about the emotional lives of their subjects. The author's baby brother was very ill, in the 1870s or so, and his mother's ability to help the child was limited by the family's near-destitution. The father was out of work, and they were surviving on the ministrations of a kind landlady and the mother's home work assembling cardboard boxes.

> Gradually my brother grew worse. Instead of reading, my father and I could only sit and watch my mother as she nursed the child in her arms, trying to still its fitful cries by strange, sweet, soothing invocations.
>
> My mother had never appeared to be particularly tender, and it was a revelation to me, this unfolding of the great, loving, maternal instinct. She would work like one possessed, her dexterous fingers molding box after box almost too quickly for the eye to follow—and all for the paltry twopence-farthing a gross complete! . . . Although her head was bent over her work apparently oblivious of all else, she would start up at the least cry from the ailing child, and rock it to her bosom until she could lay it down, enjoining silence on us all, and then resume her work as if her life depended on it. . . . All Saturday morning I could see by my mother's terrible anxiety that the child was worse.

The mother dispatched her husband to fetch a doctor, and the baby seemed to fall asleep in his mother's arms. "Suddenly a look of fear came into her face. She seemed afraid of something; then, bracing herself as if for some frightful task, inclined her ear to the child's mouth. She gave a piercing scream, and whispered brokenly, 'My God, he's dead!' " By the time the doctor arrived (having kept the desperate father waiting some hours), the mother was stupefied with grief. What the professional man saw were her stiff movements, her glassy eyes, and her mechanical comment: "Yes, better now; he's dead."[6] If he had been given to writing about his reflections of life among the poor, as some slum doctors were, his commentary on this scene might have been: "The mother of the dead baby registered no emotion; the poor are utterly fatalistic." The mother's work for this child was, sadly, over; through it she had made her statement about mother love, but the physician had not been there to witness it.

In family stories and the oral histories and autobiographies that are partly based on them, the mother as guardian of children's lives makes frequent appearances. The children's accounts tell of her anguish, sleeplessness, and labor, as well as her power (for these children did get well). The description of a mother's heroic home nursing of a son ill with typhoid, a good example of this kind of tale, entered the Eldred family's own oral tradition, to be retold in his autobiography by the boy, John. The mother, in a tenement off Walworth Road in the late 1880s, nursed her boy with the help of a kind doctor. "She fought for me like a tigress, as I heard jolly Aunt Betty, her sister, assure an assembled company in later years, 'pulled that young Johnny through just in the nick.'" As John Eldred, who worked his way into a career in journalism, recalled, "I believe mother never took off her clothes during the entire term of my illness, but snatched what sleep she could in a bedside chair." Selig Brodetsky, growing up in Whitechapel where he, his mother, and four siblings had arrived from the Ukraine to join his father in 1893, often heard the story of his mother's brilliant rescue of her son from the jaws of death. What began as a cut thumb, so the story went, became infected and eventually left the small boy paralyzed. The doctor gave him up for dead, but Mrs. Brodetsky persisted. She subjected the child to repeated hot baths, so scalding that she herself could not bear to put the boy in them; she begged her own mother to do it instead, and Selig did recover—with a lifelong sense of his mother's determination and skill in protecting her children, as well as a powerful debt of gratitude to her.[7]

MEDICINE AND MOTHERS

Some of the most advanced hospitals in the contemporary world were available to the London poor, and so were district nurses with the most up-to-date training, and despite much nervousness, the mothers rushed to use these services. But people also freely drew on forms of medical advice and practice that were no longer orthodox among their social betters in St. John's Wood or Hampstead: ancient herbal recipes, the advice of druggists who freely prescribed remedies for their clients, the warm touch of a spiritualist healer.

Allopathic Medicine Before the Twentieth Century

Medical doctors and hospitals were important elements in the health care strategies of poor mothers. The London public had already had, well before 1900, considerable contact with orthodox medical treatment and personnel. (The quality and effectiveness of that contact are, of course, another matter; the average waiting time at the London Hospital outpatient clinic in the 1870s was seven hours.) London teaching hospitals, their medical education functions expanding after the establishment of the Medical Register in 1858, provided more and more free hospital outpatient care for those Londoners willing to become "teaching material." In 1887, about a fifth of the population of Greater London used a hospital outpatient or emergency service at one of the region's ninety-one hospitals. In 1901, a quarter of all Londoners used the services of ninety-two hospitals, and over 300,000 more took advantage of charity or poor-law dispensaries.[8] The London hospitals also, of course, accommodated thousands of inpatients, and the Poor Law Medical Service, much improved after the 1867 Metropolitan Poor Act, at least in a handful of British towns, accommodated thousands of inpatients in its infirmaries.[9]

From the 1870s, if not earlier, Londoners of all classes thought of medical doctors or hospitals as the ones to call on in cases of serious illness or injury. Even the down-and-out inmates of a Flower and Dean Street lodging house in the 1870s, both men and women, had been repeatedly urging that the very emaciated four-year-old son of two residents needed a doctor's care. In another early case, Ellen Radley, a thirteen-year-old girl, testified at the Old Bailey in 1872 that when she came home in St. Pancras Road and found her mother with a gaping wound in her throat, she immediately went to fetch a doctor: "Nobody told me to go; I went of my own accord." A generation later, a baby in Deptford who looked too thin was the subject of a conversation between its mother and its aunt: One wanted to bring him to a doctor, and the other suggested a charitable dispensary.[10]

Women and children were the great majority of applicants for the free care available at many London medical institutions. At the Royal Kent Dispensary in Deptford, where patients in the mid-1870s complained of long waits, the majority of the protests were from women, "the most numerous and more noisy" of the patients. At a Tottenham dispensary in the 1890s, all but 40 of the 254 adult patients were women: Indeed, over half of the adult patients were married women under forty seeking medical help for themselves or their children. Hospital waiting rooms, too, were filled mostly with women and children. A description from about 1870 archly mentioned the "many introductions" and "much gossip" with which the patients wiled away the long hours of waiting at one of them. According to one estimate around the turn of the twentieth century, fully half of the outpatients brought to hospitals were infants under a year old.[11]

From the 1880s, the COS, supported by the British Medical Association, went on the warpath against this "medical mendicity," as they termed Londoners' assumption that in- and outpatient hospital care was a right rather than a privilege. Charles Booth observed that this widespread notion was partly related to the massive fund-raising "Hospital Sundays" and "Hospital Saturdays" to which even quite poor people contributed. Those quintessential London characters, the "pearlie" kings and queens, seem in fact to have originated in the 1880s with the elaborate processions used to collect hospital donations in working-class districts.[12] By the 1890s, the COS was training a new kind of social worker who would discourage free hospital visits, and by 1903 there were "almoners" installed in seven London hospitals. These officials would direct those who could afford it to private doctors or clinics. Mary Stewart, the young North St. Pancras COS district secretary assigned to the Royal Free Hospital in 1895 as the first of these almoners, was unable to advance her sponsor's cause. After interviewing hundreds of prospective patients in crowded waiting rooms, she found that only a small proportion—well under 20 percent—were in any position to actually pay for their medical care. Although in some hospitals, aggressive, bullying almoners, like the ex-policeman who served at St. Mary's, may have kept the numbers down, some of them found that their zeal only earned them the hostility of medical staffs always eager for more "cases."[13]

Poor people did use private doctors occasionally, however, despite their relative scarcity in poor districts (In Bethnal Green in about 1900 there was one medical doctor per 3,000 residents, compared with one per 480 in Kensington). About a quarter of the families below the poverty line who had children at the Great Ormond Street Hospital for Children in 1909–1910 had consulted private doctors (an average of four times each) before resorting to the hospital. Private care was not always prohibitively expensive, as the 1910–1916 career of the idealistic if erratic "threepenny doctor of Hackney," Dr. Jelley, indicates. In the 1880s, Mr. B., a doctor with one of the "oldest and most respectable practices in the East India Road," charged a more typical 3s. 6d. fee for a visit, including medicine,[14] a sum that a well-paid worker earning 25 to 40s. a week could occasionally afford. A Walworth household could obtain a doctor's home visit plus a bottle of medicine in the 1890s for only 6d., whereas the Great Ormond Street families had to pay doctors an average of a shilling per visit.[15]

The doctor was often, however, the health care professional of last resort, rather than the central health adviser. George Palmer King, a widower caring for his two children with the help of his Clerkenwell landlady in the late 1870s, tried a series of home remedies for some weeks as his son lay ill with a cold and cough. He gave the child castor oil, magnesia and syrup of rhubarb, mustard poultices, weak brandy and water, plus a variety of fortifying foods: fried fish, mutton broth, stewed eels, eggs and rice, sherry—all on the advice of the landlady. Though these methods had certainly seen millions through respiratory infections like this, in this case the little boy's illness was severe. He developed gangrene in one lung, which killed him. Though both caretakers were loving and conscientious, they did not think of bringing a doctor in during the two weeks of the illness, only calling one as the child obviously neared death. In the summer of 1897, district nurses in the New Kent Road area visited a household in which Benjie, the little son, was very sick with bronchitis and pneumonia, yet the father's unemployment meant that no doctor was called. When the nurse entered, the boy was delirious, having run a very high temperature for two or three days. In a later example, when Alice Linton was a girl in Shoreditch in the 1910s, her rheumatic fever was left untreated for a long time, for as the 2 shillings for a doctor's visit were hard to come by, the doctor was called in only once.[16]

Fear of an inquest in the event of a child's death rather than real confidence in doctors surely motivated some mothers finally to call in a physician. As the Kensington MOH put it in 1875, the calls came mostly from a "desire to avoid a fuss about a certificate of the cause of death." Edward Berdoe, a freethinking slum doctor deeply sympathetic to his patients, saw them in the 1890s as people whose terrors of illness were simply compounded by dread of "the inquisitorial visit of the coroner's officer."[17]

Ladies in Uniform

District nursing, which developed in the metropolis in the 1870s, was probably as important as the hospital to the medical care of the London poor. Ellen Ranyard, whose nonconformist working-class Bible women had been going door to door in inner London since 1858, introduced a nursing program ten years later, the first of many such services established in the late Victorian years. The Ranyard nurses, usually recruited from among the Bible women, were residents of the neighborhoods they were serving, women who were known for their helping and managing skills; there were eighty-two working in London by 1894. Their nursing training, provided by cooperative physicians, was at first only six and a half months long, though by the turn of the twentieth century it was more extensive. The Ranyard system of recruiting charismatic local women as nurses was unique, for as the district nursing movement grew in the 1870s and 1880s, it was an arena deliberately set aside for ladies who could afford to pay for one or more years of training. The East London Nursing Association was founded in 1868, Florence Lees' Metropolitan and National Nursing Association in 1875, and a series of other district-organized services were introduced later. The Queen's Jubilee Nurses, funded by Queen Victoria for her Jubilee in 1887 at the urging of Lees and other nursing activists, rapidly expanded throughout the country.[18]

Accustomed to paying needy neighbor women when they needed nursing, poor Londoners were astounded at these trained nurses who worked for free. Patients assumed that they were women who had come down in the world and warmly offered them advice on how to better themselves. All this misunderstanding was frustrating to district nursing leader Florence Lees, the founder and first superintendent-general of the Metropolitan and National Nursing Association. Lees accepted only probationers (trainees) who demonstrated a "love for the poor" but complained in the late 1870s that "the poor never seem to have an idea that we are *ladies*."[19]

The district nurse, an "apostle of sanitary science" to the unsanitary poor, did a lot of preaching about the value of open windows, the uses of legumes in nutritious meals, and the importance of cleanliness in the home; and many of these teachings had the potential to save lives. She also, at a point when even grave illnesses were cared for at home (only 27 percent of London deaths took place in hospitals in 1895, for example),[20] shared the material work and sometimes the emotional burdens of the wives for whom nursing sick husbands or children was a major charge. Nurses often carried on for missing family members, as in the home of a Soho printer's wife temporarily abandoned with a newborn baby in the late 1870s. The district nurse came nearly daily, lit the fire, and prepared breakfast for the woman. In a Wandsworth case, in 1893, a woman whose seven-year-old son Willie was at home for some time with an abscess that needed frequent poulticing, went to work each day knowing that a Ranyard nurse would be there daily for several hours to care for the child. Housekeeping was actually the first responsibility of the district nurse—"them char ladies" Finsbury women had first called them when they were introduced there by a local general practitioner. A nurse's regular routine involved washing the patient, making the bed, sweeping and dusting the room, cleaning the hearth, carrying out the ashes, fetching water, and filling the kettle—all jobs that belonged to the servants in the homes from which most of the nurses came. Marcella Boyce's two years as a Soho district nurse in Mary Ward's *Marcella* (1894) were both fulfillment and—because they involved danger, filth, and drudgery—penance.[21]

The soberly uniformed nurses (the Metropolitan and National nurses in the 1870s wore a "brown holland gown and black bonnet with blue ribbons," and the Ranyard nurses from the 1890s on wore a gray-blue dress with a dark blue cloak and bonnet) enjoyed much popularity and relative safety as they moved about even the poorest streets, protection that was attached to their liminal position. The costume transformed a lady into a civic institution. Working men gave up their seats to uniformed nurses in the 1870s, even in the third-class coaches of the underground. Nurse Williams, who had worked in the semicriminal Old Nichol for fifteen years, told Charles Booth's investigators around the turn of the century that because of her distinct clothing, she never had any fear for her safety. When another uniformed midwife found she had no bus fare in 1895, a workman offered to pay it for her: "I holds with midwives. I do," he explained. Midwifery student Katherine Roberts recorded her pleasure at the freedom of movement the uniform gave her as she did her "district work," and she even kept it on during a holiday so as to enjoy more fully her night in a West End hotel.[22]

The grateful mother was a well-used trope in the new journals for professional nurses, many of which were founded in the 1880s. The readiness of poor women to carry out the nurses' instructions, whether that meant opening long-sealed windows or fashioning a croup tent with coats and blankets, made the nurses feel useful and effective. An 1889 journal column devoted to the light side of nursing told of the length and detail with which slum mothers described their children's illnesses to impatient nurses and doctors. Cockney loquaciousness—an overeagerness to cooperate—was a ready source of amusing (and overall quite affectionate) sketches in nursing journals. Rose Petty, one of the first school nurses (in the late 1890s), asserted that Hoxton mothers were anxious to learn how to treat the ailments diagnosed at school medical inspections. "The most encouraging part of the nurse's work is the response of the mothers," she wrote in the *Nursing Times,* journal of the Royal College of Nursing, in 1905.[23]

The image of the grateful mother had political dimensions as a defense of the working-class woman against her detractors, the well-to-do men who had taken the offensive in debates over Infant Life Protection (in the 1870s and again in the 1890s) and in the wake of the 1903–1904 parliamentary "deterioration" hearings. Finally, the grateful mother image alludes to another issue for the middle-class women who found themselves caring at one remove for the children of the poor: their only half-conscious claim to be better "mothers" to these children than were the slum women who cared for them everyday. The mothers' gratitude was acknowledgment of this superiority.

Medical Terrors

Compliance with medical advice and even with public health regulations was limited by the fundamental differences between the health ideas of the poor and those of the medically educated practitioners they encountered. Londoners thought of many medical procedures and technologies—injections, thermometers, surgery, hospitalization—as unnatural and dangerous assaults on bodily integrity. District medical officers repeatedly complained that parents refused to relinquish to institutions the sick children whom doctors thought needed hospitalization or who came under local compulsory quarantine laws created under the 1875 Public Health Act.[24] To their interlocutors among the poor, doctors literally spoke a foreign language. Working-class patients, usually absorbing the doctors' Latin and Greek terms aurally and rapidly, heard and reproduced them willingly but inaccurately in their own conversation. Lulu, a three-year-old in Kennington, had a disease that her mother pronounced "intersections," saying the word, middle-class visitors thought, "with awe and respect." Nurses working for the Fern Street Settlement in Poplar learned about such diseases as "comic asthma, yellow jarments, S. Viper's Dance, pisis, pig styes, nervous ability, accepted knee, apathetic fits, diarrhoea in 'is ear, dialectic trouble, an experiment in his speech, two burglars in his chest, firebrick gums, bronical bronchitis and bronical pumonia." Many of these malapropisms suggest the Poplar residents' capacity for assimilating new into old words, and they betray their assumption that medical talk had a family resemblance to other kinds of highfalutin language, hence their conflation, as in "an experiment in his speech," or their confusion, as with the Hoxton mothers who said "baptism" when they meant vaccination.[25]

In London, as elsewhere in Britain, smallpox vaccination was viewed with fear and suspicion, though it had been compulsory since 1871 and parents who refused it were liable for fines and imprisonment. The opposition position was an old and respectable one, with support from Peel, Cobbett, Gladstone, William E. Forster (who introduced the 1870 Education Act), and feminist Millicent Fawcett.[26] After 1871, as the antivaccination movement grew, it gathered mass support in some working-class districts, notably in Mile End Old Town. A door-to-door survey carried out (probably in the 1880s) in another neighborhood, riverside Rotherhithe, by the London Society for the Abolition of Compulsory Vaccination (founded in 1880) uncovered 1,321 households as "believing in vaccination," 1,463 as "disbelieving," and an overwhelming majority against compulsion. A female rent collector in Deptford in the 1890s unwisely formed an alliance with the local vaccinator, who, despite an epidemic of smallpox in the area, was viewed with hostility. The proportions of London children "not finally accounted for" by the vaccinators gradually grew, reaching about 25 percent in 1900, a time when procedures for official exemption were still restrictive and cumbersome. Borough policies on vaccination, carried out by local poor-law guardians, differed widely, as did popular views of the dangers and value of the procedure. In 1898, for example, only about 19 percent of Whitechapel infants but almost 69 percent of those in Shoreditch were not vaccinated. Even after 1907, when years of campaigning had achieved easy facilities for conscientious objection and about a quarter of infants nationally were exempt from being vaccinated, the figures for unvaccinated children in many London boroughs were far higher. Over half of the babies in Shoreditch, Bethnal Green, Camberwell, and Hackney had not been vaccinated in 1910.[27]

The terror that such a simple device as a thermometer could generate is a good indication that years of exposure to doctors and hospitals had not transmitted the culture of medicine intact into working people's homes. Nurses in 1905 found London mothers who refused to let them put a thermometer under a child's arm. "I ain't going to have my child cut, I tell you," said one. Another mother, convinced that a similar thermometer had killed her husband, also refused on her daughter's behalf: "If Lizzie theer 'as to die, well let 'er die natural." District nurse Edith May found that people on a street where she had successfully treated a neighbor attributed magical powers to her thermometer. " 'She puts that little glass thing in your mouth, and it tells her *everythink,* you can't keep nothink from her,' " was the nurse's report of what they were saying about her. Margaret Loane, another district nurse, believed that many of her rural patients simply did not know what a thermometer did or whether it was better to have a "high" or "low" temperature.[28]

Folk Medicine in London

Allopathic medicine both competed and coexisted with the promises and offerings of many other schools of health care: spiritualism, herbalism, commercial prepackaged medicines, pharmacists, and traditional home remedies and techniques, all of which I lump together here as "folk medicine." Spiritualist healers, many of whom mixed mesmerism and the laying on of hands with traditional herbal cures, practiced in great numbers in London especially in the early decades of this study. The celebrated Chandos Leigh Hunt and Mrs. Olive, among others, held free sessions for the London poor.[29] Although hostility to medical science was by no means limited to workers,[30] nonmedical curing clearly flourished in London's crowded industrial districts. The variety of competing and philosophically incompatible diagnoses and treatments at women's disposal around the turn of the century indicates that at that point, women had not yet begun to acknowledge medicine as the supreme authority in the care of children but, rather, as one among many kinds of resources. A trust in heterodox remedies was, however, perfectly compatible with the use of the resources of the formal medical system. Even a believer in spiritualism, plagued by hemorrhoids in 1905, got the message from her medium that "now is the safe time for your operation."[31]

Metropolitan life had changed and weakened the older village-based knowledge of medicinal formulas and dosages without destroying it. City dwellers lost the easy access to the medicinal herbs growing near country towns and villages that gifted preindustrial healers had used, such as juniper, savin, and aloes, which some women knew how to make into abortifacients. Some herbal knowledge must have remained alive in the city, though, for in the early autumn of 1878 an Epping Forest outing for poor London mothers was an opportunity for some of them to gather medicinal plants, and a mother raised in a Wiltshire country town retained her knowledge of herbal medicines in the East London slums in the 1890s and 1900s. In Cambridge Heath, women passed around written prescriptions for home mixtures on "odd bits of paper."[32] "Queer remedies," as one unsympathetic commentator put it in 1904, continued to abound in London health care: teabags for swollen eyes (which worked and still works), onion syrup, necklaces or scarves to prevent colds and sore throats.[33] One mother's extensive regime of home remedies, as described by her oldest daughter (born in 1898), was based on ingredients provided by the chandler and the pharmacist and formulated at home. "My mother was our doctor," Alice Cordelia Davis wrote:

> If our bowels were out of order, liquourice powder was prescribed; it had a most revolting taste. A spoonful was mixed in water, when it would turn a nasty-greeny-gray colour. . . . For pimples she prescribed brimstone and treacle, which was mixed in a jam jar. . . . For sore throats a piece of flannel was put around our necks and we were made to gargle with salt water. For chesty colds it was Russian tallow. A large piece of brown paper was well smeared with tallow. It resembled creamy-yellow candlegrease. This paper was put across our chest and back and tied on with a warm scarf; we were then put to bed with a cup of warm milk. For a cough mother prescribed glycerine, paragoric, and syrup of squills: this was mixed in a medicine bottle at a cost of five (old) pence. For a feverish cold a dose of quinine was recommended. This was taken in water: it would turn the water milky white and was dreadfully bitter. All these things seemed to work.[34]

Not all traditional remedies were benign. In the 1870s, a mustard-and-vinegar plaster that neighbors had helped a young mother prepare for her two-year-old son's chest disease had created, by the time the Ranyard nurses arrived, a large, hand-sized open wound on the infant's chest. In the 1880s, Metropolitan and National nurses were referred to an eighteen-year-old girl with typhoid who had had to contend with a large piece of raw bacon around her neck for three weeks as a sore-throat remedy.[35]

Self-remedies clustered most around diseases or conditions against which medicine was useless, as in the case of the common cold today. Whooping cough is a good Victorian/Edwardian example, as F. B. Smith has pointed out. A frightening childhood disease that killed nearly half of its victims then, whooping cough was most deadly to children under two, and in 1910 there were nearly nine thousand whooping cough deaths nationally in Britain. The medicines prescribed by physicians were mostly nothing but harsh emetics, but nonmedical methods abounded: bringing children to the gas works to breathe in the fumes or to the river at low tide when it smelled sulphurous or (more conveniently) simply using the fumes of a household gas meter.[36]

Women passed recipes, protocols, and diagnostic advice rapidly through neighborhoods and kin groups. Health was, as it has continued to be, a central theme in neighborhood and family gossip. One East London woman loved to tell the story of the way a neighbor's advice saved her baby in the 1890s when the doctor had given up on the case. The propensity of East London women to be "injudicious" in this way in their choices of conversational topics was something an early twentieth-century midwife there deplored. "They are extremely fond of regaling their neighbours who are expectant mothers with all sorts of horrors reminiscent of their own past obstetrical experiences." As Emilia Kanthack, the midwife, reported, mothers with jaundiced newborns were often frightened by their neighbors' dire comments on a quite benign condition.[37] Health was always an acceptable conversational gambit. A district nurse overheard a discussion in a railroad car between two women (whom she described as lower middle class) who had just met, each woman traveling with a small child. "This one has been laid out twice for dead," said its mother. "I'll tell you how I cured her." The recipe, a nauseating concoction based on pulverized snails, was a classic in her family (and broke the ice between the two travelers). When an aunt paying a weekly visit to Jane Bark's Poplar household a little before 1900 noticed that the youngest baby had "a lump on her tongue," a numerous relatives and neighbors were involved in consultations about the diagnosis and treatment.[38]

Neighborhood health care networks were a system that the organized medical profession disapproved of and tried to destroy. The 1878 amendment to the 1858 Medical Act prohibited unqualified practitioners from charging money or advertising. The allopathic medical profession waged war on spiritualist and other unorthodox healers throughout the 1870s and 1880s. Yet when members of the "Peculiar People," a Christian sect centered in the South London engineering districts of Plumstead and Woolwich, which rejected doctors and all forms of medical technology (and which had some overlap with spiritualism), were prosecuted for failing to provide medical care for children ill with smallpox, doctors in the late Victorian years could not in good faith affirm that medical intervention could have saved the children. As a doctor testified in one of these cases in the early 1880s, in answer to a question about whether medical attendance could have prevented the smallpox death of an eight-year-old Woolwich boy, "I can only answer that by saying that it might have been—ours is not a positive science—it might have been averted if medical aid had been called in at any earlier stage; I am unable to say whether it probably would."[39] Medical models of health care continued to have strong competition until later in the twentieth century when physicians were able to make stronger claims for their own superiority as healers.

CARING FOR SICK AND DYING CHILDREN

Mothers, especially among the poor, did not see a long, healthy life as the birthright of each of their children, for they knew that many forces that parents could not control could thwart their development. At birth, infants' survival was still tentative, and as the babies grew, their mothers knew that attempting to save them from accidents or diseases would be among their most taxing and heartbreaking jobs.

Sick Children

In nineteenth-century Russia or Japan, where food, warmth, and rest were far more scarce than they were for London working people, sickly or cranky children were actually often selected at birth for neglectful mothering. This "selective neglect," which anthropologists have noted among some Third-World shantytown dwellers today,[40] seems rare among married pre–World War I London mothers, though it may be more accurate to say that it remained almost unremarked and unnamed.

Yet sickness and health, "fine" or "delicate" children were certainly the terms in which mothers observed and classed their children. In *Maternity,* a woman described her children's health problems with careful attention to the developmental markers of which she was aware, milestones that indicated the potential for health and survival: "Nearly all my children were delicate," she began. "They were nearly all two years before they ran; my eldest girl was three years before she ran. I never thought she could live, but, thank God, she has lived, and is nearly twenty-two." Women giving information about their earlier children to the General Lying-In Hospital staff in the 1880s recalled precisely such markers of healthy development as teething, walking, or running. "Was delicate. walked at 3½. then strong," reads one casebook entry. Another child was described as "now 2. alive and cannot walk by itself, all its teeth have appeared, but have rotted away again."[41] Other areas of child development were seldom noted because they were less revealing of a child's physical vigor. Speech is an accomplishment that is easy to chart: mothers in more recent generations have routinely registered and noted their children's first words. Yet women were not questioned about, and never mentioned, talking when describing their children's early years.

Instead, a mother charted out her success and geared her anxiety mainly based on her young child's size, number of teeth, and ability to walk, which told her of its chances of survival.[42]

Working-class children's health in London and in most other parts of Britain left a great deal to be desired by the standards of today and, indeed, even by those of the late Victorian and Edwardian middle classes. Respiratory disease was ubiquitous, from chronically runny noses to bronchitis, pneumonia, or whooping cough (the latter two continue to be major killers of children and infants worldwide). A month after leaving the General Lying-In Hospital in 1886, three of a group of twenty newborn babies already had had their first colds, though infants normally remain free of viral diseases for several months after birth. Also common among children were rickets, skin diseases, impaired hearing and eyesight, painful and debilitating tooth decay, and accidental cuts and scalds. In the 1870s, about a third of poor children in large cities like London or Manchester had obvious signs of rickets, though many cases can be detected only by X-rays.[43] Epidemic diseases such as measles and scarlet fever were, of course, serious threats to children as well.

Although individual mothers could certainly improve specific health problems for specific children, they made this attempt under general conditions over which they had very little control. Thus, as Chapter 2 noted, British children's weights and heights were directly correlated with their fathers' earnings. Infant death rates, as the next section of this chapter shows, were also correlated with income and employment.

Many households contained disabled children: blind, deaf, or mentally or otherwise handicapped. Some of these children had begun to receive some care in special poor-law schools, asylums, and homes for "idiots," but most remained with their families and needed extra care. A sweet-tempered three-year-old in the Covent Garden area in the late 1890s was paralyzed on his left side and unable to talk but was cared for at home by his mother and siblings. The help the family could offer him was limited, but the child did well enough at home. The boy "sits quite patiently on a hard wooden chair . . . and kicks about his one strong leg, and combs his curly hair, and crows and gurgles." The story of Mrs. G., as told by the nurses who aided her in the 1900, illustrates the strain that still more seriously disabled children represented to their mothers. Described in the Ranyard nurses' magazine as "a strong made woman, with rather hard features and a strained look in her eyes," Mrs. G. had the care of her seriously handicapped nine-year-old son in her South London house. They boy was deaf, dumb, and blind, and his limbs were "twisted and drawn up." The mother had been caring for him for two years since his discharge from a hospital. The child sometimes screamed all night, and the neighbors had understandably been urging Mrs. G. to send the child to the infirmary, but she refused. "I'm the only one he knows," she explained. The overtaxed mother got assistance from the Ranyard nurses, and her other children helped with household errands, as the poor woman was "too nervous now to go across the street."[44]

Household accidents were frequent and destructive to children. Homes themselves were often dangerous, with steep, dark staircases, open fires, kettles of boiling water within reach of toddlers, and adults cooking while small children swarmed at their feet. The Ranyard nurses working in and around Clapham in the early 1880s were often called in to deal with burns: a girl burned when a tin tub, placed too near the fire, got too hot; children scalded on the arms and legs by pea soup that had spilled on them; a seven-year-old boy scalded by "bacon fat which his father spilt as he was taking it out of the oven." A women in Kennington, preoccupied by the confusion of a bath night for a large family, ordered a daughter to warm up the bath water with some fresh boiling water, which landed on a child's leg and severely burned it. Burns were especially common among toddlers, who frequently were left at home unsupervised or watched only by siblings as young as five or six. Margaret Loane, the district nurse, who accepted this child care practice as normal if not ideal, included in her manual on home health care such suggestions for child safety as using fireguards and leaving cold water within easy reach so that thirst would not tempt a child to grab a kettle or saucepan. But these precautions did not work for Catherine Delany, who left her two-year-old with an older daughter, age twelve, in February 1888, as the *East London Advertiser* reported. The fire got low, and the older girl went out to try to find more fuel, leaving the baby alone with the remaining fire still lit, which burned her to death.[45] Marie Kelly Welsh lost a seven-year-old sister in the 1900s when her mother left the girl at home with the lit copper filled with laundry while she went out shopping. Road accidents, always something of a hazard, became a greater risk after about 1910 when automobiles began to challenge children for the use of the streets. On a typical workday in 1911, over nineteen thousand mechanical vehicles of all kinds, plus fifty thousand horse-drawn vehicles, were out in the streets of London. In 1914 in Britain, the more than thirteen hundred motor vehicle casualties outstripped the number caused by horse-drawn vehicles. In June 1914, Mary Ward complained to Christopher Addison, M.P. for Hoxton, about the recent enormous increase in street accidents involving children.[46]

Matters of Life and Death

Motherhood presented women with an emotional paradox: During infancy and early childhood, at those times when mothers were "working for" their children the hardest, the lives of their babies were the most precarious. In turn-of-the-century London at least 15 percent of all babies died in their first year, of problems of prematurity, measles and whooping cough, or diarrheal diseases. London's tally was by no means extremely bad for England at that time,[47] but by our standards these are huge losses, over ten times as high as those of most industrialized countries today. Figures from the eighteenth and early nineteenth centuries were even more staggering, estimated variously (for children from birth to age five) as high as 75 percent in the early eighteenth century and falling to about 30 percent in the early nineteenth century. By the 1850s or so, infant death rates had improved. But whereas mortality rates for other age groups continued to drop steadily during the following decades, the rates for infants barely changed for at least half a century, until the period between 1905 and 1910.[48] Not only was infant mortality high, but deaths between the ages of one and five also were frequent, though these did decrease by about a third between the 1870s and the 1900s.[49]

Statistics for London as a whole disguise the experience of its poorest inhabitants. Infant mortality varied enormously by district and hence by class, the contrast growing with each passing month of infants' lives.[50] In well-off Hempstead, as Table 6–1 shows, the rate in 1901–1903 was close to 90 per thousand (deaths of infants under one year per thousand live births). In Hackney, a borough including many better-off workers, the figure was 131 per thousand; in Southwark, 160; and in Shoreditch, 186 per thousand. (The contrasts among boroughs in the 1920s were less marked.) Within boroughs there also were huge contrasts. To take one among many possible examples: In Kensington, one ward (the northwest) had an infant mortality rate of 286 per thousand in 1895, whereas that of another (the central) was only 134. Ten years later the Kensington medical officer reported that in the very poor Norland Ward (Notting Dale), with a population of about 4,000, the rate was a staggering 432 per thousand. By 1910, when Kensington was reporting much lower death rates in general for infants, the enormous disparities among subdistricts remained. Similar disparities existed, and continue to exist, throughout England, marking the material limits on mothering.[51]

In the 1870s through the 1890s the experiences of the General Lying-In Hospital's mothers, mostly from North Lambeth and the Borough suggest that the death of two or more of a family's children was a common ordeal. The 256 (nearly all married) women aged thirty-five or over who had had babies with the hospital's outpatient service between 1877 and 1882 had compiled an astonishing record of children lost to stillbirths or disease at later ages (see Table 6–2). Only around a fifth had lost no children, and another fifth had lost only one child. A horrendous 62 percent had had two or more children die. In fact, more than

TABLE 6–1. The Decline in Annual Infant Mortality in Some London Boroughs, Early Twentieth Century (rates per thousand live births)

London Borough	1901–1903*	1910	1915	1920–1922
Bermondsey	147	126	151	93
Camberwell	136	94	108	74
Chelsea	143	101	100	67
Finsbury	166	133	128	83
Hackney	131	98	107	73
Hammersmith	136	99	102	75
Hampstead	92	60	76	57
Holborn	115	103	96	73
Poplar	157	118	134	81
Shoreditch	186	146	144	102
Southwark	160	116	132	85
Stepney	156	112	114	86
St. Marylebone	145	108	96	69
St. Pancras	145	102	104	75
Westminster	123	84	92	70
Woolwich	120	85	95	62

*Rates for these years are similar to those prevailing in London throughout the last four decades of the nineteenth century.

Sources: Janet Campbell and E. W. Hope, *Report on the Physical Welfare of Mothers and Children: England and Wales* (2 vols.) (Liverpool: Carnegie U.K. Trust, 1917), vol. 1, p. 212 (1901–1903 and 1915 figs.); Report of the MOH of the County (of London), in LCC, *Annual Reports,* 1910, vol. 3, p. 20 (1910 figs.). The 1920–1922 figures are from W. J. Martin, "Vital Statistics of the County of London in the Years 1902 to 1951," *British Journal of Preventative Social Medicine* 9 (1955): Table VIII, p. 132.

40 percent of the whole group of women had lost three or more of their babies and children. The General Lying-In midwifery program was conducted as a charity and included most of the poorest parts of inner London. It may be seen as reasonably representative of a group of "poor" and "very poor" (in Booth's terms) London mothers who exhibited, in these years, a pattern of high birthrates and high infant death rates. A much larger sample of women aged thirty-five and over, 1,314 women, who used the Guy's Hospital midwifery service (also shown in Table 6–2) for home births from 1892 to 1894 display the same pattern in a more muted form (which may be a result both of Guys' more careless

TABLE 6–2. Frequency of Children's and Infants' Deaths for a Group of South London Mothers Using Two Outpatient Maternity Programs

Hospital	Number of Women Aged 35 or Over with Dead or Stillborn Children (percentage)			
	None	*1*	*2 or More*	*Total*
General Lying-In Hospital, 1877–1882	49 (19)	49 (19)	158 (62)	256
Guy's Hospital, 1892–1896	644 (49)	228 (17)	442 (34)	1314

Sources: General Lying-In Hospital, Registers of Outpatients, July 1877–November 1882 (Greater London Record Office, HI/GLI/B22, vol. 1); and Guy's Lying-In Charity, Outpatient Maternity Record, 1892–1896 (Greater London Record Office, H9 GY B22/15). Figures for both hospitals are based on patients aged 35 and over.

record keeping—many blanks on the forms—and of the later dates of these data).

Figures tell their story. "The one great need is simply—*money*" was how Pember Reeves put the matter at a Women's Labour League conference in 1912. Thus it was possible to correlate infant death rates in London and elsewhere in England directly with the father's unemployment and with household income, as Barbara Drake did in her study of infant mortality in Westminster in the 1900s. Indeed, during World War I, infant deaths declined dramatically, especially in such inner-London boroughs as Shoreditch, Bermondsey, Stepney, and Bethnal Green. "The prime agency at work" saving the babies' lives, according to J. M. Winter, "was a rise in family incomes, especially among the poorest sections of the population."[52] Working-class mothers knew how to turn their wartime earnings directly into longer lives for many of their children.

A Tentative Attachment

Maternity obviously involved an awareness that a new baby's hold on life was tentative. In working-class opinion, according to the medical people who attended them, and in the practice of the law as well, newborns (the term, as I am using it, extending through the first few weeks of life) were not officially viewed as persons and were not always loved as children. In the first months of an infant's life, Londoners spoke of its existence tentatively, emotionally hedging their bets. In the early 1880s, district nurses talked with a pale, thin Drury Lane woman who made a distinction between giving birth to babies and being able to "rear" them.

"I have lost *seven,* and do so long to rear this one," she said of her newest child, who was sent to a convalescent home with its mother and did well there. In Grace Foakes's pre–World War I Wapping, when a new baby was presented to neighbors, they asked, "Has it come to stay?" At the birth of a weak little boy, Foakes's mother clearly prepared herself and her family for its likely death, telling them: "He hasn't come to stay; he's only lent to us for a little while." A Bow woman, also early in the twentieth century, revealed the conditional quality of her attachment to a new baby in a letter to settlement worker Clara Grant: "You ask me to name the baby and if God spares it i will name it Vilet [Violet]." This sense of the need for some detachment from very new babies is demonstrated in a later anecdote, from the 1920s. When a woman made a great fuss of her baby nephew in public in bustling East Street, Walworth, a passerby warned, "Now mother, don't make too much fuss of him because you are sure to lose him."[53]

Recent studies of very young babies emphasize their capacity for creating attachment among surrounding adults at first by gazing and later by smiling. Very sickly or irritable babies who are unresponsive discourage this attachment. A stronger mother–infant relationship develops in the second month when the child can smile at its caretakers and remain in eye contact. Thus it is quite possible that in the nineteenth and early twentieth centuries, adults did form shakier ties to infants too "delicate" or "sickly" to enteract with their caretakers. Then, as today, in any case, infant deaths were concentrated in the very earliest weeks of life. To cite the figures compiled for St. Pancras: In 1876, 68 percent of infant deaths there took place within the first three months, and in 1901, the proportion had risen to 77 percent, because the rates among older infants had declined somewhat.[54]

Anthropologist Nancy Scheper-Hughes, talking with a group of shantytown mothers in northeast Brazil in the early 1980s, in a district with extremely high infant mortality rates, identified a set of mothering practices that the women seldom articulated and about which local health officials knew nothing. Though part of a culture in which motherhood was revered, the women practiced "selective neglect accompanied by maternal detachment" toward specific babies whose chances of survival looked poor. The Brazilian example, as well as others that anthropologists and historians have only recently begun to describe, illuminates ways in which material deprivation may structure mothering and calls into question notions of nurturance, attachment, and bonding as universal or biological.[55]

A London baby's welcome had a great deal to do with the circumstances into which it was born. Many single women giving birth, for example, knew that in order to earn their living, they would have to hand over their babies to foundling hospitals, relatives, or, most often, paid nurse mothers. The painful struggles of single mothers, together with the twofold higher London death rates for illegitimate infants, also make a powerful statement about the advantages of marriage—despite all its troubles—for women and children. A single woman who gave birth in a North London workhouse in the 1870s focused her fear and anger on the newborn infant. She called her baby "a little devil" and "a little demon" and apparently had tried to smother it in bed. The single women among her patients in the early 1900s, as we have seen, spoke readily to nurse Katherine Roberts of not wanting their babies, and many were openly relieved if their babies were born dead.[56]

Married women with many children already could also be reluctant to form bonds with a new baby, and as Chapter 4 explains, women in this category often sought abortions in later pregnancies. Weak infants who, like so many of the neglected Brazilian shantytown infants, looked like they would not live long, filled the mothers with terror, to judge by their reactions during stays at the General Lying-In Hospital in the 1880s. An Old Kent Road married woman, twenty-five and having her first child, is one example of a patient whose spirits improved after the death of a sickly baby. Her boy was born on March 19, 1886, and within a few days was apparently too weak to nurse well. Though he was being bottle fed, he had become lighter and thinner by March 24: "Mother fretting about it a good deal, hoping it is going to die evidently." While the hospital staff labored to sustain the sick baby's life, its mother had regular "fits of hysterics." The baby's death unleashed more hysterics, but by March 30, the mother had found some peace: "Mother is very well, is very cheerful; sat by fire today."[57]

Few were so outrightly callous as the East London workhouse matron who said of the infants born there that "they all look best in their wooden overcoats," but medical attendants were quite matter-of-fact about very early infant deaths. At the General Lying-In Hospital in the 1880s, the death of a baby was noted in the patient's record without much comment unless the mother's distress made her feverish. At this time, the hospital's reputation was based on its maternal death figures, not those of its infants. Viviana Zelizar speculates that legislators in late nineteenth-century Britain were also more matter-of-fact about the reality of infant and child deaths than were those in the United States, where in contrast to the few British efforts, there were at least eighty legislative attempts between 1890 and 1902 to prohibit or restrict the practice of insuring children's lives.[58]

Even though the distinction between the deaths of newborns and those of older babies and children had never existed formally in the law, in practice, for hundreds of years, these deaths were treated quite differently. In the first decades of the nineteenth century, concealment of a birth, which was punished with a two-year prison term, was often the verdict in cases that outside observers thought were infanticides. Juries simply did not want to convict when the dead child was a newborn, and married women were especially likely to be exonerated.[59] Capital punishment was not imposed, in fact, for a mother's murder of a child of any age after the execution of Rebecca Smith in 1849, and her crime was a remarkably horrible one: She confessed to killing *seven* of her eleven children with rat poison. In 1864 the Home Office adopted the policy of advising the commutation of the death penalty for all cases in which a woman was convicted of killing her own infant under a year old.[60] Some of the later nineteenth-century Old Bailey "not guilty" verdicts for women whose newborn babies had died are indeed astonishing, and very short prison sentences for those who were found guilty were common.

Infanticide among the working classes had been the subject of a journalistic and official panic in the 1860s and early 1870s, stimulated in part by a few spectacular mass murders by "baby farmers" and in part by two energetic and crusading medical men who served in succession as coroners for Central Middlesex, which included the heavily servant-keeping districts of St. Marylebone and Paddington. Rumors of secret but widespread infant killing were reported to parliamentary commissions on midwifery in 1892 and 1909, at which untrained birth attendants were mentioned as particularly willing to dispose of unwanted children, and in the three parliamentary hearings on infant life protection (discussed in Chapter 5) as a proclivity of some criminal or incompetent nurse-mothers. London infants, were, in fact, being abandoned and killed at a slow but regular rate throughout the later nineteenth century. In the Metropolitan and City Police District, 231 dead infants (not all under a year old) were found in the street in 1895, a figure lower than that for 1870, which was 276. The Hampstead Police Division reported 69 dead babies, mostly newborn, given to the police in 1877.[61] The Coroner's Court for the Central Division of Middlesex found around 60 annual "willful murders" of infants under a year old in the 1860s and 1870s, after which the number declined to 25 or 30 annually by the late 1880s. The killing of infants made up a good proportion, about a quarter, of the official murders in pre–World War I London (a number that was extraordinarily low).[62]

A reading of Central Criminal Court cases for the late nineteenth century provides some examples of the circumstances in which mothers or fathers of newborn babies deliberately smothered, drowned, or abandoned them. In 1874, a former prostitute had her second child taken from her by a man who appears to have been a brothel keeper; he exposed the baby outdoors in the cold (without the mother's knowledge) until it was near death. An unmarried servant from the country and her married lover, having taken a room for some weeks in London, killed their new baby and threw it out of a train window near Manor House. (This was also the woman's second child; in both cases, the first children were alive and continued to be provided for by their mothers.) In the 1890s another former servant, returning to her mother's house from the workhouse where she had given birth to a second illegitimate child, was told that she could not stay, as the mother did not have enough work to support her daughter and two grandchildren. Soon afterward, the daughter apparently drowned the newborn. Clarence Henry Longman, a young man out of work and forced to marry his sweetheart because of her pregnancy, drowned their baby when it was three months old.[63]

Although single parents were apparently much more likely to try to kill their infants than married parents were, official interest in stamping out infanticide among the poor coalesced in the 1890s around the question of overlaying, or accidentally suffocating, babies sleeping in their parents' bed. Coroners, doctors, and medical officers of health had only gradually identified overlaying as a problem and gathered data to show that it was a serious one. Medical officers' records first included suffocation deaths by age group in 1876; as a category, suffocation in bed was first introduced in the London MOH reports in 1891. If they are at all accurate, these figures, based on the death certificates that doctors signed or the results of coroners' inquests, reveal overlaying as a distinct but relatively minor cause of infant deaths: In London as a whole in 1905, 462 infant deaths were classed as the result of overlaying. In Hackney in 1875 (whose MOH kept these figures before he was required to), 11 infants died of suffocation, but far more died of other causes: 43 of whooping cough, 17 of measles, and 78 of diarrhea.[64] In late nineteenth-century Paddington, as Table 6–3 shows, the figures similarly show suffocation to be a serious cause of death, but less so than measles and whooping cough. What gave energy to the debates—in medical jour-

TABLE 6–3. Causes of Death of Small Children in Paddington, 1876 and 1894

	1876 (Numbers)		1894 (Numbers)	
	Under 1	*Ages 1–5*	*Under 1*	*Ages 1–5*
Suffocation	13	0	10	0
Whooping cough	29	25	18	23
Measles	20	65	16	48
Diarrhea	53	6	38	4

Source: Paddington MOH, *Annual Reports,* 1876, Table III, and 1895, p. 256.

nals, at parliamentary hearings, and at conferences on infant mortality—was its focus on the intimate lives of the poor. The discussion had a distinctly prurient quality, as it scrutinized such matters as sleeping arrangements, breast feeding, and other such details.[65]

The overlaying figures surely included some deliberate infanticides, but the evidence provided by contemporaries suggests that smothering in bed was nearly always an accident, that today some of these deaths would undoubtedly be labeled "crib deaths." The figures for overlaying were larger in winter and were clustered on weekends, particularly Saturday night and Sunday morning. Thus in Limehouse in 1898, twelve of seventeen overlaying deaths for which coroner's inquests were held took place on Friday, Saturday, or Sunday.[66] Some deaths occurred, I would speculate, when parents went to sleep with alcohol in their system and thus lost the usual semiconscious vigilance that protected the infants at night. A recent theory explaining some crib deaths as a result of hyperthermia squares with the seasonality of these statistics. In the 1908 Children Act, however, a piece of legislation incorporating many of the themes of the previous decade's high-level discussions of infant welfare, a kind of criminal negligence theory of overlaying was adopted, and it became a penal offense if it happened after a parent had drunk alcohol.[67]

A Child's Death

Children's deaths occupied an ordinary part of maternal language. For a long time the dead children were counted by their mothers among their children. (" 'E only died last year," said a daughter explaining why her mother still counted Billy as her son, "and mother always reckons him in when she's counting them up.") Funerals for babies and children were, of course, common and visible reminders of child death; in many working-class districts for most of this period, as many as half of all deaths involved a child under school age. Somers Town children, according to a school headmaster early in the twentieth century, played "Funerals" as often as they played "Father and Mother." A toddler in a Ratcliff nursery pretending to be a mother was trying to decide one day in the 1870s whether to play "cradles" or "coffins" with her doll.[68] The nearly universal habit of buying death insurance for small children on weekly payments of a penny or, occasionally, two to cover the cost of a respectable funeral speaks of the necessity of imagining such deaths. In the 1890s the coroner of East London reported that three quarters of the infants on whose deaths he held inquests were insured in this way; four fifths of England's poor infants were insured according to a guess made in the 1900s.[69]

The possibility of their children's dying often entered women's speech. In the 1870s a woman had complained that "the children are so tiresome," also saying to a neighbor that she would "not mind if they all lay dead at her feet." (But when her infant boy was seriously scalded in an accident at home, the distraught mother mustered all her resources to save him.) Journalist Charles Morley heard a woman say of a schoolboy whose repeated truancy had caused the family enormous trouble: "I wish he were dead—Lord forgive me, sir, but I do." In the 1900s, Clara Grant recorded a number of such comments by the mothers with whom she worked so closely from the turn of the century. One woman, whose hard life was punctuated by crises and tragedies, "looking round at her little flock one gloomy day, . . . said, 'Oh, you'd better be all of you dead.' " Mothers' bitterness, their hopelessness about their children's lives, was expressed in remarks like "It's a blessing the Lord took my other five' or "Well, I've buried eight out of thirteen and I sometimes wish I'd buried the other five."[70]

But these sources lend themselves to readings that, taken together, contradict the view that the frequency of (non-newborn) infant and child deaths among the poor made them less painful to those around them.[71] Despite the ubiquity of the deaths, the burial insurance that everyone bought for children, and the tiny coffins on display down the street, the death of a formerly healthy baby or child was still a surprise and a grievous blow. As one girl explained when her baby sister died: "It just wasn't possible. Not our baby. Other people's babies died, but not ours."[72]

Credible descriptions of parents' encounters with the death of a baby or child, like those quoted at the opening of this chapter, are quite rare for the generations we are portraying, and mothers' own stories are still rarer. Walter Southgate's heartbreaking account of the last hours of his nine-year-old sister in the mid-1890s, like George Acorn's narrative of his infant brother's death, is from the child's vantage point. We are left wondering about the grief of the mother who had to leave her dying daughter to go to work and, later, to comfort her little son as he looked into the coffin laid out in the front parlor. In Southgate's wrenching narration:

> She was the same little sister who had taken me to school on my first day, who held my hand and kept reminding me on the way to be "a good boy." . . . She died when mother was out charing. I recall that I crept up into mother's bedroom where Florrie lay crying and in pain. Her face was tear stained and its alabaster colour was heightened by her black raven locks. I climbed on to the bed and comforted her until she fell asleep. The next thing I knew she was laying there in the coffin sleeping her last sleep with an angelic face and mother telling me, as a comforting thought, that her soul had gone to join the angels in heaven.[73]

Fleeting descriptions by sympathetic observers, mostly nurses, convey a tiny part of the intensity of mothers' grief at a "lost" baby or child. One woman came under the care of the Ranyard nurses when, fainting on hearing of her ten-year-old daughter's drowning, she fell into the fire and was severely burned. Another Ranyard patient was angry and depressed at a baby's death. She had been (in evangelical terms) "very rebellious since her last baby died, and tried to forget about good things" but was revived a bit by an older child's return from the hospital. Mrs. Layton, a Women's Cooperative Guild member whose married adulthood was spent in Cricklewood, credited her involvement with the guild for keeping her from "the drink habit" when her second child, an infant boy, died after a long illness. A Bethnal Green mother whose golden-haired four-year-old daughter died suddenly in 1924 of meningitis sat for weeks afterward, as her daughter remembered, near her equally silent husband "with folded hands, not even knitting, just doing nothing, a thing I'd never seen before." The elderly Lambeth women whom Mary Chamberlain interviewed in the 1970s and 1980s about their babies' deaths that had occurred sixty years ago were choked with tears in the retelling.[74]

As David Vincent has observed in his study of nineteenth-century working-class autobiographies, "pure" grief was uncommon among mourners. Rather, a death was usually coupled with debts contracted during a long illness or with the loss of a child's money contributions, domestic help, or companionship. A district nurse attending a nineteen-year-old with rheumatic fever in the late 1870s gave a dramatic account of a mother's misery when she learned that her son had little hope of recovering, grief that conveyed her appreciation for the particular ways in which this son had helped her: "It would be impossible to describe the agony on the poor mother's face. She said 'he is the handsomest and best of them all, and has been such a comfort and help to me, and now to lose him!'" In 1897, the Ranyard nurses reported on another mother, whose surviving teenagers were "not turning out as they should." After two years, the mother still sadly mourned the son who had offered her so much, a boy who had died of heart disease at age fourteen. "She says he was so loving and good; so very different to the others."[75]

Women often conveyed their grief through their bodies. Illness and depression were strikingly common in women whose children had died, though it is impossible to separate the grief from the exhaustion and semistarvation of the weeks of the child's illness or from injuries of pregnancy and childbirth as the precipitating causes. Some of the women who contributed letters to *Maternity* in the immediate prewar years and those who were General Lying-In Hospital patients in the 1880s reported long periods of depressed semi-invalidism following a child's death or a stillbirth. Mrs. Bullen, a Lying-In patient who was "always rather weakly," had been in bed for five years after the stillbirth of her first child (because of a craniotomy performed by the obstetrician) and for four months more recently, "presumably with consumption," after her next, a premature child who also died. Another South London woman, a felt-slipper maker in her twenties, had already had four unsuccessful pregnancies, two ending in miscarriages and two in stillbirths. After the last, she "has been ill and attending St. Thomas's ever since [for "indigestion"]. In Campbell Road, Islington, Jane Munby, a hard-drinking Covent Garden flower seller, already crushed and a little crazy after the deaths of nine of her thirteen children, took to her bed for good when her son died on the Western Front in 1917. Munby almost literally forced a remaining teenage daughter to look after her until her own death in 1919.[76]

Bereaved mothers took comfort where it was available, with the press of other duties and especially in the belief that they had "done all they could" to ward off the death and comfort the dying child. Grief was seldom, it seems, mixed with self-blame. The London mothers seemed to consider that their responsibility for their children extended as far as their resources could stretch, but no further. A Drury Lane woman's comment to a nurse in the winter of 1883 suggests that she was not only trying to please the nurse but also recalling what her circumstances had been during the previous summer when she had lost two children: "I can't help feeling if my little ones that died in the summer had had different treatment they would have lived; but we did not know you then." A woman in Hampstead, in the same year, commented similarly to her district nurse on the death of her little boy of pneumonia sometime in the past: "I did the best I could for him, but if I had known then what I know now . . . or if you had been there, my boy need not have died."[77]

A decent funeral was the only thing left to offer the dead child. Parents with an ounce of remaining morale took the child's burial very seriously. Funerals were expensive, requiring a coach and at least two horses; "walking" funerals were a thing of the quaint past, as few burials took place in inner-London cemeteries after the middle of the nineteenth century. Funeral expenses rose throughout these years and the Life Assurance Companies Act of 1870 set unrealistically low maximums payable for children's death benefits.[78] The debt incurred by the funeral expenses, which was paid off slowly over the following months, was a reminder of the dead boy or girl. For a frugal, mean funeral—even if it circumvented the hated poor-law burials—only compounded the grief of the living. Pember Reeves described the very inexpensive and especially sad funeral of a three-year-old girl who had died of tuberculosis at a time when her father, a carter, was out of work. The unemployed man had borrowed £2 5s. for a cut-rate burial.

The funeral cortege consisted of one vehicle, in which the little coffin went under the driver's seat. The parents and a neighbour sat in the back part of the vehicle. They saw the child buried in a common grave with twelve other coffins of all sizes. "We 'ad to keep a sharp eye out for Edie," they said, "she were so little she were almost 'id."[79]

The funerals of children were distinguished by the kinds of wreaths that people contributed, portraying a favorite pet or toy. For infants under a year old, a special white coffin was used. Black clothing for the survivors was also required, even if it were only dyed or borrowed for the mourning period. To support them in their grief and help them bury the child respectably, relatives, neighbors, and workmates contributed flowers, cash, and help, like the Old Kent Road woman who stayed up all night in the 1890s sewing frills for a child's burial gown. A Poplar mother describing her funeral plans for her little son was proud that they could do their best for him. As the woman reported:

We shan't bury 'im till Friday. We don't want to 'urry 'im off, do we. . . . The insurance was only £10 but the funeral will cost £15. It'd be cheaper if we 'ad 'im squeezed in the front of the carriage under the coach-man [as in Edie's funeral], but if 'e's goin' to the Lord 'e may as well go in liberty and freedom. I shouldn't like 'im to go PINCHED![80]

The careful adherence to the rules of etiquette with respect to the dead child, sometimes against all reason and economy, reveals the same determination to do one's duty, as did other forms of care for the living child.

Unlike a child's sickbed and unlike the care of well children, a child's death was as much a father's as a mother's affair. Although women generally paid the whole family's burial insurance out of their household money, men's workmates were just as likely to contribute toward a child's funeral as were a woman's neighbors. Men employed in the Hoxton furniture trades, for example, in 1910 took up a collection for an impoverished Wilmer Gardens colleague who had just lost a baby. Art Jasper's account of his little niece's death from pneumonia in Hoxton just before World War I shows his sister Mary's husband Gerry (a heavy drinker and small-scale thief) as actively involved in mourning his first baby, though with different functions from the mother's. The father fetched his relations when the baby was gravely ill, made arrangements with the undertaker, and then found money to pay him.

Little Jo' died during the night. Their eyes were red with crying and loss of sleep. Mum pulled everyone together and we all went back to our place. Gerry was left to make arrangements with the local undertaker. I am sure little Jo' was not insured. Gerry had to appeal to the boss's son Harry, to help him out, which he did. After the funeral Mary and Gerry moved to a flat in Hackney Road. The place they had gave too many memories of the baby.[81]

The loss of a child could unleash emotions about the meaning of fatherhood that had remained largely hidden during the children's lives. Fathers were, it appears, as grief stricken as mothers in the hours and days following a child's death. Autobiographies by children abound with memories of their fathers' sufferings at the deaths of one of their children. Frank Steel, writing as an old man in 1939, described the death of a baby soon after the family, newly impoverished by a bankruptcy, had moved to "Ditcher's Row" in northeast London. Steel remembered "my father's cry of anguish as he went, with me in his arms, to look [at the dead baby] for the last time." Similarly, both the father and the grandfather were very demonstrative in their mourning for a fifteen-month-old boy who died of pneumonia in the 1920s. The father's crying may have been more memorable because of his seeming lack of interest in his living children or because a man in tears was so uncommon. A girl in 1924 indeed heard "the unbelievable, a man crying, deep shaking sobs that frightened us all" the night her sister died. In this case, the tears were those of a tender young doctor at his patient's bedside.[82]

CHAPTER 7

"The Value of Babies"
Transforming Motherhood,
1900–1918

"UNPAID NURSEMAID OF THE STATE"

In the first two decades of the twentieth century, London working-class mothers were the objects of an unprecedented attempt by a cluster of governmental bodies and private associations to transform the way in which they cared for their infants and children. Collectively, these efforts comprise what contemporaries called the Infant Welfare movement. Some of these programs offered mothers help, some threats. Some began with sympathy and admiration for London's "working women"; others accused them of ignorant, even vicious, child care practices. But they all added up to a reconfiguration of their motherhood. Women of the middle classes had much earlier embraced child nurturing as a private identity and a public duty. The Infant Welfare reformers sought to generate this consciousness in the majority of British women who were poor and who regarded material survival and daily household management as more central charges than the motherly supervision of their children's development.[1] Although much maternal passion and interest went into keeping the children fed and well, and mothers' relationships with their children could be intimate and satisfying, women's principal identity during this period remained that of managers of their households rather than nurturers of their children. The "maternalist" Infant Welfare reformers, on the other hand, thought that mothering as child nurture should require new kinds of work, some of it defined by doctors, and should occupy a more central position in an adult woman's identity.[2]

The Infant Welfare movement belonged to the decade of imperialist agitation preceding World War I in which women's reproductive capacity and men's fighting capability became matters of government interest and activity as never before. Church-based visitors and mothers' meetings, missionaries, Bible sellers, and others had been circulating throughout inner London for many decades. What was new in the twentieth century was the exclusive focus on mothers and child care, the sheer size, number, and organization of the programs, the extent to which medical personnel and nomenclature were involved, and the series of coercive laws that now accompanied the programs.

This chapter builds on contributions by historians of the welfare state, of working-class women, and of medicine[3] and demonstrates the unprecedented scope of the Infant Welfare campaign, particularly in London, and the intensity of its involvement with mothers. Mothers' and babies' clinics, extensive (at least in many of the boroughs) health visiting systems, and expanded volunteer School Care Committees were the Infant Welfare movement's efficient and confident cadres. Although my argument is compatible with a loosely conceived medicine-as-social-control-position incorporating Donzelot and Foucault,[4] my main aim is to present a phenomenology of the confrontation between the mothers and the widely diffused new medical culture. This discussion injects a voice often absent in treatments of the Infant Welfare movement—that of the mothers themselves. The reformers' ideas and demands were directed toward disrupting long-standing neighborhood-based women's health care and childrearing methods, practices that, for all their failings, were interwoven with wider survival strategies. So although working-class mothers gladly, in the hopes of improving their children's health, complied with some of the prescriptions of the professionals, they were just as likely to ignore or reorder them. Because much of the campaign was staffed by volunteers and the coercive power of the state in enforcing its directives was often muted, many of the women could speak their minds, confident of their own logic.

The campaign eventually succeeded in one of its aims, that of making the medical system the central authority (though never the only one) to which mothers looked for advice and help. Its effectiveness in lowering infant mortality rates is still being debated. As Chapter 6 outlined, infant death rates were clearly correlated with income. Yet teaching antiseptic ways of preparing baby bottles and food and identifying diseases that doctors could competently treat likely contributed at least a few percentage points to the fall in infant mortality that began during this era.[5]

This chapter owes a great deal to the caustic observations of a contemporary, Anna Martin, who viewed the Infant Welfare era through the prism of gender. Feminist, suffragist, social worker, and birth control advocate, she was a member of the nonconformist Bermondsey Settlement from 1898 until her death in the 1930s. From her vantage point at Beatrice House in Rotherhithe, Martin commented on the proliferation of national legislation and local regulation that, to her way of thinking, placed even more duties on the sagging shoulders of working-class wives. Sanitary officers, school personnel, medical officials all seemingly conspired to press working-class wives beyond the limits of their endurance, both physically and financially. G. K. Chesterton's iconoclastic *Eye Witness* and its successor, *The New Witness,* similarly attacked the Education Acts and the Children Act as parts of a "campaign for the regimentation of the poor." For these radical Catholic libertarians, the mother was the emblem of state oppression.[6] Many socialists and feminists, on the other hand, tried to transform the terms of the Infant Welfare movement into a series of state and municipal supports for mothers and children, grouped under the concept of the "Endowment of Motherhood," briefly discussed in the Conclusion of this book. Anna Martin's maverick feminist scrutiny of this era was compatible with the "Endowment" position, but with an angrier feminist bite. For Martin, the Infant Welfare era legislation represented a tacit arrangement between ruling-class and working-class men to deposit the social responsibility for the nation's health in mothers' laps. It was easy, she thought, for population-minded legislators and the mostly male representatives of the working classes to agree on new measures that would not cost men—as husbands or as taxpayers—anything. Commenting on nearly two decades of such reforms, Martin observed: "Personally the writer has never heard of a single man who contributed even an extra shilling a week. . . . As therefore the regular wage-earning portion of the community would refuse to foot the bill, Parliament has, in effect, decreed that the mothers must undertake the responsibility."[7]

The twentieth-century pressures combined but also conflicted with mothers' responsibilities for providing their families' basic comforts: the traditional Sunday dinner versus spectacles for a schoolchild. As recent demographic work suggests, child health and infant survival are parts of community ecologies, unlikely to change very much without dramatic cultural shifts. The reformers were, as the mothers saw it, simply demanding that the fixed number of household resources be shifted from some parts of the family to others. Given the divide between male and female monetary streams in most working-class households, the wherewithal to meet the new definitions of maternal care would come out of the mother's own food, money, rest, and health. For wives, the price of noncompliance was "countless humiliations" and occasionally fines, jail sentences, or the loss of child custody. To be a mother in these circumstances was, in Anna Martin's terms, to be little more than "the unpaid nursemaid of the State."[8]

THE STATE AND FERTILITY

The decade under consideration here, from 1904 to World War I, saw fertility rates drop in inner-London boroughs more rapidly than they had in the three previous decades of much slower decline. As Table 4–2 illustrated, fertility in the wealthier boroughs like Hampstead and Kensington fell the earliest and the fastest; in Poplar and Southwark, working-class boroughs, the decline in the last two decades of the century was 10 percent or less. In a later twenty-year interval, however, which spanned the turn of the century, inner-London declines had become more dramatic and more widespread. There was a 23 percent drop in Poplar between 1890–1891 and 1909–1911, and one about the same size in Southwark. Still more dramatic declines in fertility took place in the 1910s and 1920s.[9]

This discussion of the Infant Welfare movement proposes that early twentieth-century state policies (local and national, official and non-official) of all kinds—many not usually viewed as relevant to questions of fertility—could be over time extremely far-reaching in reorganizing the experience of the mother–child relationship, one that is surely a basic one in any consideration of fertility as a social issue. Theories of general cultural diffusion are not necessary to understand transformations in popular assumptions about child care and the obligations of mothers. Ideas about limiting births did not have to "trickle down" to the poor in order to generate new kinds of behavior among the latter; they could be laid down with a sledgehammer.[10] A combined effort by national and local governments, supplemented by thousands of enthusiastic and well-connected volunteers, was capable—the experience of the early twentieth century demonstrates—of making its presence felt in nearly every home in the metropolis where a mother and child could be found. By 1919 Anna Martin was sure that taken together, the policies of the Infant Welfare years had created a social and material climate that discouraged women from having babies. As a Rotherhithe working woman commented: "Sometimes I hanker after another baby, but then I say to myself the pleasure of it would only last a year or two, and afterwards *there'd be nothing but worry.*"[11]

THE "DETERIORATION" HEARINGS

Political as much as scientific advances in medicine and public health ensured that doctors and health workers would serve as spokespeople for new conceptions of childhood and "mothercraft." Medicine in fact provided the main discourse in which a wide area of public policy was formulated in the years around 1904, and medical officers of health and other health experts were prominent in debates on national welfare.[12] Hygiene as state policy partly reflected real advances in medicine and bacteriology, as medicine had become powerful enough to justify new forms of official regulation of the poor as well as unprecedented kinds of public generosity (like the levying of taxes to pay for school dinners for poor children).

Two axioms in medical discourse had special relevance to the policies and practices of the Infant Welfare movement: the separation of health care from more general charity, and individual responsibility for illness and health. In regard to the first axiom, medicine had indeed once been but a branch of charity and only gradually in the eighteenth and nineteenth centuries was severed from the offer of food, fuel, clothing, or shelter. Edwin Chadwick and Southwood Smith had campaigned for medical and sanitary reform as means of eliminating poverty by keeping wage earners healthy, and the rupture between medical care and general help for the disabled and elderly poor was never complete, as the increasingly elaborate and professional poor-law infirmary and fever hospital system under the post-1871 local government board indicates. By the twentieth century, though, the distinction between medical care and charitable help for the poor was generally taken for granted. Marion Kozak's remarkable study of health care in East London in the 1920s and 1930s describes the dilemmas of personnel faced with the strict political boundary between "health" and "welfare." Hospitals offered long-term and expensive inpatient treatment for the sick, but their staffs knew that the illnesses they witnessed were often the result of a lack of decent food. Handouts of bread, meat, and vegetables would have been considerably cheaper to supply than were months of hospital care. Medical agencies sometimes brought themselves to offer vitamins, yeast, or cod-liver oil, but they could not stretch their definitions of medical attention any further.[13]

The idea of individual responsibility was more ambiguous. Epidemiology and public health as professions are, after all, based on the possible environmental transmission of disease and on the duty of government bodies to intervene when individuals cannot. Today's government-sponsored AIDS campaigns and anticancer and anti–heart disease diets—all of which place responsibility for health in the hands of individuals—tend to obscure the extent to which workplace and environmental toxins and carcinogens, which are mostly beyond the control of individuals, pose the greatest public health threats.[14] Similarly, one of the goals of the Infant Welfare movement was to instill in mothers a sense of their own responsibility for their children's health, despite the unhealthy overall environments that most of them were powerless to change.

From the beginning, the Infant Welfare movement's goals were thus at cross-purposes with the needs that working-class women articulated. Activists campaigned for trained childbirth attendants, systems of "advice" on infant feeding and infant care, and better access to medical care for mothers and babies—all with the aim of lowering national infant mortality statistics. But what the women actually seemed to need was not always medicine but food for themselves and their families; the information they craved was about birth control or abortion rather than bottle feeding; and the material suffering that nonfatal illnesses caused in mothers and children were issues as essential to the mothers as was the actual "wastage" of infant lives through death.[15]

A national forum in which medically trained people could intervene was presented in the debates on national "deterioration" that began with General J. F. Maurice's 1902–1903 series of apocalyptic journal articles claiming that the British race had so badly "deteriorated" that it was no longer producing enough men who could serve as soldiers. An Inter-Departmental Committee on Physical Deterioration, made up of civil servants, was appointed to investigate the matter and issued its celebrated report in 1904. The report covered all bases but singled out infant mortality as a major national problem, and the issue was discussed by the registrar-general at some length in his *Annual Report* for that year. Although infant mortality had long been a concern among British health officials of all kinds, it now became a major political issue.[16] Indeed, by November 1904, a Manchester town councillor referred to the subject of physical deterioration as "getting somewhat threadbare by now." Infants, children, and mothers were studied intensely during the next decade, and it was in the interest of lowering infant death rates in poor districts that health visiting schemes, milk depots, and mothers' and babies' clinics were established, all within a few years or even months of the 1904 report.[17]

Local and national legislation also followed, an unwieldy mixture of regulation and service. Earlier child welfare legislation, like the 1889 Prevention of Cruelty to Children Act, was focused on abandoned, delinquent, or abused children. The new legislation was directed at all working-class children. The 1906 Education (Provision of Meals) Act increased the supply of dinners (still means tested, however) for London schoolchildren, and in the early months of World War I, the act was considerably extended. The 1907 Education (Administrative Provisions) Act required school authorities to carry out medical inspections twice during children's school careers. In 1907, under the Notification of Births Act, local authorities were empowered to require the birth attendant or the father to notify the district MOH of all live births within thirty-six hours.[18] The LCC enacted such a measure immediately, and its borough registrars were thus sources of information for the voluntary health visiting organizations that proliferated during this period. The 1908 Children Act, best known for its creation of a separate system of juvenile justice in England, was a grab bag of middle-class theories about the failings of working-class parents, mothers especially, and was strongly opposed by the organized working class. Among its seemingly unrelated provisions, it outlawed children's (under age fourteen) going into pubs; it provided penalties for parents whose children were killed owing to a lack of fireguards in their homes or as a result of overlaying if "at the time of going to bed the person was under the influence of drink"; and for the first time it labeled and penalized parental neglect. The National Insurance Act of 1911 with its Maternity Benefit was legislated, too, in a climate partly created by the "deterioration" discussions.[19] One might say that this era concluded with the passage of Fisher's Maternity and Child Welfare Act of 1918, the product of a major wartime campaign by feminist and suffrage organizations. This legislation offered grants to local authorities for a wide variety of services for mothers and children.

The "ignorant" or "feckless" mother whose personal failings made her children sick was a central trope in "deterioration" discourse.[20] Good mothers could save English babies, create healthy children, and regenerate the nation. It is illuminating to compare the British "deterioration" debates with contemporaneous discussions in France, with its far larger population crisis and greater poverty. Late nineteenth- and early twentieth-century French discussions focused on infant (rather than child) mortality, just as the British did. In both countries poverty, unemployment, poor sanitation, and other environmental forces were acknowledged as factors in infant mortality, though this recognition was obscured by maternalist language. Yet the policy implications of similar data and assumptions were read very differently. French experts concluded that women were returning to work too soon to continue breast feeding, and ultimately, a 1913 law provided paid leave for women for eight weeks following a birth, sometimes longer. In Britain, where married women's paid work was badly underreported in the census[21] and where there was a wide official consensus against it, the infant death figures simply became indications of mothers' need for expert supervision and education.[22] The British predilection, based on a negative image of mothers, was for coercive rather than welfare legislation whenever possible.

Medical concepts structured the services supplied in the 1900s and 1910s, appearing not only in such obvious areas as the search for the causes of infant diarrhea but also in somewhat less expected settings. At the St. Pancras School for Mothers, for example, free dinners for pregnant and nursing mothers were available only "as a medical prescription" and were conditional on the mothers' regularly bringing their babies to be weighed. The committees providing dinners for schoolchildren often used the meals as a way of supplying, according to the latest nutritional theories, adequate "proteid matter" in the children's diets. Some weighed the children before and after a series of feedings, and others administered cod-liver oil along with, or instead of, actual food. The concept of child neglect also was extended in the Children Act to include failure to provide state-of-the-art medical care, for which parents could lose custody of their children to the courts or be subject to misdemeanor prosecutions.[23]

GUILT AND RESPONSIBILITY

The combined legislative and propaganda assault of the years after the turn of the century helped create the cultural conditions for what we would now call the "guilty" mother; Anna Martin thought of her as "worried." The new proposition was that mothers did—if they carefully enough followed the instructions of health visitors or doctors—have full power over their children's life and death. A speaker at the 1906 National Conference on Infant Mortality, for example, spoke of instilling "a civic religion that will make the loss of a child something of a social stigma as well as a racial sin." But the female working-class public was accustomed to toil and worry over sick children, mourning and regret over dead ones, but not self-blame or social stigmatization. The mothers had rightly refused to take full responsibility for the deaths of their children.[24]

To get a sense of what maternal "guilt"—an anachronistic term, it is true—might mean in practice in the pre–World War I years, we can turn to one of the best known of the mothers' and babies' clinics that sprang up after 1904. The St. Pancras School for Mothers, founded in 1907, with its premises at 37 Chalton Street, Euston Road, was named the Mothers' and Babies' Welcome to avoid intimidating local women with the word *school*. Despite its policymakers' feminist sympathies, they were caught partway in the rhetorical grid of the Infant Welfare movement. The clinic straddled a rather uncomfortable fence on the question of whom to blame for infant deaths, as the contradiction between the beginning and end of this excerpt from one of their official publications indicates:

The great bulk of the ailments of infants under twelve months old depend on mismanagement in some direction. It is true that raging epidemics, respiratory diseases and the more insidious tubercle bacillus slay their thousands, but the victims of faulty hygiene fall by the wayside in tens of thousands, whether the fault lies with the mother, the child's food and clothing, or its surroundings.[25]

The St. Pancras staff showed sympathy and admiration for the mothers of their district and offered them help in the form of food and medical care as well as the conventional cooking and sewing lessons. But they also wanted mothers to develop a capacity for guilt about whether they as individuals were doing enough, and the proper things, for their children.

Clinic workers were distressed by the number of women who refused responsibility. As one of them wrote:

> The despair of the institution is the unsuccessful mother who comes in and goes out smiling whate'er befall. After an intermittent attendance, a vacant reception of the doctor's advice, and then some absence, she will turn up dressed in new black to tell you how baby died of "erasmus." In one case twins died, one after the other, of "erasmus," but the mother did not seem to think she had any great part in it. The only way in cases like these is to show such gentleness that the girl may be drawn to come back as soon as she finds she is to expect a baby again, and put herself and her foolish mind into good keeping all the way through. There *is* the affection to work with if only it can be controlled and directed.[26]

The assumption that individuals can exercise control over their own or their families' health tends to be rejected today by the poorest patients. Those who are poor, sociological surveys show, are more likely than others to refuse to take responsibility for health. One can read this as fatalism related to the "culture of poverty" or as a response to an awareness of material constraints that constantly interfere with doing, buying, or eating the healthiest things. In any case, in the early 1900s, several decades of public health studies implicating income, housing, type of plumbing, and so on in morbidity and mortality supported the mothers' approach.[27] Mothers had only very limited control over their environments. Even such modest and effective measures as more hand washing around babies and more thorough cleaning of their utensils would have demanded, in many households, different quarters, more fuel, and better plumbing.[28] But the Infant Welfare movement's rhetoric had poor mothers coming and going, suggesting that they had powers that they actually lacked and holding them morally and sometimes legally responsible for deeds they could not do.

"IGNORANT OLD WOMEN" OR "MEDICAL SUPERVISION"

The professionals' standards of infant and child health and physical comfort were much higher than those prevailing among working-class

mothers. They were based partly on the experience of middle-class social worlds in which children were larger; better fed; less anemic; freer
of rashes, chilblains, and sniffles; and less prone to more serious diseases.
They represented, too, a conception of infants as particularly "precious," whereas working-class mothers had fuller vocabularies of appreciation for older children who helped at home or earned cash for their
families.[29] The professionals' health standards, too, emanated from a
culture that equated physical health with goodness, a culture that from
the mid-nineteenth century on was obsessed with health. The new
thinking about mothering was also, however, based on a rapidly proliferating body of scientific literature. The 1880s, following Robert Koch's
discovery of the typhoid bacillus in 1880, was a period of intense activity in bacteriology, and the same might be said of the 1890s and the
three following decades in regard to the study of nutrition and human
and animal metabolism.[30]

The newly professional fields of nursing and epidemiology that were
so central to the Infant Welfare and child health campaigns worked to
disseminate some pieces of this body of knowledge. They taught the
value of antisepsis for the home care of wounds and in preparing baby-
feeding bottles; the superior value, based on its digestibility as well as
its purity, of mothers' versus cows' milk in its commercially available
forms; the importance of protein in the diet; methods of preventing the
spread of tuberculosis from one infected family member to another; and
the identification and easy treatment of such common and unpleasant
childhood diseases as tooth decay, conjunctivitis, and nearsightedness.
These proponents of a more medical child care obviously had something
substantive to teach. We must remember, however, that they were not
always right. Margaret McMillan was proud, for example, that her clinic
had carried out "over 700 operations" to remove adenoids and tonsils in
one year early in this century; most of these painful procedures would
today be viewed as unnecessary. Thousands of London children in these
years had their skulls heavily irradiated, too, as a treatment for a wholly
nonlethal if disagreeable condition, ringworm.[31]

Medical advice was to replace that of grandmothers and neighbors.
Infant welfare specialists all over the country waged an active campaign
against "old wives" administering gin and pickles or opiates to small
babies, "ignorant old women who have buried 10 out of 14 or 15," as
one social worker put it.[32] As Infant Welfare educator Emilia Kanthack
declared in 1907, health visitors would have to contend with the fact
that the mothers were by and large "pitiably ignorant and superstitious,
full of prejudices, and often stuffed with dreadful advice from terrible
old gamps and dowagers in their immediate vicinity." What was needed,
wrote a commentator in the *Toynbee Record,* were young mothers "who

are able to launch out into the experiences of motherhood unchained by superstition and vulgar prejudice." Infant deaths, Dr. Janet Lane-Claypon wrote in 1909, are more likely "when women take the advice of their neighbours or of some old woman, persons who have had much experience with children but who have no knowledge of the really important points. . . . Even the healthiest baby should have medical supervision."[33]

The impulse to "supervise" mothering among the poor was often, it seems, overpowering. The biscuits offered in friendship to mothers by the St. Pancras personnel were, for instance, watched by the staff's "vigilant eyes . . . to stop [their] being administered to infants in long clothes." And settlement worker Clara Grant must have been the scourge of Bow as she went about the streets snatching pacifiers from babies. Her proud recital of these rather obnoxious deeds stemmed from her certainty that protecting the babies from the microbe-laden comforters was indisputably healthier for them. The Finsbury Milk Depot—which the borough medical officer, George Newman, had been active in founding in November 1904—put its babies entirely under "medical supervision." Mothers in the program received an elaborate twelve-item instruction sheet listing the intervals at which babies of each age were to be fed and including instructions for disinfecting the depot-supplied nipples. All infants were to be weighed regularly, even though the weighing station on Goswell Road was open only for a few hours on Wednesday afternoons. Home visits, essential to full supervision, were made weekly by a trained nurse-midwife with the aid of volunteers.[34]

The desire for more control over working-class childhood sometimes went further. Dr. Lewis Hawkes, the Finsbury general practitioner with a penchant for overstatements about the poor, candidly admitted his urge to remove Finsbury children from their parents. As he told the Inter-Departmental Committee on Physical Deterioration: "After I had been working about eighteen months in the Metropolitan Dispensary [Fore Street in the City] my own idea was to take every child as soon as it was born and put it away in a Government home of some kind." C. W. Saleeby, another physician involved in the Infant Welfare movement, dreamed in 1905 of public crèches for preschool children, offering them the sort of care "which their own parents cannot be trusted to exhibit."[35] Indeed, one of the sources of support for the public education of children from age three was the superiority of the school to the home environment. As Helen Dendy of the COS explained in 1895, the years of schooling were the children's "one chance of civilisation." Even Margaret McMillan, a very different figure who loved poor children and respected their mothers, dreamed of one day establishing "some one authority" to engage in the "continuous supervision of the childhood of the nation."[36]

Working-class mothers did not always welcome middle-class teaching and teachers. Thus the people of Hoxton, one nursery worker there remarked in 1904, were "very independent" and reluctant to admit charity workers to their homes. "I do not think that my Hoxton mothers would let a lady in if she said: 'I hear that you have got a baby and I want to teach you about it.'" Investigators doing a well-intentioned study of widows' receipt of outrelief in Lambeth in the 1900s found a suspiciously high number not at home. Not even district nurses, probably the most popular of all those who visited the homes of the poor, were always desired in working-class homes. Finsbury women relented only when the local doctor threatened to refuse his services to those who would not admit the nurses, and there were scattered reports of hostility elsewhere as well. One school nurse (outside London) even had to have a police escort, so much hatred had her delousing activities generated.[37]

Infant Welfare workers were usually conscious of their lack of welcome. A physician working with the City of Westminster Health Society ruefully warned trainee health visitors in 1906 that they would experience "many disappointments." The Fabian Women's Group's weekly visitors in Kennington, beginning their study of "the effect on mother and child of sufficient nourishment before and after birth," were also painfully aware of the wary courtesy they were offered by their clients. Florence Petty, the resourceful nutritionist attached to the St. Pancras School for Mothers, worked hard to sidestep the uncomfortable role of "visitor" in the homes of Somers Town. Instead, she solicited invitations from clients, first chatting with them at the school's cooking classes "and then offering to drop in and show [them] how to make a lentil stew, or, as in one case, 'a suet pudding without a saucepan.' "[38]

Nonetheless, although many forms of "visiting" had been discredited by sophisticated social thinkers like the Liberal C. F. G. Masterman, those with health—particularly that of infants and children—as their mission could still feel confident of the value of their work. The "deterioration" discussion had given them a mandate, one that rephrased into questions of health and hygiene older fears about the national danger posed by a "residuum" of unruly poor. Health experts rather than good samaritans were the ones to deal with a problem posed in these terms, and there was a fairly broad consensus in the early twentieth century that the agencies of the national and local state as "Overparent" (in L. T. Hobhouse's phrase) were the most efficient means of social regeneration. The permission that Victorian charity workers believed they had to invade the homes of the poor was, in the early twentieth century, requested on a new basis.[39]

"IN CAME THE LADY WITH THE ALLIGATOR PURSE": HEALTH VISITING[40]

In addition to such nineteenth-century health workers as sanitary inspectors, medical officers of health, and district nurses, new ones proliferated after 1904: school doctors (officially called medical inspectors), School Care Committees with many responsibilities for the scholars' health, infant welfare clinics, and health visitors. In Bermondsey, to give one example of the pace of their deployment, the borough medical officer advocated municipal milk depots in his 1904 annual report, along with the education of mothers. By 1908, the borough got its first paid health visitor, who was to follow up "selected cases" among Bermondsey's four thousand annual births. In 1910 a second health visitor was added, and two more in 1917. Between 1908 and 1915, two municipal and four voluntary baby clinics as well had been established in the borough.[41]

Courses of lectures for the public or for the new semiprofessionals, often by district medical officers or hospital consultants, spread over London like a medical Great Awakening. Borough health societies, such as the one in St. Pancras, sponsored series for the volunteer health visitors whom they were training, as well as for the mothers themselves. By its third year of existence, for example, the National League for Physical Education and Improvement, with its headquarters at Denison House, Vauxhall Bridge Road, could boast hundreds of lecture courses that its thirteen London branches had established. The Islington Health League, an affiliate, with only twelve lady and gentlemen members, had set up public lectures on health, first aid, infant care, and home nursing. In 1908 alone it had run fifty separate courses with six to twelve lectures per series, and this in addition to the many other courses of lectures with other sponsors in Islington.[42]

The 1907 Notification of Births Act, a permissive law that was immediately adopted in twenty of London's twenty-nine boroughs, made possible the elaborate system of home visits to infants and mothers that in some boroughs included every child born into a non–middle-class household. As Blanche Gardiner, the newly appointed sanitary inspector for the Prevention of Infant Mortality in St. Pancras, reported in 1908, the act made it possible for authorities to send an "advice card" to each mother "within a few days" of every birth in the borough. Her colleague Dora Bunting put it more graphically in her description of the St. Pancras Mothers' and Infants' Society: "Directly a baby was heard of they pounced down upon it." By 1910, there were only three boroughs (Islington, Camberwell, and Greenwich) where there was no infant visiting. In ten boroughs, on the other hand, 60 percent or more of the homes of newly registered births were visited by a combination of paid sanitary inspectors, professional health visitors, and volunteers. Clinics, schools for mothers, and similar institutions had sprouted by then in all but a handful of the twenty-nine boroughs.[43] In 1915, when there were about three thousand births in the borough, Kensington's three women health visitors, two of whom were away for part of the year doing "military work," nonetheless managed to pay well over five thousand visits in that year. The North Islington School for Mothers, founded in 1913, listed by 1917 a staff of three visiting women doctors, five nurses, and thirty-seven volunteers, the majority of whom acted as visitors. They had even trained seven women as home helpers, among the first in the country.[44]

The earliest prenatal care for working-class women in London began after 1904. This care occasionally included extra meals for the pregnant women and help with arrangements for the birth, but more often it involved visitors supplying advice. The City of Westminster Health Society used its connections with local hospitals—its trustees included a number of hospital almoners—to obtain lists of women expecting babies. Society workers could thus begin infant care lessons earlier, and they could sometimes arrange for extra help in the home during the confinement. By 1914, the society proudly announced that they had visited about a third of the borough's new mothers prenatally, even persuading dozens of the expectant mothers to attend "mothercraft" classes. The Health Society's general industry is registered in Westminster's borough figures for proportions of notified births visited in 1910: 94 percent, topped only by the much less populous city of London's 100 percent. As Ann Oakley's *The Captured Womb* argues, the goal of prenatal care then as now was to reduce infant morbidity and mortality statistics; meeting the somewhat different needs that the pregnant women defined for themselves was a subsidiary project.[45]

The membership lists of the Westminster society show a rank and file of nurses, school managers, and representatives of such organizations as the Children's Country Holiday Fund and the Invalid Children's Aid Association. By 1912, the organization had a paid staff of six women working out of two offices in Westminster, all with appropriate training (which was required after 1908 for borough-appointed health visitors). Miss Cover, the superintendent of the head office in Greek Street, Shaftesbury Avenue, had a National Health diploma; others had nursing, midwifery, or Royal Sanitary Institute certificates. The working members tended to be young; a district nurse referred to the arrival of a "girl health visitor" to instruct a mature woman in child care as a distinct insult, and surely this provided one kind of barrier among many others to their real communication with their clients.[46]

By the 1890s a number of districts in Britain had salaried health visitors, as they were eventually called,[47] but all the London health visiting schemes originated after 1904. Unlike district nurses, health visitors were usually instructed to do nothing in the homes they visited, not even to wash or dress babies. After a new mother was no longer under the care of a midwife or other childbirth attendant—that is, somewhere between one and two weeks after the birth—the health visitor was to call, observe, advise, and report to local medical authorities. Health visitors were to introduce into the homes of the London poor such concepts as antisepsis, the value of breast feeding, the dangers of overlaying, and the prevention of rickets. But their main mission was to create "responsible" mothers, women who would seek medical advice in routine infant and child care, not just in matters of life and death.[48] Emilia Kanthack's six 1906 lectures for St. Pancras volunteer health visitors were designed to draw attention to many conditions that the visitors labeled as part of the domain of doctors, such as when pregnant women had swollen extremities, fits, or pelvic deformities; when mothers were bottle feeding their babies; or when babies developed severe diarrhea or had signs of rickets.[49] The mothers themselves would have defined only some of these conditions as occasions for a doctor's visit. Also, doctors at this point did not have proven treatments for all of these problems.

Health visiting was an enterprise in public health research as well as in education. The Westminster Health Society carried out studies of infant care practices and children's health status and gathered records on which others could conduct research. Blanche Gardiner, the St. Pancras sanitary inspector specializing in infant welfare, did a study of infant health in Somers Town for the Home Office in the 1900s. Miss Gauntlett, Kensington's first salaried health visitor, also gathered information on feeding methods, house accommodation, mothers' work, and the like but was unhappy with her observer's role in homes where there was so much "distress" crying out for more active, material help.[50] According to a nurse who wrote to Sylvia Pankhurst's *Women's Dreadnought* in 1917, it was mostly these research functions that "frightened" so many working-class women and that made the visitors seem "officious."[51] Health visitors usually reported to medical and government authorities (usually borough medical officers of health). Even though they often acted as advocates of the poor—badgering landlords, for example, into fixing leaks, cleaning toilets, or disinfecting drains—to their clients they were bound to seem "officious."

MEDICAL "DEFECTS" AND
THE SCHOOL CARE COMMITTEES

School medical examinations were another effort to reshape mothers' assumptions and practices regarding children's health. The 1907 Education (Administrative Provisions) Act required that district education authorities organize annual medical examinations of all school entrants and leavers. Supported by women's and labor groups as well as by the public health establishment, the act had been violently opposed by the British Medical Association as a disastrous incursion into the livelihood of private physicians.[52] For the metropolis, with its three quarters of a million public school children, the inspection was a truly gargantuan undertaking, and the project got off to a poor start. But in the following years the school medical staff was augmented. There were ninety LCC school nurses by 1910 and, by the summer of 1912, a corps of thirty-four full-time school doctors as well.[53]

As with earlier, less formal school supervision of children's health by teachers or visiting nurses,[54] the object of the inspections was as much the mother as the child, something that contemporaries recognized.[55] Many schools made special efforts through their associated Care Committees to persuade mothers to be present at the inspections, but the numbers who did so varied enormously from school to school. Care Committee members often attended the inspections, too, making their own claim to the children's bodies.

Whether or not the mother was present and even if the examination took literally a minute, as Marion Phillips's 1910 pamphlet charged, the inspections were still an occasion on which the child and its mothering were displayed to the authorities. Mothers usually washed and dressed up their children for the event. This meant, of course, as one school medical officer complained in 1910, that "the assessment of clothing . . . is not of great value, as, having been officially warned, the children come in their own or borrowed clothes better than those usually worn." (Flea bites and head lice were harder to disguise.) The Bow mother who grabbed the boots from the feet of her just-inspected child for another to wear to the next inspection was amply demonstrating the pressure the occasion meant for her.[56] Nurses and doctors complacently reported the maternal failings they uncovered in the way of nails, wire, and pins on clothing in place of buttons; and many of them confiscated the evidence. Dr. Hawkes, the Finsbury physician who was also a school doctor, noted that "quite a collection of wire nails which were used as clothes fastenings had been made by the nurse" at one of his schools. At the Popham Road School in Islington, a nurse fastidiously reported to the Care Committee that a recent inspection had found 180 children who had their clothes pinned together, whereas 174 were "properly fastened."[57]

School medical examinations are a prime example of the sort of welfare measure that Anna Martin deplored: Seemingly providing a service to families and the protection of children, medical inspection involved a modest state outlay but a heavy charge on mothers. Medical inspections were bound to discover "defects" (as they were unfelicitously called) in the children and to prescribe treatment for them. In the school year ending in July 1912, the London doctors uncovered about sixty thousand eye, ear, nose, throat, and ringworm cases. Many commentators considered that the diagnoses, without some accessible and cheap way for parents to get their children treated, were a real cruelty,[58] but the 1907 act mandating the examinations provided no treatment. There were clinic systems in other towns, but the London proposals were opposed by moderates on the LCC Education Committee as too expensive, and Margaret McMillan's privately funded Deptford clinic was the only one in operation in the London schools in the prewar years.[59] Instead of providing its own medical care to the children, the LCC worked out a complicated financial and administrative arrangement with a number of private hospitals. The hospitals' locations mostly in inner London within a mile and a half of Charing Cross meant long trips into town for children from Poplar, Woolwich, or Stoke Newington, and mothers complained of these as well as the long waits at the hospitals, repeated trips, ineffective medical care, and high prices.[60]

The responsibility for supervising this mass treatment belonged to the School Care Committees. Named the Health Sub-Committees of Board School Managers in the nineteenth century, their title was changed to Relief Sub-Committees in 1900 and to Care Committees after the 1906 Education (Provision of Meals) Act, into which they were written as the main providers of the children's dinners and investigators of their families' means. Volunteer ladies and gentlemen, under 5 percent of whom were working class, according to an 1884 survey, the managers were attached to groups of schools where they helped choose teachers, enforce attendance, deal with school fees, organize school dinners, and screen the applicants. The London Education Department's Code of Regulations for managers lists, among other duties, that of seeing that the children were "brought up to habits of punctuality, of good manners and language, of cleanliness and neatness."[61]

In the twentieth century, especially after 1906, the managers' functions changed along with their name. They were less involved in administering the schools and did more welfare work among the scholars: serving meals, getting mothers to seek medical treatment for their children, and badgering parents to find apprenticeships for their school leavers rather than better-paying dead-end jobs. The East London Care Committees whose minutes and membership lists I have surveyed for the period after 1908 included a good many (nonworking) ladies and gentlemen, but more teachers, settlement house residents, clergymen, and wives of clergymen. In 1909, there were 5,500 Care Committee volunteers in London, working from one to four days a week in their schools and districts, and by 1914, at least eight thousand.[62]

These volunteers had the power to help mothers and their children, and they often exercised it. The Bay Street School Committee in central Hackney managed to make contact with an organization that supplied spectacles for poor children and paid for glasses for three local pupils in 1908; the Poplar district committees decided to supply meals on weekends and to younger siblings of school-aged children during the transport strike that caused such suffering in the area in the summer of 1911.[63]

Whether welcome or not, however, Care Committee volunteers were practically inescapable. As one cos-connected Hackney committee member wrote, "We are constantly calling in the help of every agency, whether official or voluntary, that has the right and the ability to interfere to the children's benefit." The committee members viewed medical follow-up work as particularly tedious and unrewarding, and a few committees in fact refused to do it at all.[64] But for the mother, the Care Committee visitor, no matter how kindly, was almost invariably a menacing personage. The visitor had the power to define a mother's refusal to bring a child to the hospital as a form of "neglect" and to refer the case for investigation by the NSPCC under Section 12 of the Children Act, a procedure that committees did use occasionally. Care Committee members were also often the ones to enforce Education Authority orders to "cleanse" lice-infested children at the hated borough cleansing stations.

The degree of zeal with which the committees carried out their responsibility depended on their numbers, energy, and principles. An activist West St. Pancras committee singled out ill-looking children at the school and asked them to attend medical inspections. Finding that one such boy had still not had the hospital treatment that the school doctor had prescribed, the committee delegated one of their number to take him there. When the head office informed the Curtain Road (Shoreditch) School's committee that five of its scholars had stopped their hospital treatments without getting formal discharges, the committee summoned all five sets of parents to attend a hearing.[65] Recalcitrant mothers received many informal visits before any of the committees began more formal legal action against them. Thus when Cecilia Osborne's mother, in Shoreditch, refused to have her child treated, the mother was visited twice by local committee members, and a third time by a special LCC officer who eventually urged the committee to drop the matter. A group of parents who had not yet paid for their children's eyeglasses were chased down by another Care Committee, which had also requested that the LCC authorize their sending "worrying letters."[66] For women with schoolchildren, the changing discourses, legislation, and knowledge about health, nutrition, and families probably appeared most vividly and frequently in the form of the dedicated and hardworking middle-class School Care Committee visitors.

In the stark terms in which the issue was posed during this era, better health for children meant for their mothers more work, more trouble, and less sleep. Margaret McMillan acknowledged that Deptford clinic mothers were being asked to take on extra burdens for goals they really did not accept: "Such a fuss about every little thing. They can't have a cold in their eyes without all this turn-up! With good-natured willingness to oblige, mothers bestir themselves, only half convinced, not half convinced yet, it may be. . . . We have put new burdens on parents, but they bear them kindly."[67] As Care Committee member Barbara Drake put it rather blandly in 1910, "The type of medical treatment urged by the School Doctor, treatment of eyes, ears, throat, and nose, is the type of treatment for which the average mother sees the least necessity." Prescriptions for spectacles and for dental work were directed at ailments that neither the mothers nor their husbands took seriously. To make matters worse, they sometimes required large cash outlays from the parents and often multiple medical visits.[68]

The Care Committees were thus often on the defensive as they, with their ambiguous half-volunteer, half-official status, attempted to change the way that parents looked after their children. In the winter of 1910, when a sizeable number of children from the Popham Road School in Islington were discovered to need glasses, the Care Committee found that a large minority of parents refused to cooperate. Their children's poor eyesight was simply not one of the things they worried about. One of the mothers, a Mrs. Stephen, told a committee member that she was "unable to pay, and stated that the child did not need the glasses her eyesight being quite good." A Mrs. Hollings also "disputed the necessity of the glasses." In general, for that committee, the balance sheet for the year ending in March 1911 showed a lot of parental foot-dragging on glasses or other minor problems: Of twenty-nine boys referred for treatment of various sorts, fifteen had never been, and of thirty-two girls, a third remained untreated, and at least five of the disputed cases pertained to unbought spectacles.[69]

The excuses that mothers offered for their failure to carry out the doctors' orders reveal a distinct system of maternal allegiances: to wage earning, to the housekeeping budget, and to domestic tasks over what the mothers viewed as the relatively minor needs of an older child, a child whom mothers expected to contribute money or work, not to take them away. The mothers complained repeatedly that they could not leave their paid work or their home duties to bring a child for medical treatment. As a woman in Rotherhithe who had failed to take her daughter to a hospital stated: "If I take Lizzie to the hospital, what with fares, medicine, and someone to mind the others while I'm gone, it will cost me one-and-six. *I don't see the good of taking money off the food to put it on the medicine.*"[70] Benjamin Atkins's mother told visitors in West St. Pancras in 1916 that she was "quite unable to leave her other children to take him to Treatment Centre." Among the many Popham Road School parents who refused to get glasses for their children, some said they could not pay for them, and a Mrs. Bearfield simply declared that it was "inconvenient to leave her stall to take the boy to the hospital."[71]

The ambiguities of the welfare state were quickly revealed through the encounters among mothers, school officials, Care Committees, and the state over children with lice, particularly head lice. Lice infestations can be quite mild, far less problematic than the long and nasty treatments prescribed for them before today's effective pesticides defused the issue.[72] Clearly, the louse represented a whole series of contagion fears among those, like schoolteachers, who lived on fairly intimate terms with the working classes. The rage of mothers over the health authorities' cruel and punitive treatment of lice-infested schoolchildren was certainly not new in the twentieth century; it adds a good deal of drama to the history of the introduction of compulsory education in Britain.

The 1908 Children Act, however, provided a new set of legal protocols under which parents could be compelled to have their infected children stripped, clipped, and bathed (while their clothes baked in special ovens) at public, borough-maintained cleansing stations. Schoolteachers found the antilouse campaign particularly disruptive of ordinary school routines. Scrutinizing the children's heads publicly in mass examinations in front of their classmates, the school nurses' procedure was to separate those children with possible lice, ringworm, and so forth from the others. The apparently reassuring comments of the LCC's medical officer for education reveal the terror of the nurse's visit: "The nurse uses careful measures for asepsis after each of such suspected children. She is provided with permanganate of potassium, with corrosive sublimate for a stronger disinfectant. She has also a powerful lens, and forceps for manipulation of ringworm cases, and spirit lamp sterilizer for her metal instruments."[73] Holborn headmistresses (in 1914) complained of "abusive parents" invading their schools to protest such procedures. In Peckham, the problem was that "parents defy nurses' orders and dirty [that is, lice-infested] children remain in school." On the other hand, several headmistresses reported that the sassafras treatments that mothers were ordered to use to kill the head lice created an "absolutely intolerable" smell in the classrooms when the poor victims came to school.[74]

Care Committee workers were at the center of the louse controversy. A school nurse's report in March 1910 that forty-nine of the children at the Wood Close School in Bethnal Green had been found "verminous" provided much unappreciated visiting work for members of the Care Committee there, though a number of paid officials had preceded them to the pupils' homes. All the verminous children received cards to bring home to their mothers with full instructions for delousing them, and they were reinspected a few days later. But only ten of the forty-nine were "clean" at the next inspection. The names of the rest were sent to a higher office to begin legal procedures under the Children Act. Meanwhile, the school attendance officer delivered another notice to thirty-nine of the households in question, offering them information on "voluntary" baths and the sterilization of clothes at the Finch Street Cleansing Station and threatening that those not complying would be taken there in any case. But only one parent was impressed enough to arrange a voluntary bath. Amazingly, though, at its April meeting, the committee could report that its members had visited all the homes of the lousy children and had actually brought the children to the cleansing station,[75] a triumph of the zeal of the committee workers and the state policies they enforced.

MOTHERS' AND BABIES' CLINICS

Mothers' and babies' clinics, often affiliated with health visiting programs, multiplied in the decades before 1918: There were 1,583 such centers in England and Wales by 1920.[76] The case records, reports, and propaganda of these organizations describe a crucial phase in the history of pediatrics and social medicine, but we can also view them, like the School Care Committees, as arenas of direct contact between the new scientific views of infancy and the older health ideas of working-class women. In these encounters we can find, from the clients' side, a constantly shifting mixture of gratitude, secretiveness, intimidation, and learning.

The gaps so often remarked between the offering and reception of medical advice in Third-World countries today were evident in the early twentieth-century London clinics. For instance, users of clinics and other medical services were exposed to a new conception of the domestic day as divided into uniform parcels of time, a vision of the housewife's time that was refined in the 1920s by the "scientific housekeeping" school and was extended into areas beyond infant care, such as cooking and cleaning. The clock-driven feeding instructions for breast- or bottle-fed infants imposed a rigorous discipline. Weekly baby weighings and short clinic-opening hours themselves imposed a new time-discipline on the mothers.

First-time mothers were more eager to try the new clinics than were those with more experience. At the Bell Street Infant Consultation, which was run by the borough of St. Marylebone Health Society for the highly varied population of building trades laborers, servants, and porters who inhabited the crowded streets of the Lisson Grove area to the west of Regent's Park, mothers of first children (or of first surviving children) made up a disproportionately large part of the patients—to judge from the fifty-nine patient records that have survived. These first-time mothers also made more clinic visits than did those with later children, stopping in for more of the prescribed weekly or biweekly visits during the child's first year (a median of 9.5 visits for the first mothers and only 4 for mothers of later babies). Kathleen Tampin's mother, for instance, an ironer who lived two blocks away from the clinic and already had four children, brought in her daughter when she was about two months old, not for general advice, but because the child was obviously very ill; she weighed only five and a half pounds, and her clinic visits ended with her death after only a few consultations. Little George Stafford, who was a sixth child, was brought in four times at about nine months. His mother, who was married to a heavy-drinking piano porter, made the five-minute walk from her two-room home in Dorset Square because the child weighed only eight and a half pounds and of course looked "very wasted."[77]

The histories of the St. Pancras School for Mothers and the Bell Street Centre suggest considerable social variety among clinic users. At Bell Street, although many of the women were wives of regularly employed men—shop assistants, porters, milkmen, a sprinkling of policemen—more than 40 percent of the husbands were either laborers or were unemployed.[78] At least at these two clinics, health visitors had probably been doing their job of recruiting mothers for the clinics who might otherwise have stayed away, pointing out that certain symptoms, such as emaciation, merited the attention of a doctor.[79]

At the clinic some patients were referred to hospitals, anemic children were given cod-liver oil, and mothers who allowed their babies to share their beds or to use pacifiers were exhorted not to. Dr. Christine Murrell and Dr. Flora Murray at Bell Street were, however, most interested in the contents and frequency of infant feedings. In the early years of this century, the biochemistry and physiology of infant and adult digestion and nutrition were new sciences. Vitamins were not isolated until 1906. But because the doctors knew something about nutrition and because, in any case, eating and excretion patterns are the major way in which small babies register illness, the baby appeared—as one piece of propaganda for another clinic put it—"as a complicated machine for the digestion and absorption of food." The baby weighings provided an "objective" register of the success of their treatment. The development of motor and cognitive skills, though well charted in contemporary medical writings by this time,[80] were of minor interest to the doctors. Accordingly, the Bell Street records note such milestones only twice.

The preoccupation with feeding the baby is one that the clinicians shared with the mothers they saw, yet many issues had to be negotiated during the clinic consultations: whether breast or bottle and how often, when to terminate breast feeding, and when to introduce solid foods. Bell Street was not usually a setting for struggles over breast feeding, for most of the babies arrived at the clinic too late for that. Twenty of the fifty-nine babies were being wholly or partly bottle fed at their first visits, a figure that says nothing about feeding patterns in Marylebone more generally but does suggest that the Marylebone Health Society health visitors laid special emphasis on the medical supervision of bottle-fed babies.[81] The clinic's practice at Bell Street may have, however, encouraged bottle feeding, for the doctors, like their colleagues elsewhere, prescribed special nourishing or medicinal bottle-administered emulsions to some babies. Scanty or nonexistent lactation, common in their population of overworked and underfed mothers, plus the doctors' desire to measure the amount that the infants were fed, surely also led the doctors to prescribe bottle feeding.

In Thomas Alfred Proctor's case this medical practice is very clear. Though he was a breast-fed baby when he was first brought to Bell Street at age three and a half months, Dr. Murrell thought the child "slightly ricketty" and prescribed two bottles daily containing five parts milk, three parts barley water, and five drops of cod-liver oil. By January when the baby was six months old, he was getting four bottles a day in addition to some breast feedings. In another case, a thirty-year-old charwoman with seven living children and an out-of-work husband was advised to supplement her breast milk with two bottles daily. When her latest offspring reached five months, it was often hungry on the overtired mother's breast milk alone. Indeed, eighteen (of the fifty-nine) mothers switched from breast feeding to whole or partial bottle feeding (usually cow's milk diluted with barley water) while under the clinic's care.

The clinic's feeding rules were quite different from those of their patients' mothers. "Regularity in feeding" was essential after the child's first week of life, according to medical opinion, and the Bell Street physicians constantly urged more regular but less frequent feeding. When mothers reported that they nursed their infants every two hours, they were told to feed them every two and a half hours, and so on. Drs. Murrell and Murray categorically insisted that babies be weaned when they had reached eight months. Solid foods were not to be introduced until after the sixth month, for as the medical texts explained, the infant's stomach, salivary glands, and pancreas could not handle meat or starchy foods before then.[82]

All of the clinic's quite plausible rules for infant feeding were broken routinely by most working-class mothers, as shown in Chapter 5. They tended to feed their babies whenever they cried rather than according to schedules. To make sure that the babies were "satisfied," the mothers commonly fed them supplementary foods—cereals or bread-and-milk mixtures—from the earliest weeks. If they could, the mothers were likely to nurse their babies considerably longer than eight months. At the St. Pancras center, "mothers even begged to be allowed to continue breast-feeding beyond the usual 9 to 12 months" to avoid the expense of buying cow's milk for their babies.[83] These maternal practices, as Chapter 5 explained, followed a rationality not visible to the doctors: They saved money; they kept babies quiet in overcrowded homes; and they were also intended to keep them sleeping longer at night. The work at Bell Street was organized around changing many of these traditional practices, and the mothers who kept coming were willing to cope with the extra trouble the clinic's advice caused them.

For all their regulating intentions, Bell Street and its sister clinics were, after all, public services rather than formal institutions of state discipline. Nearly all their clients were there in some sense by choice because they were worried about their babies (some few had no doubt been badgered by health visitors or NSPCC men into bringing in their children). Any hope that the clinicians had of changing working-class childrearing depended on their establishing comfortable relationships with the mothers. Mothers in modern Glasgow reported that they often stopped using a facility when they knew they were violating its "rules" or when they felt bullied by its staff, and London women who were contemporaries of the Bell Street mothers were notoriously intimidated by doctors.[84] A sign of the "success" of the Bell Street doctors and other workers in making the patients feel welcome at the clinic was the number of mothers who admitted failing to meet its standards but who kept coming in as patients.

In the short run, at least, the mothers could or would not put into practice all of the clinic's prescriptions. Despite frequent recommendations that babies be put to sleep in clothes baskets or on two chairs placed together, twenty-one Bell Street babies were still sleeping with their mothers as their period of clinic visits came to an end. Indeed, some of them had switched from cribs back to the parents' bed, for a number of the infants had begun to "sleep badly" and cry at night after being put to sleep by themselves. Compliance was (at least apparently) better on the matter of pacifiers. One mother declared that her baby used his "very little—only in church." Mrs. Dix, the wife of a bookseller's assistant who lived in a little turning only a few steps away from the clinic, was evasive when asked about her baby's pacifier. On the first two visits, she admitted that Dorothy did use one; she answered "no" the third time; "sometimes" the fourth; "yes" the fifth; and "rarely" the sixth.[85] These responses tell us about shifts in the mother's demeanor toward the clinicians as much as about the baby's changing habits. They reveal, in their own way, the common failure of the clinics to help poor mothers as their personnel desired and the inability of the mothers fully to accept their kind of help.

MEDICAL MOTHERHOOD

The activity of the Infant Welfare movement and of the local authority's health care institutions set up during and just after the First World War ultimately helped change the way that mothers thought of and cared for sick children. The postwar mothers, whose standard of living was higher than that of most of their own mothers and who had far fewer children, consulted doctors sooner in the course of a child's illness than their predecessors had, and followed the doctors' directives with more confidence. The experience of one young mother during World War I illustrates some of these changes.

Elizabeth Jemima Conner, married at eighteen in 1915, just before her young husband was shipped off to France, was a "medical mother," like the generations who have followed her into the present. Living with her mother-in-law in the eastern reaches of Canning Town, Elizabeth Conner was a faithful user of the local Elder Road Maternity clinic from the sixth month of her first pregnancy. That child, a daughter, was gravely disabled in infancy by a dizzying series of diseases: measles, pneumonia, and meningitis. The mother consoled herself, as had her predecessors with sick or dying children, by doing all she could. For Conner this also meant that she relied heavily on clinics and hospitals for advice, taking the infant "backwards and forwards to hospital. Tried every hospital I think," she remembered. "I knew in my heart that they couldn't do anything but like most mothers I thought that perhaps something could be done." Elizabeth Conner may not have been a more devoted or hardworking mother than were those in earlier generations who had sat at their children's bedsides, consulted with neighbors and relatives, administered locally proven remedies, and brought in a doctor only when frightened to death. But she was a more modern one, both in her ideas about the value of early seeking medical advice for a sick baby and in the kinds of resources on which she could draw. The London women interviewed by Jane Lewis about their early mothering years in the 1920s and 1930s universally described visits to clinics and hospitals for and with their children. Seeing doctors, trained nurses, and health visitors and trying to follow their advice had become ordinary parts of the experience of being a mother.[86]

Yet in its most fundamental sense, the health care of children has remained in maternal hands. As Hilary Graham maintains, feeding proper foods, protecting from danger, and teaching self-care are so fundamental to sustaining life and health that they are nearly invisible. And the greater role of medicine in child care has not destroyed informally cooperative female-centered health care. Even with such serious illnesses as Down's syndrome and meningitis, mothers today tend to make the initial diagnosis that there is something wrong, with their female relatives serving as their chief helpers and advisers. Female-centered neighborhood health care has been defined as a problem for medical sociologists concerned with minimizing the number of steps between the sick person and the medical system.[87] As feminist medical sociologists point out, however, it is also a vindication of mothers' work in sustaining the health of the world's children. From pediatricians with affluent clienteles to Third-World health officers demonstrating hydration techniques for infant diarrhea, medical workers are intervening in mother–child relationships, each with its distinct emotional quality, history, and material situation. Health care, far from the technical problem it is often designated, is an inextricable element of mothers' guardianship of their babies and children.

The trench warfare of the First World War, which decimated a generation of young men, taught as never before, as suffragist and Endowment of Motherhood supporter Maude Royden put it, "the value of babies." The Infant Welfare experience intersected with the urgency of wartime to generate a remarkable campaign aimed at and (to some extent also) in the name of the nation's mothers. The war years brought changes in the state's policy toward maternity. More resources both nationally and locally were channeled into services for mothers; the number of child welfare centers doubled between 1914 and 1918; the baby and its caretakers became national causes; and probaby propaganda campaigns, both private and public, were launched on an enormous scale. Sir Arthur Acland, former president of the Board of Education, organized the Infant Welfare Propaganda Fund, which paid organizers to travel around the country preaching what *The Times* called "the cult of the child." Between 1917 and 1920, wealthy women ran a "Children's Jewel Fund," to raise money for infant welfare centers: "A jewel for a baby's life," their rather tasteless slogan, raised a total of £700,000, a good chunk of which came through the sale of a pearl necklace donated by the duchess of Marlborough. In July 1917, the first of several annual National Baby Weeks featured an exhibition viewed by the queen, a guard of honor of 120 mothers and children, and a prize for the "finest" baby.[88]

Increased funding for women's and family health was among the principal aims of groups of politically organized women, especially in the war years. Dwork describes as a case study the Camberwell campaign launched by the Women's Cooperative Guild, the Women of the

ILP, and the women members of the local Trades and Labour Council to convince recalcitrant borough officials to establish a maternal and child health program. The combined pressure of these and other groups on the national level in the more receptive wartime context led to the passage of the 1918 Maternity and Child Welfare Act, which promised national reimbursement to boroughs that hired midwives, doctors, and health visitors to serve local women, ran crèches, provided meals for poor mothers and children, and so on.[89]

Advocates of infant welfare centers shared a willingness, if only out of political expediency, to separate health from the rest of women's lives. Eleanor Rathbone's Endowment of Motherhood campaign offered a different standpoint, in which children's health and well-being were mainly functions of the status and resources of their mothers—surely a position that fit far better the requirements for public welfare provision that working-class women voiced themselves. Susan Pedersen argues that despite the prewar currency of the Endowment concept, only the war's advent gave Rathbone's radically mother-centered ideas a wider audience. Indeed, the wartime separation allowances granted from the summer of 1915 onward to wives or mothers of wage earners in the armed services seemed to function as a kind of experiment, as Rathbone often observed, in the Endowment of Motherhood. The money arrived reasonably regularly, and because it went directly to the housewives, little of it went to such male luxuries as alcohol or tobacco. Social workers and school health officials nationwide were struck by the almost-overnight improvement in infant and child health that the war years brought.[90] The separation allowances, together with full wartime employment, demonstrated the truth of what the mothers and their political supporters had long been claiming, that sickly infants and scrawny children reflected not maternal fecklessness or the "degeneration" of their stock, but, as I noted in Chapter 6, simply the mother's sheer lack of the cash that would sustain life and health.

CONCLUSION
Rediscovering Motherhood

The recognition abroad since the 1880s of the key place of mothers in the sheer physical survival of their families formed the backdrop to the Endowment of Motherhood movement (the phrase was probably introduced in 1906 by H. G. Wells in his novel *In the Days of the Comet* and discussed subsequently in Fabian circles).[1] In the late-nineteenth-century atmosphere of the "discovery" of the mother, Eleanor Rathbone had formulated, as a Somerville College student in the mid-1890s, the idea that "society" rather than the "male parent" should pay directly for the "cost of its renewal." Rathbone eventually envisioned not only a well-funded set of health services for mothers and children but also a new method for the national distribution of income that acknowledged the wife-mother's social contribution. "Motherhood is a service which entitles a woman to economic independence," wrote Rathbone's associate Maude Royden. State subsidies to mothers would eliminate the demeaning "economic dependency of the married woman," which Rathbone's Family Endowment Committee saw as the badge of female "subjection."[2]

The "family wage" for which organized men had fought in the nineteenth century was to be replaced by a new system in which wages for both male and female employees would be aimed at the support of only one dependent, and state agencies would supply wives with housekeeping funds based on the number of children they cared for. The money for rent, food, and boots that women for generations had struggled to extract from unwilling husbands, or to earn themselves in exhausting low-waged jobs, would be issued to them regularly in recognition of the social value of the work they were doing as mothers. Rathbone's endowment notion, which during and immediately after the war was viewed as controversial but reasonable,[3] became her central concern when in 1919 she was elected president of the National Union of Societies for Equal Citizenship (NUSEC), Britain's largest feminist organization (in 1929 she was elected an Independent M.P. for the Combined English Universities).

By the mid-1920s, however, Rathbone's idea began to lose much of its appeal. Her alliances with advocates of eugenics and, in the 1930s, her use of the issue of child nutrition (through the Children's Minimum Council) as a strategy suggest a loss of support for her original focus on the rights of mothers to receive public resources.[4] When, sponsored by William Beveridge, a token mothers' allowance was finally granted in 1945, the endowment idea retained only the germ of its original concept. Indeed, by the 1940s, discussions about mothers' work, intelligence, and effort as social contributions had little place in public discourse. Mothers appeared mainly in literature on child development carrying out a range of delicate emotional functions that they could so easily get wrong, thereby creating maternal deprivation neurosis, juvenile delinquency, and even schizophrenia. The activities of mothers were aspects of "feminine" self-fulfillment rather than social functions. The fact that mothers continued to budget, feed, organize, clean, earn money, and structure neighborhood and community life, though well known to academic sociologists and anthropologists in the 1940s and 1950s, was kept out of the dominant discourses on family life.

In 1969, when Ann Oakley attempted to register a thesis at the University of London entitled "Work Attitudes and Work Satisfaction of Housewives," an interest that intellectuals fifty or seventy years earlier might well have shared, she was met with "patronizing jocularity" or "frank disbelief." The discussion of female work in the home had become so "psychologized" that the one professor Oakley could find who was willing to supervise such a thesis "spent the next three years trying to convince me that women's sexual satisfaction and adjustment were at the heart of the problem."[5]

Oakley's curiosity about housework as a job appeared at a moment when the rediscovery of housework and childcare as forms of productive work had become an international feminist project. A new generation was demanding recognition of the social importance of housework and childcare and was identifying the peculiar forms of oppression characteristic of wives and mothers: poverty, isolation, exhaustion, male violence. Some feminists indeed made their main targets the psychologists who insisted that "adjusted" women found full-time housework and childcare fulfilling; others aimed at economists who saw housework as "nonproductive." The "wages for housework" idea, which began as an Italian neighborhood campaign and had some resemblance to Rathbone's original concept, threaded its way through the thinking of many of these feminists—French, Italian, British, and North American.[6] The feminist exploration of motherhood has continued along many different paths into the present (as I noted in the Introduction), its common impulse to make motherhood—again, in our own time and in its many forms—visible as a social contribution and as a productive use of human effort.

Notes

INTRODUCTION

1. In *Maternal Thinking,* Sara Ruddick presents motherhood as a form of "caring labor" (the term is Nancy Hartsock's) that can and should function as a standpoint for rethinking peace and war, and the same may be said far more easily for the many specific public policy issues that involve gestation and infant/child care. See Ruddick's *Maternal Thinking: Toward a Politics of Peace* (Boston: Beacon Press, 1989), pp. 129–37. For a contemporary American and historical discussion of the claims of fatherhood, see Thomas W. Laqueur, "The Facts of Fatherhood," in Marianne Hirsch and Evelyn Fox Keller, eds., *Conflicts in Feminism* (New York: Routledge & Kegan Paul, 1990). On fatherhood in Britain, see John G. Gillis, "Bringing Up Father: British Paternal Identities, 1750–Present" (Paper presented at the Rutgers Center for Historical Analysis, October 1990).

2. Julia Kristeva, "The Maternal Body," *m/f* 5–6 (1981): 159; Nikolas Rose, "The Pleasures of Motherhood," *m/f* 7 (1982): 84.

3. Jacques Donzelot, *The Policing of Families,* tr. Robert Hurley (New York: Pantheon Books, 1979), esp. chap. 3; Michel Foucault, *Power/Knowledge,* ed. Colin Gordon (New York: Pantheon Books, 1980), chap. 9, "The Politics of Health in the Eighteenth Century," and Colin Gordon's Afterward; Michel Foucault, *The History of Sexuality,* vol. I: *An Introduction,* tr. Robert Hurley (New York: Pantheon Books, 1978).

4. Sheila Kitzinger, *Women as Mothers: How They See Themselves in Different Cultures* (New York: Vintage Books, 1980), p. 25.

5. One of the angriest critiques of the psychoanalytic disregard of motherhood is by Monique Plaza, "The Mother/The Same: Hatred of the Mother in Psycho-analysis," *Feminist Issues* 2 (Spring 1982): 75–100. The Kristeva quotations are from "Stabat Mater," reprinted in Susan R. Suleiman, ed., *The Female Body in Western Culture* (Cambridge, MA: Harvard University Press, 1986), pp. 112–13. For another discussion of the neglect of mothers in psychoanalysis and mothers' low status in general, see Ruddick, *Maternal Thinking,* chap. 2.

6. See the thoughtful review of a voluminous psychological literature on maternity that treats mothers' subjective experience so sparsely: Mary Georgina Boulton, *On Being a Mother: A Study of Women with Pre-School Children* (London: Tavistock, 1983), chap. 1.

7. Elizabeth Cowie's introduction to the section of that exhibit reproduced in *m/f*, a British Marxist–feminist journal devoted to examining feminist theory, stressed that Kelly's perspective was Marxist as well as psychoanalytical: *m/f*, nos. 5–6 (1981): 117–18). The exhibit was reproduced in book form as *Post Partum Document* (London: Routledge & Kegan Paul, 1983). The Cixous phrase from *La jeune née* is quoted in Christiane Olivier, *Jocasta's Children: The Imprint of the Mother,* tr. George Craig (London: Routledge & Kegan Paul, 1989), p. 9.

8. Adrienne Rich, *Of Woman Born: Motherhood as Experience and Institution* (New York: Bantam Books, 1977); Nancy Chodorow, *The Reproduction of Mothering: Psychoanalysis and the Sociology of Gender* (Berkeley and Los Angeles: University of California Press, 1978); Dorothy Dinnerstein, *The Mermaid and the Minotaur: Sexual Arrangements and Human Malaise* (New York: Harper & Row, 1976); Marianne Hirsch, *The Mother/Daughter Plot: Narrative, Psychoanalysis, Feminism* (Bloomington: Indiana University Press, 1989), Introduction; also Hirsch's chapter on the feminist revisions of psychoanalysis of the early 1970s, pp. 130–38. See Jane Gallop's commentary on *Of Woman Born* in her introduction to *Thinking Through the Body* (New York: Columbia University Press, 1988). Christiane Olivier's recently translated commentary on Freud's Oedipus complex, *Jocasta's Children,* also focuses on girls' development.

9. Ann Oakley, *Women Confined: Towards a Sociology of Childbirth* (New York: Schocken Books, 1980), *Becoming a Mother* (Oxford: Martin Robertson, 1979), and *The Captured Womb: A History of the Medical Care of Pregnant Women* (Oxford: Basil Blackwell, 1984). Also see Hilary Graham and Lorna McKee, *The First Months of Motherhood* (Health Education Council Monograph no. 13, 1980). This approach is also found in an interesting Canadian collection by Katherine Arnup, Andrée Levesque, and Ruth Roach Pierson, eds., *Delivering Motherhood: Maternal Ideologies and Practices in the 19th and 20th Centuries* (London: Routledge & Kegan Paul, 1990); and also in Jo Garcia, Robert Kilpatrick, and Martin Richards, eds., *The Politics of Maternity Care* (Oxford: Clarendon Press, 1990). Also, among a huge literature, see Barbara Katz Rothman, *Recreating Motherhood: Ideology and Technology in a Patriarchal Society* (New York: Norton, 1989); Emily Martin, *The Woman in the Body: A Cultural Analysis of Reproduction* (Boston: Beacon Press, 1987); and Michelle Stanworth, "Birth Pangs: Conceptive Technologies and the Threat to Motherhood," in Marianne Hirsch and Evelyn Fox Keller, eds., *Conflicts in Feminism* (New York: Routledge & Kegan Paul, 1990).

10. For a discussion of this "work" group, see Boulton, *Being a Mother,* pp. 28–29. Also Ann Oakley, *The Sociology of Housework* (Oxford: Martin Robertson, 1974) and *Housewife* (London: Allen Lane, 1974); and Hannah Gavron and Helena Lopata, *Occupation Housework* (New York: Oxford University Press, 1971). The "work" framework is stretched and expanded in Meg Luxton, *More Than a Labour of Love: Three Generations of Women's Work in the Home* (Toronto: Women's Press, 1980); Janet Finch and Dulcie Groves, eds., *A Labour of Love: Women, Work, and Caring* (London: Routledge & Kegan Paul, 1983); and Ann Ferguson, *Blood at the Root: Motherhood, Sexuality and Male Dominance* (London: Pandora Books, 1989). Maternal work as shaping a particular kind of consciousness remains a theme in Ruddick's *Maternal Thinking.*

Two other sociological studies focused on mothers are Miariam M. Johnson's

Strong Mothers Weak Wives (Berkeley and Los Angeles: University of California Press, 1988); and Linda Rennie Forcey, *Mothers of Sons: Toward an Understanding of Responsibility* (New York: Praeger, 1987). In this group I would also place the provocative article by Linda Blum, "Mothers, Babies and Breastfeeding in Late Capitalist America: The Shifting Context of Feminist Theory," *Feminist Studies* 19 (Spring 1993).

11. Elisabeth Badinter, *Mother Love: Myth and Reality* (New York: Macmillan, 1980); see the review by Rose, "The Pleasures of Motherhood." The family history classics mentioned earlier are Jean-Louis Flandrin, *Families in Former Times: Kinship, Household and Sexuality,* tr. Richard Southern (Cambridge: Cambridge University Press, 1976); Edward Shorter, *The Making of the Modern Family* (New York: Basic Books, 1975); and Lawrence Stone, *The Family, Sex and Marriage in England 1500–1800* (New York: Harper & Row, 1977). A less well known exception is by Randolph Trumbach, *The Rise of the Egalitarian Family* (New York: Academic Press, 1978).

12. Linda A. Pollock, *Forgotten Children: Parent–Child Relations from 1500 to 1900* (Cambridge: Cambridge University Press, 1983); Valerie Fildes, *Breasts, Bottles and Babies* (New York: Columbia University Press, 1989); Judith Schneid Lewis, *In the Family Way: Childbearing in the British Aristocracy* (New Brunswick, NJ: Rutgers University Press, 1986); Christina Hardyment, *Dream Babies* (Oxford: Oxford University Press, 1984); Elizabeth Roberts, *A Woman's Place: An Oral History of Working-Class Women 1890–1940* (Oxford: Basil Blackwell, 1984); Jane Lewis, *The Politics of Motherhood: Child and Maternal Welfare in England, 1900–1939* (London: Croom Helm, 1980); Carl Chinn, *They Worked All Their Lives: Women of the Urban Poor in England, 1880–1939* (Manchester: Manchester University Press, 1988); Denise Riley, *War in the Nursery: Theories of the Child and Mother* (London: Virago, 1983); Deborah Dwork, *War Is Good for Babies and Other Young Children: A History of the Infant and Child Welfare Movement in England 1898–1918* (London: Tavistock, 1987).

13. On class as a category in historical thinking today, see Geoff Eley, "Is All the World a Text? From Social History to the History of Society Two Decades Later" in Terence McDonald, ed., *The Historic Turn in the Human Sciences* (Ann Arbor: University of Michigan Press, 1993).

14. The "family as a bulwark" position in nineteenth-century British history is represented by Jane Humphries, in "The Working Class Family: A Marxist Perspective," in Jean Bethke Ehlstain, ed., *The Family in Political Thought* (Amherst: University of Massachusetts Press, 1982). A refutation of this position, focusing on wage-earning women, is by Harold Benenson, "The 'Family Wage' and Working Women's Consciousness in Britain, 1880–1914," *Politics and Society* 19 (March 1991): 71–108.

15. Carolyn Kay Steedman, *Landscape for a Good Woman: A Story of Two Lives* (New Brunswick, NJ: Rutgers University Press, 1987).

16. As one example of the way that the terms of social history changed drastically in the course of the 1980s, see two very different critical readings of Thompson's classic, *The Making of the English Working Class:* Joan W. Scott, "Women in *The Making of the English Working Class,*" in her *Gender and the Politics of History* (New York: Columbia University Press, 1988); and Renato Rosaldo, *Culture and Truth: The Remaking of Social Analysis* (Boston: Beacon Press, 1989).

17. Robert F. Berkhofer, Jr., "The Challenge of Poetics and Politics to (Normal) Historical Practice" (Unpublished paper, University of Michigan, 1986). See also Berkhofer's contribution to Paul Hernadi, ed., *The Rhetoric of Interpretation and the Interpretation of Rhetoric* (Chapel Hill, NC: Duke University Press, 1989). Joan Scott's

Gender and the Politics of History has been tremendously influential among historians of women, though when it was published it was reviewed quite critically by women's historians. See the reviews by Claudia Koonz in *Women's Review of Books,* January 1989, pp. 6, 19–20; Linda Gordon in *Signs* 15 (Summer 1990): 853–58; and Catherine Hall, "Politics, Poststructuralism and Feminist History," *Gender and History* 3 (Summer 1991): 204–10. On anthropologists and theory, see Sherry Ortner, "Theory in Anthropology Since the Sixties," *Comparative Studies in Society and History* 26 (January 1984): 126–66; James Clifford, "Introduction: Partial Truths," in James Clifford and George Marcus, eds., *Writing Culture: The Poetics and Politics of Ethnography* (Berkeley and Los Angeles: University of California Press, 1986); Rosaldo, *Culture and Truth;* Richard A. Shweder, *Thinking Through Cultures: Expeditions in Cultural Psychology* (Cambridge, MA: Harvard University Press, 1991). But also see Frances E. Mascia-Lees, Patricia Sharpe, and Colleen Ballerino Cohen, "The Postmodernist Turn in Anthropology: Cautions from a Feminist Perspective," *Signs* 115 (Autumn 1989): 7–33. The concept of "artful realism" is discussed by Shweder, *Thinking Through Cultures,* in the Conclusion. See also the clear-headed description of the "paradigm shift in feminist thought from the 1970s to the 1990s in Michèle Barrett and Anne Phillips, eds., *Destabilizing Theory* (Stanford, CA: Stanford University Press, 1992), Introduction.

18. See E. P. Thompson's Preface to *The Making of the English Working Class* (New York: Vintage Books, 1966), p. 12. The dangers of nostalgia and the reactionary political uses to which it has been put are convincingly exposed in Roger Bromley's *Lost Narratives: Popular Fictions, Politics and Recent History* (London: Routledge & Kegan Paul, 1988), and also by Carolyn Steedman in *Landscape for a Good Woman*. For two sharp critiques of the epistemological assumptions of social history, see Denise Riley, *"Am I That Name?": Feminism and the Category of "Women" in History* (Minneapolis: University of Minnesota Press, 1988); and Joan Scott, "The Evidence of Experience," *Critical Inquiry* 17 (Summer 1991): 773–97.

CHAPTER 1

1. Patrick Brantlinger, *Rule of Darkness: British Literature and Imperialism, 1830–1911* (Ithaca, NY: Cornell University Press, 1988), p. 100; Raymond Williams, *The Country and the City* (New York: Oxford University Press, 1973), pp. 217–18, 220; Asa Briggs, *Victorian Cities* (Harmondsworth: Penguin Books, 1977), pp. 13–15; Flora Lucy Freeman, *Polly: A Study of Girl Life* (Oxford: A. R. Mowbray, 1904), p. 9; Beatrice Webb, *My Apprenticeship* (Cambridge: Cambridge University Press, 1979), p. 265. On the poor as a distinct "race," see Gertrude Himmelfarb, *The Idea of Poverty: England in the Early Industrial Age* (New York: Random House, 1985), pp. 307–400.

2. Charles Booth, *Life and Labour of the People in London,* 1st ser.: *Poverty,* 5 vols. (1902), reprint ed. (New York: Augustus M. Kelley, 1969), vol. 1, Table I, p. 35. See also vol. 2, p. 21, for his London-wide poverty figures. On Booth as a student of poverty, see E. P. Hennock's "Concepts of Poverty in the British Social Surveys from Charles Booth to Arthur Bowley," in Martin Bulmer, Kevin Bales, and Kathryn Kish Sklar, eds., *The Social Survey in Historical Perspective 1880–1940* (Cambridge: Cambridge University Press, 1991). For another recent discussion of Booth, see Gertrude Himmelfarb, *Poverty and Compassion: The Social Ethic of the Late Victorians* (New York: Knopf, 1991), bk. 2. The notion of a "residuum" or under-

class distinctly criminal and enmeshed in a "culture of poverty" from generation to generation was widespread in the late nineteenth century and very influential in the formation of public policy, but sociologically it was probably not true. The very poor were not fundamentally different from their less poor neighbors. For a defense of this position, see Jennifer Davis, "Jennings' Buildings and the Royal Borough: The Construction of the Underclass in Mid-Victorian England," in David Feldman and Gareth Stedman Jones, eds., *Metropolis/London: Histories and Representations Since 1800* (London: Routledge & Kegan Paul, 1989). Also note the efforts of the "Harding" family to fit into the "posher" neighborhood to which they moved in 1902 when the children of the family began to earn: See Raphael Samuel, *East End Underworld: Chapters in the Life of Arthur Harding* (London: Routledge & Kegan Paul, 1981), pp. 63–64. Jerry White, in *The Worst Street in North London: Campbell Bunk Islington, Between the Wars* (London: Routledge & Kegan Paul, 1986), argues for the existence of a separate *lumpenproletariat* with its own self-perpetuating culture. The extraordinarily rich detail in his study could, however, support the other position as well.

3. This according to Jonathan Schneer, *Ben Tillett: Portrait of a Labour Leader* (London: Croom Helm, 1982), p. 11. In 1890, London received 18 percent of the ships docking at Britain's many ports, though by the late nineteenth century London was the destination of a declining number of international vessels.

4. On London (and suburban) industries, see Raphael Samuel, "The Workshop of the World: Steam Power and Hand Technology in Mid-Victorian Britain," *History Workshop Journal* 3 (Spring 1977): 6–72; and Gareth Stedman Jones, *Outcast London: A Study in the Relationship Between Classes in Victorian Society* (Harmondsworth; Penguin Books, 1976), chap. 1. On the language of rich and poor, see Williams, *Country and the City*, pp. 22, 220. For a discussion of neighborhood "respectability" in the London context, see Ellen Ross, " 'Not the Sort That Would Sit on the Doorstep': Respectability in Pre-World War I London Neighborhoods," *International Labor and Working Class History* 27 (Spring 1985): 39–59.

5. This paragraph is based on the Introduction to Paul Thompson's *Socialists, Liberals and Labour: The Struggle for London 1885–1914* (London: Routledge & Kegan Paul, 1967), one of the few places where the dizzying number of administrative entities that made up the urban entity called London is lucidly explained. More thorough treatments are those by David Owen et al., *The Government of Victorian London, 1855–1899: The Metropolitan Board of Works, the Vestries and the City Corporation* (Cambridge, MA: Harvard University Press, 1982); and Ken Young and Patricia L. Garside, *Metropolitan London: Politics and Urban Change, 1837–1901* (London: Holmes & Meier, 1982). On the urban development of London, for some of the paragraphs that follow, my description is based on Briggs, *Victorian Cities*, pp. 311–19; Stedman Jones, *Outcast London*, chaps. 1, 6, and 11; and Donald J. Olsen, *The City as a Work of Art: London, Paris, Vienna* (New Haven, CT: Yale University Press, 1986), pp. 132–37; 159–65; 183–85.

6. Calculations are based on 1871 Census, PP 1873, vol. 71, pt. 1, Table 1, p. 3; Census of London, 1901, LCC, *London Statistics,* 1903, pp. 12–13. The 1901 figures for proportions of the population aged fifteen and under are Shoreditch 36 percent, Bethnal Green 38 percent, Finsbury 35 percent, Hampstead 24 percent, and Stoke Newington 27 percent. The modern figures (1981) are based on Office of Population Censuses and Surveys, *Census of 1981 Key Statistics for Local Authorities, Great Britain* (London: HMSO, 1984).

7. Henry Nevinson's remarkable short story, "Sissero's Return," about a mar-

riage between a black sailor and a red-headed docker's daughter is reprinted in P. J. Keating, ed., *Working-Class Stories of the 1890s* (London: Routledge & Kegan Paul, 1975). On the Italians, see Maude A. Stanley, *Work About the Five Dials* (London: Macmillan, 1878) and the *Annual Reports* of the City of Westminster Health Society (founded in 1904), whose target population included Soho with its many Italian needlewomen. My remarks on the Irish are based on Lynn Hollen Lees, *Exiles of Erin: Irish Migrants in Victorian London* (Manchester: Manchester University Press, 1979); Hugh McLeod, *Class and Religion in the Late Victorian City* (London: Croom Helm, 1974), p. 40, n. 35, and pp. 72–80; K. S. Inglis, *Churches and the Working Classes in Victorian England* (London: Routledge & Kegan Paul, 1963), chap. 3; Colin G. Pooley, "Segregation or Integration? The Residential Experience of the Irish in Mid-Victorian Britain," in his *The Irish in Britain 1815–1939* (Savage, MD: Barnes & Noble, 1989); and Chaim Bermant, *London's East End: Point of Arrival* (New York: Macmillan, 1975), chap. 6. On the Jews in London, see Bermant, *London's East End,* chaps, 9–11; and David Feldman, "The Importance of Being English: Jewish Immigration and the Decay of Liberal England," in Feldman and Stedman Jones, eds., *Metropolis/London,* esp. p. 56.

8. H. J. Dyos, *Victorian Suburb: A Study of the Growth of Camberwell* (Leicester: Leicester University Press, 1977), p. 111; Schneer, *Ben Tillett,* p. 13.

9. Deborah E. Nord, "The Social Explorer as Anthropologist: Victorian Travellers Among the Urban Poor," in William Sharpe and Leonard Wallock, eds., *Visions of the Modern City: Essays in History, Art, and Literature* (New York: Proceedings of the Heyman Center for the Humanities, Columbia University, 1987). Frank Prochaska has pointed out that foreign missionary charities were among the most successful mid-century causes. See F. K. Prochaska, "Philanthropy," in F. M. L. Thompson, ed., *The Cambridge Social History of Britain 1750–1950,* vol. 3: *Social Agencies and Institutions* (Cambridge: Cambridge University Press, 1990), pp. 367–68.

10. Rev. Harry Jones, *East and West London: Being Notes of Common Life and Pastoral Work in Saint James's, Westminster, and in Saint George's-in-the-East* (London: Smith, Elder, 1875), p. 5; George Sims, *How the Poor Live* (1889), selection in Peter Keating, ed., *Into Unknown England 1866–1913* (London: Fontana/Collins, 1976), p. 65.

11. Stedman Jones, *Outcast London,* pp. 291–94. The events of "Bloody Sunday" are well recounted by Yvonne Kapp in *Eleanor Marx* (2 vols.) (New York: Pantheon 1976), vol. 2, chap. 5. Kapp's detailed biography of a figure who was tireless as a speaker and labor organizer, especially for the Gas Workers and General Labourers Union (of which she started a branch for the women in the industry) throughout London's working-class movements, gives a vivid sense of how much a fixture in West End life the processions, demonstrations, and meetings at these two locations were. Clerkenwell Green, Mile End Waste, and Victoria Park were also popular as sites of public meetings, but here the demonstrators were on their own turf.

12. *The Star,* August 21, 1889, p. 5; August 26, p. 2. On the strike, see the good short discussion in Schneer, *Ben Tillett,* pp. 40–46; also John Lovell, *Stevedores and Dockers: A Study of Trade Unionism in the Port of London, 1870–1914* (London: Macmillan, 1969).

13. These demonstrations were described in the London newspapers in late August (agitation for the passage of legislation) and early November (anger at the way the legislation was being implemented), 1905. The Social Democratic Federation was central in organizing them, and its newspaper, *Justice,* had the fullest coverage. For some journalistic accounts of the procession to Whitehall on November 5, see

Daily News, November 7, 1905, p. 4; *Daily Chronicle,* November 7, p. 6; and *Justice,* November 11, pp. 2, 4, 5.

14. On the causes of the wave of strikes in this era, see Richard Price, *Labour in British Society* (London: Routledge & Kegan Paul, 1990), pp. 114–30; and Eric Hobsbawm, "Economic Fluctuations and Some Social Movements Since 1800," in his *Labouring Men* (New York: Basic Books, 1964). On suffrage pageantry, see Lisa Tickner, *The Spectacle of Women: Imagery of the Suffrage Campaign 1907–1914* (London: Chatto & Windus, 1987). Tickner suggests that working-class mothers were seldom represented in suffrage banners and posters, though poor working women, sometimes depicted with children, were among the female types portrayed by the predominantly middle-class suffrage artists (pp. 174–81).

15. See F. K. Prochaska, *Women and Philanthropy in Nineteenth Century England* (Oxford: Clarendon Press, 1980); Anne Summers, "A Home from Home—Women's Philanthropic Work in the Nineteenth Century," in Sandra Burman, ed., *Fit Work for Women* (London: Croom Helm, 1979); and Dorothy Thompson, "Women, Work and Politics in Nineteenth-Century England: The Problem of Authority," in her *Equal or Different: Women's Politics 1800–1914* (London: Basil Blackwell, 1987).

16. For romances of this kind, see Walter Besant's *Children of Gibeon* (New York: Harper Bros., 1889); Honnor Morten and H. F. Gethen, "The Story of a Nurse," in their *Tales of the Children's Ward* (London: Sampson Low, 1894); Richard Free's story of the socialite, Sophronia Lesage, and the slum clergyman in *On the Wall: Joan and I in the East End* (London: John Lane, 1907); and George Gissing, *The Unclassed* (1884) (Brighton, Sussex: Harvester Press, 1976), pp. 219–20.

17. Constance Battersea, *Reminiscences* (London: Macmillan, 1922), chap. 20; Beatrice Webb, *My Apprenticeship* (1926) (Cambridge: Cambridge University Press, 1979), pp. 274, 285; Enid Huws Jones, *Mrs. Humphry Ward* (London: Heinemann, 1973), pp. 102–3; Andro Linklater, *An Unhusbanded Life: Charlotte Despard, Suffragette, Socialist, and Sinn Feiner* (London: Hutchinson, 1980), p. 59 and *passim.* See also Ellen Chase, *Tenant Friends in Old Deptford* (London: Williams & Norgate, 1929), pp. 23–24, 16.

18. Dame Katharine Furse (born 1875), *Hearts and Pomegranates: The Story of Forty-Five Years 1875 to 1920* (London: Peter Davies, 1940), p. 156; Mary Stocks, *My Commonplace Book* (London: Peter Davies, 1970), pp. 47, 51, 58.

19. Deborah Epstein Nord, *The Apprenticeship of Beatrice Webb* (Amherst: University of Massachusetts Press, 1985), p. 124. On the contribution of settlement-house dwellers, men and women, and church-affiliated activists to London politics, see Thompson, *Socialists, Liberals, and Labour,* pp. 21–25. On women settlement workers, see Martha Vicinus, *Independent Women: Work and Community for Single Women 1850–1920* (Chicago: University of Chicago Press, 1985), chap. 6. For a shrewd discussion of the failure of this generation of women social workers to capture the more prestigious reaches of the new academic discipline of sociology, see Seth Koven, "The Dangers of Castle Building: Surveying the Social Survey," in Bulmer et al., eds., *Social Survey in Historical Perspective.*

20. Norman Douglas, *London Street Games* (London: St. Catherine Press, 1916).

21. Joan Vincent, *Anthropology and Politics: Visions, Traditions, and Trends* (Tucson: University of Arizona Press, 1990), pp. 56–59; James Urry, "The Ethnographic Survey of the United Kingdom," in George W. Stocking, ed., *Functionalism Historicized: Essays on British Social Anthropology* (Madison: University of Wisconsin Press, 1984); Rosalind Coward, *Patriarchal Precedents: Sexuality and Social Relations* (London: Routledge & Kegan Paul, 1983); George W. Stocking, Jr., "Radcliffe-Brown and

British Social Anthropology," in Stocking, ed., *Functionalism Historicized;* Elizabeth Fee, "The Sexual Politics of Victorian Social Anthropology," in Lois Banner and Mary S. Hartman, eds., *Clio's Consciousness Raised* (New York: Harper & Row, 1974).

22. Gustave Doré and Blanchard Jerrold, *London: A Pilgrimage* (1872) (reprint, New York: Dover, 1970), "Travels in the East," in *One Dinner a Week and Travels in the East* (1884), reprint ed. (High Wycombe: Peter Marcan, 1987); George Sims, ed., *Living London* (3 vols.) (London: Cassell, 1902).

23. For some examples of this "male gaze" at working-class interiors, see Doré and Jerrold, *Travels in the East,* pp. 84–91; Mary Booth, *Charles Booth: A Memoir* (1918), reprint ed. (Farnborough: Gregg Press, 1968), pp. 105–30; and Henry Nevinson, *Changes and Chances* (London: Nisbet, 1923), p. 115.

24. "A Lady Resident" "Sketch of Life in Buildings," in Booth, *Life and Labour of the People in London,* 1st ser., vol. 3, pp. 37–57; A. L. Hodson, *Letters from a Settlement* (London: Arnold, 1909), pp. 161–62.

25. Bonnie Smith, *On Writing Women's Work* (pamphlet, European University Institute Working Papers in History, Florence, 1991). This discussion of women's talking is based on Smith's paper and on conversations with her (1987). Anna Martin, *The Married Working Woman: A Study* (London: NUWSS, 1911), p. 21; Maud Pember Reeves, *Round About a Pound a Week* (1913; reprint ed., London: Virago, 1979), p. 16; and Margaret Loane, *From Their Point of View,* as cited by Ross McKibbon in "Class and Poverty in Edwardian England," from his *The Ideologies of Class: Social Relations in Britain 1880–1950* (Oxford: Oxford University Press, 1990), p. 181. For McKibbon's discussion of Loane, see pp. 179–81.

26. Chase, *Tenant Friends,* pp. 172–73, 186–87, 190–91, 198.

27. Katherine Roberts, *Five Months in a London Hospital* (Letchworth: Garden City Press, 1911), pp. 60, 63, 131–33.

28. Margaret Nevinson, *Life's Fitful Fever* (London: A. & C. Black, 1926), p. 91. Nevinson, who lived a short walk away from the buildings, also served for a time in the mid-1880s as a rent collector with Pycroft. A fur puller's job was to pluck the longer coarser hairs from pelts, which were often badly cleaned and covered with congealed blood. See Edith Hogg, "The Fur-Pullers of South London," *The Nineteenth Century* 42 (November 1897): 739.

29. See the discussion of Dendy in McKibbon, "Class and Poverty in Edwardian England," pp. 171–77.

30. Smith, *Writing Women's Work.* Also see Naomi Black, *Social Feminism* (Ithaca, NY: Cornell University Press, 1989); Jill Liddington and Jill Norris, *One Hand Tied Behind Us* (London: Virago, 1978); and Tickner, *Spectacle of Women,* pp. 174, 179, 181.

31. James Hammerton, "Victorian Marriage and the Law of Matrimonial Cruelty," *Victorian Studies* 33 (Winter 1990): 269–92; see also his "The Limits of Companionate Marriage: Middle-Class Husbands and Patriarchal Authority in Victorian England" and Gail Savage's "Marital Conflict Among the Respectable: Middle-Class Divorce in Victorian England" (Papers presented at the annual meeting of the American Historical Association, December 1989); Roberts, *Five Months,* p. 65. See also Chapter 3, n. 7.

32. On Holl, see Julian Treuherz, *Hard Times: Social Realism in Victorian Art* (London and Mt. Kisco, NY: Lund Humphries and Moyer Bell, 1987), chap. 9.

33. On Booth's fascinating private expeditions into the poor homes of London, where as a lodger and only in partial disguise, he lived the family lives of the poor,

see Booth, *Charles Booth*. His *Life and Labour* approaches poverty mainly from the vantage point of wages and jobs, but it does discuss household consumption, as in chap. 5 ("Poverty") of vol. 1 (1st ser.).

34. The British Board of Trade canvassed, much more briefly, working households in four London districts in the 1880s. A massive survey of standards of living in several European countries was carried out by the United States Department of Labor, completed in 1890, and a similar one was commissioned by the government of Belgium. In England in the early 1890s, the Economics Club carried out thirty-eight fairly detailed budget studies of families ranging from middle class to desperately poor. All of these efforts are discussed in Henry Higgs, "Workmen's Budgets," *JRSS* 56 (June 1893): pt. II.

35. B. S. Rowntree, *Poverty: A Study in Town Life* (London: Macmillan, 1902). See also L. Chiozza Money, *Riches and Poverty* (London: Methuen, 1905). Other income/expenditure studies emphasizing the role of wives are those by May Kendall and B. S. Rowntree, *How the Labourer Lives: A Study of the Rural Labour Problem* (London: Thomas Nelson, 1913); D. N. Paton, J. C. Dunlop, and Elsie Inglis, *On the Dietaries of the Labouring Classes of the City of Edinburgh* (Edinburgh: O. Schultze, 1901); and Dr. Thomas Oliver, "The Diet of Toil," *The Lancet*, June 29, 1895, pp. 1929–35.

36. Booth, *Life and Labour,* 1st ser., vol. 1, p. 50; Higgs, "Workmen's Budgets," p. 269. In an article published the next year, Ada Heather-Bigg, an activist charity worker, suffragist, and secretary of the Women's Employment Association, pointed out that the contributions wives made as wage earners to household earnings as a whole were actually quite substantial. See her "The Wife's Contribution to Family Income," *Economic Journal* 4 (1894): 51–58.

37. Gareth Stedman Jones, "Working-Class Culture and Working-Class Politics in London 1870–1900: Notes on the Remaking of a Working Class," in his *Languages of Class: Studies in English Working Class History 1832–1982* (Cambridge: Cambridge University Press, 1983), p. 183.

38. Richard Hoggart, *The Uses of Literacy* (New York: Penguin Books, 1977); Michael Young and Peter Willmott, *Family and Kinship in East London* (New York: Penguin Books, 1983); Stedman Jones, "Working-Class Culture"; and Eric Hobsbawm, "The Formation of British Working-Class Culture," in his *Worlds of Labour: Further Studies in the History of Labour* (London: Weidenfeld & Nicolson, 1984).

39. David Vincent, *Bread, Knowledge and Freedom: A Study of Nineteenth-Century Working Class Autobiography* (London: Methuen, 1981); Jeremy Seabrook, *Mother and Son: An Autobiography* (London: Victor Gollancz, 1979), p. 7; Carolyn Steedman, *Landscape for a Good Woman: A Story of Two Lives* (New Brunswick, NJ: Rutgers University Press, 1987). Other excellent treatments of working-class autobiography are those by Mary Jo Maynes, "Gender and Narrative Form in French and German Working-Class Autobiographies," in Personal Narratives Group, ed., *Interpreting Women's Lives: Feminist Theory and Personal Narratives* (Bloomington: Indiana University Press, 1989); Ruth Behar, "Rage and Redemption: Reading the Life Story of a Mexican Marketing Woman," *Feminist Studies* 16 (Summer 1990): 223–58; and Reginia Gagnier's *Subjectivities: A History of Self-Representation in Britain, 1832–1920* (New York: Oxford University Press, 1991). Unfortunately, this last book arrived on my desk a little too late for me to assimilate it properly in my own readings of working-class autobiographies. On biography and autobiography more generally, see L. L. Langness and Geyla Frank, *Lives: An Anthropological Approach to Biography* (Novato, CA: Chandler & Sharp, 1981).

40. The act was a product of enormous activity by the thirty-one local societies for the Prevention of Cruelty to Children, which, led by the brilliant lobbyist and propagandist Benjamin Waugh, formed a national organization in 1889. Under the act that they promoted, guardians of children (defined as girls under sixteen, boys under fourteen) who were "ill-treated, neglected, abandoned, or exposed, in a manner likely to cause . . . unnecessary suffering, or injury" could be fined or imprisoned for up to two years. Parents could not use children for begging or performing on the street, and parents convicted under the act could lose custody of their children. See Ivy Pinchbeck and Margaret Hewitt, *Children in English Society* (2 vols.) (London: Routledge & Kegan Paul, 1973), vol. 2, pp. 623–29; also see George Behlmer, *Child Abuse and Moral Reform in England 1870–1908* (Stanford, CA: Stanford University Press, 1982). Waugh's campaign against child abuse never focused particularly on the poor, whom he did not think crueler than any other part of the population, nor were bad mothers the particular object of his campaign.

41. David Rubinstein, *School Attendance in London 1870–1904: A Social History* (Hull: University of Hull Publications, 1969), p. 19; Brian Simon, *Education and the Labour Movement 1870–1920* (London: Lawrence & Wishart, 1974), chap. 4.

42. On children's contributions to their households and the disruption generated by compulsory schooling, see Joy Parr, *Labouring Children: British Immigrant Apprentices to Canada, 1869–1924* (London: Croom Helm, 1980), chap. 1; Stephen Humphries, *Hooligans or Rebels? An Oral History of Working-Class Childhood and Youth 1889–1939* (Oxford: Basil Blackwell, 1981), chap. 6; Rubinstein, *School Attendance,* chap. 4; Hurt, *Elementary Schooling,* pt. III. The most comprehensive of these studies is Anna Davin's, *"Little Women": The Childhood of Working-Class Girls in Late Nineteenth-Century London* (London: Routledge & Kegan Paul, 1994). Separate chapters are devoted to child minding as a children's (largely girls') duty, errands, home manufacturing, and outside paid work for children.

43. The reference is to Tamara Hareven, *Family Time and Industrial Time: The Relationship Between the Family and Work in a New England Industrial Community* (Cambridge: Cambridge University Press, 1982).

CHAPTER 2

1. The term *awsome responsibility* is Linda Rennie Forcey's and is a central one in her contemporary American study, *Mothers of Sons: Toward an Understanding of Responsibility* (New York: Praeger, 1987). The control of money is discussed more thoroughly in Chapter 3.

2. Cases of starvation deaths "upon which a Coroner's Jury have Returned a Verdict of Death from Starvation, or Death Accelerated by Privation" were reported annually for the country and included in the Parliamentary Papers. London's local and metropolitan newspapers also gave ample details on many cases.

3. For a few examples among hundreds that could be cited on food, food "entitlement," and revolution, see E. P. Thompson, "The Moral Economy of the English Crowd in the Eighteenth Century," *Past and Present* 50 (February 1971): 76–136; Olwen Hufton, "Women in Revolution, 1789–1796," *Past and Present* 53 (November 1971): 90–108; Barbara Clements, "Working-Class and Peasant Women in the Russian Revolution," *Signs* 8 (Winter 1982): 215–35; Temma Kaplan, "Female Consciousness and Collective Action: The Case of Barcelona, 1910–1918," *Signs* 7 (Spring 1982): 545–66; Louise A. Tilly, "Food Entitlement, Famine and Conflict,"

Journal of Interdisciplinary History 14 (Autumn 1983): 333–49; Paul R. Hanson, "The 'Vie Chere' Riots of 1911: Traditional Protests in Modern Garb," *Journal of Social History* 22 (Spring 1988): 463–81; Amartya Sen, *Poverty and Famines: An Essay on Entitlement and Deprivation* (Oxford: Clarendon Press, 1981).

4. Hilary Graham, *Women, Health and the Family* (Brighton: Wheatsheaf Books, 1984), pp. 120–21; W. M. Frazer, *A History of English Public Health 1834–1939* (London: Balliere, Tindall, 1950), pp. 263–64.

5. See the discussion of Richards and other early anthropologists of food and meals in Jack Goody's *Cooking, Cuisine and Class: A Study in Comparative Sociology* (Cambridge: Cambridge University Press, 1982), chap. 2. Mary Douglas's classic statement is probably "Deciphering a Meal," *Daedalus* 101 (Winter 1972): 61–81. See also the chapter "Food as a System of Communication" in Douglas's *In the Active Voice* (London: Routledge & Kegan Paul, 1982). The Barthes quotation is from his "Toward a Psychosociology of Contemporary Food Consumption," in Robert Forster and Orest Ranum, eds., *Food and Drink in History* (Baltimore: Johns Hopkins University Press, 1979), pp. 167–68. A useful feminist perspective on the study of food can be found in Nickie Charles and Marion Kerr, *Women, Food and Families: Power, Status, Love, Anger* (Manchester: Manchester University Press, 1988), pp. 2–5. The classic feminist study is by Christine Delphy, "Sharing the Same Table: Consumption and the Family," tr. Diana Leonard, in *The Sociology of the Family: New Directions for Britain* (Sociological Review Monographs, no. 28, University of Keele, 1979). For a creative look at meals and getting them (and a plea for a new way of conceptualizing the domestic) by a sociologist, see R. E. Pahl, "Concepts in Context: Pursuing the Urban of 'Urban'," in Derek Fraser and Anthony Sutcliffe, eds., *The Pursuit of Urban History* (London: Arnold, 1983). Jack Goody and Sidney Mintz, among many other anthropologists, do take a more material position on food. An ethnography connecting food, gender, and religion is Anna S. Meigs, *Food, Sex, and Pollution: A New Guinea Religion* (New Brunswick, NJ: Rutgers University Press, 1984). There is an American sociological study by Marjorie L. De-Vault, *Feeding the Family: The Social Organization of Caring as Gendered Work* (Chicago: University of Chicago Press, 1991).

6. These struggles come to life in Anna Clark, "Womanhood and Manhood in the Transition from Plebeian to Working-Class Culture: London, 1780–1845" (Ph.D. diss., Rutgers University, 1988).

7. Special Committee of the COS on Soup Kitchens and Dinner Tables, *Minutes of Evidence* (London: Spottiswoode, 1887), p. 40; E. Robinson, "I Remember . . ." Unpublished manuscript, 1960–70, Brunel University Library, unpaginated; Grace Foakes, *My Part of the River* (London: Futura Books, 1976), p. 71; an account by Gracie Tarbuck, in Mary Chamberlain, *Growing Up in Lambeth* (London: Virago, 1989), p. 98.

8. A. S. Jasper, *A Hoxton Childhood* (London: Centerprise, 1969), p. 68, also see pp. 46–47.

9. Ey, Old Bailey, vol. 77 (1872–1873), no. 70, p. 87. See also Tritner, Old Bailey, vol. 89 (1878–1879), no. 203, p. 279.

10. Herbert Morrison, *An Autobiography by Lord Morrison of Lambeth* (London: Odhams Press, 1960), p. 16.

11. See Marjorie Shostak's remarkable oral history, *Nisa: The Life and Words of a !Kung Woman* (New York: Vintage Books, 1983), the autobiography of a hunter-gatherer who does indeed live hand to mouth. Nisa recaptures the major events of her life—her infancy, marriages, children—almost entirely in terms of food and eat-

ing. Food created emotions, marked them, and celebrated them.

12. Joseph Williamson, *Father Joe: The Autobiography of Joseph Williamson of Poplar and Stepney* (London: Hodder & Stoughton, 1963), p. 28.

13. Dorothy Scannell, *Mother Knew Best: Memoir of a London Girlhood* (New York: Pantheon Books, 1974), p. 37.

14. Roy Busby, *British Music Hall: An Illustrated Who's Who* (London: Paul Elek, 1976), pp. 33–34. The songs may be found in Peter Davison, *Songs of the British Music Hall* (New York: Oak Publications, 1971); and William Matthews, *Cockney Past and Present* (London: Routledge & Kegan Paul, 1938), pp. 141–42.

15. References to the "docker's dinner" as a theme in strikers' placards appear in the *East London Observer*, August 24, 1889, p. 5, and *The Star*, August 19, 1889, p. 3.

16. Sidney W. Mintz, "Time, Sugar, and Sweetness," *Marxist Perspectives* 2 (Winter 1979–80): 60.

17. Researchers working on the meanings and uses of food in a U.S. project in the late 1970s and early 1980s used "key kitchen persons" for shoppers/cooks and sometimes even "food events" for snacks or meals. See Mary Douglas, *Food and the Social Order: Studies of Food and Festivities in Three American Communities* (New York: Russell Sage Foundation, 1984), p. 17. The phrase *human occasions,* E. P. Thompson's, is used this way in Sidney Mintz, *Sweetness and Power: The Place of Sugar in Modern History* (New York: Viking Penguin, 1985), p. 69.

18. Marvin Harris, *Good to Eat: Riddles of Food and Culture* (New York: Simon & Schuster, 1985), chap. 1. See also Nick Fiddes, *Meat: A Natural Symbol* (London: Routledge & Kegan Paul, 1991).

19. *Missing Link,* November 1919, pp. 183–84; an account by Fred Cant, who moved to the Island district of Clapham in 1913, in Hackney People's Autobiography, *"The Island": The Life and Death of an East London Community 1870–1970* (London: Centerprise, 1979), p. 50. See also Raphael Samuel, *East End Underworld: Chapters in the Life of Arthur Harding* (London: Routledge & Kegan Paul, 1981), p. 28.

20. D. J. Oddy, "Working-Class Diets in Late Nineteenth-Century Britain," *Economic History Review* 23 (1970): 318, Table 1.

21. Ivy Pinchbeck and Margaret Hewitt, *Children in English Society* (2 vols.) (London: Routledge & Kegan Paul, 1973), vol. 2, p. 456; Margaret Nevinson, *Life's Fitful Fever* (London: Black, 1926), p. 94; Betty McNee, "Trends in Meat Consumption," in T. C. Barker, J. C. Mckenzie, and John Yudkin, eds., *Our Changing Fare: Two Hundred Years of British Food Habits* (London: MacGibbon & Kee, 1966), p. 81; F. B. Smith, *The People's Health 1830–1910* (New York: Holmes & Meier, 1978), p. 207.

22. W. E. Eide and F. C. Steady, "Individual and Social Energy Flows: Bridging Nutritional and Anthropological Thinking About Women's Work in Rural Africa, Theoretical Considerations," in Norge W. Jerome et al., eds., *Nutritional Anthropology: Contemporary Approaches to Diet and Culture* (Pleasantville, NY: Redgrave, 1980). For a summary of an enormous number of studies of household food allocation worldwide, see, in the same volume, E. M. Rosenberg, "Demographic Effects of Sex-differential Nutrition." An almost convincing political critique of meat eating is Carol J. Adams, *The Sexual Politics of Meat: A Feminist–Vegetarian Critical Theory* (New York: Continuum, 1990).

23. Laura Oren, "The Welfare of Women in Laboring Families: England, 1860–1950," in Mary Hartman and Lois W. Banner, eds., *Clio's Consciousness Raised* (New York: Harper & Row, 1974), pp. 227–28; Oddy, "Working-Class Diets," pp. 320–

21. See the detailed dietaries that Oliver collected, and his commentary on them, in *The Lancet,* June 29, 1895, pp. 1629–35.

24. Mrs. Benjamin, born in London Fields (Hackney) in 1905, oral history, manuscript transcript, Hackney People's Autobiography, unpaginated.

25. Harris, *Good to Eat,* p. 240; Maud Pember Reeves, *Round About a Pound a Week,* reprint ed. (London: Virago, 1979), p. 156; see also Oren, "Welfare of Women," pp. 238–40.

26. Eide and Steady, "Individual and Social Energy Flows," p. 66.

27. Family Life Archive, no. 216, p. 9; no. 240, p. 7; and (this quotation) no. 298, p. 3. The Limehouse mother, whom Paul Thompson calls Mrs. Durham, is discussed and quoted at some length in Thompson's *The Edwardians: The Remaking of British Society* (St. Albans: Paladin Books, 1977), pp. 162–76.

28. Scannell, *Mother Knew Best,* p. 100; Roberts, *Classic Slum,* p. 112.

29. On the use of the "docker's dinner," see *East London Observer,* August 24, 1889, p. 5, and *The Star,* August 19, 1889, p. 3. A "docker's baby" emblem depicting a skinny infant also was seen occasionally in the processions: Herbert Llewellyn-Smith and Vaughn Nash, *The Story of the Dockers' Strike,* extract, in Eric Hobsbawm, ed., *Labour's Turning Point 1880–1900* (Brighton: Harvester Press, 1974), p. 85.

30. Burns's speech: *The Star,* August 27, 1889, p. 2. London Cottage Mission provides separate meals for women and children (*The Star,* August 27, p. 2); Charrington collects money to feed "a thousand wives and children a day" (*The Star,* August 28, p. 2); a comment on "thousands of destitute women and children" (*The Star,* September 12, p. 2); free breakfasts during the 1911 dock strike (Mrs. Benjamin, transcript, p. 44).

31. Guardians feeding strikers' children (*East London Observer,* October 12, 1911, p. 5); Anna Martin, "The Mother and Social Reform," *The Nineteenth Century and After* 73 (May 1913): 1079; LCC, *Minutes of Proceedings,* July to December 1912, pt. I, pp. 90, 267, 362. A. M. Carr-Saunders did think the charities helped the strikers to hold out longer (*Toynbee Record,* July–September 1912, p. 146).

32. Pember Reeves, *Round About a Pound,* pp. 113–14; the interpolations are mine. See the outraged comments on this gendered disparity in a review of the book by S. Gertrude Ford in *The Vote,* January 30, 1914, pp. 235–36, referring to men's better meals as "a gastronomic injustice to women."

33. Family Life Archive, no. 225, pp. 13–14; and, no. 296, p. 13; Lillian Hine, "A Poplar Childhood," *East London Record* no. 3 (1980): 35; Family Life Archive, no. 236, p. 29; H. John Bennett, *I Was a Walworth Boy* (London: Peckham Publishing Project, 1980), p. 22.

34. Scannell, *Mother Knew Best,* pp. 99–100; also see Pember Reeves, *Round About a Pound,* pp. 171–72.

35. M. E. Bulkley, *The Feeding of School Children* (London: G. Bell, 1914), p. 200; R. W. Kittle, Letter to the Editor, *Toynbee Record,* December, 1897, p. 45. For more on school dinners, see Ellen Ross, "Hungry Children: Housewives and London Charity, 1870–1918," in Peter Mandler, ed., *The Uses of Charity: The Poor on Relief in the Nineteenth Century Metropolis* (Philadelphia: University of Pennsylvania Press, 1990).

36. Anna Martin, *The Married Working Woman: A Study* (London: NUWSS, 1911), p. 20.

37. C. Anne Wilson, *Food and Drink in Britain from the Stone Age to Recent Times* (London: Constable, 1973), p. 213; E. J. T. Collins, "The 'Consumer Revolution' and the Growth of Factory Foods: Changing Patterns of Bread and Cereal-Eating in

Britain in the Twentieth Century," in Derek Oddy and Derek Miller, eds., *The Making of the British Diet* (London: Croom Helm, 1976), p. 36.

Oatmeal was relished by working-class families in Barrow and Lancaster. See Elizabeth Roberts, "Working-Class Standards of Living in Barrow and Lancaster, 1890–1914," *Economic History Review* 30 (1977): 313. But even in Glasgow, nutritionists deplored the development of a taste for bread and jam in place of the classic Scottish breakfast. See Mintz, *Sweetness and Power*, p. 68; *Missing Link*, June 1878, p. 166.

38. Pember Reeves, *Round About a Pound a Week*, pp. 57–58.

39. "Impressions of Camp," *Toynbee Record*, October 1909, pp. 12–13; A. R. Price, "Meals for School Children," *Toynbee Record*, January 1893, p. 43; Bulkley, *The Feeding of School Children*, p. 201; test. Honnor Morten, Special Sub-Committee of the London School Board, 1898, app. I, p. 12 (GLRO SBL/1469).

40. Robert Bocock, *Ritual in Industrial Society: A Sociological Analysis of Ritualism in Modern England* (London: Allen & Unwin, 1973), p. 36. Bocock stresses that ritualism is social, a demonstration by individuals or groups for each others' sake.

41. Edward Ezard, *Battersea Boy* (London: William Kember, 1979), pp. 21, 23; Bennett, *Walworth Boy*, p. 7.

42. Frederick Willis, *101 Jubilee Road: A Book of London Yesterdays* (London: Phoenix House, 1948), pp. 70–71.

43. Venables, Old Bailey, vol. 76 (1872), no. 581, p. 347; (Florence) Petty et al., *The Pudding Lady: A New Departure in Social Work* (London: Stead's Publishing, 1910), p. 46; Mary Douglas, *Implicit Meanings: Essays in Anthropology* (London: Routledge & Kegan Paul, 1975), pp. 250–51; Willis, *101 Jubilee Road*, p. 77.

44. Sally F. Moore and Barbara Myerhood, "Introduction" to their *Secular Ritual* (1977), cited by John Gillis in *For Better, for Worse: British Marriages, 1600 to the Present* (New York: Oxford University Press, 1985), p. 324, n. 8. On Sunday meals, see Foakes, *My Part of the River*, p. 101; Family Life Archive, no. 284, p. 17; Ezard, *Battersea Boy*, p. 24; Family Life Archive, no. 216, p. 8, and no. 225, p. 42.

45. Family Life Archive, no. 225, p. 16, and no. 215, p. 67. For other examples of discipline at meals when the father was present, see Peckham People's History, *Times of Our Lives* (London: Peckham Publishing Project, 1983), p. 45; interviews with Mr. Causon and with Mrs. Bradford, whose father was a small shopkeeper, Samuel oral histories; also, Family Life Archive, no. 215, p. 16; and no. 70, pp. 9–10.

46. Janet Blackman, "Changing Marketing Methods and Food Consumption," in Barker et al., eds., *Our Changing Fare*, p. 41; John Burnett, *Plenty and Want: A Social History of Diet in England from 1815 to the Present Day* (London: Scholar Press, 1979), p. 101; Paul Thompson, with Tony Wailey and Trevor Lummis, *Living the Fishing* (London: Routledge & Kegan Paul, 1983), p. 112. Fried fish, sold with a piece of bread, had been available on the streets of London for decades or even centuries (as a convenient way to sell fish that was going "off"). The sale of fish with fried potatoes, however, cooked on special frying ranges manufactured in Lancashire, seems to have originated not much earlier than the 1880s. See W. H. Chaloner, "Trends in Fish Consumption," in Barker et al., eds., *Our Changing Fare*, *passim* and pp. 109–10. Also see John K. Walton, "Fish and Chips and the British Working Class, 1870–1930," *Journal of Social History* 23 (Winter 1989): 243–66. On bread, see John Burnett, "Trends in Bread Consumption," in Barker et al., eds., *Our Changing Fare*, p. 64.

47. Smith, *People's Health,* pp. 203–11; Burnett, *Plenty and Want,* chap. 10 and p. 100.

48. Burnett, *Plenty and Want,* pp. 156, 99, 186, 93; Rufus S. Tucker, "Real Wages of Artisans in London, 1729–1935," *Journal of the American Statistical Association* 31 (March 1936): 80.

49. Mintz, *Sweetness and Power.*

50. D. J. Oddy, "A Nutritional Analysis of Historical Evidence: The Working-Class Diet, 1880–1914," in Oddy and Miller, eds., *Making of the English Diet,* pp. 222, 230; Consumption and Cost of Food in Workmen's Families in Urban Districts in the U.K., PP 1905, vol. 84, pp. 6–8.

51. Graham, *Women, Health and the Family,* pp. 128–29.

52. In 1981, food accounted for about a quarter of the weekly expenses for households subsisting on less than £120 per week. See Graham, *Women, Health and the Family,* pp. 120, 123. See also Emma A. Winslow, "Changes in Food Consumption Among Working-Class Families," *Economica* 2 (1922), which is an analysis of a 1920 TUC survey of households from all classes and districts in Great Britain, whose food expenditures, on average, totaled just under half of weekly income.

53. Clara Grant, *Farthing Bundles* (London: Fern Street Settlement, 1930), p. 77; Henry Higgs, "Workmen's Budgets," *JRSS* 56 (June 1893): 284–85; and also the Jewish East London slipper maker's budget, p. 283.

54. Enid Gauldie, *Cruel Habitations: A History of Working-Class Housing 1780–1918* (New York: Barnes & Noble, 1974), p. 157; John Burnett, *A Social History of Housing 1815–1985* (London: Methuen, 1986), pp. 150–51. Also on housing, see A. S. Wohl, *The Eternal Slum: Housing and Social Policy in Victorian London* (London: Arnold, 1977); David Englander, *Landlord and Tenant in Urban Britain 1838–1918* (Oxford: Clarendon Press, 1983); and Richard Rodger, *Housing in Urban Britain 1780–1914: Class, Capitalism and Construction* (London: Macmillan, 1989). The observation about landlords was made by Gareth Stedman Jones in *Outcast London: A Study in the Relationship Between Classes in Victorian Society* (Harmondsworth: Penguin Books, 1976), p. 284.

55. Burnett, *Social History of Housing,* pp. 153–54, 150–51; M. J. Daunton, *House and Home in the Victorian City: Working-Class Housing 1850–1914* (London: Arnold, 1983), p. 80. Housing in such rapidly growing working-class London suburbs as Willesden, Walthamstow, East Ham, and Wood Green was much cheaper than in the central city, but train fares added a great deal to the cost. See A. S. Wohl, "The Housing of the Working Classes in London 1750–1914," in Stanley Chapman, ed., *The History of Working Class Housing: A Symposium* (Newton Abbot: David and Charles, 1971), pp. 17; 29–36.

56. Burnett, *Social History of Housing,* p. 147; Tucker, "Real Wages ot Artisans in London," p. 76; Wohl, "Housing of the Working Classes," p. 26; David Rubinstein, *School Attendance in London, 1870–1904: A Social History* (Hull: University of Hull Publications, 1969), p. 57, citing the 1891 and 1901 censuses. Newcastle was closest to the London figure, at 6 percent, but most other towns had far smaller proportions of one-room dwellers.

57. J. Hasloch Potter, *Inasmuch: The Story of the Police Court Mission 1876–1926* (London: Williams & Norgate, 1927), p. 70; V. de Vesselitsky, *Expenditure and Waste* (London: G. Bell, 1917).

58. Burnett, *Plenty and Want,* p. 198; Michael Young, "Distribution of Income Within the Family," *British Journal of Sociology* 3 (December 1952): 307–8; A. E. Dingle, "Drink and Working-Class Living Standards in Britain, 1870–1914," *Eco-*

nomic History Review, 2nd ser., 25 (November 1972): 608–22. See also Dingle's history of an important branch of the temperance movement, *The Campaign for Prohibition in Victorian England* (London: Croom Helm, 1980).

59. Dingle, "Drink and Working-Class Living Standards," pp. 608–11. Per-capita U.S. alcohol consumption in the 1890s was less than half the British figure. See Joseph Rowntree and Arthur Sherwell, *The Temperance Problem and Social Reform,* 7th ed. (New York: Truelove, Hanson and Comba, 1900), pp. 70, 15.

60. Thomas P. Whittaker, *The Economic Aspects of the Drink Problem* (London: Lees and Raper Memorial Trustees, 1902), p. 11; Philip Snowden, *Socialism and the Drink Question* (London: ILP, 1908), p. 36; Burnett, *Plenty and Want,* p. 199; Brian Harrison, "Pubs," in H. J. Dyos and Michael Wolff, eds., *The Victorian City: Images and Realities* (2 vols.) (London: Routledge & Kegan Paul, 1973), vol. 1, p. 162. In the administrative county of London, which excluded most suburbs, there was a pub for every fifty inhabitants, according to one alarmist calculation. See Rowntree and Sherwell, *The Temperance Problem,* p. 77.

61. Jack Welch, untitled oral history, Hackney People's Autobiography, p. 5; Anna Martin, "Working Women and Drink, Part II," *The Nineteenth Century and After* 79 (January 1916): 97; Jasper, *Hoxton Childhood,* pp. 63–64.

62. Booth citation from Oddy, "The Working-Class Diet," p. 216; Norman B. Dearle, *Problems of Unemployment in the London Building Trades* (London: Dent, 1908), pp. 67–69 and 79, n. 1; LCC, *London Statistics* 3 (1892–1893): 352–57; Raphael Samuel, "Comers and Goers," in Dyos and Wolff, eds., *The Victorian City,* vol. 1, pp. 132–37.

63. Paul Thompson, *Socialists, Liberals and Labour: The Struggle for London 1885–1914* (London: Routledge & Kegan Paul, 1967), p. 12, citing PP 1887, vol. 71, pp. 312–13; Beatrice Webb and Sidney Webb, *English Local Government,* reprint ed. (London: Frank Cass, 1963), vol. 9, pp. 631–69. Also COS, Special Committee on Unskilled Labour, *Report and Minutes of Evidence* (London: COS, 1908), p. 13. For employment figures by trade, see, for example, LCC, *London Statistics* 3 (1892–1893): 352–57.

64. James C. Adderley, "Some Results of the Great Dock Strike," *Economic Review* 11 (April 1892): 205, 209; A. L. Bowley, *Wages and Income in the United Kingdom Since 1860* (Cambridge: Cambridge University Press, 1937), pp. 43–44; Dearle, *Unemployment in the London Building Trades,* pp. 134–35; Oddy, "Working-Class Diet, 1880–1914," p. 215. Bowley calculated that about 58 percent of full-time industrial workers in the United Kingdom earned 25 shillings or under in 1886 and about 32 percent in 1906. See Bowley, *Wages and Income,* p. 42.

65. Dearle, *Unemployment in the London Building Trades,* p. 142; Bowley's figures are cited in W. Hamish Fraser, *The Coming of the Mass Market, 1850–1914* (Hamden, CT: Archon Books, 1981), p. 22.

66. James A. Schmiechen, *Sweated Industries and Sweated Labor: The London Clothing Trades 1860–1914* (Urbana: University of Illinois Press, 1984), pp. 66–72. Much of the material that follows on married women and widows in paid work, particularly as they appear in the 1911 census, is based on a 1990 paper by Andrew August, Columbia University, "Wives and Widows in the Work Force: London, 1911," a preview of his doctoral dissertation. My thanks to Andy for supplying me with this material.

67. See Sally Alexander, Anna Davin, and Eve Hostettler, "Labouring Women: A Reply to Eric Hobsbawm," *History Workshop Journal* 8 (1979): 174–82; Catherine Hakim, "Census Reports as Documentary Evidence: The Census Commentaries

1801–1951," *Sociological Review,* new ser., 28 (August 1980): 551–80; and Edward Higgs, "Women, Occupations and Work in the Nineteenth Century Censuses," *History Workshop Journal* 23 (Spring 1987): 59–80. Also see the comments in August, "Wives and Widows."

68. Arthur Sherwell, *Life in West London* (London: Methuen, 1897), pp. 59, 65–68; 80–81; COS, *Report of the Committee on Unskilled Labour* (London: COS, 1908), p. 7; Patricia Malcolmson, *English Laundresses: A Social History, 1850–1930* (Urbana: University of Illinois Press, 1986), p. 15; and Patricia Malcolmson, "Getting a Living in the Slums of Victorian Kensington," *London Journal* 1 (May 1975): 28–55.

69. V. de Vesselitsky, *The Homeworker and the Outlook: A Descriptive Study of Tailoresses and Boxmakers* (London: G. Bell, 1916), p. 4; Schmiechen, *Sweated Industries,* pp. 72 and *passim.*

70. Grant, *Farthing Bundles,* p. 81; *Report by Dr. Crichton-Browne and Mr. J. G. Fitch upon the Alleged Over Pressure of Work in Public Elementary Schools* (London: Hansard, 1884), p. 9.

71. Frank Steel, *Ditcher's Row: A Tale of the Older Charity* (London: Sidgwick & Jackson, 1939), p. 5; interview with Mrs. Mac, born 1905, typescript, p. 15, Samuel oral histories.

72. On household ornaments as a kind of collateral to be pawned in hard times, see Paul Johnson, "Credit and Thrift and the British Working Class, 1870–1939," in Jay Winter, ed., *The Working Class in Modern British History* (Cambridge: Cambridge University Press, 1983). Also see Paul Johnson, *Saving and Spending: The Working Class Economy in Britain 1870–1939* (Oxford: Oxford University Press, 1985).

73. C. A. Cuthbert Keeson, "Pawnbroking London," in George R. Sims, ed., *Living London* (3 vols.) (London: Cassell, 1902), vol. 2, pp. 36–41; Melanie Tebbutt, *Making Ends Meet: Pawnbroking and Working-Class Credit* (London: Methuen, 1984), esp. chap. 2. London's peak in licensed pawnbroking was in about 1900. Unlicensed "dolly" shops were probably far more numerous than the legal shops. See Helen Bosanquet, "The Burden of Small Debts," *Economic Journal* 6 (1896): 212–23; V. de Vesselitsky and M. E. Bulkley, "Money-Lending Among the London Poor," *Sociological Review* 9 (Autumn 1917): 129–38.

74. Grant, *Farthing Bundles,* p. 77; Newham History Workshop, *A Marsh and a Gasworks: One Hundred Years of Life in West Ham* (London: Parents' Centre Publications, 1986), p. 54.

75. Thompson, *The Edwardians,* p. 179; Henry Higgs, "Workmen's Budgets," *JRSS* 56 (June 1893): 269; account by Minnie Ferris, who moved to the Island in 1907, in Hackney People's Autobiography, *The Island,* p. 31. See also the Luton description of the fate of a Sunday dinner during World War I: Sunday roast, Monday cold meat and pickles, Tuesday meat flecks in rissoles, Wednesday meat bones in a soup. See Edith Hall, *Canary Girls and Stockpots* (Luton: WEA Luton Branch, 1977), p. 7.

76. "Board School Children and their Food," *Toynbee Record,* February 1895, pp. 61–68.

77. Trish Hall, "Stretching Low-Cost Food Budgets," *New York Times,* September 16, 1987, p. C1.

78. Burnett, "Trends in Bread Consumption," p. 72; Oddy, "Working-Class Diets," p. 318.

79. Olive Christian Malvery, *Baby Toilers* (London: Hutchinson, 1907), p. 48; *Missing Link,* November 1, 1878, p. 332; Pember Reeves, *Round About a Pound,* p. 96; Margaret McMillan, *The Nursery School* (New York: Dutton, 1921), p. 53.

80. Burnett, "Trends in Bread Consumption," p. 97; M. E. Bulkley, *The Feeding of School Children* (London: G. Bell, 1914), pp. 200–201; Bay Street School Care Committee, minutes, February 25, 1908, EO/WEL/2/ vol. 1, GLRO; test. Miss Deverell, PP 1904, vol. 32, Q. 7981.

81. Daunton, *House and Home in the Victorian City*, pp. 241–42, 245, Table 10.4; Pember Reeves, *Round About a Pound*, p. 59; Logbook, Maidstone Street School, July 21, 1902, cited by Anna Davin in *Little Women: The Childhood of Working-Class Girls in Late Nineteenth-Century London* (London: Routledge & Kegan Paul, 1994), chap. 6; Petty et al., *Pudding Lady*, p. 18.

82. Test. Mr. Thomas Bird, Royal Commission on the Housing of the Working Classes, PP 1884–1885, vol. 30, Q. 4962; Henry Jephson, *The Sanitary Evolution of London* (Brooklyn, NY: A. Wessels, 1907), pp. 160–61, 361–62, 405–6, and *passim;* David Owen, *The Government of Victorian London 1855–1889* (Cambridge, MA: Harvard University Press, 1982), pp. 137–40; Burnett, *Social History of Housing*, pp. 158–61; Gauldie, *Cruel Habitations*, p. 215.

83. Test. Mr. T. Jennings, PP 1884–1885, vol. 30, Qq. 2908–11; Daunton, *House and Home*, p. 242. See also the example described in Fenner Brockway, *Bermondsey Story* (London: Allen & Unwin, 1949), p. 12.

84. Interview with Mrs. Stone, born in 1884, raised near Brick Lane, Samuel oral histories, pp. 6–7; also C. H. Rolph, *London Particulars* (Oxford: Oxford University Press, 1980), p. 75; Petty et al., *Pudding Lady*, p. 15.

85. Report of the MOH of the County [of London], in LCC, *Annual Reports* 1910, vol. 3, pp. 101–4; London MOH, *Annual Reports*, 1900, app. 1, pp. 3–14.

86. Margaret Loane, *An Englishman's Castle* (London: Arnold, 1909), p. 183. See also Grant, *Farthing Bundles*, p. 104. On low-income shoppers today, see, for example, Marcus Alexis, George H. Haines, Jr., and Leonard Simon, *Black Consumer Profiles: Food Purchasing in the Inner City* (Ann Arbor: Graduate School of Business Administration, University of Michigan, 1980). The U.S. Department of Agriculture's Human Nutritional Information Service spokeswoman commented that the poor are "better food shoppers, and they get more nutrients per dollar spent". See *New York Times*, September 16, 1987, p. C1.

87. Roberts, *Classic Slum*, p. 115; W. Hamish Fraser, *The Coming of the Mass Market, 1850–1914* (Hamden, CT: Archon Books, 1981), pp. 134–46, 206–7, and *passim.* Also see Peter Mathias, *The Retailing Revolution* (London: Longmans Group, 1967).

88. Test. Miss Deverell, PP 1904, vol. 32, Qq 7978–79; "Special Report of a Case of Food Poisoning at Homerton," Hackney MOH, *Annual Reports*, 1895, pp. 24–26.

89. Fraser, *Coming of the Mass Market*, p. 100–101; also see Davin, *Little Women,* chap. 6; Petty et al., *The Pudding Lady*, pp. 31–32.

90. On shops and shopkeepers, see Thea Vigne and Alun Howkins, "The Small Shopkeeper in Industrial and Market Towns," in Geoffrey Crossick, ed., *The Lower Middle Class in Britain* (London: Croom Helm, 1977); Janet Blackman, "The Corner Shop: The Development of the Grocery and General Provision Trade," in Oddy and Miller, eds., *The Making of the British Diet;* Hugh McLeod, *Class and Religion in the Late Victorian City* (London: Croom Helm, 1974), p. 15; Charles Booth, *Life and Labour of the People in London*, 1st ser. (5 vols.) (1902), reprint ed. (New York: Augustus M. Kelley, 1969), vol. 2, pp. 45–80.

91. McLeod, *Class and Religion*, p. 15; *Bethnal Green News*, May 4, 1895, p. 3. (The street is probably Cambridge Heath Road in Bethnal Green.) Also see George

Sims, *How the Poor Live and Horrible London,* combined ed. (London: Chatto & Windus, 1889), pp. 126–27; Pember Reeves, *Round About a Pound,* pp. 39–40.

92. *The Star,* August 28, 1889, p. 2; August 27, p. 2; August 23, p. 2; and issues throughout the strike.

93. Family Life Archive, no. 70, p. 24; *The Star,* November 12, 1889.

94. Women's Labour League Baby Clinic File, pamphlet 12/3, Labour Party Library, London. Rickets was underdiagnosed eighty years ago because it is hard to detect in its early stages. See Charles Singer and E. Ashworth Underwood, *A Short History of Medicine,* rev. ed. (New York: Oxford University Press, 1962), p. 614.

95. City of Westminster Health Society, *Annual Reports,* 1913, pp. 18–21, Westminster City Archive; Report of the Medical Officer (Education), in LCC, *Annual Reports,* 1910, vol. 3, pp. 136–39.

96. H. Henry Mosley and Lincoln C. Chen, *An Analytical Framework for the Study of Child Survival: Strategies for Research* (Cambridge: Cambridge University Press, 1984), p. 30. See also T. J. Marchione, "Factors Associated with Malnutrition in the Children of Western Jamaica," in Jerome et al., eds., *Nutritional Anthropology,* p. 226; Anne Burgess and R. F. A. Dean, eds., *Malnutrition and Food Habits: Report of an International and Interprofessional Conference* (New York: Macmillan, 1962), p. 5.

97. Smith, *People's Health,* p. 183; Arthur Greenwood, *The Health and Physique of School Children* (London: P. S. King, 1913), app. A, ser. A and B; *The School Child,* March 1913, p. 1; *Toynbee Record,* January 1912, p. 48.

98. Report of the Medical Officer (Education), 1910, pp. 133, 149. For a recent comprehensive study of the heights and weights of working-class Britons, see Roderick Floud, Kenneth Wachler, and Annabel Gregory, *Height, Health and Human History* (Cambridge: Cambridge University Press, 1990).

99. Test. Dr. Hawkes, PP 1904, vol. 32, Q. 12970; Joan Jacobs Brumberg, *Fasting Girls: The Emergence of Anorexia Nervosa as a Modern Disease* (Cambridge, MA: Harvard University Press, 1988); Charles Shorter, "The First Great Increase in Anorexia Nervosa," *Journal of Social History* 21 (Fall 1987): 69–96; Helena Michie, *The Flesh Made Word: Female Figures and Women's Bodies* (New York: Oxford University Press, 1987), esp. pp. 12–13.

100. Evelyn M. Bunting, Dora E. L. Bunting, Annie E. Barnes, and Blanche Gardiner, *A School for Mothers* (London: Horace Marshall, 1907), pp. 29–30, 25–27; Beatrice Webb, *Health of Working Girls* (1917), quoted in Angela Woollacott, *On Her Their Lives Depend: Munitions Workers in the Great War* (Berkeley and Los Angeles: University of California Press, forthcoming), chap. 3.

101. Martin, *Married Working Woman,* pp. 13, 15. See also Charles and Kerr, *Women, Food and Families,* p. 180; and Delphy, "Sharing the Same Table."

102. Family Life Archive, no. 236, p. 36; Scannell, *Mother Knew Best,* p. 37. On overall contrasts between male and female diets, see Oren, "Welfare of Women in Labouring Families"; Oddy, "A Nutritional Analysis of Historical Evidence"; and Burnett, *Plenty and Want,* pp. 122–24, 144.

103. Williamson, *Father Joe,* p. 22.

CHAPTER 3

1. For studies focusing on working-class gender relationships in London in the years under scrutiny here, see John Gillis, *For Better, for Worse: British Marriages 1600*

to the Present (New York: Oxford University Press, 1985) (based on much London research); Patricia Malcolmson, *English Laundresses: A Social History 1850–1930* (Urbana: University of Illinois Press, 1986), chap. 1; Nancy Tomes, " 'A Torrent of Abuse': Crimes of Violence Between Working-Class Men and Women in London, 1840–1875," *Journal of Social History* 11 (Spring 1978): 329–45; and Jerry White, *The Worst Street in North London: Campbell Bunk, Islington, Between the Wars* (London: Routledge & Kegan Paul, 1986).

2. The term *sexual antagonism* is introduced and illustrated in Marilyn Strathern's *Women in Between* (London: Seminar Press, 1972), esp. pp. 296–314; and in Ann Whitehead, "Sexual Antagonism in Herefordshire," in D. L. Barker and S. Allen, eds., *Dependence and Exploitation in Work and Marriage* (London: Longman Group, 1976). Although the concept continues to be used by anthropologists, many of its premises have been recently challenged by Strathern herself, based on her reading of two decades of feminist writing about gender. See Marilyn Strathern, *The Gender of the Gift* (Berkeley and Los Angeles: University of California Press, 1988), esp. chap. 3.

3. Florence Roberts, *The Ups and Downs of Florrie Roberts* (London: Peckham Publishing Project, 1980), p. 8. On the "swell" genre in music hall, see Christopher Pulling, *They Were Singing* (London: George G. Harrap, 1952), chap. 2; Anthony Bennett, "Music in the Halls," in J. S. Bratton, ed., *Music Hall: Performance and Style* (Milton Keynes: Open University Press, 1986), pp. 16–18; and Peter Bailey, "The Swell Song," in Bratton, ed., *Music Hall.* On music-hall music and drama in London's working-class culture, see Bratton's introduction to *Music Hall;* her earlier *The Victorian Popular Ballad* (Totowa, NJ: Rowman & Littlefield, 1975), chap. 6; and Patrick Joyce, *Visions of the People: Industrial England and the Question of Class 1848–1914* (Cambridge: Cambridge University Press, 1991), chap. 13. Also see Peter Bailey, ed., *The Victorian Music Hall: The Business of Pleasure* (Milton Keynes: Open University Press, 1987).

4. Sung by Gus Elen (1862–1940), lyrics in Colin MacInnes, *Sweet Saturday Night* (London: MacGibbon & Kee, 1967), pp. 37–38.

5. Peter Gammon, ed., *Best Music Hall and Variety Songs* (London: Wolfe, 1972).

6. Dorothy Scannell, *Mother Knew Best: Memoir of a London Girlhood* (New York: Pantheon, 1974), pp. 97–98.

7. See, among many other possible sources, A. James Hammerton, "Victorian Marriage and the Law of Matrimonial Cruelty," *Victorian Studies* 33 (Winter 1990); 269–92; A. James Hammerton, *Cruelty and Companionship: Conflict in Nineteenth Century Married Life* (New York: Routledge & Kegan Paul, 1992); and Pat Jalland, *Women, Marriage and Politics 1860–1914* (Oxford: Clarendon Press, 1986), esp. pt. I.

8. On family and marriage in other contemporaneous parts of Britain, see Elizabeth Roberts, *A Woman's Place; An Oral History of Working-Class Women 1890–1940* (Oxford: Basil Blackwell, 1984); Paul Thompson, with Tony Wailey and Trevor Lummis, *Living the Fishing* (London: Routledge & Kegan Paul, 1983), pt. III; Gillis, *For Better, for Worse,* pt. III; Trevor Lummis, "The Historical Dimension of Fatherhood: A Case Study 1890–1914," in Margaret O'Brien and Lorna McKee, eds., *The Father Figure* (London: Tavistock, 1982); Keith McClelland, "Some Thoughts on Masculinity and the 'Representative Artisan' in Britain, 1850–1880," *Gender and History* 1 (Summer 1989): 164–77.

9. See Michele Barrett and Mary McIntosh, "The 'Family Wage': Some Problems for Socialists and Feminists," *Capital and Class* 2 (Summer 1980): 51–72. On

poverty in old age, see, for example, Charles Booth, *The Aged Poor in England and Wales* (London: Macmillan, 1894), pp. 14–15.

10. Paul Thompson, *Socialists, Liberals and Labour: The Struggle for London 1885–1914* (London: Routledge & Kegan Paul, 1967), pp. 69–72.

11. John Springhall, *Coming of Age: Adolescence in Britain 1860–1960* (Dublin: Gill & Macmillan, 1986), pp. 81–87; and the thorough study of work for young men and of the problem of "boy labour": Harry Hendrick, *Images of Youth: Age, Class, and the Male Youth Problem, 1880–1920* (Oxford: Clarendon Press, 1990); "Children on Outdoor Relief," Royal Commission on the Poor Laws, app. II, PP 1910, vol. 52, p. 153. On middle-class men, see J. A. Mangan and James Walvin, eds., *Manliness and Morality: Middle-Class Masculinity in Britain and America 1800–1940* (New York: St. Martin's Press, 1987). See the examination of this issue in Wally Secombe, "Patriarchy Stabilized: The Construction of the Male Breadwinner Wage Norm in Nineteenth-Century Britain," *Social History* 11 (January 1986): 53–76.

12. J. S. Bratton, "Jenny Hill: Sex and Sexism in the Victorian Music Hall," in Bratton, ed., *Music Hall,* p. 105. The daughter of a Marylebone cab driver, Hill had been a cleaner and performer in a country pub before she returned to London in her early twenties. Her attempt at a straightforward statement of a wife's viewpoint in this number was thwarted by critics who insisted that this was a "comic" number or that Hill appeared in the character of a drunken wife; the refrain "("I've been a good woman to you") was labeled "self-satisfied." On Hill, also see Wilson Disher, *Winkles and Champagne: Comedies and Tragedies of the Music Hall* (London: Batsford 1938, pp. 19–20. On "female interest" in the domestic context, see Christine Stansell, *City of Women: Sex and Class in New York 1789–1860* (New York: Knopf, 1986), pp. 79–83.

13. John Hasloch Potter, *Inasmuch: The Story of the Police Court Mission, 1876–1926* (London: Williams & Norgate, 1927), pp. 67–68; Doris M. Bailey, *Children of the Green* (London: Stepney Books, 1981), p. 18.

14. Jane Lewis, *Women in England 1870–1950* (Brighton: Wheatsheaf Books, 1984), p. 157. National marriage figures from *Papers of the Royal Commission on Population, vol. 2: Reports and Selected Papers of the Statistics Committee* (London: HMSO, 1950), Table 5, p. 311. The borough figures are from 1881 Census E. and W., PP 1883, vol. 80, Table 8, pp. 10–11; and 1911 Census of PP 1912–1913, vol. 113, Table 9, pp. 321–35. For his generously offered advice on this section (most of which I was unequipped to follow), I am very grateful to Michael Haines, Department of Economics, Colgate University.

15. The mean marriage age in the country in 1888 was 26.3 for men and 24.7 for women. Among the "professional and independent class," the means were 31.2 for men and 26.4 for women. See William Ogle, "Marriage Rates and Marriage Ages, with Special Reference to the Growth of Population," *JRSS* (June 1890): 273; Table F, p. 274, and Table C, p. 267.

16. The figures are for St. Matthews Church, Bethnal Green, for the years 1879 through 1912, and for St. Peter's, Liverpool Street, for the years 1887 through 1904. Marriage registers in the GLRO. The total number of marriages for the three selected periods in Bethnal Green was 1,062, and for St. Peters for the two selected periods the total was 439. For full references, see the sources for Table 3–3.

17. These 1911 borough mean ages of marriage are actually "singulate means," which I calculated not from the marriage registers themselves but from the proportions remaining single in different age cohorts between fifteen and fifty. They are often used in describing national marriage patterns. On the procedures and justifi-

cation for this technique, see John Hajnal, "Age at Marriage and Proportions Marrying," *Population Studies* 7 (1953): 111–36, app. 3.18. Calculations are based on LCC, *London Statistics,* vol. 3 (1893–1894); and *Statistical Abstract for London 1905,* vol. 8, pp. 86–87.

18. Gillis, *For Better, for Worse,* p. 232, summarizing Charles Booth's late nineteenth-century findings on this. Mayhew had found "tally" marriages common among costermongers in the 1850s, and London city missionaries were distressed by the low marriage rates for poor districts in Deptford. See Henry Mayhew, *London Labour and the London Poor* (4 vols.) (London: Bohn, Griffin, 1861–1862), vol. 1, pp. 20–21; *London City Mission Magazine,* August 1855, pp. 187–88; and Donald M. Lewis, *Lighten Their Darkness: The Evangelical Mission to Working-Class London, 1828–1860* (Westport, CT.: Greenwood Press, 1986), pp. 140–49.

19. "Life in Spitalfields," *Bethnal Green News,* May 11, 1895, p. 6; PP 1904, vol. 32, Qq. 8425 and 13179; test. Robert Ernest Moore, Royal Commission on Divorce and Matrimonial Causes, PP 1912–1913, vol. 18, Q. 4813. See also Charles Booth, *Life and Labour of the People in London,* 3rd ser.: *Religious Influences* (7 vols.) (London: Macmillan, 1902), vol. 1, p. 55.

20. Clergymen did remark on this phenomenon to Booth's investigators (*Life and Labour,* 3rd. ser., vol. 1, p. 55); Guy A. Aldred, *No Traitor's Gait* (Glasgow: Strickland Press, 1955), pp. 9, 22. Aldred became a journalist as a teenager, joined the Christian Social Mission, and eventually became a freethinker, SDF member, and, finally, anarchist. He was tried in 1922 for publishing birth control pamphlets.

21. Interviews with rectors at All Saints, Stoke Newington; and at St. James the Great, Bethnal Green, reported in Fulham Papers, London Visitations, 1883, Lambeth Palace, London. On the nurse-mother case, see Spaul, Old Bailey, vol. 76 (1872), no. 687, p. 404.

22. Booth, *Life and Labour,* 3rd ser., vol. 1, p. 55. See also test. of Miss Deverell, PP 1904, vol. 32, Qq. 7988, 8081; also see Gillis, *For Better, for Worse,* p. 234. On the Matthew Peters case, see Peters, Old Bailey, vol. 80 (1874), no. 367, p. 32. As in similar bigamy cases in which one partner had lost track of the other for many years, the verdict in Peters's case was not guilty.

23. "The Boy I Love Is Up in the Gallery," written and composed by George Ware, discussed in MacInnis, *Sweet Saturday Night,* p. 20. See also Pulling, *They Were Singing,* p. 201. The song is reprinted in John M. Garrett, ed., *Sixty Years of British Music Hall* (London: Chappell, 1976).

24. Macinnis, *Sweet Saturday Night;* Peter Davidson, *Songs of the British Music Hall* (New York: Oak Publications, 1971); Pulling, *They Were Singing.*

25. Gillis, *For Better, for Worse,* p. 277. "Mrs. 'Awkins" is reprinted in Gammon, ed., *Best Music Hall and Variety Songs.* Also, Goldthorpe, Old Bailey (1873–74), vol. 80, no. 433, p. 133; and "Young Roughs Who Frequent Bow Road," *Bethnal Green News,* March 16, 1895, p. 8. See also George Sims, "London Sweethearts," in his *Living London* (3 vols.) (London: Cassell, 1902), vol. 2, pp. 18–19.

26. "The Old Bachelor" mourned his dead sweetheart for his entire adult lifetime in an Albert Chevalier love song. For a crush on the vicar, see Alice Linton, *Not Expecting Miracles* (London: Centerprise, 1982), pp. 55–56. On love letters, see Chaim Bermant, *London's East End: Point of Arrival* (New York: Macmillan, 1975), p. 198.

27. Gillis, *For Better, for Worse,* p. 278; Arthur Seymour (b. 1879), "Childhood Memories" (Manuscript autobiography, Brunel University Library).

28. Gillis, *For Better, for Worse,* p. 284; Emmeline Pethick-Lawrence, *My Part in a Changing World* (London: Victor Gollancz, 1938), p. 82.

29. Marie Kelly Welsh, born in Norfolk Gardens, Hoxton, in 1904, typescript oral history, Hackney People's Autobiography, p. 43; Family Life Archive, no. 225, p. 93; Pethick-Lawrence, *Changing World,* p. 82.

30. Hugh McLeod, *Class and Religion in the Late Victorian City* (London: Croom Helm, 1974), pp. 7–8, Table 4, pp. 296–97; Louise A. Tilly and Joan W. Scott, *Women, Work and Family* (New York: Holt, Rinehart and Winston, 1978), pp. 191–92; Geoffrey Crossick, *An Artisan Elite in Victorian Society: Kentish London 1840–1880* (London: Croom Helm, 1978), p. 123.

31. Interview with Mr. and Mrs. Mac and with Ethel Vango, Samuel oral histories; Linton, *Not Expecting Miracles,* chap. 8; Edward Ezard, *Battersea Boy* (London: William Kember, 1979), p. 30. See also Family Life Archive, no. 124; and John Bennett, *I Was a Walworth Boy* (London: Peckham Publishing Project, 1980).

32. Gillis, *For Better, for Worse,* p. 264; interview with Mrs. Henman, Samuel oral histories, tape 1, side 2. See also Family Life Archive, no. 412, p. 19.

33. Family Life Archive, nos. 412, and 333. May Surrey is a pseudonym.

34. Linton, *Not Expecting Miracles,* p. 72 (in this later autobiography, the couple did have a white wedding, in 1928, at Hoxton Parish Church); Gillis, *For Better, for Worse,* p. 293; London Visitations, 1883, St. Mary's Spital Square; St. John's, Cubitt Town. See also Helen Dendy, "Marriage in East London," in Bernard Bosanquet, ed., *Aspects of the Social Problem* (London: Macmillan, 1895).

35. "Angels Without Wings," sung by Vesta Tilly in her favorite male drag and written and composed by George Dance: see Garrett, ed., *Sixty Years of British Music Hall;* "The Bachelor of Sixty Two," in W. Henderson, ed., *Victorian Street Ballads* (London: Country Life, 1938), pp. 133–34.

36. Anna Martin, "Working-Women and Drink, Part II," *The Nineteenth Century and After* 79 (January 1916): 98; Family Life Archive, no. 126, p. 26. Mrs. H., born in Canning Town in 1895, recounted her mother's leaving her neglectful husband with three children: "There you are, she said . . . now you can keep them children, she said, I'm off." The husband eventually found her, returned the children, and promised to reform. Edwin Pugh, in his collection of stories *The Cockney at Home,* turns this situation into comedy in "Woman's Work," *The Cockney at Home* (London: Chapman & Hall, 1914).

37. Ellen Ranyard, *Nurses for the Needy, or Biblewomen Nurses in the Homes of the London Poor* (London: James Nesbet, 1875), p. 24; Doris M. Bailey, *Children of the Green* (London: Stepney Books, 1981), p. 16.

38. James Greenwood, "Pawnbrokery in London," *Hours at Home* 7 (1868): 116. I owe this reference to Jan Lambertz, "Male–Female Violence in Late Victorian and Edwardian England" (B.A. thesis, Harvard University, 1979).

39. Plampton, Old Bailey, vol. 99 (1883–1884), no. 301, p. 533; A. S. Jasper, *A Hoxton Childhood* (London: Centerprise, 1974), pp. 17, also pp. 69–70.

40. Grace Foakes, *My Part of the River* (London: Futura Books, 1978), p. 114; Scannell, *Mother Knew Best,* p. 96. See Marion Glastonbury on the power of these homey sayings: "The Best Kept Secret—How Working-Class Women Live and What They Know," *Women's Studies International Quarterly* 2 (1979): 171–81.

41. Bailey, *Children of the Green,* p. 53; Foakes, *My Part of the River,* p. 114; Scannell, *Mother Knew Best,* p. 96; interview with Mrs. Mac, side 2, p. 1, Samuel oral histories. Tales of women who had tricked their husbands by serving them food that had been mauled by cats or had fallen in the street are regular elements of working-class female storytelling. Another example, told to a Somers Town housing manager by a woman born in 1902, is Margaret White, *And Grandmother's Bed*

Went Too: Poor but Happy in Somers Town (Richmond: St. Pancras Housing Association, 1988), p. 25.

42. Thomas Holmes, *Known to the Police* (London: Arnold, 1908), pp. 48–49; James Greenwood, *Prisoner in the Dock: My Four Years' Daily Experiences in the London Police Courts* (London: Chatto & Windus, 1902), p. 184. Men were apparently getting three-month jail sentences instead of the much longer hospital treatment for which magistrates and court officials had lobbied as a remedy for female offenders. See Geoffrey Hunt, "Wretched, Hatless and Miserably Clad: Women and the Inebriate Reformatories from 1900–1913" (Unpublished paper, Polytechnic of North London, 1989), which looks at the case records of Farmfield, the LCC's asylum. See also Robert Thorne, "The Movement for Public House Reform 1892–1914," in Derek J. Oddy and Derek S. Miller, eds., *Diet and Health in Modern Britain* (London: Croom Helm, 1985); and on the use of dangers to infants in a stepped-up campaign against women's drinking in the 1900s, see David W. Gutzke, " 'The Cry of the Children': The Edwardian Medical Campaign Against Maternal Drinking," *British Journal of Addiction* 79 (1984): 71–84. Also see Patrick M. McLaughlin, "Inebriate Reformatories in Scotland: An Institutional History," in Susanna Barrows and Robin Room, eds., *Drinking: Behavior and Belief in Modern History* (Berkeley and Los Angeles: University of California Press, 1991).

43. Neale and Neale, Old Bailey, vol. 105 (1887), no. 253, p. 325.

44. The phrases used by Beatrice Potter in her account book describing tenants in the Katharine Buildings, for which she was a rent collector from 1885 until 1889. See "Received of the Inhabitants During the Years 1885–1990. Begun by Mrs. Sidney Webb . . . " LSE Manuscript Collection, Coll. Misc. 43, R (S.R.) 1017.

45. Edith Hall, *Canary Girls and Stockpots* (Luton: WEA, 1977), p. 16.

46. The term is used by Jessie Bernard in her essay by that title in Jo Freeman, ed., *Women: A Feminist Perspective,* 2nd ed. (Palo Alto, CA.: Mayfield, 1979).

47. "Unoccupied Women: The Result of a Day's Canvassing in a New District," *Woman's Dreadnought,* May 30, 1914, p. 44. Emphasis in the original.

48. Gardener, Old Bailey, vol. 80 (1873–1874), no. 477, p. 207. See also Green, Old Bailey, vol. 80 (1873–1874), no. 533, p. 280; and Boddy, Old Bailey, vol. 90 (1879), no. 886, p. 821.

49. Stan Shipley, "Tom Causer of Bermondsey: A Boxer Hero of the 1890s," *History Workshop* 15 (Spring 1983): 28–59; Charles P. Korr, "West Ham United Football Club and the Beginnings of Professional Football in East London, 1895–1914," *Journal of Contemporary History* 13 (April 1978): 211–32.

50. Ross McKibbin, "Working-Class Gambling in Britain 1880–1939," in his *The Ideologies of Class: Social Relations in Britain 1880–1950* (Oxford: Clarendon Press, 1990); see also David C. Itzkowitz, "Victorian Bookmakers and Their Customers," *Victorian Studies* 32 (Autumn 1988): 6–30.

51. (Florence) Petty et al., *The Pudding Lady: A New Departure in Social Work* (London: Stead's Publishing House, 1910), p. 34. See Iris Minor's "Working-Class Women and Matrimonial Law Reform, 1890–1914," in David E. Martin and David Rubinstein, eds., *Ideology and the Labour Movement* (Totowa, NJ: Rowman & Littlefield, 1979), pp. 115–16.

52. Thomas Saunders, *Metropolitan Police Court Jottings* (London: Horace Cox, 1882), pp. 15–17. Saunders served as a police court magistrate years before the Summary Jurisdiction (Married Women) Act of 1895, which permitted separations to wives on more lenient grounds than previously. According to one observer writing in 1899, "no recent Act has brought so much work" to the courts. See

C. H. D., "An East End Police Court," *Toynbee Record,* February 1899, pp. 70–71.

53. See Minor, "Working-Class Women and Matrimonial Law Reform"; also "An East End Police Court," *Toynbee Record,* February 1899, pp. 70–71. On maintenance orders, see Griselda Rowntree and Norman H. Carrier, "Resort to Divorce in England and Wales 1858–1957," *Population Studies* 11 (March 1958): 190–93, 198; and V. M. Shillington, "Maintenance Grants Under Separation Orders," *Women's Industrial News,* new. ser., 16 (January 1913): 106–10.

54. Tritner, Old Bailey, vol. 89 (1878–1879), no. 203, p. 279.

55. Margaret Loane, "Husband and Wife Among the Poor," *Contemporary Review* 87 (February 1905): 222; Jack Welch, born in 1903 in Norfolk Gardens, Hoxton, oral history transcript, p. 4, Hackney People's Autobiography. Also see George Acorn (pseud.), *One of the Multitude: An Autobiography by a Resident of Bethnal Green* (London: Heinemann, 1911), p. 2. As Nancy Tomes has remarked, a man's "right" to assault his wife was one that magistrates began increasingly to doubt toward the end of the nineteenth century (Tomes, " 'Torrent of Abuse' ").

56. Mary Ann Ford case cited in Tomes, " 'Torrent of Abuse,' " p. 332.

57. "Woman, Lovely Woman," sung by James Fawn in the late 1880s, in Pulling, *They Were Singing,* pp. 70–71.

58. Jasper, *Hoxton Childhood,* pp. 31, 51–52, also p. 40.

59. Ivy Pinchbeck, *Women Workers and the Industrial Revolution, 1750–1850,* reprint ed. (New York: Augustus M. Kelley, 1969), pp. 1, 312; Alice Clark, *Working Life of Women in the Seventeenth Century,* reprint ed. (New York: Augustus M. Kelley, 1969), p. 54. On teetotalers' payments to wives, see George Duckworth's discussion with P. C. Ryland, Hoxton Subdivision of the G Division of the Metropolitan Police, Charles Booth ms., ser. B., vol. 352, LSE Manuscript Collection. See also Anne Gray, "The Working Class Family as an Economic Unit," in Chris Harris, ed., *The Sociology of the Family: New Directions for Britain* (Sociological Review Monographs, University of Keele, 1979).

On the use of the term *wages* for wives, see Laura Oren, "The Welfare of Women in Labouring Families: England 1860–1950," *Feminist Studies* 1 (Winter–Spring 1973): 112–13; Family Life Archive, no. 368; Elizabeth Roberts, "Working Class Women in the North West," *Oral History* 5 (Autumn 1977): 13; E. Robinson (born in Camberwell in 1894), "I Remember" (1960–70) (Typescript, Brunel University Library), p. 7. For another arrangement, see Malcolmson, *English Laundresses,* p. 40.

60. Hilary Land, "Poverty and Gender: The Distribution of Resources within the Family," in M. Brown, ed., *The Structure of Disadvantage* (London: Heinemann, 1983), p. 52; Michael Young, "Distribution of Income Within the Family," *British Journal of Sociology* 3 (1952): 309; Hilary Land, *Large Families in London: A Study of 86 Families,* Occasional Papers on Social Administration, no. 32 (London: G. Bell, 1969), p. 66; Hilary Graham, *Women, Health and the Family* (Brighton: Wheatsheaf Books, 1984), pp. 102, 104; Gray, "The Working-Class Family," pp. 196–99.

61. Petty et al., *Pudding Lady;* V. de Vesselitsky, *Expenditure and Waste* (London: G. Bell, 1917), pp. 9–10, 45. A similar estimate was offered by the trade unionist A. G. Markham in 1902 to the Select Committee of the House of Lords on Betting: Of a wage earner's 30 shillings per week, "he would give the wife 20s. to 25s." Quoted in McKibbin, "Working-Class Gambling," p. 125. See also in this book, Chapter 2, "The Battle over Alcohol."

62. H. A. Mess, *Casual Labour at the Docks* (London: G. Bell, 1916), p. 35; Henry Iselin, "The Story of a Children's Care Committee," *Economic Review* 22 (1912): 46. In Middlesbrough, over a third of the wives interviewed by Lady Bell had not

figured out how much their husbands earned. See Lady Florence Bell, *At the Works* (1907), reprint ed. (London: Virago, 1985), p. 78. On Rowntree's study, see Michael Young, "Distribution of Income Within the Family," *British Journal of Sociology* 3 (1952): 307; Michael Young and Peter Wilmott, *Family and Kinship in East London* (Harmondsworth, Penguin Books, 1962), pp. 18, 26–27; Gray, "The Working-Class Family"; see also, on recent domestic arrangements, R. E. Pahl, *Divisions of Labour* (Oxford: Basil Blackwell, 1984), chaps. 9 and 10.

63. Oren, "Welfare of Women," pp. 111–12; Peter N. Stearns, "Working Class Women in Britain, 1890–1914," in Martha Vicinus, ed., *Suffer and Be Still* (Bloomington: Indiana University Press, 1972), p. 116; Standish Meacham, *A Life Apart: The English Working Class 1890–1914* (Cambridge, MA: Harvard University Press, 1977), chap. 3.

64. Acorn, *One of the Multitude,* p. 5; Linton, *Not Expecting Miracles,* p. 6. Anna Martin, "Working-Women and Drink, Part II," *The Nineteenth Century and After* 79 (January 1916): 86; Land, "Poverty and Gender," p. 56; Young, "Distribution of Income Within the Family," pp. 313 ff; Lucy Syson and Michael Young, "Poverty in Bethnal Green," in Michael Young, ed., *Poverty Report* (London: Temple Smith, 1974), p. 110.

65. Land, "Poverty and Gender," p. 53; Margaret Loane, "Husband and Wife Among the Poor," *Contemporary Review* 87 (February 1905): 226.

66. T. E. Harvey, *A London Boy's Saturday* (Birmingham: Saint George Press, 1906), p. 12 (reference generously supplied by Anna Davin and Jerry White); Raphael Samuel's interview with Mrs. Mac.

67. John Benson, *The Penny Capitalists: A Study of Nineteenth-Century Working-Class Entrepreneurs* (Dublin: Gill & Macmillan, 1983), p. 134; Linton, *Not Expecting Miracles,* pp. 5–6; Scannell, *Mother Knew Best,* pp. 97–99; Lillian Hine, "A Poplar Childhood," *East London Record* 3 (1980): 43.

68. E. P. Thompson, "Time, Work-Discipline, and Industrial Capitalism," *Past and Present* 36 (December 1967): 77; Hine, "Poplar Childhood," p. 38; Bailey, *Children of the Green,* p. 17; Hall, *Canary Girls,* p. 6.

69. Walter Southgate, *That's the Way It Was: A Working Class Autobiography 1890–1950* (London: New Clarion Press, 1982), p. 67.

70. George Rushbrook, "Memories" (1974), typescript, Tower Hamlets Local History Library, p. 4; Octavia Hill, *Homes of the London Poor* (New York: Charities Aid Association, 1873), p. 41.

71. Davison, *Songs of the British Music Hall,* pp. 208–10; Foakes, *My Part of the River,* p. 113; Linton, *Not Expecting Miracles,* p. 2.

72. Southgate, *The Way It Was,* pp. 65–66.

73. Like pub use by women, the pawnshop's reputation varied enormously by district. Pledging appears to have been both common and socially acceptable in much of East London. Arthur Sherwell's study of West London family budgets demonstrates the function of pawning when employment was so irregular. See his *Life in West London* (London: Methuen, 1897). Also see the references on pawning cited in Chapter 2, "Money and Food."

74. The police had succeeded in getting several others in Hoxton closed down. George Duckworth's tour of the area (the Hoxton subdivision of the G. or Finsbury Division of the Metropolitan Police) with P. C. Ryland, May 1898. Charles Booth Papers, B 352, p. 113, LSE Manuscript Collection. See also C. R. Cuthbert Keeson, "Pawnbroking London," in George Sims, ed., *Living London* (3 vols.) (London: Cassell, 1902), vol. 2, pp. 37, 3; and Grant, *Farthing Bundles,* p. 98.

75. Keeson, "Pawnbroking London," pp. 37, 39; Grant, *Farthing Bundles,* p. 98; Melanie Tebbutt, *Making Ends Meet: Pawnbroking and Working-Class Credit* (London: Methuen, 1984), p. 42; Greenwood, *Prisoner in the Dock,* pp. 225–26. Also Jasper, *Hoxton Childhood,* p. 75.

76. Pawn tickets themselves, as opposed to the items they represented, had a market value of a few cents. See Helen Bosanquet, "The Burden of Small Debts," *Economic Journal* 6 (1896): 217. For women at police court because of lost pawn tickets, see *London City Mission Magazine,* October 1864, p. 206. For the case of a servant who stole three pawn tickets from her landlady and sold two of them to another woman, see Mary Blaney, Worship Street Police Court, "May 1874" bundle; for a young woman sentenced to twenty-one days in jail for stealing three sheets from her landlady, pawning them, and selling the pawn tickets, see Sophia Cooper, Worship Street, "Feb–March 1874" bundle. All are from Middlesex County Police Court depositions from 1855 to 1889, GLRO.

77. Pat Thane, "The Working Class and State 'Welfare' in Britain, 1880–1914," *Historical Journal* 27 (1984): 891; Catherine Webb, *The Woman with the Basket: The Story of the Women's Cooperative Guild 1883–1927* (Manchester: Cooperative Whole-sale Society, 1927), p. 89. The cooperative movement's well-known position against credit buying and pawning was violated by a majority of the local societies, a proportion that grew larger from the 1880s to the 1910s. See Paul Johnson, *Saving and Spending: The Working-Class Economy in Britain 1870–1939* (Oxford: Clarendon Press, 1985), pp. 133–35.

78. Thomas Wright, *The Pinch of Poverty: Sufferings and Heroism of the London Poor* (London: Isbister & Co., 1892), p. 301; Perry, Hollingsworth, and Black, Old Bailey, vol. 110 (1889), no. 531, p. 849. For an example of a mixed-sex group of thieves, in which the women did the group's pawning, see Thames Police Court, "Feb–March 1873" bundle.

79. Bosanquet, "Burden of Small Debts," p. 224; Jasper, *Hoxton Childhood,* p. 23. Also, on pawning as a skill, see Wright, *Pinch of Poverty,* p. 301.

80. John C. Blake, *Memories of Old Poplar* (London: Stepney Books, 1977), p. 11; also Arthur Hadley, "Penny Plain: Autobiography of a Bethnal Green Boy" (1947) (Typescript, Tower Hamlets Local History Library).

81. Interview with Mr. Causon, born in Donald Street, Bromley-by-Bow, in 1891, Samuel oral histories; Scannell, *Mother Knew Best,* p. 42; William Sanson, Introduction, in his *Victorian Life in Photographs* (London: Thames & Hudson, 1974), photo no. 92.

82. Lil Smith, "A Child's Saturday Work in 1920," *Working Lives: Volume One, 1905–45* (London: Hackney WEA and Centerprise, n.d.), p. 62.

83. Cited in Tomes, " 'Torrent of Abuse, " p. 337; Pethick-Lawrence, *Changing World,* p. 82.

84. Tomes, " 'Torrent of Abuse,' " p. 330. On the decline in official figures for violent crimes, see V. A. C. Gatrell, "The Decline of Theft and Violence in Victorian and Edwardian England," in V. A. C. Gatrell, Bruce Lenman, and Geoffrey Parker, eds., *Crime and the Law: The Social History of Crime in Western Europe Since 1500* (London: Europa Publications, 1980), pp. 284–301, and Tables A1 and A2.

85. French, Old Bailey, vol. 79 (1874), no. 301, pp. 389–90; Montague Williams, *Round London: Down East and Up West* (London: Macmillan, 1892), p. 79; Anna Martin, "The Mother and Social Reform," *The Nineteenth Century and After* 73 (May 1913): 1071–72. Williams on "drunken and brutal husbands" is quoted in Thomas

Holmes, *Pictures and Problems from London Police Courts* (London: Arnold, 1900), p. 62. See also R. E. Corder, *Tales Told to a Magistrate* (London: Andrew Melrose, 1925), pp. 205–6. On the courts as a popular method of adjusting problems for working people, see Jennifer Davis, "A Poor Man's System of Justice: The London Police Courts in the Second Half of the Nineteenth Century, *Historical Journal* 27 (1984): 309–35.

86. Tomes, " 'Torrent of Abuse,' " pp. 336–38; Hancock, Old Bailey, vol. 89 (1879), no. 250, p. 321; also Holmes, *Pictures and Problems,* pp. 62–63. On similar patterns in New York City in the early nineteenth century, see Stansell, *City of Women*, pp. 76–83.

87. Palmer, Old Bailey, vol. 89 (1869), no. 218, p. 267; Shipley, "Tom Causer of Bermondsey," pp. 39 and app. II, p. 55.

88. The term *threshold* describing wives' tolerance for domestic violence is developed in Lambertz, "Male–Female Violence." William Fitzsimmons's comments are from his testimony at the Royal Commission on Divorce and Matrimonial Causes, pp 1912–1913, vol. 19, Qq.19,473 ff.

89. See O. R. McGregor, *Divorce in England: A Centenary Study* (London: Heinemann, 1957), pp. 17–34, esp. pp. 22–26; Hammerton, "Victorian Marriage and the Law of Matrimonial Cruelty"; Margaret May, "Violence in the Family: An Historical Perspective," in John Powell Martin, ed., *Violence and the Family* (New York: Wiley, 1978).

90. Charles Welch, *An Autobiography* (Banstead: Berean Publishing, 1960), pp. 31, 39, 41. Welch was born in 1880 in Fair Street, Bermondsey.

91. Frank Galton, "Autobiography" (Typescript, 1939–1944), p. 23, Coll. Misc. 315, LSE Manuscript Collection. Galton, born in 1867 in Camden Town, lived mostly near Regents Park as a child. In 1886 he got involved with the Fabian Society and eventually became a secretary and assistant to the Webbs.

92. Johnson, *Saving and Spending*, p. 157; for piano sales in Bethnal Green, see Booth, *Life and Labour*, 3rd ser., vol. 2, p. 16; Ezard, *Battersea Boy*, p. 53; Jasper, *Hoxton Childhood;* Family Life Archive, no. 225, p. 2.

93. "A Christmas Party," *East London Observer*, January 2, 1869, p. 2; Family Life Archive, no. 225, p. 33; Booth manuscripts B349, pp. 219, 223; see also B350, p. 7.

94. Elizabeth Rignall, "All So Long Ago" (Typescript, unpaginated, Brunel University Library). The author was born in 1894. Her autobiography describes not only her childhood but also her work as a board schoolteacher and then as a clerical worker in the Ministry of Munitions during World War I.

95. James Ashley, untitled and undated typescript autobiography, Brunel University Library. Will Ashley eventually became chairman of the Political Science and Economics Department at the University of Toronto and then Birmingham University; Percy a lecturer at the London School of Economics.

96. Anna Martin, *The Married Working Woman: A Study* (London: NUWSS, 1911), p. 24; Pember Reeves, *Round About a Pound*, p. 16; Southgate, *The Way It Was*, p. 12; Frank Steel, *Ditcher's Row: A Tale of the Older Charity* (London: Sidgwick & Jackson, 1939), pp. 28–29. Steel's mother qualified her statement somewhat when she said, "I would never again sit back worshipping masculine wisdom and holding my piece till the mischief was done." Happy families in East Anglian fishing communities are described in Lummis, "The Historical Dimension of Fatherhood," in O'Brien and McKee, *The Father Figure*.

97. Aldred, *No Traitor's Gait;* Cranwell, Old Bailey, vol. 81 (1874–1875), no.

93, pp. 150–67; Boddy, Old Bailey, vol. 90 (1878–1879), no. 886, p. 821; "A Lucky Rescue," *East London Observer,* July 22, 1911, p. 3.

98. MacInnis, *Sweet Saturday Night,* p. 130. The workhouse gate setting often used as the backdrop when this song was performed, was, of course, a particularly sharp indictment of a poor-law system that separated lifelong couples in their last years.

99. W. MacQueen-Pope, *The Melodies Linger On: The Story of Music Hall* (London: Allen, 1950), p. 326; Bratton, "Jenny Hill." To make it more interesting, some of these tunes were also sung by elaborately transdressed performers, as in Vesta Tilley's "Angels Without Wings." See Garrett, *Sixty Years of British Music Hall.* On the growth of music-hall respectability, see Penelope Summerfield, "The Effingham Arms and the Empire: Deliberate Selection in the Evolution of Music Hall in London," in Eileen Yeo and Stephen Yeo, eds., *Popular Culture and Class Conflict* (Brighton: Harvester Press, 1981).

CHAPTER 4

1. General Lying-In Hospital (GLI, Medical Officers' Case Books, January–September 1881, no. 48; January–March 1884, no. 34.

2. Report of the Royal Commission on Population, PP 1948–1949, vol. 19, p. 26, Table 17; Census of England and Wales, PP 1911, vol. 13, pt. 2, pp. xlii–xliii, Table 16. Because the 1911 census questioned only those women whose spouses were still alive, it missed those whose childbearing had been cut short by separation or widowhood and thus overestimated the national fertility rate.

3. Patricia Branca, *Silent Sisterhood: Middle-Class Women in the Victorian Home* (London: Croom Helm, 1979), chap. 7; Dennis Wrong, "Class Fertility Differentials Before 1850," *Social Research* 25 (1958): 81; A. Newsholme and T. H. C. Stevenson, "The Decline in Human Fertility in the United Kingdom and Other Countries," *JRSS* 69 (March 1906): 66–67.

4. T. A. Welton, "A Study of Some Portions of the London Census for 1901," *JRSS* 65 (September 1902): 493, Tables 3 and 8; see also the comparisons among groups of London boroughs in Newsholme and Stevenson, "Decline in Human Fertility," p. 67.

5. Report of the MOH of the County [of London], in LCC, *Annual Reports* (1910), vol. 3, p. 12. London's legitimate fertility rate declined by 25 percent during these years, with the illegitimate rate falling by a whopping 45 percent.

6. For references to contemporaries' associations between stillbirths and miscarriages, and syphilis, see Susan Kingsley Kent, *Sex and Suffrage in Britain, 1860–1914* (Princeton, NJ: Princeton University Press, 1987), pp. 105–10. Most of the hospital material cited in this chapter dates from the 1870s and 1880s. In the twentieth century, the hospitals whose outpatient maternity records I examined kept no detailed childbearing histories; they simply used the now-standard designation of women as either "multiparous" or "nulliparous" without further details.

7. J. W. B. Douglas, "Social Class Differences in Health and Survival During the First Two Years of Life; the Results of a National Survey," *Population Studies* 5, pt. I (July 1951): 35–58; Hilary Graham, *Women, Health and the Family* (Brighton: Wheatsheaf, 1984), pp. 49–50.

8. Kate Moody (a pseudonym), a Lambeth mother interviewed in her old age in 1982 by Mary Chamberlain, distinguished between her "first" child" and her

"very first" child, which was stillborn during World War I and which she forgot to mention at first to a very patient and sympathetic interviewer. My thanks to Mary Chamberlain for sharing her interview transcripts. Much of this material was incorporated into her *Growing Up in Lambeth* (London: Virago, 1989). On unofficial burials of stillborn infants, see Margaret Hewitt, *Wives and Mothers in Victorian Industry,* reprint ed. (Westport, CT: Greenwood Press, 1975), pp. 104–5; and F. B. Smith, *The People's Health 1830–1910* (New York: Holmes & Meier, 1979), pp. 67–68. Also, on prematurity and stillbirths, see test. Florence Willey, Royal Commission on Venereal Disease, PP 1914, vol. 49, Qq. 11,577–11,580.

9. John Gillis, *For Better, for Worse: British Marriages 1600 to the Present* (New York: Oxford University Press, 1985), chap. 11; Maud Pember Reeves, *Round About a Pound a Week* (1913); reprint ed. (London: Virago, 1979), p. 193; Alexander Paterson, *Across the Bridges: A Study of Social Life in South London* (London: Arnold, 1911), p. 210.

10. Ellen Holtzman, "The Pursuit of Married Love: Women's Attitudes Toward Sexuality and Marriage in Great Britain, 1918–1938," *Journal of Social History* 16 (Winter 1982): 39–51; Pat Jalland, *Women, Marriage and Politics 1860–1914* (Oxford: Clarendon Press, 1986), p. 139; Katherine Roberts, *Five Months in a London Hospital* (Letchworth: Garden City Press, 1911), pp. 80, 16, 72.

On the birth control movement in the 1920s, see Richard A. Soloway, *Birth Control and the Population Question in England 1877–1930* (Chapel Hill: University of North Carolina Press, 1982); Norman Himes, "British Birth Control Clinics," *Eugenics Review* 20 (October 1928): 157–65; Griselda Rowntree and Rachel M. Pierce, "Birth Control in Britain Since the First World War," pt. I, *Population Studies* 15 (1961–1962): 3–31; Mary Breed and Edith How-Martin, *The Birth Control Movement in England* (London: J. Bale, 1930).

11. Ruth Hall, ed., *Dear Dr. Stopes: Sex in the 1920s* (Harmondsworth: Penguin Books, 1978), p. 17; Marie Stopes, ed., *Mother England: A Contemporary History Self-Written by Those Who Have Had No Historian* (London: John Bale, Sons and Danielsson, 1929), pp. 110–11, 116, 28. For samples of Canadian letters on birth control from the 1920s, see Angus McLaren, " 'Keep Your Seats and Face Facts': Western Canadian Women's Discussion of Birth Control in the 1920s," *Canadian Bulletin of Medical History* 8 (1991): 189–201.

12. C. P. Blacker, *Birth Control and the State* (London: Kegan Paul, Tench, Trubner, 1926), p. 36. For a nursing student's encounter with this fatalism two decades earlier, see Roberts, *Five Months,* p. 31. W. Somerset Maugham's novel *Of Human Bondage* (1915) is based on his years as a medical student of Guy's (Harmondsworth: Penguin Books, 1963), p. 559.

13. Christopher Pulling, *They Were Singing* (London: George G. Harrap, 1952), pp. 70–71; Colin MacInnis, *Sweet Saturday Night: Songs of the 1890's* (London: MacGibbon & Kee, 1967), p. 5.

14. The "trousers" story is told by a woman born in Canning town in 1895; her mother had nineteen children, of whom only seven survived (Family Life Archive, no. 126, p. 25); Margaret Nevinson, *Life's Fitful Fever* (London: A. and C. Black, 1926), p. 95.

15. Eileen Baillie, *The Shabby Paradise* (London: Hutchinson, 1959), pp. 205–6; also see W. Payne, *The Cruelty Man* (London: NSPCC, 1912), p. 151.

16. GLI Medical Officers' Case Books, December 1881–April 1882, no. 20; Jan-

uary–April 1888, nos. 92 and 103. Also see the Thomas Coram Foundling Hospital cases discussed by Françoise Barret-Ducrocq in *Love in the Time of Victoria,* tr. John Howe (London: Verso, 1991), chap. 3.

17. Elizabeth Flint, *Hot Bread and Chips: The Story of a Family Living in London's East End* (London: Museum Press, 1963) p. 95; Family Life Archive, no. 92, p. 17; no. 333, p. 26; no. 299, p. 31.

18. Interview with Mr. and Mrs. Mac, Samuel oral histories, p. 3; Dorothy Scannell, *Mother Knew Best: Memoir of a London Girlhood* (New York: Pantheon, 1974), p. 69; Frances Widdowson, "Childbirth in Greenwich Hospital 1930s and the Walworth Road Clinic" (Dittoed oral history transcript, Goldsmith's College, London). Similar experiences for women in three northern towns may be found in Elizabeth Roberts, *A Woman's Place: An Oral History of Working-Class Women 1890–1940* (Oxford: Basil Blackwell, 1984), chap. 3; and, for Birmingham primarily, Carl Chinn, *They Worked All Their Lives: Women of the Urban Poor in England, 1880–1939* (Manchester: University of Manchester Press, 1988), pp. 141–45.

19. Anna Martin, "The Mother and Social Reform," *The Nineteenth Century and After* 73 (May 1913): 1061; test. Fitzsimmons, Royal Commission on Divorce and Matrimonial Causes, PP 1912–13, vol. 19, Q. 19,522.

20. Scannell, *Mother Knew Best,* p. 11; Edith Hall, *Canary Girls and Stockpots* (Luton: WEA, 1977), p. 15; also Kathleen Woodward, *Jipping Street: Childhood in a London Slum* (1928), reprint ed. (London: Virago, 1983), p. 98; Margaret Llewelyn Davies, ed., *Maternity: Letters from Working Women* (1915) reprint ed. (New York: Norton, 1978), esp. pp. 65–66, 99.

21. Angus McLaren, *Birth Control in Nineteenth-Century England* (London: Croom Helm, 1978), p. 247; Tottenham History Workshop, *How Things Were: Growing Up in Tottenham 1890–1920* (London: n.p., n.d.), p. 23; Letter from Isabel Peterkin, October 15, 1976, p. 7, Women's Labour League Baby Clinic File, Labour Party Library. The clinic staff, like many of their contemporaries, thought of contraception as a practice that would give men "liberty to overtax or mollest [*sic*]" their wives (as physician Ethel Bentham put it) and so refused all such requests for information.

22. Lella Secor Florence, *Birth Control on Trial* (London: Allen & Unwin, 1930), pp. 68, 109; McLaren, *Birth Control,* p. 224; Widdowson, "Childbirth in Greenwich Hospital 1930s." Florence's book is a study of the first three hundred applicants at a birth control clinic opened in Cambridge in 1925. It was an affiliate of the Society for the Provision of Birth Control Clinics that had, as early as 1921, opened a clinic in Walworth, London. On the early birth control clinics, see Diana Gittins, *Fair Sex: Family Size and Structure, 1900–1939* (London: Hutchinson, 1982), chap. 6; also see Jane Lewis, *The Politics of Motherhood: Child and Maternal Welfare in England, 1900–1939* (London: Croom Helm, 1980), chap. 7.

23. E. Lewis-Faning, *Report on an Enquiry into Family Limitation and Its Influence on Human Fertility During the Past Fifty Years,* Papers of the Royal Commission on Population, vol. I (London: HMSO, 1949), pp. 4, 5, 7; Newsholme and Stevenson, "Decline in Human Fertility," pp. 67–69. On class differences in birth control use, also see Judah Matras, "Social Strategies of Family Formation: Data for British Female Cohorts Born 1831–1906," *Population Studies* 19 (November 1965): 167–81; and, for a slightly later period, Rowntree and Pierce, "Birth Control in Britain."

24. McLaren, *Birth Control,* chap. 12; *The Declining Birth-Rate: Its Causes and Effects* (Proceedings of a conference organized by the National Birth-Rate Commis-

sion) (London: Chapman & Hall, 1916), p. 136; John Peel, "The Manufacture and Retailing of Contraceptives in England," *Population Studies* 17 (1964): 116–19; test. Dr. Lewis Hawkes, Report of the Interdepartmental Committee on Physical Deterioration, PP 1904, vol. 32, Q. 13177.

25. This crucial issue has often been neglected in treatments of contraception as an issue. But for the period under review, see the useful discussions in Jane Lewis, *Women in England 1870–1950: Sexual Divisions and Social Change* (Brighton: Wheatsheaf Books, 1984), pp. 18–20; Roberts, *A Woman's Place;* and Paul Thompson, *The Edwardians: The Remaking of British Society* (St. Albans: Granada, 1977), p. 72. Wally Seccombe deals with husbands directly in his "Men's 'Marital Rights' and Women's 'Wifely Duties': Changing Conjugal Relations in the Fertility Decline," in John Gillis, Louise Tilly, and David Levine, eds., *The European Experience of Declining Fertility, 1850–1970* (Cambridge: Basil Blackwell, 1992).

26. Davies, *Maternity*, pp. 115, 73–74.

27. Elizabeth Rignall, "All So Long Ago" (Typescript autobiography, unpaginated, Brunel University Library).

28. See, for example, Angus McLaren, *Reproductive Rituals: The Perception of Fertility in England from the Sixteenth Century to the Nineteenth Century* (London: Methuen, 1984), chaps. 4 and 5; Rosalind Petchesky, *Abortion and Woman's Choice: The State, Sexuality, and Reproductive Freedom* (New York: Longman Group, 1984); and Carroll Smith-Rosenberg, "The Abortion Movement and the AMA, 1850–1880," in her *Disorderly Conduct: Visions of Gender in Victorian America* (New York: Knopf, 1985).

29. As in, for example, "Self Induced Instrumental Abortion," *BMJ*, September 17, 1898, p. 841; "The Traffic in Abortifacients," *BMJ*, January 14, 1899, p. 110; and "The Sale of Abortifacients," *BMJ*, December 2, 1899, p. 1583.

30. McLaren, *Reproductive Rituals;* Edward Shorter, *A History of Women's Bodies* (New York: Basic Books, 1982), chap. 8; Barbara Lesley Brookes, "Abortion in England, 1919–1939: Legal Theory and Social Practice" (Ph.D. diss., Bryn Mawr College, 1982).

31. McLaren, *Reproductive Rituals*, p. 104; *The Declining Birth-Rate*, pp. 140, 173, 279; McLaren, *Birth Control*, p. 242; Shorter, *Women's Bodies*, p. 212.

32. Roberts, *Woman's Place*, pp. 98–100; McLaren, *Birth Control*, p. 232. Medical practitioners reiterated that these were useless; see *BMJ*, January 14, 1899, p. 110.

33. Roberts, *Five Months*, p. 104; Tottenham History Workshop, *How Things Were*, p. 23; McLaren, *Birth Control*, chap. 13; Norman E. Himes, *Medical History of Contraception* (New York: Schocken Books, 1970), pp. 327–28 (on the 1920s); Barbara Brookes, "Women and Reproduction," in Jane Lewis, ed., *Labour and Love: Women's Experience of Home and Family, 1850–1940* (Oxford: Basil Blackwell, 1986); Blacker, *Birth Control*, p. 26; Barret-Ducrocq, *Love in the Time of Victoria*, pp. 129–31. Journals like Bradlaugh and Besant's *National Reformer* and *The Malthusian*, of course, were filled with advertisements for abortifacient drugs throughout the pre–World War I decades.

34. Shorter, *Women's Bodies*, pp. 191–95; 207–8; *The Declining Birth Rate*, testimony of Mrs. Ring of the Women's Industrial Council, pp. 277–81 (see also that of Miss Martin, a midwife working in an industrial suburb of Birmingham, pp. 273–77); Stopes, quoted in Gittins, *Fair Sex*, pp. 162–64. Also see Mary Chamberlain, *Old Wives' Tales: Their History, Remedies, and Spells* (London: Virago, 1981), p. 119.

35. Shorter, *Women's Bodies*, p. 195. See also Brookes, "Abortion in England," pp. 18–20, on the operations of abortionists around the turn of the century. Also

William F. J. Whitley, "Criminal Abortion and Abortifacients," *Public Health,* February 1915, p. 108; and Blacker, *Birth Control,* p. 36.

36. See test. Robert Reid Rentoul, Report from the Select Committee on Midwives' Registration, PP 1892, vol. 14, Q. 571; and Jean Donnison, *Midwives and Medical Men: A History of Inter-Professional Rivalries and Women's Rights* (New York: Schocken Books, 1977). The Guy's and General Lying-In's outpatient records suggest that some staff person (student, nurse, or midwife) had interviewed each woman once during her pregnancy, apparently at about the fifth month. On prenatal care, see Ann Oakley, *The Captured Womb: A History of the Medical Care of Pregnant Women* (Oxford: Basil Blackwell, 1984), chaps. 2 and 3; and Jalland, *Women, Marriage and Politics,* p. 141.

37. GLI Medical Officers' Case Books, January–April 1888, no. 96 and January–March 1884, no. 28; Stopes, *Mother England,* pp. 29–30. In common law, of course, for many centuries a pregnancy began only with quickening, and it was only after that point that a woman risked prosecution if she attempted to abort the fetus. See McLaren, *Reproductive Rituals,* chaps. 4 and 5, on the place of quickening in the history of abortion law in England.

38. The one-fifth guess is based on Paddington MOH, *Annual Reports,* 1905, p. 6.

39. Marie Kelly Welsh oral history transcript, Hackney People's Autobiography, p. 47A; Family Life Archive, no. 215, p. 66.

40. Foakes, *My Part of the River.* Also see Family Life Archive, no. 333, p. 26; and Scannel, *Mother Knew Best,* p. 181. Two middle-class studies are Jalland's *Women, Marriage and Politics,* p. 41; and M. Jeanne Peterson,, *Family, Love, and Work in the Lives of Victorian Gentlewomen* (Bloomington: Indiana University Press, 1989). See Roberts, *A Woman's Place,* for accounts of girls' first menstrual periods and their mothers' reactions to them.

41. Margaret Llewelyn Davies, *Life as We Have Known It: By Co-Operative Working Women* (1931), reprint ed. (New York: Norton, 1975), pp. 34–35; Dora Bunting et al., *The School for Mothers* (London: Horace Marshall, 1907), p. 37; Mrs. Pember Reeves, "Provision for Maternity," in *The Needs of Little Children: Report of a Conference on the Care of Babies and Young Children* (London: Women's Labour League, 1912), p. 15.

42. GLI Medical Officers' Case Books, January–September 1881, no. 68; January–March 1884, nos. 22, 25, 32, 34, and 45. The comments on the sixty-five-patient group are based on the GLI January–March 1884 Case Book.

43. GLI Medical Officers' Case Books, January–March 1884, nos. 20 and 11; January–September 1881, nos. 32 and 20.

44. Based on GLI Medical Officers' Case Books, January–April 1888.

45. See Report from the Select Committee of the House of Lords on the Infant Life Protection Bill [H.L.] and the Safety of Nurse Children Bill [H.L.], PP 1896, vol. 10, Qq. 1086–87; Janet E. Lane-Claypon, *Report on the Provision of Midwifery Service in the County of London,* Reports to the Local Government Board on Public Health and Medical Subjects, no. 111 (London: HMSO, 1917), p. 48; and test. Alexander D. L. Napier, Select Committee on Midwives' Registration, PP 1892, vol. 14, Q. 13. The prices noted are averages for England and Wales as a whole.

46. Anna Martin, *The Married Working Woman: A Study* (London: NUWSS, 1911), p. 43; Davies, *Maternity,* p. 165; Clementina Black, ed., *Married Women's Work* (1915), reprint ed. (London: Virago, 1983); George A. Simpson, *My Life and Family Reminiscences* (London: J. Truscott, 1931), p. 33; Kensington MOH, *Annual Reports,* 1915, pp. 11–12.

47. GLI Medical Officers' Case Books, January–March 1884, nos. 2, 14, and 29; George F. McCleary, *Life in the Laundry* (London: Fabian Society, 1902), p. 7.

48. Sylvia Pankhurst, *Save the Mothers* (London: Knopf, 1930), p. 29; Newham History Workshop, *A Marsh and a Gasworks: One Hundred Years of Life in West Ham* (London: Parents' Centre Publications, 1986), p. 59.

49. Truda Gordon, "The Feelings of Poor Patients," *Nursing Times,* October 14, 1905, p. 467; Family Life Archive, no. 215, p. 69; GLI Medical Officers' Case Books, January–September, 1881, no. 68.

50. *Biblewomen and Nurses,* February 1897, p. 33; E. J. Morris, "Report of a Visit to the District Maternity Charity with Miss Nicholls, District Midwife" (typescript) (1922), Tower Hamlets Health District Archives, London Hospital, p. 8; Lane-Claypon, *Provision of Midwifery Service,* p. 39.

51. Based on GLI Medical Officers' Case Books, January–April 1886; GLI Hospital *Annual Report,* 1885; Elizabeth Garrett Anderson, "Deaths in Childbirth," *BMJ,* September 17, 1898, p. 839.

52. GLI Medical Officers' Case Books, January–March 1884, nos. 7 and 48; January–April 1886, nos. 20 and 53; January–April 1888, no. 48.

53. GLI Medical Officers' Case Books, December 1881–April 1882, no. 31; January–March 1884, no. 51; January–April 1888, nos. 53 and 132.

54. Roberts, *Five Months,* p. 40.

55. Alice Linton, *Not Expecting Miracles* (London: Centerprise, 1982), p. 35; Mrs. Bartholomew, interviewed by Anna Davin, summer 1973, transcript, p. 3; Roberts, *Five Months,* p. 125; see also p. 135 and pp. 126–28. Blacker, however, wrote of the occasional very sudden delivery that was witnessed by the other children (*Birth Control,* p. 38).

56. A. S. Jasper, *A Hoxton Childhood* (London: Centerprise, 1969), p. 11; Lillian Hine, "A Poplar Childhood," *East London Record* 3 (1980): 40–41; Morris, "Report of a Visit to the District Maternity Charity," p. 7.

57. Jalland, *Women, Marriage and Politics,* p. 144; Roberts, *Five Months,* pp. 142–43; Davies, *Maternity,* p. 47.

58. Ellen Ranyard, *Nurses for the Needy of Bible Women Nurses in the Homes of the London Poor* (London: James Nesbet, 1875), p. 204; Davies, *Maternity,* p. 113.

59. *Nursing Times,* October 28, 1905, pp. 547–48; October 13, 1906, p. 173; Mrs. Layton's account in *Life as We Have Known It,* p. 50; and test. Mrs. Elizabeth Malleson, PP 1892, vol. 14, Q. 1123.

60. Roberts, *Five Months;* test. George Brown, PP 1892, vol. 14, Q. 1660; Davies, *Life as We Have Known It,* p. 31.

61. Emilia Kanthack, *The Preservation of Infant Life* (London: H. K. Lewis, 1907), pp. 2–3; Peckham People's History, *The Times of Our Lives: Growing Up in the Southeast Area 1900–1945* (London: Peckham Publishing Project, 1983), p. 57; Christian Social Union, *Report on an Inquiry into Employment of Women After Childbirth* (London, 1905), Tuckwell Collection, TUC Archives, pp. 3–4. About a quarter of the women in the Christian Social Union study were from towns outside London. Herzlich and Pierret argue that illness today is defined primarily as an inability to do paid work, which marks the illness of housewives as ambiguous at best. See Claudine Herzlich and Janine Pierret, *Illness and Self in Society,* tr. Elborg Forster (Baltimore: Johns Hopkins University Press, 1987), chap. 10.

62. Black, *Married Women's Work,* pp. 10–11; Linton, *Not Expecting Miracles,* p. 71.

63. Winifred Stamp, *Dr. Himself: An Unorthodox Biography of Harry Roberts, M.D.* (London: Hamish Hamilton, 1949), p. 66; Chamberlain's interview with Kate Moody; Lane-Claypon, *Report on the Provision of Midwifery Service*, p. 46; Lewis, *In the Family Way*, chap. 6.

64. Newspaper clipping no. 603–14 (Cooperative Guild Memo), Tuckwell Collection; Donnison, *Midwives and Medical Men*, pp. 107–8, 142. See also City of Westminster Health Society, *Annual Report*, 1911, p. 20.

65. Grace L. Meigs, *Maternal Mortality from All Conditions Connected with Childbirth in the United States and Certain Other Countries* (Washington, DC: U.S. Department of Labor, 1917), Table XIII, p. 56. F. B. Smith argues convincingly that actual figures for the years before 1918 must have been higher than the official ones, for all the personnel involved in childbirth—from hospital officials, to doctors, to untrained midwives—had an interest in disguising maternal deaths (Smith, *People's Health*, pp. 13–14, and, more generally, chap. 1). Also see Irvine Loudon, "Deaths in Childbed from the Late Eighteenth Century to 1935," *Medical History* 30 (January 1986): 3–4, 14–16 (Tables 2 and 3). Donnison's figures (*Midwives and Medical Men*, p. 93) support the view that midwives with formal training were the safest of all birth attendants. See also Ornella Moscucci, *The Science of Woman: Gynaecology and Gender in England, 1800–1929* (Cambridge: Cambridge University Press, 1990), p. 185; also of interest, chaps. 2 and 3.

66. Simpson, *My Life and Family Reminiscences*, p. 34; *Biblewomen and Nurses*, May 1910, p. 96; Roberts, *Five Months*, p. 45; Margaret Loane, *The Queen's Poor: Life as They Find It in Town and Country* (London: Arnold, 1909), p. 163. For examples of women alone in childbirth, see Ranyard, *Nurses for the Needy*, p. 15; and *Missing Link*, June 1, 1878, p. 174. For an example of a country woman who came to London to give birth secretly and found help there, see Dilley and Rainbow, Old Bailey, vol. 90 (1879), no. 698, pp. 484 ff.

67. See test. Dr. James Edwards, PP 1892, vol. 14, Q. 1478; "Maternity Charities," *The Lancet*, November 3, 1906, p. 1227. See also the 1903 survey of means testing in maternity cases by the almoner of the Royal Free Hospital (Almoners' Reports, July 25, 1903, and December 31, 1905, Royal Free Hospital Archive).

68. Lt. Col. Montefiore, "Uses and Abuses of Medical Charities," *Charity Organisation Review*, new ser., 14 (July 1903): 16–36; "Outpatients at London Hospitals," *BMJ*, January 2, 1904, pp. 44–45.

69. *Nursing Notes*, March 1907, p. 40; the statement about increasing medical referrals is by Donnison, *Midwives and Medical Men*, p. 185. Figures from District Case Books, City of London Maternity Hospital, GLRO, October 1913–September 1916: From October 18, 1913, to October 18, 1915, 1,479 patients were seen regularly for the first two postpartum weeks, but there were only 33 referrals of any kind for mothers or babies.

70. By the early 1900s, eight London boards of guardians, mostly in areas not serviced by the big teaching hospitals, guaranteed payment to physicians brought in under the stipulations of the Midwives Act. See "Midwives in England, Especially in Relation to the Medical Profession," *St. Bartholomew's Hospital Journal* 15 (November 1907): 42. Under the Midwives Act of 1918, all local authorities were required to pay doctors' fees when patients could not (Donnison, *Midwives and Medical Men*, p. 185). On doctors' hostility to midwives, see Roberts, *Five Weeks*, p. 68; and Donnison, *Midwives and Medical Men*, p. 161.

71. Smith, *People's Health,* pp. 17–18, 23–24; test. M. W. H. Fenton, M.D., pp 1892, vol. 14, Q. 1678. See also Marie Stopes, *The First Five Thousand* (London: John Bale, Sons and Danielsson, 1923), p. 32. The medical student was writing in the *BMJ,* March 5, 1892, p. 524. For blood letting in labor, see test. Mr. George Brown, pp 1892, vol. 14, Q. 1659–60 (Brown was president of the General Practitioners' Alliance); also Donnison, *Midwives and Medical Men,* p. 131; and M. Jeanne Peterson, *The Medical Profession in Mid-Victorian London* (Berkeley and Los Angeles: University of California Press, 1978), p. 279.

72. Stamp, *Doctor Himself,* p. 66.

73. The activities of the General Lying-In Hospital's midwives are described in the hospital's registrar of "Midwives' Out Door Cases, 1886–1888," and the functioning of their own program is discussed occasionally in the *Guy's Hospital Gazette* (both in the GLRO). Also on the length of midwives' visits, see *Nursing Notes,* June 1, 1894, p. 77, and July 1, 1894, p. 93.

74. Donnison, *Midwives and Medical Men,* n. 43, p. 216; n. 11, p. 218; p. 110; Smith, *People's Health,* p. 48; *Nursing Times,* May 20, 1905, p. 51; Report of the London MOH, 1910, p. 89. Also see Anne Summers, "The Mysterious Demise of Sarah Gamp: The Domiciliary Nurse and Her Detractors, c. 1830–1860," *Victorian Studies* 32 (Spring 1989): 365–86.

75. Hall, *Canary Girls,* p. 15; Peckham People's History, *Times of Our Lives;* Lane-Claypon, *Provision of Midwifery Service,* p. 47. Also see Linton, *Not Expecting Miracles,* p. 1.

76. Interview with Mrs. Henman, side 2, Samuel oral histories; Walter Southgate, *That's the Way It Was* (Oxted: New Clarion Press, 1982), p. 11.

77. Interview with Mrs. Henman, side 2, Samuel oral histories; Tottenham History Workshop, *How Things Were,* p. 11; Report from Dr. A. E. Thomas, Finsbury MOH, in Janet Campbell and E. W. Hope, *Report on the Physical Welfare of Mothers and Children, England and Wales* (2 vols.) (Liverpool: Carnegie U.K. Trust, 1917), vol. 1, p. 275. See also the comments in Lane-Claypon, *Provision of Midwifery Service,* p. 20.

78. Davies, *Life as We Have Known It,* p. 31. For another similar history, from the 1870s, see Maude A. Stanley, *Work About the Five Dials* (London: Macmillan, 1878), pp. 133–41.

79. Donnison, *Midwives and Medical Men,* pp. 156, 172–73, 181; J. M. Munro Kerr, R. W. Johnstone, and Miles H. Phillips, *Review of British Obstetrics and Gynaecology 1800–1950* (Edinburgh: Livingstone, 1954), p. 337; Loane, *Simple Introductory Lessons in Midwifery,* p. vi.

80. Ranyard, *Nurses for the Needy,* pp. 82–85. On the history of gynecology as a profession in nineteenth-century Britain and for some information on hospital practices, see Moscucci, *Science of Woman.*

81. GLI Medical Officers' Case Books, December 1881–April 1882, nos. 12, 14, and 31; Matron's Weekly Reports, April 1881–April 1912. This from the May 24, 1882, entry; see also November 28, 1883.

82. GLI Medical Officers' Case Books, December 1881–April 1882, nos. 23 and 4; January–March 1884, no. 4. On women's fears (across all classes) of contracting syphilis from their husbands and transmitting it to their babies, see Gail Savage, " 'The Wilful Communication of a Loathsome Disease": Marital Conflict and Venereal Disease in Victorian England," *Victorian Studies* 34 (Autumn 1990): 35–54. See also Kent, *Sex and Suffrage,* pp. 105–10.

83. Report of the London MOH, 1910, p. 15.

84. On childbirth as a "shock" and postpartum depression and illness, see Mary Georgina Boulton, *On Being a Mother: A Study of Women with Pre-School Children* (London: Tavistock, 1983), p. 1; Hilary Graham and Lorna McKee, *The First Months of Motherhood* (London: Health Education Council, 1980), pp. 23–24; and Ann Oakley, *Women Confined: Towards a Sociology of Childbirth* (New York: Schocken Books, 1980), esp. chaps. 5 and 6.

85. Eleanor Rathbone, "The Remuneration of Women's Services," *Economic Journal* 27 (March 1917): 66. On the health of working-class married women in the 1920s and 1930s, see Lewis, *Politics of Motherhood,* pp. 45–46; Margery Spring Rice, *Working-Class Wives* (1939), reprint ed. (London: Virago, 1981); Innes H. Pearse and Lucy H. Crocker, *The Peckham Experiment: A Study in the Living Structure of Society* (London: Allen & Unwin, 1943), chap. 6. On the care of first children, see Douglas, "Social Class Differences in Health and Survival," p. 47. On depression and its treatment in general in this era, see Janet Oppenheim, *"Shattered Nerves": Doctors, Patients, and Depression in Victorian England* (New York: Oxford University Press, 1991).

86. Black, *Married Women's Work,* p. 10; Shorter, *Women's Bodies,* p. 275; and on prolapsed uterus and its treatments, see Shorter, *Women's Bodies,* pp. 273–81.

87. Royal Free Hospital Archive, Doctors' Casebook (Mrs. Willey), 1911–1913, pp. 477, 507, 509, 517.

88. GLI Medical Officers' Case Books, January–September 1881, no. 48.

89. Black, *Married Women's Work,* pp. 90–92.

CHAPTER 5

1. Judith Schneid Lewis, *In the Family Way: Childbearing in the British Aristocracy, 1760–1860* (New Brunswick, NJ: Rutgers University Press, 1986), esp. chaps. 1 and 2.

2. On childhood during this period, see Joy Parr, *Labouring Children: British Immigrant Apprentices to Canada, 1869–1924* (London: Croom Helm, 1980), chap. 1; Stephen Humphries, *Hooligans or Rebels? An Oral History of Working-Class Childhood and Youth 1889–1939* (Oxford: Basil Blackwell, 1981), chap. 6; James Walvin, *A Child's World: A Social History of English Childhood 1800–1914* (Harmondsworth: Penguin Books, 1982); Carol Dyhouse, *Girls Growing Up in Late Victorian and Edwardian England* (London: Routledge & Kegan Paul, 1981); Anna Davin, *Little Women: The Childhood of Working-Class Girls in Late Nineteenth-Century London* (London: Routledge & Kegan Paul, 1994); Carolyn Steedman, Cathy Urwin, and Valerie Walkerdine, eds., *Language, Gender and Childhood* (London: Routledge & Kegan Paul, 1985); Pat Thane, "Childhood in History," in Michael King, ed., *Childhood, Welfare and Justice: A Critical Examination of Children in the Legal and Childcare Systems* (London: Batsford, 1981); Peter Coveney, *The Image of Childhood, the Individual and Society: A Study of the Theme in English Literature* (Harmondsworth: Penguin Books, 1967). There are, in addition, dozens of more specialized studies of education, scouting, children's literature, child labor, juvenile delinquency, and so on during this period.

3. Jeremy Seabrook, *Working-Class Childhood* (London: Victor Gollancz, 1982), pp. 12–13; Viviana Zelizer, *Pricing the Priceless Child: The Changing Social Value of Children* (New York: Basic Books, 1985); Barbara Caine, *Destined to Be Wives: The Sisters of Beatrice Webb* (Oxford: Clarendon Press, 1986), pp. 124, 127. Yet the Potter

sisters were generally not affectionate mothers; Theresa Cripps was the only exception (Kate and Beatrice did not have children).

4. *Biblewomen and Nurses,* April 1897, p. 70; Joseph Williamson, *Father Joe: The Autobiography of Joseph Williamson of Poplar and Stepney* (London: Hodder & Stoughton, 1963), p. 21. The Poplar guardians at that point included George Lansbury and Will Crooks, both elected in 1893; Crooks is the person who confronted Mrs. Williamson. Also see Sylvia Pankhurst, *The Home Front: A Mirror to Life in England During the World War* (London: Hutchinson, 1932), p. 402. Another statement is in Clara Grant, *Farthing Bundles* (London: Fern Street Settlement, 1931), p. 104.

5. H. John Bennett, *I Was a Walworth Boy* (London: Peckham Publishing Project, 1980), p. 28; Dorothy Scannell, *Mother Knew Best: Memoir of a London Girlhood* (New York: Pantheon, 1974), pp. 63–65.

6. (George Acorn), pseud., *One of the Multitude: An Autobiography by a Resident of Bethnal Green* (London: Heinemann, 1911); Kathleen Woodward, *Jipping Street: Childhood in a London Slum* (1928), reprint ed. (London: Virago, 1983); Elizabeth Rignall, "All So Long Ago" (Typescript, Brunel University Library, unpaginated); interview with Mr. and Mrs. Mac, Samuel oral histories, pp. 13–14.

7. Scannell, *Mother Knew Best,* pp. 32, 67–68; Williamson, *Father Joe,* p. 22.

8. Walter Southgate, *That's the Way It Was: A Working Class Autobiography 1890–1950* (Oxted: New Clarion Press, 1982), p. 12; interview with Mrs. Mac, Samuel oral histories, side 2, p. 46; Marie Kelly Welsh, typescript oral history, Hackney People's Autobiography, p. 6; A. S. Jasper, *A Hoxton Childhood* (London: Centerprise, 1969), pp. 9–10.

9. Williamson, *Father Joe,* p. 19; for another clear example, see Family Life Archive, no. 215, p. 48.

10. Williamson, *Father Joe,* p. 20; Doris M. Bailey, *Children of the Green: A True Story of Childhood in Bethnal Green 1922–1937* (London: Stepney Books, 1981), p. 53; Scannell, *Mother Knew Best,* p. 96 and *passim.* Marion Glastonberry discusses the significance of this talk in "The Best-Kept Secret: How Working-Class Women Live and What They Know," *Women's Studies International Quarterly* 2 (1979): 171–81.

11. Clara Grant, *From 'Me' to 'We': Forty Years on Bow Common* (London: Fern Street Settlement, 1940), p. 136; Southgate, *That's The Way It Was,* pp. 28, 12; Grant, *Farthing Bundles,* p. 104; *Nursing Times,* November 25, 1905, p. 593; General Lying-In Hospital (GLI), Medical Officers' Case Books, January–April 1886, no. 28; Michael Young and Peter Willmott, *Family and Kinship in East London* (Harmondsworth: Penguin Books, 1957), p. 25. The children's names were compiled by Andy August from his copies of census enumerators' books.

12. On churching, see Alice Linton, *Not Expecting Miracles* (London: Centerprise, 1982), p. 71; Mary Chamberlain's interview with "Kate Moody," whose first child was born during World War I, November 25, 1982 (also see Chapter 4, n. 8); Edith Hall, *Canary Girls and Stockpots* (Luton: WEA, 1977), p. 16; Jeffrey Cox, *The English Churches in a Secular Society: Lambeth, 1879–1930* (New York: Oxford University Press, 1982), p. 99. Also see Peter Rushton, "Purification or Social Control? Ideologies of Reproduction and the Churching of Women After Childbirth," in Eva Gamarnikow, David Morgan, June Purvis, and Daphne Taylorson, eds., *The Public and the Private* (London: Heinemann, 1983), pp. 125–27. On churching among aristocrats in a somewhat earlier period, see Lewis, *In the Family Way,* pp. 201–3.

Churching was abolished by the Catholic church after Vatican II, but the Church of England continued to offer this ritual. See Robert Bocock, *Ritual in Industrial Society: A Sociological Analysis of Ritualism in Modern England* (London: Allen & Unwin, 1974), p. 126; and John Gillis, "The Feminization of Fertility Among the British Middle Classes," in John Gillis, David Levine, and Louise Tilly, eds., *The Quiet Revolution: Western Europeans in an Age of Declining Fertility* (Oxford: Basil Blackwell, 1992).

13. Christenings are found in Southgate, *The Way It Was,* pp. 11–12; Hackney People's Autobiography, *'The Island': The Life and Death of an East London Community 1870–1970* (London: Centerprise, 1979), p. 20; Ellen Chase, *Tenant Friends in Old Deptford* (London: Williams & Norgate, 1929), pp. 108–9; Lillian Hine, "A Poplar Childhood," *East London Record,* no. 3 (1980), p. 41; and Mrs. Layton, "Memories of Seventy Years," in Margaret Llewelyn Davies, ed., *Life as We Have Known It,* reprint ed. (New York: Norton, 1975), p. 24. See also Donald M. Lewis, *Lighten Their Darkness: The Evangelical Mission to Working-Class London, 1828–1860* (Westport, CT: Greenwood Press, 1986), pp. 125–26. Catholics were more likely to have their babies christened than Anglicans were.

14. The vicar of St. Barnabas, Bethnal Green, a parish of about 14,000, reported in the late 1890s that he performed 150 baptisms and 200 churchings in a year, according to Hugh McLeod, University of Birmingham, who plumbed his notes on the Booth manuscripts on my behalf (B 205, p. 171). The discussion of baptism in Bermondsey is based on the work of Alan Bartlett, who very generously sent me a chapter of his dissertation (Birmingham University, 1988), "The Church of England in the 'Golden Age' of the Parish c. 1880–1914." Also see Muriel Wragge, *The London I Loved* (London: James Clarke, 1960), pp. 37–38.

15. Southgate, *The Way It Was,* p. 12; Jasper, *Hoxton Childhood,* p. 73. Also see the comments by Cox, *English Churches in a Secular Society,* p. 98.

16. For example, Hine, "Poplar Childhood," p. 41; Coulson, Old Bailey, vol. 80 (1874), no. 430, p. 119.

17. Henry W. Nevinson, "Mrs Simon's Baby," in his *Neighbours of Ours* (Bristol: J. W. Arrowsmith, 1895); Charles Booth, *Life and Labour of the People in London,* 1st ser.: *Poverty* (1902), reprint ed. (5 vols.) (New York: Augustus M. Kelley, 1969), vol. 2, p. 80; Grace Foakes, *My Part of the River* (London: Futura Books, 1978), p. 63; test. Deaconess Gilmore, head of the Deaconesses' Institution of the Diocese of Rochester, Clapham Common, Report from the Select Committee of the House of Lords on the Infant Life Protection Bill [H.L.] and the Safety of Nurse Children Bill [H.L.], PP 1896, vol. 10, Qq. 2194–2200; "Report on the Baby-farming System and Its Evils," *BMJ,* March 21, 1896, p. 747 (part of a series running weekly from February 22 through March 28, 1896).

18. Bethnal Green Board of Guardians, Settlement Examinations, Rough, February 1889–January 1890, GLRO; Olive Christian Malvery, "Music in the By Ways," *Pearson's Magazine* 19 (January–June 1905): 157.

19. George Sims, *How the Poor Live and Horrible London,* combined ed. (London: Chatto & Windus, 1889), p. 89.

20. Anna Martin, *The Married Working Woman: A Study* (London: NUWSS, 1911), p. 32; Ada Bennett, "In the Workhouse," in Peckham People's History, *The Times of Our Lives: Growing Up in the Southwark Area 1900–1945* (London: Peckham People's History, 1983), p. 85; Lillian Hine, "A Poplar Childhood," *East London Record* 3 (1980): 33.

21. Test. Miss Eves, Inter-Departmental Committee on Physical Deterioration, PP 1904, vol. 32, Q. 7558; Outdoor Relief in Lambeth, Royal Commission on the Poor Laws and the Relief of Distress, PP 1910, vol. 50, p. 151; Christian Social Union, *Report. (n.d.) quoted in Patricia E. Malcolmson, "Laundresses and the*

Laundry Trade in Victorian England," Victorian Studies 24 (Summer 1981): 57.

22. On the involvement of Lydia Becker, see "Report on the Baby Farming System and Its Evils," *BMJ,* February 22, 1896, p. 489.

23. Test. Isabel G. Smith, LCC Infant Life Protection Inspector, Select Committee of the House of Lords on the Infant Life Protection Bill, Qq. 1086–87; test. Wynne Edwin Baxter, Coroner for East London, Q. 1508; test. Deaconess Gilmore, Qq. 2186–2238.

24. *East London Observer,* July 11, 1868, p. 3; test. Gilmore, PP 1896, vol. 10, Qq. 2264–65. The conventional 5-shilling weekly fee was modest, but the cash coming in a lump sum each week was a welcome boost to a subsistence household budget (test. Smith, Qq. 1086–87; test. Gilmore, Qq. 2271 and 2342).

25. Inquiry by General Relieving Officer, St. Olave's Union, BBG 539/1, case 11, 1896, GLRO.

26. Ann R. Higgenbotham, "The Unmarried Mother and Her Child in Victorian London, 1834–1914" (Ph.D. diss., Indiana University, 1985), p. 286; *Report of the Proceedings of the [Second] National Conference on Infantile Mortality* (London: P. S. King, 1908), p. 100 (address by Miss Isabel Smith, LCC inspector under the Infant Life Protection Act).

27. Francis, Old Bailey, vol. 100 (1883–1884), no. 905, pp. 619–20; Powney, vol. 101 (1884), no. 272, pp. 600–11.

28. *The Nurses' Journal,* May 1891, p. 33; Martin Daunton, *House and Home in the Victorian City: Working-Class Housing 1850–1914* (London: Arnold, 1983), p. 243.

29. William George Perry, *A West Ham Life: An Autobiography* (Newham: Parents' Centre Publications, 1984), p. 48; *Biblewomen and Nurses,* May 1910, p. 87. On laundering at home, see also Patricia E. Malcolmson, *English Laundresses: A Social History, 1850–1930* (Urbana: University of Illinois Press, 1986), chap. 1. See also Maud Pember Reeves, *Round About a Pound a Week* (1913), reprint ed. (London: Virago, 1979). A huge 1942 national survey, the Heating of Dwellings Inquiry, found that three fourths of housewives were still heating laundry water by hand, in a copper, gas boiler, or kettle on a grate or stove. See Caroline Davidson, *A Woman's Work Is Never Done: A History of Housework in the British Isles 1650–1950* (London: Chatto & Windus, 1982), p. 160.

30. Rose Petty, *Cleanliness in Children* (London: Scientific Press, n.d.), p. 14; Christina Hardyment, *Dream Babies: Childcare from Locke to Spock* (Oxford: Oxford University Press, 1984) pp. 23, 135–36; Foakes, *My Part of the River,* p. 78; also Mary Chamberlain, *Growing Up in Lambeth* (London: Virago Books, 1989), p. 94.

31. Hardyment, *Dream Babies,* p. 60; Catherine Storr, "Freud and the Concept of Parental Guilt," in Arlene Skolnick and Jerome Skolnick, eds., *Intimacy, Family and Society* (Boston: Little, Brown, 1974), pp. 377–83. Grace Foakes (*My Part of the River,* p. 135) remembered dozens of toddlers attending school early in the twentieth century who were incompletely toilet trained, and the Newsons' study of childrearing in the early 1960s found that unskilled workers' wives were less likely to try to train their children very early (before age one) than were higher-class mothers. See John and Elizabeth Newson, "Infant Care in an Urban Community," in J. A. Banks, ed., *Studies in British Society* (New York: Crowell, 1968).

32. "Care of an Infant for the First Twenty-Four Hours of Life," *British Journal of Nursing,* October 21, 1905; pp. 332–24; Foakes, *My Part of the River,* p. 78; Chamberlain, *Growing Up in Lambeth,* p. 95.

33. Dora Bunting et al., *The School for Mothers* (London: Horace Marshall, 1907), pp. 47–48; City of Westminster Health Society, *Annual Reports,* 1914, p. 12; D. L.

Thomas (MOH for Limehouse), "On Infant Mortality," *Public Health,* September 1899, p. 814; Foakes, *My Part of the River,* p. 79.

34. See the advice offered by Eric Pritchard in *Infant Education* (London: Henry Kempton, 1907); and by Truby King, the New Zealand pediatrician and popular infant care writer, mostly after World War I. King is discussed in Ann Dally, *Inventing Motherhood: The Consequences of an Ideal* (New York: Schocken Books, 1984). Upper-class nurseries could be bleak places, according to Thea Thompson, *Edwardian Childhoods* (London: Routledge & Kegan Paul, 1981). For a progressive position on childrearing, see the works by Margaret McMillan, for example, *Early Childhood* (London: Swan Sonnenschein, 1900).

35. On prams, see Margaret Llewelyn Davies, ed., *Life as We Have Known It,* reprint ed. (New York: Norton, 1975), p. 4; Foakes, *My Part of the River,* p. 113; and (the case cited here) Hibbard, Old Bailey, vol. 120 (1893–1894), no. 745, p. 1087.

36. On schoolchildren being kept up by crying babies, see *Report by Dr. Crichton-Browne and Mr. J. G. Fitch on Alleged Over-Pressure in Elementary Schools* (London: Hansard, 1884), pp. 26–27. The Old Bailey case mentioned is Longman, vol. 111 (1889–1890), no. 53, pp. 99 ff.

37. Brown (1894–1960) was a Labour M.P. for Wolverhampton 1929–1931, and represented Rugby (Independent) in 1942. W. J. Brown, *So Far* (London: Allen & Unwin, 1943), p. 12; (Florence) Petty et al., *The Pudding Lady: A New Departure in Social Work* (London: Stead's Publishing House, 1910, p. 73.

38. See Terry Parssinen, *Secret Passions, Secret Remedies: Narcotic Drugs in British Society 1820–1930* (Philadelphia: Institute for the Study of Human Issues, 1983); also Virginia Berridge and Griffith Edwards, *Opium and the People: Opiate Use in Nineteenth-Century England* (London: Allen Lane, 1981), pp. 99–104, 120, 130; and Frances B. Smith, *The People's Health 1830–1910* (New York: Holmes & Meier, 1979), p. 98. On the issue of mothers' use of opiates, see also Margaret Hewitt, *Wives and Mothers in Victorian Industry,* reprint ed. (Westport, CT: Greenwood Press, 1975), pp. 142–49.

39. Berridge and Edwards, *Opium and the People,* p. 131; [Second] *National Conference on Infantile Mortality,* 1908. Baby minders were, however, occasionally associated with the use of laudanum (a morphine mixture), as in F. S. Toogood, "The Role of the Crèche or Day Nursery," in Theophilus N. Kelynack, ed., *Infancy* (London: Robert Culley, 1910), p. 82.

40. The 1908 Children Act, among its many other provisions, prohibited children under fourteen from entering pubs. The ban was aimed at keeping women away as well as children. See Stanley B. Atkinson, "The Care of Children Neglected by Drunken Parents," *[Second] National Conference on Infantile Mortality,* 1908, pp. 147–53; and George R. Sims, *The Cry of the Children* (London: The Tribune, 1907), p. 14. This subject is treated thoroughly in David W. Gutzke, " 'The Cry of the Children': The Edwardian Medical Campaign Against Maternal Drinking," *British Journal of Addiction* 79 (1984): 71–84.

41. Hall, Old Bailey, vol. 90 (1879), no. 787, p. 662; and Carter, Old Bailey, vol. 80 (1874), no. 454, p. 439.

42. An estimate of two thirds of infants breast fed at six months is made by D. J. Oddy in "The Health of the People," in Theo Barker and Michael Drake, eds., *Population and Society in Britain 1850–1980* (London: Batsford, 1982), pp. 125–26. London statistics from Paddington MOH, *Annual Reports,* 1905, pp. 5–6; and G. F. McCleary, *Early History of the Infant Welfare Movement* (London: M. K. Lewis,

1933), p. 82. For Kensington figures, see Kensington MOH, *Annual Reports*, 1910, p. 9; and the table in Westminster Health Society, *Annual Reports*, 1906, p. 6.

43. Pember Reeves, *Round About a Pound*, p. 169. On lactation problems and women's lives today, see Hilary Graham, *Women, Health and the Family* (Brighton: Wheatsheaf, 1984), p. 171. A different position, offered by two medical anthropologists, is that of Judith Gussler and Linda Briesemeister, "The Insufficient Milk Syndrome: A Biocultural Explanation," *Medical Anthropology* 4 (Spring 1980): 145–64.

44. Moore, Old Bailey, vol. 89 (1878–1879), no. 172, p. 214; Lilian Westall's autobiography, "The Good Old Days," is included in John Burnett, ed., *Useful Toil* (Harmondsworth: Penguin Books, 1974), pp. 215–16; also see Doris M. Bailey, *Children of the Green* (London: Stepney Books, 1981), p. 11.

45. Pember Reeves, *Round About a Pound*, p. 102 and *passim*; Lara Marks, " 'Dear Old Mother Levy's': The Jewish Maternity Home and Sick Room Helps Society 1895–1939," *Social History of Medicine* 3 (1990): 61–88; *Toynbee Record*, January 1911, p. 57.

46. Arthur Newsholme, *Fifty Years in Public Health* (2 vols.) (London: Allen & Unwin, 1935), vol. 1, p. 372; Ian Buchanan, "Infant Feeding, Sanitation and Diarrhoea in Colliery Communities, 1880–1911," in Derek J. Oddy and Derek S. Miller, eds., *Diet and Health in Modern Britain* (London: Croom Helm, 1985), p. 160; on middle-class breast feeding, see Agnes Hunt, *This Is My Life* (New York: Putnam, 1942), p. 19. On the feeding views of advice books, see Hardyment, *Dream Babies*, p. 94.

47. The work of the Bell Street Clinic is discussed in Chapter 7.

48. Nursing journals were filled with patent food advertisements; so were, among many others, Ada Ballin's *Baby*, written for middle-class readers, and the progressive *Child Study*, founded in 1908. On infant foods, see Ian G. Wickes, "A History of Infant Feeding," pt. 4, *Archives of Disease in Childhood* 28 (1953): 421–22; and Anthony Wohl, *Endangered Lives: Public Health in Victorian Britain* (Cambridge, MA: Harvard University Press, 1983), p. 20.

49. Carol Dyhouse, "Working-Class Mothers and Infant Mortality in England, 1895–1914," *Journal of Social History* 12 (Winter 1978): 255–56. On condensed milk, see Jane Lewis, *The Politics of Motherhood: Child and Maternal Welfare in England, 1900–1939* (London: Croom Helm, 1980), pp. 73–75; and Smith, *People's Health*, p. 61. On the popularity of various patent infant foods, see Smith, *People's Health*, p. 93; and Thomas, "Infant Mortality," p. 811.

50. On milk drinking among workers, see H. M. Burton, *There Was a Young Man* (London: Geoffrey Bles, 1958), p. 45; Family Life Archive, no. 215, p. 48; Grant, *Me to "We,"* p. 19; Pember Reeves, *Round About a Pound*, p. 99; and Janet Blackman, "Changing Marketing Methods and Food Consumption," in T. C. Barker, J. C. McKenzie, and John Yudkin, eds., *Our Changing Fare* (London: McGibbon & Kee, 1966), p. 40.

51. Buchanan, "Infant Feeding," p. 159; Smith, *People's Health*, p. 90; Sir Arthur Newsholme, *Fifty Years in Public Health* (London: Allen & Unwin, 1935), p. 42; Deborah Dwork, *War Is Good for Babies and Other Young Children: A History of the Infant and Child Welfare Movement in England 1898–1918* (London: Tavistock, 1987), pp. 26–51. The information on the current state of knowledge about infant diarrhea was supplied by W. R. Glendon, M.D. On the infamous long-tube bottle, see Smith, *People's Health*, p. 89; Westminster Health Society, *Annual Reports*, 1906, p. 7.

52. Helen Bosanquet, in *The School Child* 1 (March 1910): 10, called the Infant Welfare movement "the most successful piece of social work which has been done in the last ten years." Also Newsholme, *Fifty Years in Public Health,* pp. 331, 372; and McCleary, *Early History of the Infant Welfare Movement.* My position on the culpability of the medical profession was held by some contemporaries. See Janet Lane-Clapon, "The Waste of Infant Life," *The Nineteenth Century and After* 65 (January 1919): 52; and Kensington MOH, *Annual Reports,* 1910, p. 10.

53. For advice on infant feeding, see George Newman, *A Special Report on an Infants' Milk Depot Established Under the Auspices of the Finsbury Social Workers Association* (London: Thomas Bean, 1905), p. 24; A. M. Dick, "The Work of Women as Sanitary Inspectors," *Journal of the Royal Sanitary Institute* 25 (1904): 882; *Missing Link,* November 1, 1878, p. 332; Mary D. Scharlieb, "The Hygiene of the Nursery in Relation to Tuberculosis," in Theophilus N. Kelynack, ed., *Tuberculosis in Infancy and Childhood* (London: Balliere Tindall & Cox, 1908). On working-class feeding practices, see test. Isabel Smith, PP 1896, vol. 10, Q. 1085; test. Dr. Hawkes, PP 1904, vol. 32, Q. 12976; Kensington MOH, *Annual Reports,* 1905, p. 60.

54. Westminster Health Society, *Annual Reports,* 1906, p. 7. On the introduction of solid foods today, see Graham, *Women, Health, and the Family,* p. 171.

55. Smith, *People's Health,* p. 94; Katherine Roberts, *Five Months in a London Hospital* (Letchworth: Garden City Press, 1911), p. 56; *Toynbee Record,* January 1911, p. 56; Pember Reeves, *Round About a Pound,* chap. 12. There are intriguing essays on time and motherhood in Frieda Johles Forman and Caoran Sowton, eds., *Taking Our Time: Feminist Perspectives on Temporality* (Oxford: Pergamon Press, 1989).

56. In addition to the autobiographies cited in this section, see Edward Brown, untitled London autobiographical manuscript, Brunel University Library, p. 1; Bennett, *Walworth Boy,* p. 4; and Linton, *Not Expecting Miracles,* p. 1. A vivid story of a child's loss at this moment a hemisphere away is told by Nisa, a !Kung Bush woman interviewed by Marjorie Shostak (also see Chapter 2, n. 10). When Nisa's mother was pregnant with the child who would become her baby brother, Nisa was already four. Her histrionics were so impressive and her grief so great that her mother (moved by the child's suffering but perhaps just a master of child psychology) dramatically offered to kill the baby at birth. Begging her mother to spare the baby, Nisa made him her own special charge and friend. See Marjorie Shostak, *Nisa: The Life and Words of a !Kungwoman* (New York: Vintage Books, 1983), pp. 51–56.

57. Jasper, *Hoxton Childhood,* pp. 6, 12–13.

58. Dr. Charles Porter, the Marylebone MOH, referred to "ex-babies" in quotation marks (Janet Campbell and E. W. Hope, *Report on the Physical Welfare of Mothers and Children. England and Wales* (2 vols.) (Liverpool: Carnegie U.K. Trust, 1917), vol. 1, p. 383; Wragge, *The London I Loved,* p. 54.

59. N. S. Scrimshaw, C. E. Taylor, and J. E. Gordon, *Interaction of Nutrition and Infection,* cited in Milton Lewis, "The Problem of Infant Feeding: The Australian Experience from the Mid-Nineteenth Century to the 1920s," *Journal of Medical History* 35 (1980): 175–76.

60. On the poor health of older babies, see Bunting, *School for Mothers;* Pember Reeves, *Round About a Pound;* Petty et al., *Pudding Lady,* pp. 2, 22. On services for the ex-babies, see Bunting, *School for Mothers,* p. 6; Campbell and Hope, *Physical Welfare of Mothers and Children,* vol. 2, p. 102.

61. Pember Reeves, *Round About a Pound,* chap. 8; *Missing Link,* June 1883, p. 257; Petty et al., *Pudding Lady,* pp. 38, 188; Clementina Black, ed., *Married Women's*

Work (1915), reprint ed. (London: Virago, 1983), pp. 80, 120; Margaret Loane, *From Their Point of View* (London: Arnold, 1908), p. 133.

62. Nanette Whitbread, *The Evolution of the Nursery–Infant School* (London: Routledge & Kegan Paul, 1972); see also Clara Grant, "Needlework in Infants' Schools," *Child Life*, new ser., no. 15 (1902): 172–73.

63. *Toynbee Record*, February 1894, p. 70; November 1904, p. 30; November 1905, pp. 21, 24; *Child Life*, October 1902, pp. 218–20; Margaret McMillan, *The Nursery School* (London: Dent, 1919), p. 85; Carolyn Steedman, *Childhood, Culture, and Class in Britain: Margaret McMillan 1860–1931* (New Brunswick, NJ: Rutgers University Press, 1990), chap. 11.

64. Margaret McMillan, "Guy and the Stars" and "I Saw the Stars," in her *Nursery School*, also pp. 129–30 and 185. On McMillan's and her generation of socialist women's view of childhood and for a wonderful account of McMillan's Deptford years, see Steedman, *McMillan*, chaps. 9–11. I discuss the rivalry between middle-class professionals and working-class mothers in my "Good and Bad Mothers: Lady Philanthropists and London Housewives Before the First World War," in Kathleen McCarthy, ed., *Lady Bountiful Revisited: Women, Philanthropy and Power* (New Brunswick, NJ: Rutgers University Press, 1990); reprinted and revised in Dorothy O. Helly and Susan Reverby, eds., *Beyond Dichotomy: Public and Private Spheres in Historical Perspective* (Ithaca, NY: Cornell University Press, 1992).

65. Honnor Morten and H. F. Gethen, *Tales of the Children's Ward* (London: Sampson Low, Marston, 1894), pp. 25–26; Muriel Wragge, "News of the Woolwich Mission Kindergarten," *Child Life*, April 1901, p. 100; see also Campbell and Hope, *Physical Welfare of Mothers and Children*, vol. 2, pp. 130–31. The NSPCC campaigned not only against cruelty toward children but also for milder forms of discipline for them. Fathers more than mothers were the usual culprits in its propaganda. See George K. Behlmer, *Child Abuse and Moral Reform in England, 1870–1908* (Stanford, CA: Stanford University Press, 1982).

66. P. A. Heard, *An Octogenarian's Memoirs* (Elms Court: Arthur H. Stockwell, 1974), p. 40; interview with Mrs. Winifred Prentice, born in 1905, sides 1 and 2, Samuel oral histories.

67. "Our Settlement Guest House," *The Vote*, August 4, 1916, p. 1127.

68. Whitbread, *Nursery–Infant School*, pp. 44–45. More generally, see Second Report of the Royal Commission Appointed to Enquire into the Working of the Elementary Education Acts, England and Wales, PP 1887, vol. 29; and Report of a Board of Education Consultative Committee upon the School Attendance of Children Below the Age of Five, PP 1908, vol. 82.

69. Whitbread, *Nursery–Infant School*, p. 66, Table 3; p. 68, Table 4; David Rubinstein, *School Attendance in London 1870–1904: A Social History* (Hull: University of Hull Publications, 1969), p. 110; on the new LCC Education Committee and the politics of the 1902 Education Act, see Steedman, *McMillan*, pp. 49–51, 169.

70. Beatrice B. Whiting and John W. M. Whiting, *Children of Six Cultures: A Psycho-Cultural Analysis* (Cambridge, MA: Harvard University Press, 1975), pp. 83, 105–8; Beatrice B. Whiting, ed., *Six Cultures: Studies of Child Rearing* (New York: Wiley, 1963). There is already a large literature on the work of Victorian and Edwardian children, and so in this section I treat this subject only enough to clarify the relationship between child and mother. Anna Davin, in *Little Women*, fully explores children's household labor, emphasizing the heavier domestic responsibilities of girls.

71. Southgate, *The Way It Was*, pp. 41, 50; Scannell, *Mother Knew Best*, pp. 45,

56; Foakes, *My Part of the River,* p. 21; Stephen "Johnny" Hicks, *Sparring for Luck: Autobiography of the East End Boxer-Poet* (London: Tower Hamlets Arts Project, 1982), p. 18; and Family Life Archive, no. 412, p. 13.

72. Southgate, *The Way It Was,* p. 50; T. E. Harvey, *A London Boy's Saturday* (Birmingham: Saint George Press, 1906); Edith Hogg, "School Children as Wage Earners," *The Nineteenth Century* 42 (August 1897): 235–44; Arnold Freeman, *Boy Life and Labour: The Manufacture of Inefficiency* (London: P. S. King, 1914) (based on a Birmingham study); Reginald Bray, *Boy Labour and Apprenticeship* (London: Constable, 1912), pp. 105–13, on the paid work of schoolboys. Also see Michael J. Childs, "Boy Labour in Late Victorian and Edwardian England and the Remaking of the Working Class," *Journal of Social History* 23 (Summer 1990): 783–802, a summary of developments during this period. The quotation is from Catherine Webb, "The Committee on Wage-earning Children," *Economic Review* 14 (April 1904): 210.

73. Charles Morley, *Studies in Board Schools* (London: Smith, Elder, 1897), p. 42; Rubinstein, *School Attendance,* pp. 8, 112–13; Thomas Gautrey, *"Lux Mihi Laus": School Board Memories* (London, Link House, 1937), pp. 36, 152–53.

74. On the distinction between the mother's power and her authority in the home (based on Max Weber's definitions), see Miriam M. Johnson, *Strong Mothers Weak Wives: The Search for Gender Equality* (Berkeley and Los Angeles: University of California Press, 1988), pp. 5–8. On angry mothers, see Atkinson, "The Care of Children," p. 145; Southgate, *The Way It Was,* p. 44; interview with Mrs. Prentice, side 1, and with Mrs. Ada Stone, p. 36, both in Samuel oral histories.

75. Interview with Mrs. Mac, side 2, Samuel oral histories, pp. 1–2; Alexander Paterson, *Across the Bridges: A Study of Social Life in South London* (London: Arnold, 1911), p. 210. See the discussion of mothers who set up their husbands as objects for their children to fear in Judy Blendis, "Men's Experiences of Their Own Fathers," in Nigel Beail and Jacqueline McGuire, eds., *Fathers: Psychological Perspectives* (London: Junction Books, 1982), pp. 203–4.

76. Murphy, Old Bailey, vol. 86 (1876–1877), nos. 413–14, pp. 4–5. Obviously this does not exhaust the subject of child abuse in this era, which is better approached through the records of the agencies that monitored it, such as the National Vigilance Association (NVA) and the NSPCC. The NVA campaigned for decades for an incest bill aimed at protecting girls from fathers' sexual abuse, which was finally legislated in 1908. See Sheila Jeffreys, *The Spinster and Her Enemies: Feminism and Sexuality 1880–1930* (London: Pandora, 1985), chaps. 3 and 4.

77. Lilian Westall, in *Useful Toil,* pp. 215–16. The pub was along the Pentonville Road, Kings Cross. Begg is a pseudonym for a man born in 1884, one of ten children of a Battersea woodworker (Family Life Archive, no. 225). Also see Bennett, *Walworth Boy,* p. 41. Bushnell, another pseudonym, was born in 1900; he is quoted in Stephen Humphries, "Steal to Survive: The Social Crime of Working Class Children 1890–1940," *Oral History* 9 (Spring 1981): 31.

78. *Missing Link,* June 1883, pp. 170–71; Humphries, *Hooligans or Rebels?* pp. 151–53.

79. Family Life Archive, no. 299 (Rose Albert is a pseudonym), p. 28; Frank Steel, *Ditcher's Row: A Tale of the Older Charity* (London: Sidgwick & Jackson, 1939), pp. 43, 48; Olive Christian Malvery, *Baby Toilers* (London: Hutchinson, 1907), pp. 45–48.

80. Anna Martin, "The Irresponsibility of the Father, Part II," *The Nineteenth Century and After* 85 (March 1919): 555–56; Marie Kelly Welsh, oral history transcript, Hackney People's Autobiography, p. 9; Hogg, "School Children as

Wage Earners"; James A. Schmiechen, *Sweated Industries and Sweated Labor: The London Clothing Trades, 1860–1914* (Urbana: University of Illinois Press, 1984), app. A, pp. 194–97; and Harvey, *London Boy's Saturday, passim* (the term *mother's work*).

81. Charles E. B. Russell and Lilian M. Rigby, *Working Lads' Clubs* (London: Macmillan, 1908), pp. 256–57, describing big brothers and their smaller ones at a summer camp for Hackney children. Also Morley, *Studies in Board Schools,* pp. 17–18. A few examples from oral history/autobiographical literature are Bennett, *Walworth Boy,* pp. 54–55; and Jasper, *Hoxton Childhood.* Several of these are quoted in Chapter 2.

82. Nancy Chodorow, *The Reproduction of Mothering: Psychoanalysis and the Sociology of Gender* (Berkeley and Los Angeles: University of California Press, 1978). D. H. Lawrence's *Sons and Lovers* (1913) is the classic literary representation of this relationship. For a searing story of a later Nottingham working-class mother–son pair (from the 1930s and 1940s), which consumed the son entirely for his first thirty years, see Jeremy Seabrook, *Mother and Son: An Autobiography* (London: Victor Gollancz, 1979). A loving and appreciative son's autobiography revolving around the glowing figure of his South London schoolteacher mother is that by Richard Church, *Over the Bridge: An Essay in Autobiography* (London: Heinemann, 1955).

83. Mary A. Ward, *Play-Time of the Poor* (London: Smith, Elder, 1906), p. 7; Davin, *Little Women;* Paterson, *Across the Bridges,* pp. 82–83; R. E. Roper, ed., *Organized Play at Home and Abroad* (London: National League for Physical Education and Improvement, 1911); Russell and Rigby, *Working-Lads' Clubs;* Michael Rosenthal, *The Character Factory: Baden-Powell's Boy Scouts and the Imperatives of Empire* (New York: Pantheon, 1984).

84. John Springhall, *Coming of Age: Adolescence in Britain 1860–1960* (Dublin: Gill & Macmillan, 1986), pp. 130–32; Patrick A. Dunae, "Penny Dreadfuls: Late Nineteenth-Century Boys' Literature and Crime," *Victorian Studies* 22 (Winter 1979): 133–50; Kristin Drotner, *English Children and Their Magazines, 1751–1945* (New Haven, CT: Yale University Press, 1988). For some boys who were ardent readers of these publications, see Church, *Over the Bridge,* p. 74; Edward Ezard, *Battersea Boy* (London: William Kember, 1979), p. 98; Edward Brown, untitled autobiography, p. 4; Frank Galton, *Autobiography,* typescript version, LSE Manuscript Collection, Coll. Misc. 315, p. 5a.

85. *Biblewomen and Nurses,* November 1906, p. 197; Grant, *Farthing Bundles,* p. 95; Rubinstein, *School Attendance,* p. 8; Davin, *Little Women,* chap. 9, "Needed at Home." See also Family Life Archive, no. 215, p. 30.

86. May Craske, "Girl Life in a Slum," *Economic Review* 18 (April 1908): 186–87. Also see Report of the Medical Officer for Education, in LCC, *Annual Reports,* 1910, vol. 3, p. 130; Malvery, *Baby Toilers,* pp. 60–63; Dyhouse, *Girls Growing Up,* chap. 3; test. Dr. Alfred Eichholz, PP 1904, vol. 32, Qq. 720, 729; test. Maude Stanley, PP 1904, vol. 32, Qq. 13378, 13451, 13456–59.

87. Morley, *Studies in Board Schools,* pp. 42–43. For a parallel study of turn-of-the-century American children, see David Nasaw, *Children of the City at Work and at Play* (Garden City, NY: Doubleday Anchor, 1985). See also Anna Davin's *Little Women,* chap. 8, "Caretakers or Schoolchildren?" The "Violet Harris" quotation is from Chamberlain, *Growing Up in Lambeth,* p. 45.

88. Cold, harsh, and/or unloved mothers appear in such autobiographies as Linton, *Not Expecting Miracles;* Acorn, *One of the Multitude;* Woodward, *Jipping Street;* and Mrs. Benjamin, oral history transcript, Hackney People's Autobiography.

89. Rebecca Jarrett's typescript autobiography was generously supplied by Pamela Walker (Rebecca Jarrett File, Salvation Army Heritage Center, London). See the chapter on "The Maiden Tribute" episode in Judith Walkowitz, *City of Dreadful Delight: Narratives of Sexual Danger in Late Victorian London* (Chicago: University of Chicago Press, 1992). Colin Ward, *The Child in the City,* cited in Nasaw, *Children of the City,* p. 20; Iona Opie and Peter Opie, *The Lore and Language of Schoolchildren* (Oxford: Oxford University Press, 1959), esp. chap. 18, on pranks; and Iona Opie and Peter Opie, *Children's Games in Street and Playground* (Oxford: Clarendon Press, 1969); Norman Douglas, *London Street Games* (London: St. Catherine Press, 1916), "Cold Meat Mutton Chops," p. 40; also Alice B. Gomme, "The Antiquity of Children's Singing Games," *Child Life,* April 1901, pp. 72–83.

90. "Sketch of Life in Buildings," in Booth, *Poverty,* vol. 3, p. 40; Chase, *Tenant Friends in Old Deptford,* p. 129.

91. *East London Observer,* March 9, 1889, p. 5, and July 11, 1868, p. 3; John Hasloch Potter, *Inasmuch: The Story of the Police Court Mission 1876–1926* (London: Williams & Norgate, 1927), pp. 67–68; J. A. R. Cairns, *Drab Street Glory: Impressions of Life in the Slums* (London: Hutchinson, 1934), p. 125. On neighborhood suspiciousness of reputed "baby farmers," also see PP 1896, vol. 10, Q. 171 and Q. 1037.

92. Interview with Mrs. Henman, Samuel oral histories; Hine, "Poplar Childhood," p. 33; Boswell, Old Bailey, vol. 71 (1869–1870), no. 91, p. 115; Sims, *How the Poor Live,* p. 95; "Starvation in Shoreditch," *Justice,* August 12, 1905, p. 3; Martin, *Married Working Woman,* p. 31; Scannell, *Mother Knew Best,* p. 76.

93. Elizabeth Flint, *Hot Bread and Chips* (London: Museum Press, 1963), p. 27.

94. Flint, *Hot Bread and Chips,* pp. 29, 74; Woodward, *Jipping Street.*

95. Leonore Davidoff, "The Separation of Home and Work? Landladies and Lodgers in Nineteenth- and Twentieth-Century England," in Sandra Burman, ed., *Fit Work for Women* (London: Croom Helm, 1979); Cranwell, *Old Bailey,* vol. 81 (1874–1875) no. 93, p. 158; Wallace, Old Bailey, vol. 71 (1869–1870), no. 80, pp. 94 ff.

96. Parker, Old Bailey, vol. 79 (1873–1874), no. 123, p. 157; Inquirey in Certain Unions into Causes of Refusal of Out-Relief, Royal Commission on the Poor Laws and Relief of Distress, PP 1910, vol. 52, pp. 41–42.

97. Acorn, *One of the Multitude,* pp. 41–43.

98. Interview with Mrs. Henman, Samuel oral histories; R. E. Corder, *Tales Told to the Magistrate* (London: Andrew Melrose, 1925), p. 14.

99. Prosser, Old Bailey, vol. 69 (1868–1869), no. 337, pp. 410–11; Family Life Archive, no. 225, p. 53; Harvey, *London Boy's Saturday,* p. 7.

100. Henry Turner Waddy, *The Police Court and Its Work* (London: Butterworth, 1925), pp. 9, 7; Corder, *Tales Told to the Magistrate,* p. 141.

101. Family Life Archive, no. 296, p. 22 (describing the 1890s and 1900s); Ezard, *Battersea Boy,* p. 28; James H. Robb, *Working-Class Anti-Semite: A Psychological Study in a London Borough* (London: Tavistock, 1954), p. 62.

102. Patterson, *Across the Bridges,* p. 32. On budget studies and mothers' standard of living, see, for example, Arthur L. Bowley and A. R. Burnett-Hurst, *Livelihood and Poverty* (London: Ratan Tata Foundation, 1915). Some examples of a child's income changing the family standard of living are Frank Galton autobiography, p. 20; National Birth-Rate Commission, *The Declining Birth-Rate: Its Causes and Effects* (London: Chapman & Hall, 1916), p. 204; Family Life Archive, no. 412, p. 15; and Scannell, *Mother Knew Best,* p. 66.

103. The phrase is from A Medical Secretary, "Care Committees: Following Up in Medical Work," *The School Child,* January 1913, p. 6.

104. Martin, *Married Working Woman,* p. 15; Black, *Married Women's Work,* p. 91; Nasaw, *Children of the City,* chap. 9.

105. Chase, *Tenant Friends in Old Deptford,* pp. 172–73. See also Rosemary Arthman, "Labor Force Participation, Life Cycle, and Expenditure Patterns: The Case of Unmarried Female Factory Workers in Berlin (1902)," in Ruth-Ellen B. Joeres and Mary Jo Maynes, eds., *German Women in the Eighteenth and Nineteenth Centuries* (Bloomington: Indiana University Press, 1986).

106. Notebooks of Rev. Arthur O. Jay (February 1889), Charles Booth Papers, B80, LSE Manuscript Collection. See also Florrie Roberts, *The Ups and Downs of Florrie Roberts* (London: Peckham Publishing Project, 1980), p. 5.

107. Acorn, *One of the Multitude,* pp. 106–7; E. Robinson (b. 1894), "I Remember (1960–1970)" (Typescript, Brunel University Library). Also see Bennett, *Walworth Boy,* p. 41.

108. George Haw, *From Workhouse to Westminster: The Life Story of Will Crooks M.P.* (London: Cassell, 1911), pp. 3, 7; Family Life Archive, no. 284, p. 52. Also see *Missing Link,* November 1, 1878, pp. 330–31.

109. *Missing Link,* October 1878, p. 299; Hackney People's Autobiography, *The Island,* pp. 15–16.

110. John Gillis, "The Evolution of Juvenile Delinquency in England 1890–1914," *Past and Present* 67 (May 1975): 96–126. Also on definitions of juvenile delinquency, see Humphries, *Hooligans or Rebels,* chap. 7. On parents' resorting to the magistrates courts, see Davis, "A Poor Man's System of Justice," p. 332; Jasper, *Hoxton Childhood,* p. 45; and Hackney People's Autobiography, *The Island,* p. 26. On women police volunteers, see Lucy Bland, "In the Name of Protection: The Policing of Women in the First World War," in her *Women-in-Law: Explorations in Law, Family, and Sexuality* (London: Routledge & Kegan Paul, 1985).

111. Rubinstein, *School Attendance,* p. 33; Donald Read, *Edwardian England 1901–1915: Society and Politics* (London: Harrap, 1972), pp. 160–61; Pat Thane, *Foundations of the Welfare State* (London: Longman Group, 1982), p. 201.

112. Family Life Archive, no. 215, p. 19; Marie Kelly Welsh, Autobiography, pp. 4–5.

113. Mrs. Mac, Samuel oral histories, pp. 5–6.

114. Mrs. Benjamin, oral history.

115. Flint, *Hot Bread and Chips,* pp. 68, 98, 108–11.

CHAPTER 6

1. Summer diarrhea accounted for about a quarter of all infant deaths in England and Wales throughout the years of this study. See Anthony S. Wohl, *Endangered Lives: Public Health in Victorian Britain* (Cambridge, MA: Harvard University Press, 1983), p. 23; and for a discussion of the changing ratio of diarrhea deaths to those from other causes, see R. I. Woods, P. A. Watterson, and J. H. Woodward, "The Causes of Rapid Infant Mortality Decline in England and Wales, 1861–1921," pt. I, *Population Studies* 42 (1988): 343–66.

2. The sense that the medical profession could offer newer and safer ways of caring for children, which gradually structured the thinking of U.S. mothers, is well outlined in Nancy Schrom Dye and Daniel Blake Smith, "Mother Love and Infant

Death, 1750–1920," *Journal of American History* 73 (September 1986): 329–53.

3. Edward Berdoe, "Slum-Mothers and Death-Clubs: A Vindication," *The Nineteenth Century*, April 1891, p. 562; Mrs. Marvin, "Physical Inspection," *Journal of the Royal Sanitary Institute* 26 (1905): 72; Margaret McMillan, *The Nursery School* (London: Dent, 1919); The Baby Clinic, *First Annual Report* (1911), p. 12, Women's Labour League Baby Clinic File, Labour Party Library.

4. Berdoe, "Slum Mothers," p. 562; Margaret Llewelyn Davies, *Maternity: Letters from Working Women* (1915), reprint ed. (New York: Norton, 1978), p. 45.

5. Maud Pember Reeves, *Round About a Pound a Week* (1913) reprint ed. (London: Virago, 1979), pp. 90–91; *The Hospital*, January 13, 1906, p. 232.

6. George Acorn (pseud.), *One of the Multitude: An Autobiography by a Resident of Bethnal Green* (London: Heinemann, 1911), pp. 35–38.

7. John Eldred (born in 1885), *I Love the Brooks* (London: Skeffington, 1955), p. 16; Selig Brodetsky, *Memoirs: From Ghetto to Israel* (London: Weidenfelt & Nicolson, 1960), p. 23.

8. F. B. Smith, *The People's Health 1830–1910* (New York: Holmes & Meier, 1979), p. 255; Lt. Col. Montefiore, "Uses and Abuses of Medical Charities," *Charity Organisation Review*, new ser., 14 (July 1903): 18. On the dispensaries, see the excellent Ph.D. dissertation by Mary Jean Chamard, "Medicine and the Working Class: The Dispensary Movement in London, 1867–1911," University of Toronto, 1984.

9. Jeanne L. Brand, *Doctors and the State: The British Medical Profession and Government Action in Public Health, 1870–1912* (Baltimore: Johns Hopkins University Press, 1965). The Metropolitan Asylums Board, also formed as the result of the Metropolitan Poor Act, had six thousand beds in its own hospitals in 1900, mostly for victims of contagious diseases; the forty-four poor-law infirmaries in the metropolitan area had a total of over twelve thousand beds in 1893 (p. 96 and p. 254, n. 29).

10. Miney and Waghorn, Old Bailey, vol. 76 (1871–1872), no. 668, p. 371; Radley, no. 686, p. 397; Curme, vol. 105 (1886–1887), no. 504, pp. 623–24.

11. Chamard, *Dispensary Movement*, pp. 217, 129b, 121, 154. See also E. C., "Outpatient Departments and the Rearing of Children," in C. S. Loch, ed., *Methods of Social Advance* (London: Macmillan, 1904), p. 8. General practitioners today in Britain also see a preponderance of women patients. See Ann Oakley, "Women and Health Policy," in Jane Lewis, ed., *Women's Welfare, Women's Rights* (London: Croom Helm, 1983), p. 103, and Table 6.1, p. 104.

12. Charles Booth, *Life and Labour of the People in London*, vol. 17: *Notes of Social Influences and Conclusion*, reprint of the 1902–1904 ed. (17 vols.) (New York: AMS Press, 1970), p. 151; Raphael Samuel and Gareth Stedman Jones, "Pearly Kings and Queens," in *Patriotism: The Making and Unmaking of British National Identity*, vol. 3: *National Fictions*, ed. Raphael Samuel (3 vols.) (London: Routledge & Kegan Paul, 1989), p. 68.

13. Brian Abel-Smith, *The Hospitals 1800–1948* (Cambridge, MA: Harvard University Press, 1964), pp. 174–75; Royal Free Hospital, Almoner's Reports, Royal Free Hospital Archives. Also see E. Moberly Bell, *The Story of the Hospital Almoners: The Birth of a Profession* (London: Faber & Faber, 1961), pp. 19–21; and H. G. N., "The Work of a Hospital Almoner," in Loch, ed., *Methods of Social Advance;* "An Almoner's Work in a General Hospital," *The Hospital*, May 1907, pp. 434–35; and Ronald D. Walton, *Women in Social Work* (London: Routledge & Kegan Paul, 1975), pp. 43–47.

14. Census figures cited by Frank Prochaska in "Body and Soul: Bible Nurses

and the Poor in Victorian London," *Historical Research* 60 (October 1987): 342; Chamard, *Dispensary Movement,* p. 222.

15. Stewart Johnson, "The Health and Medical Treatment of the Uninsured," *JRSS* 76 (March 1913): 410–14; Inner City Theatre Company, *The Threepenny Doctor: Doctor Jelley of Hackney* (London: Centerprise, 1983); Chamard, *Dispensary Movement,* p. 222; Eldred, *I Love the Brooks,* p. 16. Also, on the use of private physicians, see Smith, *People's Health,* pp. 372–74; and M. Jeanne Peterson, *The Medical Profession in Mid-Victorian London* (Berkeley and Los Angeles: University of California Press, 1978).

16. King, Old Bailey, vol. 87 (1877–1878), no. 103, pp. 131–32; *Biblewomen and Nurses,* August 1897, p. 156; Alice Linton, *Not Expecting Miracles* (London: Centerprise, 1982), p. 23.

17. Kensington MOH, *Annual Report,* 1875, p. 12; Berdoe, "Slum-Mothers," p. 562.

18. Elspeth Platt, *The Story of the Ranyard Mission 1857–1937* (London: Hodder & Stoughton, 1937); Mary Stocks, *A Hundred Years of District Nursing* (London: Allen & Unwin, 1960); Prochaska, "Body and Soul"; Ellen Ranyard, *Nurses for the Needy, or Bible Women Nurses in the Homes of the London Poor* (London: James Nesbet, 1875), pp. 31, 45; Betty Cowell and David Wainwright, *Behind the Blue Door: The History of the Royal College of Midwives 1881–1981* (London: Balliere Tindall, 1981). On the low status of Ranyard's nurses, see Cowell and Wainwright, *Blue Door,* p. 45. Also on district nursing, see Lee Holcombe, *Victorian Ladies at Work* (Newton Abbott: David and Charles, 1973), pp. 89–91; and Brian Abel-Smith, *A History of the Nursing Profession* (London: Heinemann, 1960).

19. Metropolitan and National Nursing Association for Providing Trained Nurses for the Sick Poor (MNNA), Hon. Inspector's Reports, 1876–1880, fol. 35–47, Guildhall Manuscript Library (emphasis in the original). The report for 1886 contains a very negative evaluation of a new nurse probationer, on the grounds that she was unable to work with the poor; also see Superintendent's Reports, 1912–1915.

20. E. Margery Homersham, "The Spread of Sanitary Knowledge by District Nurses," *Nurses' Journal,* May 1891, p. 33; LCC, *London Statistics,* 1898–1899, vol. 9, p. xii (based on the registrar-general's calculations, which include Londoners dying elsewhere and exclude nonresidents of London who died in London institutions). The numbers for that year were a total of 87,298 deaths, of which 23,282 were in workhouses and infirmaries, Metropolitan Asylums Board hospitals, lunatic asylums, and voluntary (private) hospitals. For its time, this is a very high proportion of institutional deaths.

21. Chamard, "Medicine and the Working Class," p. 136; Maude A. Stanley, *Work About the Five Dials* (London: Macmillan, 1878), pp. 110–11; *Biblewomen and Nurses,* October 1893, p. 190, and September 1910, p. 184; test. Dr. Hawkes, PP 1904, vol. 32, Q. 12989. On the cleaning routines of the MNNA nurses, see the organization's *Annual Reports* (at the Guildhall Library), 1878, pp. 10–11, and 1879, p. 12. Mrs. Humphrey Ward, *Marcella* (1894), reprint ed. (London: Virago, 1984).

22. Stanley, *Work About the Five Dials,* p. 109; Smith, *The People's Health,* p. 261; Prochaska, "Body and Soul," p. 341. The interview with Nurse Williams is in the Booth Manuscripts, A vol. 39, LSE Manuscript Collection; *The Hospital,* September 21, 1895, p. clxv; Katherine Roberts, *Five Months in a London Hospital* (Letchworth: Garden City Press, 1911).

23. "A Plaster Party," *Nursing Record,* March 21, 1889, p. 105; Rose Petty, "School Nursing," *Nursing Times,* June 3, 1905, pp. 80–81.

24. See Kensington, MOH, *Annual Reports,* 1884, p. 24. In that year, the MOH reported, 70 of 202 infectious patients in his district refused hospitalization. See also MNNA, *Annual Reports,* 1879, pp. 14, 17. On the compulsory notification of infectious diseases and legislation dealing with "fever" hospitals, see W. M. Frazer, *A History of Public Health 1834–1939* (London: Balliere, Tindall & Cox, 1950), pp. 153. 181, 288.

25. See "Outpatient Oddities," *Nursing Times,* June 24, 1905, pp. 138–39, and December 9, 1905, p. 634; also Pember Reeves, *Round About a Pound,* p. 187; Muriel Wragge, *The London I Loved: Reminiscences of Fifty Years Social Work in the District of Hoxton* (London: James Clarke, 1960), p. 37; Clara Grant, *Farthing Bundles* (London: Fern Street Settlement 1930), pp. 83–84.

26. Roy M. McLeod, "Law, Medicine and Public Opinion: The Resistance to Compulsory Health Legislation 1870–1907," pts. I and II, *Public Law* (Summer and Autumn 1967): 107–28 and 189–211; Ann Beck, "Issues in the Anti-Vaccination Movement in England," *Medical History* 4 (October 1960): 310–21.

27. McLeod, "Law, Medicine and Public Opinion," pt. II, p. 197, n. 28; Ellen Chase, *Tenant Friends in Old Deptford* (London: Williams & Norgate, 1929), p. 184; Report of the MOH of the County [of London], in LCC, *Annual Reports,* 1910, vol. 3, pp. 28–29.

28. *Nursing Times,* January 24, 1905, p. 138, and October 28, 1905, p. 558; Edith E. G. May, *True Tales of a District* (London: Knott, 1908), p. 36. May belonged to the Guild of St. Barnabas for Nurses and worked in Central London. Margaret Loane, *From Their Point of View* (London: Arnold, 1908), p. 84.

29. Logie Barrow, *Independent Spirits: Spiritualism and English Plebeians 1850–1910* (London: Routledge & Kegan Paul, 1986), chap. 7; Alex Owen, *The Darkened Room: Women, Power and Spiritualism in Late Victorian England* (Philadelphia: University of Pennsylvania Press, 1990), pp. 127, 113–21. For an earlier period, see J. F. C. Harrison, "Early Victorian Radicals and the Medical Fringe," in W. F. Bynum and Roy Porter, eds., *Medical Fringe and Medical Orthodoxy 1750–1850* (London: Croom Helm, 1987).

30. The antivivisection movement and the opposition to the Contagious Diseases Acts (partly an antidoctor movement) were largely middle class, as was much of the leadership of the antivaccination movement. See Richard D. French, *Vivisection and Medical Science in Victorian Society* (Princeton, NJ: Princeton University Press, 1975), chap. 9. On spiritualists' actions against compulsory vaccination, see Owen, *Darkened Room,* pp. 131–32.

31. *Nursing Times,* December 9, 1905, p. 633. See Lyle Saunders and Gordon W. Heiwes, "Folk Medicine and Medical Practice," in L. Riddick Lynch, ed., *The Cross-Cultural Approach to Health Behavior* (Rutherford, NJ: Fairleigh Dickenson University Press, 1969).

32. *Missing Link,* October, 1878, p. 290; Dorothy Scannell, *Mother Knew Best: An East End Childhood* (London: Macmillan, 1974), p. 87; Walter Southgate, *That's the Way It Was: A Working Class Autobiography 1890–1950* (London: New Clarion Press, 1982, p. 80.

33. Test. Miss Deverell, school inspector for West Ham, PP 1904, vol. 32, Q. 8006; Mrs. Marvin, "Physical Inspection," *Journal of the Royal Sanitary Institute* 26 (1905): 72; Tottenham History Workshop, *How Things Were: Growing Up in Tottenham 1890–1920* (London, n.d.), pp. 23, 25; *The School Child,* January 1913; McMillan, *The School Clinic Today: Health Centres and What They Mean to the People* (London: ILP and National Labour Press, 1912), p. 9; Grant, *Farthing Bundles,* p. 84.

Many of these recipes may be found in Mary Chamberlain's *Old Wives' Tales: Their History, Remedies and Spells* (London: Virago, 1981), pp. 135–36.

34. Peckham People's History, *The Times of Our Lives* (London: Peckham Publishing Project, 1983), p. 58.

35. Ranyard, *Nurses for the Needy*, p. 14; MNNA, *Annual Reports*, 1883, p. 11.

36. Smith, *People's Health*, p. 105, Table 2.8, and, p. 110; Grace Foakes, *My Part of the River* (London: Futura Books, 1976), p. 77.

37. Scannell, *Mother Knew Best*, pp. 29–30; Emilia Kanthack, *The Preservation of Infant Life* (London: H. K. Lewis, 1907), pp. 25, 55–56, 7.

38. Loane, *From Their Point of View*, pp. 141–42; Jane Bark, "Memories" (Typescript, n.d., Tower Hamlets Local History Library). See also "A Girl's Sad Story," *Women's Dreadnought*, September 4, 1914, p. 93.

39. Barrow, *Independent Spirits*, p. 215; Owen, *Darkened Room*, chaps. 5, 6, and 7. The sect, also known as the Plumstead Peculiars, was founded in London in 1838; by the 1900s there were about fifteen hundred members in clusters in South East Essex. (My thanks to Hugh McLeod for supplying this additional information.) The father in the 1882 case was pronounced guilty, but the verdict was later overturned by a higher court. See Morby, Old Bailey, vol. 95 (1881–1882), no. 363, p. 542. For a similar case with a different verdict, see Hurry, Old Bailey, vol. 76 (1871–1872), no. 435, p. 63.

40. On "selective neglect" (the term is Nancy Scheper-Hughes's), see David L. Ransel, "Infant-Care Cultures in the Russian Empire," in Barbara Clements, Barbara Engel, and Christine Worobec, eds., *Russia's Women: Accommodation, Resistance, Transformation* (Berkeley and Los Angeles: University of California Press, 1991). See also Nancy Scheper-Hughes, "Culture, Scarcity, and Maternal Thinking: Maternal Detachment and Infant Survival in a Brazilian Shantytown," *Ethos* 13 (1985): 291–317; Nancy E. Levine, "Differential Child Care in Three Tibetan Communities: Beyond Son Preference," *Population and Development Review* 13 (June 1987): 281–304; and Monica Das Gupta, "Selective Discrimination Against Female Children in Rural Punjab, India," *Population and Development Review* 31 (March 1987): 77–100. The information about the neglect of Japanese infants was supplied by Kathleen Uno of Temple University, personal communication, November 1991. This issue is discussed further later in this chapter.

41. Medical Officers' Case Books, January–September 1881, no. 73; January–April 1888, no. 49.

42. Early in the twentieth century in Britain and the United States, the Child Study movement began to encourage close attention to children's cognitive development. Pember Reeves and her researchers were somewhat attentive to small children's speech and personalities, though this approach seldom appears in the other literature of the Infant Welfare era.

43. GLI Medical Officers' Case Book, January–April 1886; J. C. Drummond and Anne Wilbraham, *The Englishman's Food: A History of Five Centuries of English Diet*, revised ed. (London: Jonathan Cape, 1957), p. 453; Lawrence K. Altman, "Childhood Death: Respiratory Ailments Are Now No. 1 Cause," *New York Times*, April 8, 1986, p. C1. Respiratory diseases (including measles, as it is usually its respiratory complications that make it fatal) now account for more deaths worldwide than does diarrhea or any other cause.

44. On the extent of poor-law services for the handicapped, see Ruth Hodgkinson, *Science and Public Health* (Milton Keynes: Open University Press, 1973); and Rachel Vorspan, "The Battle over the Workhouse: English Society and the New

Poor Law" (Ph.D. diss., Columbia University, 1975). On the home care of disabled children, see *Biblewomen and Nurses,* August 1897, p. 154, and October 1906, pp. 181–82.

45. *Missing Link,* October 1882, pp. 299–301; account by Minnie Bowles (b. 1903), in Margaret Cohen, Marion Fagan, and Hymie Fagan, eds., *Childhood Memories: Recorded by Some Socialist Men and Women in their Later Years* (London: self-published, n.d.), p. 6 (my thanks to Anna Davin, who made me a gift of this book); Margaret Loane, *Simple Sanitation* (London: Scientific Press, n.d.), p. 69; William J. Fishman, *East End 1888: A Year in a London Borough Among the Labouring Poor* (London: Duckworth, 1988), p. 127.

46. Marie Kelly Welsh (born in Hoxton in 1904), typescript oral history, Hackney People's Autobiography, p. 6. For a statistical discussion of drowning, burns, and scalds as causes of death of British children, see Richard Wall, "Health and Responsibility: Gender Roles 1900–1930" (Typescript, Cambridge Group on the History of Population and Social Structure, Cambridge). On auto accidents, see William Plowden, *The Motor Car and Politics 1896–1970* (London: The Bodley Head, 1971), p. 95 n., 97, 227; typescript letter to Addison from Mary A. Ward, June 29, 1914, Addison Papers, Box 60 (Children and Child Welfare 1914), Bodleian Library, Oxford.

47. Britain's turn-of-the-century infant mortality rates (in 1903) were higher than those of Australia, Switzerland, Denmark, Scotland, New South Wales, Ireland, Sweden, and New Zealand, but lower than those of France, Germany, Italy or Russia. See Margaret McMillan, *Infant Mortality* (London: ILP, n.d.), p. 6. On the degree to which the British figures were underreported, see Smith, *People's Health,* pp. 66–68; Wohl, *Endangered Lives,* p. 11; and, Chapter 4, "Honeymoon All Over," esp. n. 8.

48. M. W. Beaver, "Population, Infant Mortality and Milk," *Population Studies* 26 (1973): 243–54, 246. A good short description of the trends is in G. F. McCleary, *The Early History of the Infant Welfare Movement* (London: H. K. Lewis, 1933), pp. 1–3. The best recent article on the infant mortality decline in Britain is that by Woods, Watterson, and Woodward, "Causes of Rapid Infant Mortality Decline."

49. The death rates for this age group remained more or less stationary until 1915, when they subsided. See Carol Dyhouse, "Working-Class Mothers and Infant Mortality in England, 1895–1914," *Journal of Social History* 12 (Winter 1978): 248; and J. M. Winter, "Mortality Decline in England and Wales in the Period of the First World War," Conference Paper, September 1983, p. 4, on file at the Center for Population Studies, Cambridge University. See also J. M. Winter, *The Great War and the British People* (London: Macmillan, 1985), p. 124, Table 4:4.

50. The registrar-general's 1911 figures, for example, show Class V (the lowest of the occupational categories delineated) with 41 percent more infant deaths than Class I had during the first month, but 183 percent for the last three months of the first year. See Jane Lewis, *The Politics of Motherhood: Child and Maternal Welfare in England, 1900–1939* (London: Croom Helm, 1980), p. 67. There were also great urban–rural differences. See also Smith, *People's Health,* p. 123.

51. Kensington MOH, *Annual Report,* 1910, p. 8; 1895, p. 15; 1905, p. 12; 1910, p. 8. On Birmingham's contrasts, see L. G. Chiozza Money, *Riches and Poverty,* rev. ed. (London: Methuen, 1911). On the contrast among classes in the present, see Hilary Graham, *Women, Health and the Family* (Brighton: Wheatsheaf, 1984), Table 3.3, p. 50; and Nicholas Abercrombie and Alan Warde, *Contemporary British Society* (Cambridge: Policy Press, 1988), pp. 282–83, 484.

52. *The Needs of Little Children: Report of a Conference on the Care of Babies and Young Children* (London: Central London Women's Labour League, 1912), p. 14 (italics in the original); Barbara Drake, "Study of Infant Life in Westminster," as summarized by Smith in *People's Health*, pp. 124–27; J. M. Winter, "Aspects of the Impact of the First World War on Infant Mortality in Britain," *Journal of Economic History* 11 (Winter 1982): 713–38. The quotation is from p. 729.

53. MNNA, *Annual Reports*, 1883, p. 13 (emphasis in the original); Foakes, *My Part of the River*, pp. 24, 78; Clara Grant, "Fern St. Settlement," *The School Child* 1 (February 1911): 3; Florence Roberts, *The Ups and Downs of Florrie Roberts* (London: Peckham Publishing Project, 1980), p. 11.

54. For a good discussion of the literature on "attachment," see Andrea B. Eagan, *The Newborn Mother: Stages of Her Growth* (Boston: Little, Brown, 1985), chaps. 1 and 2. Eagan lists a number of recent American studies. Figures are cited in McCleary, *Early History*, pp. 32–33. Also see Kensington MOH, *Annual Reports*, 1905, p. 61.

55. See n. 40, this chapter.

56. Hall, Old Bailey, vol. 90 (1879), no. 787, p. 662; Roberts, *Five Months in a London Hospital*. In 1895 the death rate of illegitimate children under age one was an extraordinary 566 per thousand registered births in Kensington. By age five, if only *registered* births are used for the calculation, 72 percent of illegitimate children had died. See Kensington MOH, *Annual Reports*, 1895, pp. 5, 17. Clearly this method of caring for illegitimate babies was an unconscious form of "selective neglect."

57. GLI, Medical Officers' Case Books, January–April 1886, no. 67. See also January–April 1884, no. 31, and January–April 1886, no. 53.

58. Frank Steel, *Ditcher's Row: A Tale of the Older Charity* (London: Sidgwick & Jackson, 1939), pp. 199–200; Viviana A. Zelizer, *Pricing the Priceless Child: The Changing Social Value of Children* (New York: Basic Books, 1985), p. 116. Also see Lionel Rose, *Massacre of the Innocents: Infanticide in Great Britain 1800–1939* (London: Routledge & Kegan Paul, 1986), chaps. 12 and 17, on infant life protection legislation in Britain, and chaps. 15 and 16.

59. R. Sauer, "Infanticide and Abortion in Nineteenth-Century Britain," *Population Studies* 32 (1978): 82. See also Angus McLaren, *Reproductive Rituals: The Perception of Fertility in England from the Sixteenth Century to the Nineteenth Century* (London: Methuen, 1984), pp. 129–36.

60. George K. Behlmer, "Deadly Motherhood: Infanticide and Medical Opinion in Mid-Victorian England," *Journal of the History of Medicine and Allied Sciences* 34 (October 1979): 412; Catherine Damme, "Infanticide: The Worth of an Infant Under Law," *Medical History* 22 (1978): 14. Women who had been convicted of infanticide and who had been committed to Bethelem or Broadmoor were more likely to be released by order of the home secretary than was any other group of criminally insane. See Roger Smith, *Trial by Medicine: Insanity and Responsibility in Victorian Trials* (Edinburgh: Edinburgh University Press, 1981), pp. 143–50.

61. See George K. Behlmer, *Child Abuse and Moral Reform in England, 1870–1908* (Stanford, CA.: Stanford University Press, 1982), chap. 2; Rose, *Massacre of the Innocents*, chap. 7; and A. Braxton Hicks, *Hints to Medical Men Concerning the Granting of Certificates of Death* (London: William Clowes, 1889), esp. p. 15; test. Alfred Spencer, PP 1896, vol. 10, Q. 3046. See also David Jones, *Crime, Protest, Community and Police in Nineteenth-Century Britain* (London: Routledge & Kegan Paul, 1982), pp. 12, 122.

62. Behlmer, "Deadly Motherhood," fig. 2, p. 424; V. A. C. Gatrell, "The Decline of Theft and Violence in Victorian and Edwardian England," in V. A. C.

Gatrell, Bruce Lenman, and Geoffrey Parker, eds., *Crime and the Law: The Social History of Crime in Western Europe Since 1500* (London: Europa Publications, 1980), Table A1, p. 342. Nationally, the proportion of infant murder victims was somewhat lower. Babies "found dead" may have been more numerous in London, the place to which pregnant women with a birth to conceal often resorted for their confinements.

63. Alexander and Clifford, Old Bailey, vol. 80 (1874), no. 417, p. 81; Dilley and Rainbow, Old Bailey, vol. 90 (1879), no. 698, p. 484; Pearch, Old Bailey, vol. 119 (1894), no. 389, p. 508; Longman, Old Bailey, vol. 110 (1889) no. 48, p. 103.

64. According to W. H. Willcox, *BMJ*, September 24, 1904, pp. 753–55. For figures for Hackney and Paddington, see Hackney MOH, *Annual Reports*, 1875, pp. 45–46; Paddington MOH, *Annual Reports*, 1876, Table III, and 1894, p. 256.

65. See Report from the Select Committee on the Children's Life Insurance Bill [H.L.], PP 1890, vol. 13, especially the testimony of Mrs. Greenwood, of the Women Sanitary Inspectors' Association on the (lack of) relationship between overlaying and burial insurance; and the 1896 hearings in the House of Lords on the same subject, PP 1896, vol. 10. Also see Berdoe, "Slum Mothers," pp. 560–63; Wohl, *Endangered Lives*, p. 34; and Rose, *Massacre of the Innocents,* chap. 16.

66. George Newman, *Infant Mortality: A Social Problem* (London: Methuen, 1906), p. 211; D. L. Thomas, "On Infant Mortality," *Public Health,* September 1899, p. 813; and test. Dr. Hawkes, PP 1904, vol. 32, Q. 13001. See also Todd L. Savitt, "Smothering and Overlaying of Virginia Slave Children: A Suggested Explanation," *Bulletin of the History of Medicine* 49 (Fall 1975): 400–404.

67. W. H. Willcox, "Infantile Mortality from 'Overlaying'," *BMJ*, September 24, 1904, p. 754. The modern overheating theory is presented in *BMJ*, July 14, 1990, p. 85. Another modern study argues that some deaths are indeed caused by smothering (by bedding, objects in cribs, and the like), whereas others are due to hyperthermia or "shaken baby syndrome." See Millard Bass, et al., "Death-Scene Investigation in Sudden Infant Death," *New England Journal of Medicine,* July 10, 1986, pp. 100–105.

68. Grant, *Farthing Bundles,* p. 104; Mary A. Ward, *Play-Time of the Poor* (London: Smith, Elder, 1906), p. 5; Marie Hilton, *The Fourth Year of the Crèche, February 1874 to February 1875* (London: Morgan & Scott, n.d.), p. 11. See Wordsworth's "We Are Seven," the poet's poignant interview with a little farm girl who continues to count her dead sister and brother among her siblings, in *Norton Anthology of English Literature,* 5th ed. (2 vols) (New York: Norton, 1986), vol. 2, pp. 147–48. Eileen Gillooly (personal conversation, June 1992) sees Wordsworth as offering two kinds of logic in this poem: the patriarchal voice repeating that the children are dead and the voice of the mother (through her little daughter) for whom the children will always have life. For another example of maternal logic, see Elizabeth Gaskell's remark—through a character in *Cranford*—that she (who had lost a child herself) could always recognize the "wild" eyes of "mothers of dead children" (*Cranford* [Harmondsworth: Penguin Books, 1976], p. 160). Also, on the deaths of upper-class children, see M. Jeanne Peterson, *Family, Love, and Work in the Lives of Victorian Gentlewomen* (Bloomington: Indiana University Press, 1989), pp. 108–15.

69. Thomas, "On Infant Mortality," p. 813; Stanley B. Atkinson, "The Care of Children Neglected by Drunken Parents," *National Conference on Infantile Mortality, Report of the Proceedings* (London: P. S. King, 1908), p. 153.

70. *Missing Link,* March 1878, pp. 77–78; Charles Morley, *Studies in Board Schools* (London: Smith, Elder, 1897), p. 19; Grant, *Farthing Bundles,* pp. 100, 104.

71. A number of historians have taken this position describing preindustrial Europeans. See Elisabeth Badinter, *Mother Love: Myth and Reality* (New York: Macmillan, 1981), pp. 60–64; Lawrence Stone, *The Family, Sex and Marriage in England 1500–1800* (New York: Harper & Row, 1977), p. 70; and Edward Shorter, *A History of Women's Bodies* (New York: Basic Books, 1982). Note that most of the cited examples of maternal indifference to a "child's death" (all three of Mrs. Thrale's children discussed in Stone, *The Family*, p. 70) are of newborns or are the deaths of babies who had always been sickly. As Angus McLaren has pointed out, the notion that high infant or child mortality rates meant that parents felt them less was always shaky and is becoming more so as new historical work accumulates. See McLaren, *Reproductive Rituals*, p. 10.

72. Doris M. Bailey, *Children of the Green* (London: Stepney Books, 1981), p. 69.

73. Southgate, *The Way It Was*, pp. 70–71.

74. Ranyard, *Nurses for the Needy*, p. 22; *Missing Link*, February 1883, p. 39; Mrs. Layton, "Memories of Seventy Years," in Margaret Llewelyn Davies, ed., *Life as We Have Known It by Co-operative Working Women* (1931), reprint ed. (New York: Norton, 1975), pp. 37, 48; Bailey, *Children of the Green*, p. 71; oral histories collected by Mary Chamberlain, also cited in earlier chapters.

75. David Vincent, *Bread, Knowledge and Freedom: A Study of Nineteenth-Century Working Class Autobiography* (London: Methuen, 1981), p. 58; MNNA, *Annual Reports*, 1878, p. 20; *Biblewomen and Nurses*, September 1897, p. 177.

76. GLI Medical Officers' Case Books, January–March 1884, no. 17; January–April 1888, no. 87; Jerry White, *The Worst Street in North London: Campbell Bunk, Islington, Between the Wars* (London: Routledge & Kegan Paul, 1986), p. 149.

77. The common mothers' phrase is noted in Pember Reeves, *Round About a Pound*, p. 177. The statements by grieving mothers are quoted from *Round About a Pound a Week*, p. 91; *Missing Link*, April 1883, p. 110; and MNNA, *Annual Reports*, 1883, p. 12. In Dye and Smith's view ("Mother Love and Infant Death"), the belief that the child's well-being depended almost entirely on the quality of the mother's care and on her compliance with medical advice dated from sometime in the middle of the nineteenth century. The women described in my later study did not seem to accept this view, although it was one of the aims of the Infant Welfare movement to disseminate this way of thinking.

78. Family Life Archive, no. 261, p. 24. There is a reference to "walking funerals" in *Talks About Old London*, p. 12 (a collection of articles based on interviews with old workhouse inmates on their childhood, serialized in the *Evening News* between 1908 and 1910). The first fifty-eight are in the Bishopsgate Library. On funerals for adults and children, see Paul Johnson, *Saving and Spending: The Working-Class Economy in Britain 1870–1939* (Oxford: Clarendon Press, 1985), esp. pp. 12, 42, 45–56.

79. Pember Reeves, *Round About a Pound*, pp. 70–71.

80. Raphael Samuel, *East End Underworld: Chapters in the Life of Arthur Harding* (London: Routledge & Kegan Paul, 1981), p. 59; Southgate, *The Way It Was*, p. 74; Family Life Archive, no. 261, p. 24 (Mrs. C. was born in 1893); Grant, *Farthing Bundles*, p. 106. This quotation may well be from the 1920s, as the funeral prices seem very high for the prewar period.

81. Jasper, *Hoxton Childhood*, pp. 14, 49.

82. Steel, *Ditcher's Row*, p. 7; Roberts, *Ups and Downs of Florrie Roberts*, p. 10; Bailey, *Children of the Green*, pp. 69–70. See Mary O'Brien's speculations on the

psychic meaning of fatherhood in her *The Politics of Reproduction* (London: Routledge & Kegan Paul, 1981), pp. 8–15; and the references in my Introduction, n. 2.

CHAPTER 7

1. For more discussion of this issue, see especially Chapter 2. Also see Elizabeth A. M. Roberts, "Women's Strategies, 1890–1940," in Jane Lewis, ed., *Labour and Love: Women's Experience of Home and Family 1850–1940* (Oxford, Basil Blackwell, 1986).

2. The term *maternalism* is used by Deborah Dwork to characterize the contemporary position that the key to infant health lay with the mother's child care behavior. See her *War Is Good for Babies and Other Young Children: A History of the Infant and Child Welfare Movement in England 1898–1918* (London: Tavistock, 1987), esp. pp. 226–28.

3. Susan Pedersen, "The Failure of Feminism in the Making of the British Welfare State," *Radical History Review* 43 (Winter 1989): 86–110; Sonya Michel and Seth Koven, "Womanly Duties: Maternalist Politics and the Origins of Welfare States in France, Germany, Great Britain, and the United States, 1880–1920," *American Historical Review* 95 (October 1990): 1076–1108; Dwork, *War Is Good for Babies;* Jane Lewis, *The Politics of Motherhood* (London: Croom Helm, 1980); Bentley B. Gilbert, *The Evolution of National Insurance in Britain: The Origins of the Welfare State* (London: Michael Joseph, 1966); Nikolas Rose, *The Psychological Complex: Psychology, Politics and Society in England 1869–1939* (London: Routledge & Kegan Paul, 1985); Carol Dyhouse, "Working-Class Mothers and Infant Mortality in England, 1895–1914," *Journal of Social History* 12 (1978): 248–67; Anna Davin, "Imperialism and Motherhood," *History Workshop* 5 (Spring 1978): 6–66; Dorothy Porter, " 'Enemies of the Race': Biologism, Environmentalism, and Public Health in Edwardian England," *Victorian Studies* 34 (Winter 1991): 159–78; and Susan Turnball Shoemaker, *"To Enlighten, Not to Frighten": A Comparative Study of the Infant Welfare Movement in Liverpool and Philadelphia, 1890–1918* (Westport, CT: Garland, 1992). The Infant Welfare movement was a truly international one. For a few studies of other countries, see Rima Apple, *Mothers and Medicine: A Social History of Infant Feeding, 1890–1950* (Madison: University of Wisconsin Press, 1987); Richard A. Meckel, *Save the Babies: American Public Health Reform and the Prevention of Infant Mortality, 1850–1929* (Baltimore: Johns Hopkins University Press, 1990); Ann Taylor Allen, *Feminism and Motherhood in Germany, 1800–1914* (New Brunswick, NJ: Rutgers University Press, 1991); and Valerie Fildes, Lara Marks, and Hilary Marland, eds., *Women and Children First* (New York: Routledge, 1992).

4. Michel Foucault, *Power/Knowledge: Selected Interviews and Other Writings 1972–1977,* ed. Colin Gordon (New York: Pantheon, 1980), chap. 9; Michel Foucault, *Birth of the Clinic: An Archeology of Medical Perception,* tr. A. M. Sheridan Smith (New York: Vintage, 1975); Jacques Donzelot, *The Policing of Families,* tr. Robert Hurley (New York: Pantheon, 1979). For a discussion of Foucault's analysis of the mobilization of "microinstitutions" in enlisting individuals in reformulating themselves, see Mary Rawlinson, "Foucault's Strategy: Knowledge, Power, and the Specificity of Truth," *Journal of Medicine and Philosophy* 12 (1987): 371–95.

5. On the effects in the United States of differences in mothers' household health care practices on infant death rates, see Gretchen Condran and Samuel H. Preston, "Child Mortality Differences, Personal Health Care Practices, and Medical Tech-

nology: The United States, 1900–1930," in Lincoln Chen and Arthur Kleinman, eds., *Health and Social Change in International Perspective* (New York: Oxford University Press, 1992). Conversations with demographer Sheila Johansson of the University of California at Berkeley (July 1989 and November 1991) also convinced me that domestic antisepsis (and, today, a knowledge of home hydration for infants with diarrhea) can decrease infant death rates by "a few [significant] percentage points."

6. See, among many examples of their indignation on mothers' behalf in the pre–World War I years, "Lex v. the Poor" (which was a regular column), *Eye Witness*, September 12, 1912, p. 398.

7. Anna Martin, "The Irresponsibility of the Father, Part II," *The Nineteenth Century and After*, March 1919, p. 558 (one of a three-part series of articles by the same title, December 1918, March 1919, and May 1919).

8. Anna Martin, "The Mother and Social Reform, Part II," *The Nineteenth Century and After* (June 1913): 1239–40; Anna Martin, "The Irresponsibility of the Father, Part III," *The Nineteenth Century and After* (May 1919): 960. A similar argument taking the woman's side against the new welfare policies and agencies is in Anna Martin's *The Married Working Woman: A Study* (London: NUWSS, 1911), pp. 38–44. As noted in the previous chapter, the significance of cultural ecologies (support for mothers from their husbands and communities, residence with grandparents, mothers' hours out of the home, and, of course, income levels) is graphically presented in David L. Ransel, "Infant-Care Cultures in the Russian Empire," in Barbara Clements, Barbara Engel, and Christine Worobec, eds., *Russia's Women: Accommodation, Resistance, Transformation* (Berkeley and Los Angeles: University of California Press, 1991). On the state, see the Foucaultian but concrete and practical essay by Rosemary Pringle and Sophie Watson, " 'Women's Interests' and the Post-Structuralist State," in Michèle Barrett and Anne Phillips, eds., *Destabilizing Theory: Contemporary Feminist Debates* (Stanford, CA: Stanford University Press, 1992).

9. These figures are from the Report of the MOH of the County (of London) in LCC, *Annual Reports*, 1910, vol. 3, p. 12. On the fertility decline in inner London, see Chapter 4. More generally in Britain, see Diana Gittins, *Fair Sex: Family Size and Structure 1900–1939* (London: Hutchinson, 1982).

10. The origin of the cultural-diffusion theory in regard to fertility questions lies with J. A. Banks, *Prosperity and Parenthood: A Study of Family Planning Among the Victorian Middle Classes* (London: Routledge & Kegan Paul, 1954). My position looking at coercion as well as diffusion in the shaping of popular practices appears in several of the essays in Nicholas Abercrombie et al., eds., *The Dominant Ideology Thesis* (London: Allen & Unwin, 1980).

11. (Emphasis in the original) Martin, "Irresponsibility of the Father, Part III," pp. 960–61.

12. See Bruce Haley, *The Healthy Body and Victorian Culture* (Cambridge, MA: Harvard University Press, 1978). Haley's is a discussion of Victorian rather than Edwardian culture, but its comments on the use of health and illness as metaphors are pertinent to this period, too.

13. Foucault, *Power/Knowledge*, chap. 9; Donzelot, *Policing of Families*, chap. 3; Marion Kozak, "Health Care in East London in the 1920s and 1930s" (Unpublished monograph, London, 1980), kindly lent to me by the author.

14. See Roisin Pill and Nigel C. H. Stott, "Concepts of Illness Causation and Responsibility: Some Preliminary Data from a Sample of Working Class Mothers," *Social Science and Medicine* 16 (1982): 43.

15. This is the argument made by Jane Lewis in *The Politics of Motherhood* (Lon-

don: Croom Helm, 1980). See also Ann Oakley, "Women and Health Policy," in Jane Lewis, ed., *Women's Welfare, Women's Rights* (London: Croom Helm, 1983), p. 116.

16. On public health research in the nineteenth century, see John M. Eyler, "Mortality Statistics and Victorian Health Policy: Program and Criticism," *Bulletin of the History of Medicine* 50 (Fall 1976): 335–55; and M. J. Cullen, *The Statistical Movement in Early Victorian Britain: The Foundations of Empirical Social Research* (New York: Barnes & Noble, 1975). Arthur Newsholme also made a point of demonstrating the nineteenth century's attention to infant morality and diarrhea, in his *Fifty Years in Public Health* (London: Allen & Unwin, 1935), 138–39, 322–23, 336–37, 349. On the physical deterioration scare, see Bentley B. Gilbert, "Health and Politics: The British Physical Deterioration Report of 1904," *Bulletin of the History of Medicine* 39 (March–April 1965): 143–53; and Gilbert, *Evolution of National Insurance.*

17. ("Threadbare") W. F. Dearden, speech at a Manchester meeting of the Northwestern Branch of the Society of Medical Officers of Health, *Public Health* 18 (January 1905): 237. A good summary of the movement's activity by one of its leaders is that by G. F. McCleary, *The Early History of the Infant Welfare Movement* (London: H. K. Lewis, 1933); also excellent is Dwork, *War Is Good for Babies,* pt. II.

18. Pat Thane, *The Foundations of the Welfare State* (London: Longman Group, 1982), p. 76. In 1915, all stillbirths after twenty-eight weeks of pregnancy also had to be registered with local medical authorities.

19. Pat Thane, "Women and the Poor Law," *History Workshop* 6 (Autumn 1978): 47; Gilbert, *Evolution of National Insurance,* and "Health and Politics." See the comment on the Children Act in Stephen Reynolds, Bob Woolley, and Tom Woolley, *Seems So! A Working-Class View of Politics* (London: Macmillan, 1911), p. 39.

20. This point was made by Anna Martin during the war and by her contemporary, William B. Brend, in "Infant Mortality," *The Nineteenth Century and After* (March 1916): 606–26. The distortions of the "maternal failure" position and their political uses are stressed by Davin in "Imperialism and Motherhood" and by Lewis in *The Politics of Motherhood.* Their position is disputed (somewhat halfheartedly, I thought) by Dwork, in *War Is Good for Babies,* chap. 5.

21. See Catherine Hakim, "Census Reports as Documentary Evidence: The Census Commentaries 1801–1951," *Sociological Review* 28 (1980): 551–80; Edward Higgs, "Women, Occupations and Work in the Nineteenth Century Censuses," *History Workshop* 23 (Spring 1987): 59–80.

22. This French–English comparison was made by Jane Jensen in "Gender and Reproduction: Or, Babies and the State," *Studies in Political Economy* 20 (Summer 1986): 9–46; see also Mary Lynn McDougall, "Protecting Infants: The French Campaign for Maternity Leaves, 1890's–1913," *French Historical Studies* 13 (1983): 79–105; Karen Offen, "Depopulation, Nationalism, and Feminism in Fin-de-Siecle France," *American Historical Review* 89 (June 1984): 648–76; and Angus McLaren, *Sexuality and Social Order: The Debate over the Fertility of Women and Workers in France, 1770–1920* (New York: Holmes & Meier, 1983).

23. Dora Bunting, Annie Barnes, and Blanche Gardiner, *A School for Mothers* (London: Horace Marshall, 1907), p. 71. For Donzelot, what distinguished modern philanthropy from medieval and early-modern charity were in fact its medical goals and terms (see *Policing of Families,* chap. 3).

24. Martin, "The Irresponsibility of the Father, Part III," p. 961. The quotation is cited in Porter, "Enemies of the Race," p. 170. Also see Chapter 6, n. 70.

25. Bunting et al., *School for Mothers*, pp. 40–41. On the St. Pancras School for Mothers, see Dora E. Lidgett Bunting, "Schools for Mothers," in Theophilus N. Kelynack, ed., *Infancy* (London: Robert Culley, 1910); "A Comprehensive School of Mothercraft and Baby Training," in St. Pancras MOH, *Annual Reports*, 1910; McCleary, *Early History*, chap. 10; S. B. A., "A School for Mothers," *Toynbee Record*, January 1908. See the excellent discussion of this clinic in Anna Davin's "Imperialism and Motherhood," pp. 38–43.

26. Bunting et al., *School for Mothers*, p. 51 (emphasis in the original). The "responsibility" of one or the other parent was a recurring theme at the second National Conference on Infantile Mortality in London in 1908. See especially eugenicist Alice Ravenhill's "The Education of Girls and Women in the Functions and Duties of Womanhood," and the comments of Mrs. Greenwood from the Women Sanitary Inspectors' Association, who discussed (p. 166) the responsibilities of fathers, in *Report of the Proceedings of the National Conference on Infantile Mortality* (London: P. S. King, 1908).

27. On class differences in perceptions of illness and the responsibility for it, see Claudine Herzlich and Janine Pierret, *Illness and Self in Society*, tr. Elborg Forster (Baltimore: Johns Hopkins University Press, 1987), pp. 202 ff. The investigations of impure milk, flies, and so forth are described in Dwork, *War Is Good for Babies*, esp. chaps. 2 and 3. See also Chapter 6, "Matters of Life and Death." For a defense of the working-class mother against the position that "the death of every infant might, with a reasonable amount of maternal care, have been prevented," see Margaret Loane, *From Their Point of View* (London: Arnold, 1908), p. 125.

28. Some professionals also rejected the individual responsibility hypothesis. See, for example, the comments of a Shoreditch health visitor assessing maternal education as the solution to the high infant mortality rates: "I have found that the education of the mother, although an important factor, is not in itself an all-sufficient remedy for the evils which militate against infant life in this borough." She wrote about bad plumbing, not enough cash coming from fathers, and chronic poverty as major problems of her district (quoted in Second Report on Infant and Child Mortality by the Medical Officer of the Local Government Board, PP 1913, vol. 32, p. 71).

29. "Precious," used by Viviana A. Zelizer, *Pricing the Priceless Child* (New York: Basic Books, 1985). My point about the greater "value" of older children to the London mothers is made in Chapters 5 and 6.

30. Haley, *Healthy Body*, esp. chap. 1, pp. 3, 19. For a short overview of the history of medicine in this period, see Charles Singer and E. Ashworth Underwood, *A Short History of Medicine*, rev. ed. (New York: Oxford University Press, 1982).

31. Margaret McMillan, *The Nursery School* (London: Dent, 1919), p. 191; H. C. Barker, "Medical Treatment of London Children," *Toynbee Record* 24 (January 1912): 48. As one physician wrote in *The Sanitary Officer*, "Treatment by X-rays is efficacious in some cases; but as a skilled operator and costly apparatus are required for the successful application of this treatment, it is seldom available" (June 1909, p. 14).

32. Dyhouse, "Working-Class Mothers and Infant Mortality," p. 262; Helen M. Blagg, *Statistical Analysis of Infant Mortality and Its Causes in the United Kingdom* (London: P. S. King, 1910), p. 15.

33. "Obtaining medical care has assumed the value of a moral obligation," as Herzlich and Pierret put it in *Illness and Self*, p. 190. Emilia Kanthack, *The Preservation of Infant Life: A Guide for Health Visitors. Six Lectures to the Voluntary Health*

Visitors in the Borough of St. Pancras (London: H. K. Lewis, 1907), p. 4; S. B. A., "A School for Mothers," p. 54; Janet Lane-Claypon, "The Waste of Infant Life," *The Nineteenth Century and After* 65 (January 1909): 52.

34. Bunting et al., *School for Mothers,* p. 18; Clara Grant, *Farthing Bundles* (London: Fern Street Settlement, 1931), p. 83; George Newman, *A Special Report on an Infants' Milk Depot* (London: Thomas Bean, 1905), pp. 9, 40, 20. On the problem of impure milk, and the efforts to supply safe milk to children, see Dwork, *War Is Good for Babies,* chaps. 3 and 4.

35. Test. Dr. Hawkes, PP 1904, vol. 32, Q. 13017; C. W. Saleeby, "The Future of the Nurse" *Nursing Times,* July 29, 1905, p. 224. See also Anna Martin's compilation of similar statements in "The Irresponsibility of the Father, Part II," p. 561.

36. H. Dendy, "The Children of Working London," in Bernard Bosanquet, ed. *Aspects of the Social Problem* (London: Macmillan, 1895), p. 41; Margaret McMillan, "Nature vs. Nurture," in *The Needs of Little Children: Report of a Conference on the Care of Babies and Young Children* (London: Women's Labour League, 1912), p. 3.

37. Test. Miss Eves of the Maurice Hostel, PP 1904, vol. 32, Qq. 7763–64, 7700; Outdoor Relief in Lambeth, Royal Commission on the Poor Laws and Relief of Distress, PP 1910, vol. 52, app. II; test. Lewis Hawkes, PP 1904, vol. 32, Qq. 12987–99; *The Sanitary Officer,* July 1910, p. 280.

38. City of Westminster Health Society, *Annual Reports,* 1906, p. 9, Westminster City Archives; Maud Pember Reeves, *Round About a Pound a Week* (1913), reprint ed. (London: Virago, 1979), pp. 8, 16; (Florence) Petty et al., *The Pudding Lady: A New Departure in Social Work* (London: Stead's Publishing House, 1910), p. 26.

39. See Standish Meacham, *Toynbee Hall and Social Reform 1880–1914: The Search for Community* (New Haven, CT: Yale University Press, 1987), esp. chap. 4. Also see Bill Jordan, *Freedom and the Welfare State* (New Delhi: Ambika Publications, 1977), chap. 7.

40. " 'Naughty,' said the doctor; 'wicked,' said the nurse; 'wind' said the lady with the alligator purse" ("Tiny Tim," anonymous piece of children's doggerel).

41. D. M. Connan, *A History of the Public Health Department in Bermondsey* (London: n.p., 1935).

42. National League for Physical Education and Improvement, *Annual Reports,* 1908, p. 20.

43. St. Pancras MOH, *Annual Reports,* 1908, pp. 28–29; *National Conference on Infantile Mortality,* 1908, p. 69; Report of the London MOH, 1910, pp. 13–14. A reference to Jay Winter's skepticism about the availability of services for women and children in London during World War I is due here, however. See J. M. Winter, *The Great War and the British People* (London: Macmillan, 1985), pp. 189–203.

44. Kensington MOH, *Annual Reports,* 1915, p. 8; Janet Campbell and F. W. Hope, *Report on the Physical Welfare of Mothers and Children: England and Wales* (2 vols.) (Liverpool: Carnegie U.K. Trust, 1917), vol. 2, pp. 87, 90.

45. Westminster Health Society, *Annual Reports,* 1914; Report of the London MOH, 1910, p. 14; Ann Oakley, *The Captured Womb: A History of the Medical Care of Pregnant Women* (Oxford: Basil Blackwell, 1984).

46. Robert W. J. Dingwall, "Collectivism, Regionalism and Feminism: Health Visiting and British Social Policy 1850–1975," *Journal of Social Policy* 6 (1977): 302; Westminster Health Society, *Annual Reports,* 1912; Loane, *From Their Point of View,* p. 128.

47. Beatrice M. Langton, "Early Health Visiting," *Nursing Times,* October 4, 1963, pp. 1247–48; Dingwall, "Collectivism, Regionalism and Feminism." On the

construction of health visiting as a female profession, and the tendency in many authorities for better-paid sanitary inspectors to be men, see Celia Davies, "The Health Visitor as Mother's Friend: A Woman's Place in Public Health, 1900–1914," *Social History of Medicine* 1 (April 1988): 39–60.

48. Breast feeding was normally promoted on sanitary and nutritional grounds, though Kanthack and other writers of her era also made passing references to "the ethical point of view that a mother should suckle her child" and the "close companionship" nursing created between mother and baby. Kanthack, *Preservation of Infant Life*, p. 37; see also F. Cavanagh, "The Responsibility of a Maternity Nurse," *Nursing Times*, March 10, 1906, p. 196.

49. Kanthack, *Preservation of Infant Life*, pp. 26, 51, 81, 75, 58, 66.

50. Kensington MOH, *Annual Reports*, 1905, p. 59. This visitor's report, quoted by Orme Dudfield, the borough medical officer, stressed poverty as the reason that so many women in her district could not breast feed. "The malnutrition of the nursing mother [is] the principal cause of the malnutrition of the infant," she wrote. She vividly described the stage when the lack of money for milk meant that mothers sometimes fed even tiny babies bread, the only food in the house.

51. E. H. Cunliffe, "Health Visitors: A Nurse's View," *Women's Dreadnought*, September 22, 1917, p. 857.

52. Thane, *Foundations of the Welfare State*, p. 77; Newsholme, *Fifty Years in Public Health*, pp. 393–96, Bentley B. Gilbert, "The British Physical Deterioration Report of 1904," p. 149; also see Jeanne L. Brand, *Doctors and the State: The British Medical Profession and Government Action in Public Health, 1870–1912* (Baltimore: Johns Hopkins University Press, 1965), pp. 186–88. A 1906 bill had been defeated, partly because of hostile lobbying by the BMA. In the following year, after the Second International Congress on School Hygiene revealed how far Britain was lagging behind in this area, the school medical inspections were legislated, however.

53. J. D. Hirst, "A Failure 'Without Parallel': The School Medical Service and the London County Council 1907–1912," *Medical History* 25 (1981): 281–300, esp. p. 297; Report of the Medical Officer (Education), in LCC, *Annual Reports*, 1910, vol. 3, p. 149; Hirst, "School Medical Service," p. 297. A good sense of the routine activities of school medical personnel may be found in Duncan Forbes, "The School Nurse," in Theophilus N. Kelynack, ed., *Medical Examination of Schools and Scholars* (London: P. S. King, 1910). On school health and medical inspection more generally, see Smith, *People's Health*, pp. 178–88.

54. See Anna Davin, *Little Women: Girlhood in Nineteenth-Century London* (London: Routledge & Kegan Paul, 1994), chap. 10, on schools and health before 1904. In the late 1890s, a Queen's Nurse was paying rotating visits to a half-dozen poor schools in the Clare Market neighborhood. In 1898 a London School Nurses Association, organized by school board member (and trained nurse) Honnor Morten, had sent Rose Petty, a highly qualified nurse, to work at schools in Hoxton, where Petty lived as a member of the Hoxton Settlement. The first London school medical officer was appointed in 1890. Formal eye testing had begun in the London schools in 1899. See *Nursing Notes*, July 1898, p. 95, and October 1898, p. 14; Rose Petty, "School Nursing," *Nursing Times*, June 3, 1905, p. 80; and Thane, *Foundations of the Welfare State*, p. 76.

55. See, for example, *The Sanitary Officer*, March, 1911, p. 439.

56. Mothers who did attend the inspections, Marion Phillips found, might have waited as long as three hours for the minute-long sessions. See *The School Doctor and the Home: Results of an Inquiry into Medical Inspection and Treatment of School Chil-*

dren (London: Women's Labour League, 1910), p. 8; Report of the Medical Officer (Education), 1910, p. 137; Grant, *Farthing Bundles,* p. 76.

57. Dr. Hawkes, a member of the COS, longtime resident of Finsbury and general practitioner there, quoted many times in this book, testified at length before the 1903–1904 Inter-Departmental Committee on Physical Deterioration. His report to the London MOH is in the 1910 Report of the Medical Officer, p. 137. Also see Popham Road School Care Committee, minutes, 1909–1911, November 5, 1909, GLRO.

58. "The Health of the Children," *Toynbee Record* 21 (January 1909): 60–63; Margaret McMillan, *The School Clinic Today: Health Centres and What They Mean to the People* (London: ILP, c. 1909); Phillips, *School Doctor;* "Care Committees: Methods of Work," *The School Child* 2 (December 1912): 1; "Care Committees," *The School Child* 3 (March 1913): 1.

59. Phillips, *School Doctor,* p. 19. The BMA actually did agitate for a few years through about 1910 for the formation of a regular school medical service. See Brand, *Doctors and the State,* p. 188.

60. Hirst, "School Medical Service," pp. 291–92; Phillips, *School Doctor;* C. W. W., "The Treatment of School Children at Hospitals," *The School Child* 3 (February 1913): 12. On the limited number of hospital beds in East London, whose population in 1900 was about 900,000, see Smith, *People's Health,* p. 251; on the long waits, squalid hospital waiting rooms, and poor treatment available to hospital outpatients, see pp. 256–57. See also Chapter 6, "Medicine and Mothers."

61. Peter Gordon, *The Victorian School Manager: A Study in the Management of Education 1800–1902* (London: Woburn Press, 1974), pp. 152–66; Thomas Alfred Spalding, *The World of the London School Board* (London: P. S. King, 1900), p. 112.

62. See the discussions among school managers in the *Toynbee Record* during these years. A number of the Toynbee Hall residents were school managers, and regular conferences were convened there. In 1910, a more specialized journal, *The School Child,* was founded to cater to the thousands of school care workers nationwide. On the numbers of members, see James Kerr, ed., *The Care of the School Child: Lectures Delivered Under the Auspices of the National League for Physical Education and Improvement May to July 1916* (London: National League, 1916), p. 4; Anne Summers, "A Home from Home: Women's Philanthropic Work in the Nineteenth Century," in Sandra Burman, ed., *Fit Work for Women* (London: Croom Helm, 1979), p. 34.

63. Bay Street School Care Committee, minutes, March 31, 1908; on children's meals in Poplar, see LCC *Minutes of Proceedings,* July 16, 1912, p. 267, July 2, 1912, p. 90, and July 23, 1912, p. 362, GLRO.

64. J. T. Mustard, "Investigation and Co-ordination," *The School Child* 2 (June 1912): 9. See also the reports in *The School Child* 1 (July 1910): 15; and *The School Child* 3 (March 1913): 4.

65. St. Matthews (N.) School, Arlington Road, N.W., Care Committee, minutes, January 28, 1916, and March 3, 1916; Curtain Road School Care Committee, Shoreditch, minutes, May 6, 1910. As was customary, only one person, a mother, came, and she agreed to resume her daughter's eye treatments.

66. Popham Road Care Committee, minutes, April 8, 1910. The LCC refused the request. The incident is described later in this chapter.

67. McMillan, *The Nursery School,* p. 314.

68. Letter to the Editor, *The School Child* 1 (February 1910): 16. Drake was the secretary of the Charing Cross Road School Care Committee; W. M. Langdon,

"The Medical Treatment of L.C.C. School Children," *Toynbee Record* 30 (October 1912): 3–7; "Treatment of School Children at Hospitals"; Margaret Frere, "The Charitable Work of a Local Manager in a Board School," *Charity Organisation Review,* new ser., 75 (March 1903): 124.

69. Popham Road Care Committee, minutes, April 22, 1910, and June 16, 1911.

70. Emphasis is Martin's. Anna Martin, "Mother and Social Reform, Part II," p. 1242; Martin, "The Irresponsibility of the Father, Part I," *The Nineteenth Century and After,* December 1918, pp. 1100–1.

71. St. Matthews (N.) School Care Committee, minutes, January 28, 1916; Popham Road Care Committee, April 22, 1911; see also Curtain Road Care Committee, May 6, 1910.

72. On lice treatment today, see Mildred Blaxter and Elizabeth Paterson, *Mothers and Daughters: A Three-Generational Study of Health Attitudes and Behaviour* (London: Heinemann, 1982), p. 62.

73. "School Nursing in London," *The Sanitary Officer,* July, 1909, p. 34.

74. Central Consultative Committee of Head Masters and Head Mistresses, *Minutes of Miscellaneous Resolutions Subcommittee* (November 1909–June 1921), vol. 2, pp. 14, 44, 77, 88, 96, GLRO. My warm thanks to Dina Copelman for sharing with me her research notes on these minutes.

75. Wood Close School Care Committee, minutes, 1909–1910. The grisly atmosphere of the tiled cleansing stations, with their huge steam disinfectors for clothing, showers (which apparently frightened the children), and simultaneous crews visiting the children's homes to disinfect bedding and clothing certainly must have contributed to the popular resistance to this form of delousing, which was reserved mostly for children with body (as opposed to head) lice or those with very heavy infestations.

76. Janet E. Lane-Claypon, *The Child Welfare Movement* (London: G. Bell, 1920), p. 6, n. 1.

77. "66 Records of Newborn Babies from the St. Marylebone Health Society, sent by Dr. Flora Murray and Dr. Christine Murrell," 1909, Karl Pearson Papers, item 297, University College, London (my thanks to Jane Lewis for suggesting this source). See Lewis, *Politics of Motherhood,* p. 98, on the occupations of clinic users. Of those fifty-two patient records containing sufficient information to determine whether the child was the first or a later one, twenty-two women were bringing a first or first-surviving child, and thirty were bringing later children.

First mothers averaged 10.4 visits, with a median of 9.5; nonfirst mothers averaged 6.2 visits, with a median of 4.

78. The Finsbury MOH, Dr. A. E. Thomas, reported during World War I that it was women from "the better class poor, who are already solicitous for the welfare of their babies" who used the services of infant welfare centers and clinics. See Campbell and Hope, *The Physical Welfare of Mothers and Children,* vol. 1, p. 275. Of fifty-three Bell Street fathers whose jobs were listed in the records, thirteen were laborers of various kinds, and eleven were out of work or in very slack work.

79. On the clientele of the St. Pancras clinic, probably the best information, though it is just a hint, is in the case records of Petty et al., *Pudding Lady.*

80. Bunting et al., *School for Mothers,* p. 41. On knowledge about child development, see the contributions to Kelynack, ed., *Infancy,* esp. John Benjamin Hellier, "Infant Development," and William J. Thompson, "The Hygiene of Infancy."

81. See the advice of Emilia Kanthack to health visitors in *Preservation of Infant Life,* p. 51.

82. James Stewart Fowler, "The Feeding of Infants," pp. 39–40; Thompson, "Hygiene of Infancy," p. 30; and Hellier, "Infant Development," all in Kelynack, ed., *Infancy;* also Kanthack, *Preservation of Infant Life,* p. 19.

83. "Comprehensive School of Mothercraft," in St. Pancras MOH, *Annual Report,* 1910, p. 30.

84. Blaxter and Paterson, *Mothers and Daughters,* pp. 97, 136. "A Day in the Life of a [London] Woman Sanitary Inspector," *The Sanitary Officer,* June 1909, pp. 4–5, gives two examples: a mother living in LCC buildings afraid to tell the doctor that her child would not drink the milk he had prescribed for her convalescence from pneumonia, and another woman who did not take her very sick baby to the hospital for fear the staff would disapprove of her: "They don't like you to take a baby to the hospital unless it is really ill."

85. "66 Records of Newborn Babies from the St. Marylebone Health Society."

86. Family Life Archive, no. 215, p. 63; Conner is a pseudonym. Taped interviews by Jane Lewis with a group of women, who had raised young children in the 1920s and 1930s in London and elsewhere. My thanks to Jane Lewis for lending me these tapes.

87. See Hilary Graham, "Caring: A Labour of Love," in Janet Finch and Dulcie Groves, eds., *A Labour of Love: Women, Work and Caring* (London: Routledge & Kegan Paul, 1983); and especially Hilary Graham, "Providers, Negotiators, and Mediators: Women as the Hidden Carers," in her *Women, Health and Healing: Toward a New Perspective* (New York: Tavistock/Methuen, 1985). The classic statement of the issue in medical sociology is by Elliot Friedson, *Patients' View of Medical Practice* (New York: Russell Sage Foundation, 1961); also Elliot Friedson, "Client Control and Medical Practice," *American Journal of Sociology* 65 (1969): 374–82.

88. (Royden quotation) Pedersen, "Failure of Feminism," p. 90; Dwork, *War Is Good for Babies,* p. 211; Winter, *Great War,* pp. 191–93; Lewis, *Politics of Motherhood,* p. 34.

89. Dwork, *War Is Good for Babies,* p. 217; Winter, *Great War,* chaps. 6 and 7 and pp. 195–97.

90. Pedersen, "Failure of Feminism," p. 88; Winter, *Great War,* pp. 240–41; Susan Pedersen, "Gender, Welfare, and Citizenship in Britain During the Great War," *American Historical Review* 95 (October 1990): 991–1005 (on the politics and administration of the grants, in detail); and for many stories of class prejudice, inefficiency, and moralizing in their administration, see Sylvia Pankhurst, *The Home Front: A Mirror to Life in England During the World War* (London: Hutchinson, 1932).

CONCLUSION

1. Samuel Hynes, *The Edwardian Turn of Mind* (Princeton, NJ: Princeton University Press, 1968), pp. 113, 117; Susan Pedersen, "The Failure of Feminism in the Making of the British Welfare State," *Radical History Review* 43 (1989): 88.

2. Hilary Land, "Eleanor Rathbone and the Economy of the Family," in Harold L. Smith, ed., *British Feminism in the Twentieth Century* (Amherst: University of Massachusetts Press, 1990), pp. 147–48; Pedersen, "Failure of Feminism," p. 91.

3. The essays collected by Harold Smith on twentieth-century feminism refer to the issue in many different contexts. Mothers' endowment established the terms of feminist discussion in the postwar decade especially. In Smith's *British Feminism,*

see the contributions by Smith himself, Susan Kent, Deborah Gorham, Martin Pugh, Pat Thane, and Hilary Land.

4. Pat Thane, *The Foundations of the Welfare State* (London: Longman Group, 1982), pp. 216–17; Jane Lewis, "Eleanor Rathbone," in Paul Barker, ed., *Founders of the Welfare State* (London: Heinemann, 1984), p. 87. The point that advocacy of better nutrition for children in the 1930s could easily involve censure of the mothers was spotted by contemporary observers. See Elizabeth Wilson, *Women and the Welfare State* (London: Tavistock, 1977), pp. 122–23. Also on feminism between the wars, see Brian Harrison, *Prudent Revolutionaries: Portraits of British Feminists Between the Wars* (Oxford: Oxford University Press, 1987).

5. See Ann Oakley's *Telling the Truth About Jerusalem* (Oxford: Basil Blackwell, 1986), p. 218. Oakley's own work was obviously central to this project. See the references in n. 10 of the Introduction.

6. Two pamphlets tucked away in my library revived the sense of "discovery" of the social value of housework: Mariarosa Dalla Costa and Selma James, *The Power of Women and the Subversion of the Community* (London: Falling Wall Press, 1972); and Power of Women Collective, ed., *All Work and No Pay: Women, Housework and the Wages Due* (London: Falling Wall Press, 1975).

Selected Bibliography

ARCHIVES

Greater London Record Office

General Lying-In Hospital (GLI), York Road, Waterloo. Used with permission of R. Murray, Unit Administrator, Acute Services, St. Thomas's Hospital. (When I used these records in 1984–1985 they were slated for recataloging.)

Medical Officers' Case Books, new ser., January–September 1881; December 1881–April 1882; January–March 1884; January–April 1886; January–April 1888 (cataloged as HI/GLI/date).

Registers of Outpatients July 1877–November 1882 (HI/GLI/B22/vol. 1).

Midwives' Out Door Cases 1886–1888 (HI/GLI/B23/1).

Matron's Weekly Reports, April 1881–April 1912 (HI/GLI/A28/1).

City of London Maternity Hospital. Used with permission of L. V. Wood, Acute Unit Administrator, Whittington Hospital.

District Case Books, October 1913–September 1916 (HiO/CLM/B6/no. 1).

Guy's Lying-In Charity (Outpatient Maternity Record). Used with permission of Mr. Andrew Reed, Clinical Services Administrator, Guy's Hospital (HO/GY/ B22/5 (1892–1896).

School Care Committee Minutes
Bay Street, Central Hackney, 1907–1911 (EO/WEL/2/1).

Curtain Road, Shoreditch, 1909–1911 (EO/WEL/2/15).

Popham Road, Islington, 1909–1911 (EO/WEL/2/6).

St. Matthews N. School, West St. Pancras, 1916 (EO/WEL/2/17).

Wood Close, Bethnal Green, 1909–1910 (EO/WEL/2/10).

School Board for London

> Report of the Special Sub-Committee of the General Purposes Committee on Underfed Children, London School Board, 1898–1899 (SBL/1469).

Poor-Law Records

> Settlement Examinations, Rough, Bethnal Green (Be B.G. 267/41; December 1889–July 1890).

> Enquiry by General Relieving Officer, St. Olave's Union (Bermondsey) (BBG 539/1; February 1896). Households applying to take custody of children in the workhouse schools.

Marriage Registers

> St. Peters, Liverpool St., Walworth, P92/PETI/42 and 48, selected years, 1887–1904.

> St. Matthews, Bethnal Green, P72/MIW/73–74 and 78, selected years, 1879–1912.

Middlesex County Police Court Depositions, 1855–1889

> These were stored in tied bundles by court and date when I used them at the old Middlesex Record Office in 1979. They have since been recataloged. Cases from 1873 and 1874, Thames and Worship Street Courts, are cited, though I also read bundles from Worship Street 1869, 1879, 1884, and 1889 as well as cases from Thames, Clerkenwell, and Dalston.

Lambeth Palace: Fulham Papers

London Visitations (questionnaires to clergymen on church affairs), 1883: St. Mary's Spital Square; St. John's Cubitt Town; All Saints Stoke Newington; St. James the Great Bethnal Green.

London School of Economics

Passfield Papers

> Beatrice Potter and Ella Pycroft, "Received of the Inhabitants [of the Katharine Buildings] During the Years 1885–1900. Begun by Mrs. Sidney Webb," Coll. Misc. 43, R. (S.R.) 1017.

> Frank Galton, "Autobiography," typescript, 1939–1944, Coll. Misc. 314.

Charles Booth Manuscripts

> Series A (East London trades, interviews with employers, clergy, and social workers)

> Series B (interviews with school board visitors; tours of various police subdivisions by local members of the force).

Labour Party Library, London

Women's Labour League Baby Clinic File, A12 BC: *Annual Reports* of the Baby Clinic; letters and pamphlets.

Selected Bibliography

Tower Hamlets Health District Archives, London

Mr. Jonathan Pepplar, archivist

E. J. Morris, "Report of a Visit to the District Maternity Charity with Miss Nicholls, District Midwife." Typescript, 1922.

Trades Union Congress (TUC) Archives

Gertrude Tuckwell Collection, of clipping, letters, and pamphlets.

Royal Free Hospital Archive

Dr. Gilchrest, archivist

Almoners' Reports to the Hospital Board, 1893–1910.

Doctors' Case Notes (Mrs. Willey), 1911–1913.

Obstetrical (outpatient) Case Books, 1914–1917.

Guildhall Manuscript Library

Metropolitan and National Nursing Association for Providing Trained Nurses for the Sick Poor (MNNA), Inspector's Reports, 1876–1915.

Bodleian Library, Oxford, Manuscripts

Addison Papers, Box 60 (Children and Child Welfare, 1914).

University College Manuscripts Library

Karl Pearson Papers: "66 Records of Newborn Babies from the St. Marylebone Health Society, sent by Dr. Flora Murray and Dr. Christine Murrell," 1909.

Note: All offices are located in London unless another location is given.

COURT TRANSCRIPTS, OLD BAILEY

Central Criminal Court: *The Whole Proceedings, Oyer and Terminer and Goal Delivery for the City of London, and Goal Delivery for the County of Middlesex, and Parts of the Counties of Essex, Kent, and Surrey, Within the Juristiction of the Central Criminal Court,* printed series, housed at the British Library, Harvard Law Library, and a few other locations. Years and volumes used: 1869 (vols. 69–71), 1872–1873 (vols. 75–77), 1874 (vols. 79–81), 1877 (vols. 85–87), 1879 (vols. 89–91), 1882 (vols. 95–96), 1883–1885 (vols. 99–101), 1886–1887 (vols. 105–7), 1888–1889 (vols. 109–11), 1893–1894 (vols. 119–21).

PARLIAMENTARY PAPERS

Census of England and Wales
    1871: PP 1873, vol. 71.

1881: PP 1883, vol. 80.

1911: PP 1911, vol. 13, pt. 2.

Minutes of Evidence, Royal Commission on the Housing of the Working Classes, PP 1884–85, vol. 30 (C. 4402).

Second Report of the Royal Commission Appointed to Enquire into the Working of the Elementary Education Acts, England and Wales, Minutes of Evidence, PP 1887, vol. 29 (C. 5056).

"Tabulation of the Statements Made by Men Living in Certain Selected Districts of London in March 1887," PP 1887, vol. 71 (c. 5228).

Report from the Select Committee of the House of Lords on the Children's Life Insurance Bill Together with the Proceedings of the Committee, Minutes of Evidence and Appendix, PP 1890–1891, vol. 9 (C. 393).

Report from the Select Committee on the Infant Life Protection Bill, PP 1890–1891, vol. 13 (C. 346).

Report from the Select Committee on Midwives' Registration, Proceedings and Minutes of Evidence, PP 1892, vol. 14.

Report from the Select Committee of the House of Lords on the Infant Life Protection Bill (H.L.) and the Safety of Nurse Children Bill (H.L.), PP 1896, vol. 10 (C. 343).

Interdepartmental Committee on Physical Deterioration, List of Witnesses and Minutes of Evidence, PP 1904, vol. 32 (Cd. 2210).

Consumption and Cost of Food in Workmen's Families in Urban Districts in the U.K., PP 1905, vol. 84, pp. 6–8.

Special Report and Report from the Select Committee on Education (Provision of Meals) Bill, 1906, and the Education (Provision of Meals) (Scotland) Bill, 1906, Proceedings, Minutes of Evidence, Appendix (Cd. 288).

Report of the Board of Education Consultative Committee upon the School Attendance of Children Below the Age of Five, PP 1908, vol. 82 (Cd. 4259).

Women and Children in Public Houses. Information Obtained from Certain Police Forces as to the Frequenting of Public Houses by Women and Children, PP 1908, vol. 39 (Cd. 3813).

Departmental Committee Appointed by the Lord President of the Council to Consider the Working of the Midwives Act 1902, Evidence and Index, PP 1909, vol. 33 (Cd. 4822).

Royal Commission on the Poor Laws and Relief of Distress. Report, PP 1909, vol. 37 (Cd. 4499).

Royal Commission on the Poor Laws and Relief of Distress, Report on the Condition of the Children Who Are in Receipt of the Various Forms of Poor Law Relief in England and Wales. App. II: Report of an Inquiry into Cases of Children Whose Parents Were in Receipt of Outdoor Relief in Lambeth, PP 1910, vol. 52 (Cd. 5037).

Report of the Royal Commission on the Poor Laws and the Relief of Distress on an Inquiry in Certain Unions into Cases of Refusal of Out-Relief, PP 1910, vol. 52 (Cd. 5074).

Board of Education, Report on the Working of the Education (Provision of Meals) Act 1906 up to 31 March 1909, PP 1910, vol. 23 (Cd. 5131).

Minutes of Evidence Taken Before the Royal Commission on Divorce and Matrimonial Causes, PP 1912–1913, vol. 18 (Cd. 6478).

Second Report on Infant and Child Mortality by the Medical Officer of the Local Government Board, PP 1913, vol. 32 (Cd. 6909).

Royal Commission on Venereal Disease, Appendix to First Report of the Commissioners, PP 1914, vol. 49 (Cd. 7475).

Report of the Royal Commission on Population, PP 1948–1949, vol. 19 (Cmd. 7695).

AUTOBIOGRAPHIES AND AUTOBIOGRAPHICAL COLLECTIONS

Published Autobiographies and Collections

(Acorn, George), pseud. *One of the Multitude: An Autobiography by a Resident of Bethnal Green*. London: Heinemann, 1911.

Aldred, Guy. *No Traitor's Gait*. Glasgow: Strickland Press, 1955.

Bailey, Doris M. *Children of the Green: A True Story of Childhood in Bethnal Green 1922–1937*. London: Stepney Books, 1981.

Bennett, John. *I Was a Walworth Boy*. London: Peckham Publishing Project, 1980.

Blake, John. *Memories of Old Poplar*. London: Stepney Books, 1977.

Brodetsky, Selig. *Memoirs: From Ghetto to Israel*. London: Weidenfelt & Nicolson, 1960.

Brown, W. J. *So Far*. London: Allen & Unwin, 1943.

Burnett, John, ed. *Useful Toil*. Harmondsworth: Penguin Books, 1974.

Church, Richard. *Over the Bridge: An Essay in Autobiography*. London: Heinemann, 1955.

Cohen, Margaret, Marion Fagan, and Hymie Fagan, eds. *Childhood Memories: Recorded by Some Socialist Men and Women in their Later Years*. Self-published, n.d.

Davies, Margaret Llewelyn. *Life as We Have Known It: By Cooperative Working Women* (1931). Reprint ed. New York: Norton, 1975.

———, ed. *Maternity: Letters from Working Women* (1915). Reprint ed. New York: Norton, 1978.

Eldred, John (b. 1885). *I Love the Brooks*. London: Skeffington, 1955.

Ezard, Edward. *Battersea Boy*. London: William Kember, 1979.

Foakes, Grace. *My Part of the River*. London: Futura Books, 1976.

Hackney People's Autobiography, *"The Island": The Life and Death of an East London Community 1870–1970*. London: Centerprise, 1979.

Hall, Edith. *Canary Girls and Stockpots*. Luton: WEA, 1977.

Hicks, Stephen "Johnny." *Sparring for Luck: Autobiography of the East End Boxer-Poet. A Stepney Life*. London: Tower Hamlets Arts Project, 1982.

Hine, Lilian. "A Poplar Childhood." *East London Record* 3 (1980): 32–43.

Jasper, A. S. *A Hoxton Childhood*. London: Centerprise, 1969.

Linton, Alice. *Not Expecting Miracles*. London: Centerprise, 1982.

Morrison, Herbert. *An Autobiography by Lord Morrison of Lambeth*. London: Odhams, 1960.

Newham History Workshop. *A Marsh and a Gasworks: One Hundred Years of Life in West Ham*. London: Parents' Centre Publications, 1986.

Peckham People's History. *The Times of Our Lives: Growing Up in the Southeast Area 1900–1945*. London: Peckham Publishing Project, 1983.

Perry, George William. *A West Ham Life: An Autobiography*. Newham: Parents' Centre Publications, 1984.

Roberts, Florence. *The Ups and Downs of Florrie Roberts*. London: Peckham Publishing Project, 1980.

Rolph, C. H. *London Particulars*. Oxford: Oxford University Press, 1980.

Samuel, Raphael. *East End Underworld: Chapters in the Life of Arthur Harding*. London: Routledge & Kegan Paul, 1981.

Scannell, Dorothy. *Mother Knew Best: Memoir of a London Girlhood*. New York: Pantheon, 1974.

Southgate, Walter. *That's the Way It Was: A Working-Class Autobiography 1890–1950*. London: New Clarendon Press, 1982.

Steel, Frank. *Ditcher's Row: A Tale of the Older Charity*. London: Sidgwick & Jackson, 1939.

Tottenham History Workshop. *How Things Were: Growing Up in Tottenham 1890–1920*. N.p., n.d.

Welch, Charles. *An Autobiography*. Banstead: Berean Publishing, 1960.

White, Margaret. *And Grandmother's Bed Went Too: Poor but Happy in Somers Town*. Richmond: St. Pancras Housing Association, 1988.

Williamson, Joseph. *Father Joe: The Autobiography of Joseph Williamson of Poplar and Stepley*. London: Hodder & Stoughton, 1963.

Willis, Frederick. *101, Jubilee Road: A Book of London Yesterdays*. London: Phoenix House, 1948.

Woodward, Kathleen. *Jipping Street: Childhood in a London Slum* (1928). Reprint ed. London: Virago, 1983.

Working Lives: Volume One, 1905–45. London: WEA and Centerprise, n.d.

Brunel University Library, Autobiography Collection

Seymour, Arthur (b. 1879). "Childhood Memories." Manuscript.

Robinson, E. (b. 1894). "I Remember." Typescript, 1960–1970.

Rignall, Elizabeth (b. 1894). "All So Long Ago." Typescript.

Ashley, James (b. 1833). Untitled and undated typescript.

Brown, Edward (b. 1880). Untitled and undated manuscript.

Miscellaneous Autobiography and Oral History Archives and Collections

Bark, Jane (b. c. 1900). "Memories." Undated typescript. London, Tower Hamlets Local History Library.

Mrs. Bartholomew. Interviewed by Anna Davin, summer 1973. Transcript in the interviewer's possession; used with her permission and with thanks.

Mrs. Benjamin. Oral history transcript. Hackney People's Autobiography. London, Centerprise.

Jarrett, Rebecca. Typescript autobiography. London, Jarrett File, Salvation Army Heritage Center (courtesy of Pamela Walker).

Lewis, Jane. Audiotaped interviews with a group of old women from London and elsewhere, who had raised young children in the 1920s and 1930s; kindly lent to me by Jane Lewis.

Rushbrook, George (b. 1897). "Memories." Typescript, 1974. London, Tower Hamlets Local History Library.

Talks About Old London. A collection of articles from the *Evening News*, 1908–1910, based on interviews with old workhouse inmates about their childhoods. London, Bishopsgate Library.

Welsh, Marie Kelly. Oral history transcript, Hackney People's Autobiography.

Widdowson, Frances. Dittoed typescripts of interviews with women in Deptford, New Cross, and Lewisham, 1979.

Family Life and Work Experience Archive

Directed by Paul Thompson and Thea Vigne, housed at the Sociology Department, University of Essex; with permission of Paul Thompson; cited on condition that the informants remain anonymous.

No. 70. James M., born 1899, Poplar. Father a stevedore; mother a former factory hand, did laundry at home; two siblings; father and son were socialists.

No. 124. John T., born 1879, Bow. Father a builder's laborer; mother a former servant in a public house, after marriage did "nursing"; eight siblings.

No. 215. Alice G., born 1897, Custom House. Nine siblings, several of whom died as infants; mother disabled, former tailor; father a socialist and trade unionist and very involved with the household's domestic life. Mrs. G. married in 1915 and had twelve children; active in Labour politics.

No. 216. Elsie B. born 1891, Leyton. Father a clerk; one brother, three half-siblings; mother a former seamstress who did not work for pay after marriage.

No. 225. Frank S. born 1884, Hoxton. Moved to Battersea in 1886; father a woodworker; nine siblings.

No. 236. Mr. C. V., born 1899, Woolwich. Father a former soldier, then a railway laborer and Woolwich Arsenal worker; two siblings; mother a former domestic servant; parents childhood sweethearts from Hampshire.

No. 240. Mr. J. P., born 1902, Camden Town. Later moved to Hackney; four siblings; father died when he was three; widowed mother worked in a collar factory.

No. 261. Ms. C. C., born 1893, Old Kent Road. Lived mostly in Bermondsey; nine siblings but only three grew up; mother a factory box maker; father a railroad laborer and blacksmith.

No. 284. Margaret A., born 1896, Kings Cross Road. Seven siblings; father a painter/decorator; mother occasionally worked as a cook.

No. 296. Stanley W. B., born 1892, Tottenham. Seven siblings; father a Hackney cabinet maker (commuted by train); mother had emigrated from Australia; chapel goers.

No. 333. Louisa K., born Bromley-by-Bow, 1901. Father a lighterman (Thames boatman) handy at sewing and mending and fond of Dickens; another family of chapel goers; mother seldom went out.

No. 412. Mary M., born 1899 Camden Town. Thirteen siblings; father a painter-decorator; mother had lodgers for extra income; cheerful, musical family.

Samuel Oral Histories

Transcripts (some typescript, some manuscript) of interviews carried out or organized by Raphael Samuel, mostly in 1974; in his personal files; used with gratitude and with his permission. Also on file at the London History Workshop Centre, Conway Hall, 42 Queen Street, London. I supply here at least some information about each of these informants. These are their own names.

Mrs. Mac. Born 1905. Family moved often in and around Haggerston/Hackney; seven children; father a cabinet maker; mother a French polisher.

Mr. Mac. Born 1894, Boston Street, Hackney Road. Father a chair maker; ten children born in the family; five died in childhood or infancy. The Macs were interviewed both separately and together.

Mrs. Ada Stone. Born 1884, Victoria Cottages, Deal St., Bethnal Green, an enclave of regularly employed brewery workers just off Brick Lane. Family of four children; mother a former cook; father a horse keeper for Trueman's Brewery.

Ethel Vango. Born around 1890. Father a freight porter, Bishopsgate railroad station; mother a former grocery shop clerk, a laundress after marriage; lived mostly in Blackwell Buildings near Valence Park, Whitechapel; three siblings.

Winifred Prentice. Born 1905, South Row (now Southern Row), Kensal Green. Family of six children; mother a laundress; father a meat carrier.

Mrs. Henman. Born Manville Street, Isle of Dogs, about 1900. Family of eight children; mother did mangling, pawning, and confinements for neighbors.

NEWSPAPERS AND PERIODICALS (BEFORE 1918)

Baby
Bethnal Green News
British Medical Journal (BMJ)
Charity Organisation Review
Child Life
Child Study
City of Westminster Health Society, *Annual Reports,* Westminster City Archive
Daily Chronicle
Daily News
East London Observer
Economic Journal
Economic Review
Guy's Hospital Gazette
The Hospital
Hours at Home
Journal of the Royal Sanitary Institutes
Journal of the Royal Statistical Society (JRSS)
Justice

The Lancet

London City Council (LCC), *Annual Reports*

———, *London Statistics*

———, *Minutes of Proceedings,* July to December 1912, pt. I

London City Mission Magazine

The Malthusian

Medical Officers of Health (MO's H) Annual Reports: St. Pancras, Hackney, Kensington, London, London (Education), Paddington

Metropolitan and National Nursing Association (MNNA), *Annual Reports,* Guildhall Library

Missing Link Magazine, founded 1865; the title was *Biblewomen and Nurses* from 1889 through 1915

National League for Physical Education and Improvement, *Annual Reports*

National Reformer

The Nineteenth Century (and *The Nineteenth Century and After*)

Nurses' Journal (Royal British Nurses' Association)

Nursing Notes (Workhouse Infirmary Nursing Association and the Midwives' Institute)

Nursing Record (1888–1892); *Nursing Record and Hospital Journal* (1892–1902); *British Journal of Nursing* (1902–1956)

Nursing Times (Royal College of Nursing)

Paddington and Marylebone District Nursing Association, *Annual Reports*

Pearson's Magazine

Public Health

St. Bartholomew's Hospital Journal

The Sanitary Officer

The School Child

Sociological Review

The Star

Toynbee Record

The Vote

The Women's Dreadnought

Women's Industrial News

Index

303